The Bioarchaeology of the Human Head

BIOARCHAEOLOGICAL INTERPRETATIONS OF THE HUMAN PAST:
LOCAL, REGIONAL, AND GLOBAL PERSPECTIVES

UNIVERSITY PRESS OF FLORIDA

Florida A&M University, Tallahassee
Florida Atlantic University, Boca Raton
Florida Gulf Coast University, Ft. Myers
Florida International University, Miami
Florida State University, Tallahassee
New College of Florida, Sarasota
University of Central Florida, Orlando
University of Florida, Gainesville
University of North Florida, Jacksonville
University of South Florida, Tampa
University of West Florida, Pensacola

THE BIOARCHAEOLOGY
OF THE HUMAN HEAD

Decapitation, Decoration, and Deformation

Edited by Michelle Bonogofsky

Foreword by Clark Spencer Larsen

University Press of Florida

Gainesville · Tallahassee · Tampa · Boca Raton
Pensacola · Orlando · Miami · Jacksonville · Ft. Myers · Sarasota

In memory of Kathleen Forgey

First cloth printing, 2011
First paperback printing, 2015

Library of Congress Cataloging-in-Publication Data
The bioarchaeology of the human head : decapitation, decoration, and
deformation / edited by] Michelle Bonogofsky ; foreword by Clark
Spencer Larsen.
p. cm. — (Bioarchaeological interpretations of the human past)
Summary: "Explores the symbolic significance of the human head in
cultural, political, economic, and religious ritual across the world"—
Provided by publisher.
ISBN 978-0-8130-3556-7 (hardback)
ISBN 978-0-8130-6177-1 (pbk.)
1. Head—Abnormalities. 2. Head—Social aspects. 3. Skull—Artificial
deformities. 4. Cranial manipulation. 5. Beheading. 6. Human remains
(Archaeology) I. Bonogofsky, Michelle.
GN63.8.B56 2011
930.1—dc22
2011004807

The University Press of Florida is the scholarly publishing agency for the
State University System of Florida, comprising Florida A&M Univer-
sity, Florida Atlantic University, Florida Gulf Coast University, Florida
International University, Florida State University, New College of Florida,
University of Central Florida, University of Florida, University of North
Florida, University of South Florida, and University of West Florida.

University Press of Florida
15 Northwest 15th Street
Gainesville, FL 32611-2079
http://www.upf.com

Contents

List of Figures   vii

List of Tables   xi

Foreword   xiii

Preface   xvii

1. Contextualizing the Human Head: An Introduction   1
   Michelle Bonogofsky

PART I. SYMBOLIC AND CONTEXTUAL APPROACHES

2. Heads as Memorials and Status Symbols: The Collection and Use of Skulls in the Torres Strait Islands   51
   Heather Bonney and Margaret Clegg

3. Melanesian Modeled Skulls, Mortuary Ritual, and Dental X-Rays: Ancestors, Enemies, Women, and Children   67
   Michelle Bonogofsky and Jeremy Graham

4. Marquesan Trophy Skulls: Description, Osteological Analyses, and Changing Motivations in the South Pacific   97
   Frédérique Valentin and Noémie Rolland

5. The Social Lives of Severed Heads: Skull Collection and Display in Medieval and Early Modern Ireland   122
   Barra O'Donnabhain

PART II. BIOARCHAEOLOGICAL AND BIOCHEMICAL APPROACHES

6. Identifying the Origins of Decapitated Male Skeletons from 3 Driffield Terrace, York, through Isotope Analysis: Reflections of the Cosmopolitan Nature of Roman York in the Time of Caracalla   141
   Janet Montgomery, Christopher J. Knüsel, and Katie Tucker

7. Biohistory and Cranial Morphology: A Forensic Case from Spanish Colonial Georgia   179

   Christopher M. Stojanowski and William N. Duncan

8. Skull Deformation during the Iron Age in the Trans-Urals and Western Siberia   202

   Svetlana Sharapova and Dmitry Razhev

9. Marking Ethnicity through Premortem Cranial Modification among the Pre-Inca Chiribaya, Peru   228

   María Cecilia Lozada

10. Getting a Head Start in Life: Pre-Columbian Maya Cranial Modification from Infancy to Ancestorhood   241

    Pamela L. Geller

11. How the Wari Fashioned Trophy Heads for Display: A Distinctive Modified Cranium from Cuzco, Peru, and Comparison to Trophies from the Capital Region   262

    Valerie A. Andrushko

12. Nasca Trophy Head Origins and Ancient DNA   286

    Kathleen Forgey

List of Contributors   307

Index   309

Figures

1.1. Plastered skull from Neolithic Jericho 5

2.1. Map of the Torres Strait Islands 52

2.2. Modeled skull of young adult male BMNHPAHR571 collected on Naghir Island 54

2.3. Mummy collected on Darnley Island 57

2.4. Dried head of young adult male BMNHPAHR583 from the Torres Strait 57

2.5. Bamboo beheading knives 58

2.6. Evidence of termite activity in the sphenoid bone of trophy skull BMNHPAHR487 60

2.7. Cut marks on the ramus of trophy mandible BMNHPAHR509 62

2.8. Cut marks on the posterior ramus of trophy mandible BMNHPAHR560 63

2.9. Three-dimensional reconstruction of cut mark peel from mandible BMNHPAHR509 64

3.1. Skull decorated with a bamboo noseplug with rattan trim from Vanuatu 69

3.2. Map of Melanesia 70

3.3. Anterior view of child's skull from the Sepik River 72

3.4. Right lateral view of child's skull from the Sepik River 72

3.5. Right lateral oblique radiograph of child's skull from the Sepik River 75

3.6. Skull of an enemy or relative overmodeled in clay from Iatmül 78

3.7. Illustration of burial effigy *(rambaramp)* from Vanuatu 80

3.8. Skull covered with putty-nut paste and inlaid with pearl shell from Rubina, Solomon Islands 84

4.1. Map of the archipelago of Marquesas Islands 98

4.2. Trophy skull from Nuku Hiva with pig tusks 100

4.3. Young Marquesan warrior with trophy skull 102

4.4. Trophy skull from Nuku Hiva with textiles and tapa strip 103

4.5. Skull wrapped in white tapa painted with tattoo motifs from Nuku Hiva 104

4.6. Trophy skull from Hiva Oa 107

5.1. Map of Ireland and Britain showing locations mentioned in text 124

5.2. Plan of medieval Dublin showing locations mentioned in the text 124

5.3. Skull from Viking-age Dublin with perimortem cutting wounds and damage 125

5.4. The execution by hanging, drawing, and quartering of Hugh Despencer in Hereford (1326) 128

5.5. Heads of Irish rebels displayed above Dublin Castle gate (1581) 130

5.6. Public dissection from Hogarth's *Four Stages of Cruelty* (1751) 131

5.7. Detail from twelfth-century church doorway in County Clare 134

6.1. Geological sketch map, Yorkshire region 143

6.2. Map of Roman York in regional context 144

6.3. Fortress at Roman York 146

6.4. Plan view of the cemetery at 3 Driffield Terrace 147

6.5. Double burial of decapitated individuals SK15 (4146) and SK16 (4147) 148

6.6. Cleanly bisected cervical vertebra from SK17 (4130) 149

6.7. Posterior view of cervical and upper thoracic vertebrae of SK47 (4471) 149

6.8. Mandible from SK33 (4253) 149

6.9. Decapitated individual SK37 (4344) 150

6.10. Second cervical vertebra of decapitated individual SK37 (4344) 150

6.11. Age structure in populations from Driffield Terrace and Roman-age London cemetery 153

6.12. Lead concentrations and isotope ratios for Driffield Terrace Romans versus British individuals 158

6.13. Lead isotope ratios for Driffield Terrace individuals versus contemporary English burials 159

6.14. Strontium concentrations and isotope ratios of Driffield Terrace individuals   160

6.15. Strontium isotope ratios versus concentration for enamel and crown dentine of Driffield Terrace individuals   161

6.16. Strontium isotope ratio versus oxygen isotope ratio for Driffield Terrace individuals   163

6.17. Strontium isotope ratios versus oxygen isotope ratios for Driffield Terrace skeletons and contemporary Romano-British burials   165

7.1. Right lateral view of the Fort King George calvaria   181

7.2. Map of Florida and Georgia, showing Fort King George   184

7.3. Inferior view of Fort King George calvaria   186

7.4. Bivariate principal components plot   192

8.1. Map of the landscape zones of Eurasia   203

8.2. Map of central Eurasia at the beginning of the Iron Age   204

8.3. Burial of adult male from Gaevsky 1 cemetery   207

8.4. Grave goods from Gaevsky 1 cemetery   210

8.5. Arrowheads from Gaevsky 1 cemetery   211

8.6. Pottery from Gaevsky 1 cemetery   211

8.7. Luxury goods found with young woman from Abatsky 3 cemetery   214

8.8. Burial of woman 40–50 years old at Karasie 9   215

8.9. Pottery from Karasie 9 grave   216

8.10. Skulls from Abatsky 3 and Abatsky 1 cemeteries, exhibiting relatively minor deformation   219

8.11. Skull of a female 40–50 years old from Karasie 9 grave   219

9.1. Map of Peru   230

9.2. Location of sites of study   231

9.3. Fronto-occipital type of cranial modification   232

9.4. Annular type of cranial modification   232

9.5. Distribution of annular type of cranial modification at study sites   233

9.6. Distribution of fronto-occipital type of cranial modification at study sites   235

10.1. Map of the Río Bravo region   244

10.2. Map of Dos Barbaras   248

10.3. Map of Group B at Dos Barbaras   249

10.4. Individual 35 interred beneath Room 2, Structure 6 250

10.5. Frontispiece to Bulwer's *Anthropometamorphosis* (1650) 255

11.1. Map of Cuzco region sites mentioned in text 266

11.2. Perimortem cut marks, postmortem perforations 268

11.3. Lateral-view sketch of trophy skull CC 48 showing multiple modifications 269

11.4. Inferior view of cranium CC 48 with basicranial portion removed 270

11.5. Anterior view of cranium CC 48 with sweeping cut mark 271

11.6. Anterior-view sketch of trophy skull CC 48, showing multiple modifications 272

11.7. Cut nasals with multiple cut marks along nasal bridge 273

11.8. Tiny drill holes with two metal tacks on left parietal 273

11.9. Anterior view of maxilla showing prosthetic teeth 274

11.10. Lateral view of right maxilla showing prosthetic third molar 275

12.1. Nasca trophy head showing frontal perforation and posterior enlargement 288

12.2. Peru's South Coast 290

Tables

3.1. Summary of dental aging results   76

4.1. Short inventory of Marquesan trophy skulls in museum and private collections   108

6.1. Sample details of individuals examined by isotope analysis   154

6.2. Isotope data   156

6.3. Summary of isotope results   166

7.1. Comparative populations used for comparison of FKG-l21   190

8.1. Cranial sample by cemetery   206

8.2. Male cranial sample displaying evidence of cranial deformation   208

8.3. Female and subadult cranial samples displaying evidence of cranial deformation   212

8.4. Measurements of deformed and nondeformed skulls of Sargat males   217

8.5. Measurements of deformed and nondeformed skulls of Sargat females   218

10.1. Occurrence of shaped crania at centers from the Río Bravo region   245

10.2. Intentional tabular cranial shaping by sex in the Río Bravo sample   245

12.1. Chronology of the Nazca Valley   291

12.2. Mitochondrial restriction haplotype data   296

12.3. Mitochondrial DNA sequence haplotype data   296

12.4. Combined RFLP and partial HVRI sequence data   297

12.5. Combined RFLP and partial HVRI sequence data organized by valley   297

Foreword

The human head as represented by skulls has a long history of study in anthropology in general and bioarchaeology in particular. Indeed, the focus on human anatomy above the neck is a founding interest of physical anthropology, largely emphasizing biology and with little attention paid to the social dimensions of treatment of the body at the time of a person's death. Bioarchaeology—the study of human remains from archaeological contexts—is now at the forefront of an emerging understanding of social embodiment, the interplay between biology and culture, and values of a society expressed in the remains of its deceased. Past societies practiced a remarkable array of body treatments. Upon death, the bodies—especially the heads—of the deceased were frequently modified in very patterned ways. These modifications performed by the living and applied to the dead were informed by a complex interplay of religion, politics, economics, and long-standing social behaviors oftentimes associated with gender or age or both. Usually, bodies were buried near the place of death. However, "trophies" representing the body and the person (oftentimes heads) were sometimes transported over long distances.

In this remarkable book, the authors focus on the bioarchaeology of the human head, discussing the various ways in which the head was treated at the time of death as well as before and after. Treatments were not random affairs but reflect intentional and ritualized practices with significant social meaning. In addition to providing a description of these practices, bioarchaeologists use a broad array of contextual information to understand what motivated these treatments. The earliest evidence of skull treatment is represented in cut marks deriving from the removal of soft tissue on the face of the 600,000-year-old Bodo cranium from the Middle Awash Valley, Ethiopia (White 1986). In this instance, the activity associated with defleshing may have been related to ritual or cannibalism, two areas of historical interest in anthropology. Such craniofacial perimortem treatment is only rarely found before the Holocene, when humans began to practice an extensive range of craniofacial modifications, including the kinds of cut marks documented in Bodo and other Pleistocene hominids. During the Holocene, humans greatly diversified head and skull treatments, including plastering, modeling, and painting (e.g., Bonogofsky 2005). In many settings, the head was removed altogether. Decapitation, however, was motivated by multiple factors, sometimes as a form of execution. In some settings, disembodiment followed death, for the purpose of long-term curation of the skull, both for public display and as heirlooms in households. In other settings, holes were drilled or entire sections of the head or skull removed. These practices were mostly performed on the deceased, but not always.

The ethnographic and social historical records reveal a common theme involving head treatment, both for the living and for the dead. That is, the head (represented by the skull in archaeological contexts) is what Bonogofsky and others have described as "the seat of personhood," or the element of the body that displays a person's identity. We are what our heads broadcast about us as individuals, including hair treatment, facial features, facial morphology, and various material items that can be attached to it, such as strings, beads, rings, and plugs. Collectively, this montage of biological and cultural gives the person his or her identity.

Via the context of historical sources, ethnography, and archaeology, bioarchaeologists are well positioned to provide perspectives on past societies through the study of body treatment. Contrary to the notion held by some that archaeology is missing from bioarchaeology (see Goldstein 2006), the study of ancient remains from archaeological contexts is well demonstrated by the authors of this volume as successfully linking the biological with the behavioral and social dimensions of humanness. Although bones and teeth are a central focus in bioarchaeological inquiry, the questions and hypotheses that the remains allow us to address are linked to the larger study of the human condition and the multiple ways in which the human condition is preserved in mortuary settings.

This volume builds on the notion that human remains provide a window to the past and especially identity (see Knudson and Stojanowski 2009). The bioarchaeology of the skull is now much more than the typological focus that was emphasized by the founders of physical anthropology in the late nineteenth and early twentieth centuries. This volume and the growing body of literature reveal the skull as a window into identity well beyond the biological forensics. We are now beginning to dig deep into the social dimensions of human remains from mortuary settings as a profound form of symbol. This book sets new directions for and new pathways to understanding past societies and how these societies constructed themselves—an individual at a time.

Clark Spencer Larsen
Series Editor

REFERENCES CITED

Bonogofsky, Michelle. 2005. A Bioarchaeological Study of Plastered Skulls from Anatolia: New Discoveries and Interpretations. *International Journal of Osteoarchaeology* 15: 124–135.

Goldstein, Lynne. 2006. Mortuary Analysis and Bioarchaeology. In *Bioarchaeology: The Contextual Analysis of Human Remains*, edited by J. E. Buikstra and L. A. Beck, 375–387. Elsevier, Amsterdam.

Knudson, Kelly J., and Christopher M. Stojanowski, editors. 2009. *Bioarchaeology and Identity in the Americas*. University Press of Florida, Gainesville.

White, Tim D. 1986. Cut Marks on the Bodo Cranium: A Case of Prehistoric Defleshing. *American Journal of Physical Anthropology* 69: 503–509.

Preface

This is the second of two volumes based on papers presented at the 2005 and 2006 European Association of Archaeologists annual meetings, during sessions that I organized and chaired on skull collection, modification, and decoration. The first volume, *Skull Collection, Modification and Decoration* (Bonogofsky 2006), included eleven chapters (all but one of which were presented during the sessions) grouped by geographic region—Europe, the Middle East, Eurasia, Oceania, and the New World—with a focus on the human skull postmortem. The current volume includes seven papers that also were presented during the sessions, while the remaining chapters are new submissions from regional specialists. This volume compares practices such as decapitation, decoration of skulls, and deformation of the human head among various groups in the geographic regions of Oceania, Europe, the Middle East, Eurasia, and the New World. The chapters are ordered by approach—whether primarily symbolic and contextual or bioarchaeological and biochemical—then topically by treatment and geographic location of the human head pre- to postmortem, concluding with a chapter that highlights the utility of DNA analysis and serves as a roadmap to future studies. Both volumes present original research papers on human skulls recovered from ethnographic and archaeological contexts, focusing on the question of whose skulls/heads were collected/modified and why.

The current volume places emphasis on the methodology and theory of decapitation, decoration, and deformation of the human head/skull from areas as varied as Roman Britain and Spanish Colonial Georgia to the Iron Age Trans-Urals and ethnographic Polynesia. Discussions of the archaeological contexts, visual descriptions, ethnographic studies, osteological analyses, and technological investigations of such skulls were encouraged. The intent is to shed light on practices within past societies, addressing whose skulls and heads were collected and why, whether as ancestors or enemies, as insiders or outsiders, as males or females, as adults or children. This particular bioarchaeological focus on the human head/skull complements other recent large-scale publications (e.g., Bonogofsky 2006; Rakita et al. 2005 [for global case studies]; and Chacon and Dye 2007; Knudson and Stojanowski 2009 [for case studies from the Americas]; as well as Sofaer 2006 [on the body as material culture]).

The diverse tools employed to answer these questions include DNA, x-ray and isotope analysis, taphonomy, iconography, and a primary study of the skulls themselves, to determine—for example—whether the skulls belonged to ancestors or enemies, as local or nonlocal residents. It is intended that researchers in various world regions may thus benefit from shared insights derived from scientific analyses coupled with challenging questions.

The current volume, like its companion, *Skull Collection, Modification and Decoration* (Bonogofsky 2006), is deliberately wide-ranging in nature, broadly including varied approaches to heads and skulls both as biological objects and as material culture. Whether decorated, disembodied, or deformed, collected for display or hidden, or otherwise modified or curated, heads and skulls and their study serve to illustrate the potential of the vast wealth of information that can be obtained from a combined contextual and bioarchaeological analysis of this most important part of the human body.

ACKNOWLEDGMENTS

I thank Clark Spencer Larsen, series editor, for inviting me to submit this book for consideration as part of the series Bioarchaeological Interpretations of the Human Past: Local, Regional, and Global Perspectives. I thank Tim White for his rigor in preparing graduate students and his continued role as a mentor. I trust that this book reflects some aspects of the sound instruction and guidance that I received from both professors. I thank the contributors for their valuable work, with a special thank you to Kathleen Forgey and Jeremy Graham for their early correspondence and/or sharing of materials—regarding our mutual questions and varied analytical approaches concerning skulls in the Middle East, the Americas, and Oceania—which contributed to my conception of this endeavor in bringing scholars together from around the globe. I also thank James Roberts, John L. Hayes, Kathleen Tandy, Bethany Lopez, Christy Risser-Milne, Rebecca Jabbour, Joseph Noble, Arthur E. Clark, and Venkat Ganesan for their assistance. John Krigbaum and John Verano provided helpful comments and suggestions for which I am most grateful.

REFERENCES CITED

Bonogofsky, Michelle, editor. 2006. *Skull Collection, Modification and Decoration.* BAR International Series 1539. Archaeopress, Oxford, U.K.

Chacon, Richard J., and David H. Dye, editors. 2007. *The Taking and Displaying of Human Body Parts as Trophies by Amerindians.* Springer, New York.

Knudson, Kelly J., and Christopher M. Stojanowski, editors. 2009. *Bioarchaeology and Identity in the Americas*. University Press of Florida, Gainesville.

Rakita, Gordon F. M., Jane E. Buikstra, Lane A. Beck, and Sloan R. Williams, editors. 2005. *Interacting with the Dead: Perspectives on Mortuary Archaeology for the New Millennium*. University Press of Florida, Gainesville.

Sofaer, Joanna R. 2006. *The Body as Material Culture: A Theoretical Osteoarchaeology*. Cambridge University Press, Cambridge.

1

Contextualizing the Human Head

An Introduction

MICHELLE BONOGOFSKY

This book is the product of an emerging concern in bioarchaeology: the conceptual status of the human body and its parts in the past—notably, whose heads and skulls were given special treatment and why, whether as ancestor or enemy, as insider or outsider, as adult or child, or as male or female. Ancient human groups collected, buried, enshrined, disinterred, modified, and decorated entire bodies as well as selected portions, paying special attention to the human head (e.g., see Bonogofsky 2006c; Chacon and Dye 2007; Knudson and Stojanowski 2009; Rakita et al. 2005). After over a century of research, we now understand that treatment of the body was dependent upon a network of political, social, economic, and religious concerns. These concerns intersected with the biological characteristics and constraints of the body in diverse but finite ways. For archaeologists, evidence of these complex networks comes primarily in the form of cemeteries, tombs, burials, and human skeletal remains. However, as the authors in this volume demonstrate, documentary sources, iconography, and ethnographic analogy, along with bioarchaeological and biochemical analyses conducted on human remains, help us to contextualize the treatment of the body and provide more nuanced interpretations, such as whether the individuals are local or nonlocal residents (e.g., see Forgey this volume; Montgomery, Knüsel, and Tucker this volume).

Our understanding of the body is significantly informed by the now firmly established approach of bioarchaeology, which integrates biological data and archaeological context, stressing the interaction between biology and behavior of modern populations from archaeological sites (Larsen 1997, 2007). Twenty-first-century researchers are increasingly recognizing the advantages of such an integrated approach and putting it into practice in a variety of temporal and spatial contexts. Such endeavors present significant challenges for researchers, however, because they demand the study and synthesis of the evidence on several conceptual levels—that of the individual body and associated artifacts; that of the tomb, mound, or cemetery context; that of the regional landscape; and that of the larger sociocultural context. The advantage of dealing with the human body on several levels is that it provides us with the most complete picture of ancient life—from the embodied experience of the individual to the culturally mediated context of deposition and finally to the physical, cultural, and historical contexts in which individuals lived; negotiated their ages, statuses, roles, and sexualities; ritualized their beliefs and actions; and ultimately died, with their body parts collected, curated, and brought back into the community. Contributors to this volume approach the study of a specific body part—the human head—and its context through analyses based in skeletal, DNA, radiographic, isotopic, documentary, and iconographic evidence as well as in the more traditional study of material culture. In some contributions, the head itself is viewed simultaneously as a biological object—the product of physical processes—and as an object of material culture (Sofaer 2006) to be manipulated in various ways. Implicit in this approach is the recognition that body parts (the head or skull in particular) are objects vested with immense symbolic, social, religious, and political value.

Ethnographers at the forefront of the postmodern focus on gender, identity, ethnicity, and personhood, have produced compelling research that situates elements of the human body within both indigenous cultural contexts and colonialist discourses (e.g., Hoskins 1986; Rosaldo 1980; Taylor 1993). Bodies and their parts function within political economies of power and prestige and serve as social markers for family and ethnic groups. The consumption of the body, for example, can consolidate distinctions between kin groups, as among the Wari of Amazonia (Conklin 1995, 2001). Their postmortem treatment provides an arena for the display of resources and the negotiation of social relationships. However, archaeology reveals that consumption of the body can occur for completely different reasons, as among the Anasazi in the American Southwest, who butchered and cooked nearly thirty men, women, and children for their bone marrow around AD 1100 (White 1992) before abandoning their Colorado location. Bodies and their parts also take their places within mythological and ideological systems—in the reenactment of origin stories, in the dramatization of cosmological events, and in the materialization of the divine.

Individual body parts, notably the head or skull, may take on the role of the body entire, as in the symbolic phenomenon of *pars pro toto* (e.g., Bienert 1991) or may be imbued with an altogether different sort of meaning. The head (Hoskins 1986; Rosaldo 1980), hair (Leach 1958), internal organs (Lock 2002; Scheper-Hughes 2001; Sharp 1994), and various other body parts have been treated in detail (see examples in Chacon and Dye 2007; Hillman and Mazzio 1997) by ethnologists and sociologists, who have illustrated how the body can serve human interests on several social and cultural levels. Bioarchaeologists, who have long viewed the human skeleton as a source of information about the past, are now for the first time addressing how specific parts functioned within sociopolitical networks (e.g., see chapters in Chacon and Dye 2007 for Amerindian studies). This volume deals with what is almost certainly the most archaeologically visible and symbolically loaded body part—the human head.

Treatment and Deposition of the Head

The head or the skull, regarded in many societies as the seat of personhood, ancestorhood, or the soul, is most familiar to archaeologists as a highly salient object recovered in burial contexts. On occasion, burials will be excavated in which the head is missing, as with the early Nasca in Peru (e.g., DeLeonardis 2000) and during the Natufian and Neolithic periods in the Levant and Anatolia, where the cranium, or even the entire skull, was often removed after decomposition of the interred body (e.g., Bienert et al. 2004; Bonogofsky 2001b, 2004, 2006a; Kenyon 1981; Rollefson 1983: 30). Unlike the smaller and more easily overlooked bones of the hands and feet, cranial elements are rarely missed in archaeological contexts unless preservation is exceedingly poor. Ethnographic research allows us to identify several reasons that skulls might be missing from interred bodies: for example, the head may serve as a trophy taken by victorious warriors, as a memento of the deceased recovered by kin, as a political symbol of power and terror, or as a modified object for daily or ritual use.

When re-created, the face of the trophy head or loved one is one of the most concrete images of social personhood (George 1996: 91). Ethnographic examples of mortuary rituals abound in which the skull, usually after soft tissue decomposition, is retrieved from an interment, often for use by relatives or members of the same ethnic group (e.g., Arnold and Hastorf 2008: 163–166; Bonogofsky 2001b: 16–35; Bonogofsky and Graham this volume; Goodale 1985; Keesing 1982). At an early Lapita burial site in Vanuatu, in Melanesia, each interred individual was missing his or her skull, with one exception. This individual was interred with three skulls on his chest. Strontium and oxygen isotope analysis of tooth enamel further singled out this individual as a recent immigrant to the island (Bentley et al. 2007). In this case, we may be looking at an individual with a special social status—that of immigrant—which is marked in burial through the inclusion of skulls.

Sometimes the skull was manually defleshed using special tools before decomposition of the soft tissue, as it was during headhunting rituals in British New Guinea (e.g., see Bateson 1932: 408, 1958: 141) and the Torres Strait Islands (Bonney and Klegg this volume). Similarly, from the other end of the temporal spectrum, are three crania recovered from archaeological contexts in the Middle Awash Valley, Ethiopia, that had been intentionally manipulated, polished, cut, and scraped with sharp stone and obsidian tools when the head was still fresh. This early (but not earliest) evidence of defleshing of the human head dates to the intersection between the Acheulean and Middle Stone Age, 160,000–154,000 years ago (Clark et al. 2003). The three crania—belonging to an adult male, a probable adult male, and a juvenile, with clear evidence of cutting, decorating, and polishing (Clark et al. 2003)—are reminiscent of postmortem modifications found on skulls from New Guinea (White and Toth 1991). However, the earliest solid evidence for intentional defleshing of a human ancestor, offering research avenues for the investigation of the beginning of this mortuary practice, involved cut marks made by stone tools to the Middle Pleistocene Bodo cranium from Ethiopia when the bone was still fresh (White 1986).

Regardless of whether the skull was removed following soft tissue decomposition or whether the head was severed before burial, the head becomes a form of material culture—a commodity in some cases—taking on a life history of its own and entering the sociopolitical economy of the living (Appadurai 1986; Hoskins 1989; see Valentin and Rolland this volume for examples from Polynesia). In some cases, the skull may be used without alteration or decoration (Bonogofsky 2006a). More often, humans engage in extensive cultural and physical modification such as plastering, modeling, painting, and adorning with a variety of materials including lime plaster, clay, animal collagen, ochre, shell, and fiber. Sometimes these decorative materials were removed, at times leaving behind damage to the cranium in the form of striations, which can be viewed microscopically, if not macroscopically (e.g., Bonogofsky 2001a: fig. 1, 2001b: pl. 5h). The decorative materials in turn may inform on methods of preparation. For example, at Neolithic 'Ain Ghazal in Jordan, three lime plaster "masks" were found broken away—and buried separately—from the three crania over which they had been modeled (Griffin et al. 1998). Although the corresponding skulls were not found, imprints in the plaster indicated that the cranial cavities had been stuffed with grass and that a few teeth were intact in the maxilla at the time of modeling.

Examples of cranial plastering and modeling are known as well from Jericho (figure 1.1) and eight other Neolithic sites in the Middle East (Bienert 1991; Bonogofsky 2001b, 2003, 2004, 2005a, 2005b, 2006a, 2006b; Özbeck 2009), most recently at Yiftah'el in Israel (Gedalyahu 2008) and at Tell Aswad in

Figure 1.1. Plastered skull decorated with paint and shell (without its mandible), from Neolithic Jericho (D114; J5757). Scale in centimeters. Courtesy of the Jordan Archaeological Museum, Amman; photography by Mohammad Fayyez.

Syria (Stordeur and Khawam 2007). The skulls from these sites continue to be interpreted by many of their excavators and other researchers as evidence of an ancestor cult (with an attendant mythology, discussed and refuted in Bonogofsky 2001b, 2002, 2003), while overlooking evidence to the contrary (e.g., Bonogofsky 2001a, 2001b). The ancient practice first made famous by Kathleen Kenyon in the 1950s has now been documented among several cultures of Eurasia (e.g., Kaiser 2003, 2006; Shishlina 2006; Vadetskaia 2006), among the early coastal inhabitants of Chile (Arriaza 1995), and among Middle to Late Woodland period burials in the Great Lakes region of North America (e.g., Clark 1984; Ossenberg 1964, cited in Wyckoff 1978; Speal 2006: fig. 9; see also Aufderheide 2009 for additional examples from around the globe). In the

Great Lakes region, not only was clay modeling applied to adult and juvenile skulls but also holes were drilled for suspension, suggesting that such skulls were meant to be displayed and to be seen, although differential treatment of individuals by age was widespread (e.g., Clark 1984).

Other forms of modification include carving or incising the cranial vault, found among the Sepik River groups in New Guinea (Stodder 2006, 2011), and drilling or punching holes through the mandibular rami (Stodder 2006) and the bones of the calvarium in North and South America (Speal 2006; Verano 2001). The foramen magnum at the base of the skull may be purposely enlarged, as it was among the Nasca and Wari of Peru (e.g., see Andrushko this volume; Forgey this volume; Kellner 2006; Verano 1995; Williams et al. 2001). Pieces of the skull may be converted into masks, bowls, or cups (Jacobi 2007: figs. 11.12–11.15; Speal 2006; Verano et al. 1999; Webb and Baby 1957: fig. 2), and parietal disks taken from crania may be used as rattles (Jacobi 2007: 323; Williamson 2007). Conversely, Gran Chacoan warriors of South America took the entire scalp, ears, and part of the face to make drinking cups, discarding the victims' skulls, except for the teeth, which they perforated and made into necklaces (Mendoza 2006).

Deformation, Trephination, and Scalping

In some cases, radical modifications occur before death, taking advantage of the living tissue to reshape the skull. Cultural practices such as in vivo wrapping of the cranial vault and removal of a portion of the outer bone table produce modification of the skull. These procedures may be performed for aesthetic or health reasons, often leaving postmortem imprints on the skull, including the face (Anton 1989: 264), that offer clues to past social practices such as cranial deformation or trephination. Prehistoric Eurasians practiced artificial deformation, altering the shape of the skull by applying pressure during growth and development of the cranial plates. Applying a board to the head, for example, and wrapping it tightly could achieve pronounced elongation. Sharapova and Razhev (this volume) describe examples of such deformation among the Sargat people of the Trans-Urals and western Siberia. Cases are known worldwide, including among the Nasca of the southern Peruvian coast (Forgey and Williams 2005: 259), and among the pre-Inca Chiribaya in southern Peru (Buikstra et al. 2005: 77–78; Lozada and Buikstra 2006; Lozada this volume). Cranial deformation in this region has been interpreted as the intentional marking of a member of a specific ethnic group—essentially, the creation of a social person (Silverman and Proulx 2002: 69–70). The Nasca style of deformation took a bilobated form with bilateral extensions of the parietal region; a second form, similar to that of the Sargat, is more elongated and conical (Williams et al. 2001). Deformation is also known from central Saharan Libya (Ricci et al. 2008), the ancient Near East (Fletcher et al. 2008; Kurth and Röhrer-Ertl 1981; Molleson and Campbell 1995; Strouhal 1973), the Eastern Woodlands of North America (Webb and Baby, 1957: 51–53, 55), Mesoamerica (Geller this volume; Mendoza 2007: fig. 14.11), and several other cultures of the Andes (Allison et al. 1981; Blom 2005; Hoshower et al. 1995).

Skull deformation at the Near Eastern settlement of Jericho during the Neolithic period included two basic types—a lengthening of the skull backwards (*deformato tabulae oblique*) and a shortening of the skull (*deformato tabulae erectae*)—evident in both males and females well as children and adults. Kurth and Röhrer-Ertl (1981) found intentionally deformed crania in all areas of the settlement, involving skulls that had been plastered and painted as well as skulls that were otherwise untreated. The only division they noted between the two types was based on location: only artificially elongated skulls were found in the central part of the settlement, while the shortened skulls were found only in the northern and southern areas. One plastered skull—belonging to a young adult male (Bonogofsky 2001b: 147–148, tables 4.8, 5.2)—that had been excavated from the northern area, reportedly appeared trilobed with signs of healed trephination beneath the plaster on the right parietal (Kurth and Röhrer-Ertl 1981: 438, 441, pls. 57a, 57b). Elsewhere, people pierced their nasal septa and filed, ablated, incised, and inlaid their teeth (see Geller this volume; Clark and Colman 2008: fig. 2 for references to Mesoamerican use of dental modification). These manipulations of the skull and dentition literally ossify social position, making elite group membership permanently visible and thereby conveying a sense of its immanence and inflexibility. Trepanning and scalping may also mark ritual or specific events within the life of an individual.

Trephination—the surgical removal of a part of the skull, whether through scraping, drilling, cutting, or incising—is done to relieve serious medical problems such as the effects of skull fracture or some other defect or disease process that produces intracranial pressure, but the process itself can cause infection, brain injury, and even death if the dura is penetrated (Arnott et al. 2003; Aufderheide 1985; Nystrom 2006; Ortner and Putschar 1985; Stewart 1958; Weber and Czarnetzki 2001). Trephination could result in visible changes to the head and scalp, making evidence of past trauma apparent, as with a Mesolithic frontal bone from the Muge site in Portugal. This cranial bone displays a depressed fracture with clear signs of trephination (Crubézy et al. 2001: fig. 4; see Andrushko and Verano 2008 for examples from Peru). However, there are instances of trepanned crania with no evidence of fracture or concussion (e.g., Littleton and Frifelt 2006). In these cases, the procedure has been explained as a treatment for complaints such as sinusitis, epilepsy, neuralgia, and psychiatric conditions. However, the procedure may also be associated with ritual, as has been suggested for the Neolithic period in France (Aufderheide 1985: 122). There, multiple trephinations were performed on women usually lacking other signs of trauma. Small discs of bone were subsequently cut postmortem to include portions of these premortem defects and were pierced to accommodate a necklace cord, possibly to permit them to be worn as amulets.

Like trephination, scalping may result in lesions on the skull that can be detected macroscopically. Although violence is often cited as the reason for scalping, other explanations (many with support from documentary sources) include punishment, treatment of head wounds, and even as part of a ritual sequence (Mednikova 2002; see Andrushko this volume). Given the context in which some of the scalped individuals have been recovered, magical or religious acts are reasonable suppositions. Evidence for scalping seems to occur most commonly in association with other kinds of trauma, as at the Mississippian site of Orendorf, Illinois, where scalped individuals were found with others who had suffered decapitation or blunt-force cranial trauma (Steadman 2008). Similar patterns have been identified on the northern plains of North America, where women and children, as well as warrior-age males, were scalped (Owsley 1994). Although the ancient Greeks made much of scalping by the Scythians (Murphy et al. 2002), knowledge of the true extent of the practice is only now emerging through analysis of cranial remains. The practice is associated with warfare in South America (Métraux 1963), but cases of scalping are also reported from Eurasia (e.g., Mednikova 2002; Murphy et al. 2002).

Decapitation

Decapitation, or beheading, either as a perimortem action or as a form of execution, appears to have played a symbolic role in addition to its effectiveness as a mode of dispatch. In medieval and early modern European contexts, decapitation represented the literal severing of the mind from the body. In medieval Ireland, accounts of court rulings during the period of English control of Ireland (from the medieval period until the early nineteenth century) indicate that those convicted of treason were publicly hanged, drawn, and quartered, with their heads and quarters mounted on the city walls for all to view. Skulls excavated from the perimeter of high-status medieval dwellings and from along the walls of cities such as Dublin many times bear evidence of decapitation and other trauma and are thought to have been displayed similarly on walls, gates, and towers (O'Donnabhain this volume). In England, beheading physically ended the link between traitorous speech and the treacherous body and was considered a more noble—and less painful—death than drawing and quartering, with some notable exceptions (e.g., Lewis 2008). The infamous deaths of Mary, Queen of Scots, by axe and the French royal family by guillotine are two examples in which perceived treachery—either to a queen or to a cause—was ended with a blade. Throughout the English medieval period, decapitation was followed by display of the head as a preferred form of death and spectacle. Heads were occasionally retrieved from public display, as from above the gatehouse on London Bridge, and kept by relatives as relics or mementos. The head of Sir Thomas More, who was decapitated by axe on the orders of Henry VIII, was displayed on the bridge until his daughter retrieved it. It was reportedly interred with her (Anonymous n.d.).

Roman period burials in Britain (Montgomery, Knüsel, and Tucker this volume) and Iron Age bog bodies (e.g., Kelly 2006) exhibit decapitation, as do medieval remains recovered from Irish settlements (see O'Donnabhain this volume, for literary as well as skeletal evidence). Lincoln (1991) observed a similar pattern among the ancient Scythians of western Asia, who punished forswearing of oaths to the king by beheading. Loss of the head and the head as a source of luck, power, or knowledge are prominent themes in mythology (e.g., O'Flaherty 1988), and archaeologists working in the United Kingdom occasionally turn to Celtic myth as a source of interpretation. At a late Roman period burial site in Bedfordshire, excavators recovered several decapitated individuals amid more-numerous extended burials in which the heads were intact and articulated (Boylston et al. 2000). They suggested two possible explanations: first, that decapitation was the result of endemic warfare; second, that decapitation was intended to facilitate the protective role of the head after death. In support of their hypothesis, Boylston and colleagues (2000; see also Wright 1988) pointed to several myths, including that of the Celtic hero Bran, in which heads continued to guard, provide wise counsel, or otherwise benefit the living community after being severed from the body.

Decapitation has also been identified as a ritual facilitating collective representation. Two Mississippian examples, Dickson Mounds and Cahokia Mound 72 (Fowler et al. 1999), involved the headless burials of four males. Brown (2003) observes that the replacement of the heads of the deceased with distinctive ceramic vessels supports an interpretation that downplays the personhood of each man, instead highlighting the role of mythic hero in the reenactment of a cosmic event. In this example, decapitation has nothing to do with the deceased as persons, that is, the deceased were not decapitated because of their individual statuses, offenses, or roles. Rather, their final acts in ritual performance—embodying cosmic heroes who suffered decapitation—resulted in their headless interment.

Decapitated individuals may be recovered more frequently archaeologically than is perhaps realized; this relative invisibility in the literature, with some major exceptions, is perhaps the result of an apparent lack of patterning, the perplexity with which investigators regard such finds, and the absence of an osteoarchaeologist on the team. As a result, reports often fail to include pertinent data, such as whether the mandible or cervical vertebrae are included and whether the bone has been modified by cut marks or evidence of trauma, as noted by Berryman (2007: 378) among the Maya. At several sites in the United Kingdom, however, patterns in decapitation are emerging at so-called execution cemeteries. Janet Montgomery, Christopher Knüsel, and Katie Tucker (this volume) discuss a Roman period cemetery from Yorkshire in which over half of the interred were decapitated, presumably as a form of capital punishment. Anglo-Saxon, as well as Romano-British, execution cemeteries with evidence of decapitation have also been identified (Harman et al. 1981). For example, at Walkington Wold, Yorkshire, bodies and crania were buried separately and many crania exhibited occipital blade injuries (Buckberry and Hadley 2007). Farther afield, three beheaded individuals were identified in an Avar cemetery in Austria amidst a much larger (n=540) group of interments (Wiltschke-Schrotta and Stadler 2005). Significantly, in the Avar case as well as in several of the British examples, many of those individuals who were decapitated also exhibited other unusual features, such as burial in a prone position or grave goods that were qualitatively and quantitatively different from those of the rest of the cemetery population.

Human sacrifices represent a special group of decapitated individuals. Although human sacrifice took many forms in the past, decapitation appears to have been a preferred method in many state-level societies, especially when the victims were male, as with captured and sacrificed enemy rulers in the Maya area as part of a ballgame (Miller 1999: 356–357). At the Moche site of Dos Cabezas on the North Coast of Peru, a structure containing eighteen severed heads (sex unreported) was excavated. On the basis of cut marks on the anterior portions of the cervical vertebrae, either the victims had their throats slit or their heads were removed by blades entering from an anterior position (Cordy-Collins 2001). In contrast, women who were sacrificed among the Moche were usually strangled with ligatures (Verano 2001). Not a single Moche female decapitation has been reported in the literature, suggesting that among the Moche, specific modes of death were associated with one sex or the other and that the meanings attached to such deaths differed significantly.

Another example of sacrificial decapitation comes from the Shang dynasty capital at Anyang, China, which contained multiple royal tombs with both human and animal sacrifices. In at least one case, headless, sacrificed individuals were placed face down in a tomb (Chang 1983: 326–331, esp. fig. 282), while elsewhere skull pits containing as many as 33 skulls were excavated. Published photographs suggest that the skulls were interred while still fleshed, as the mandibles and crania were articulated. These pits represented the remains of at least 398 individuals, with at least 80 percent of them males (Li 1977: 256–257, figs. 258, 259). Smaller deposits to the east of the main tomb complex, interpreted as additional sacrificial pits, contained a minimum of 209 skulls; 192 postcranial skeletons, presumably the source of the skulls, were also excavated (Li 1977: 90). Clearly decapitation was considered the preferred form of sacrificial death, at least for men. The sex bias in skulls from sacrificial contexts may indicate that they belonged to war captives. Documentary evidence indicates that as many as 300 captives from the neighboring polity of Ch'iang were sacrificed in a single ritual event, and there is abundant evidence of divination to determine whether, for example, a sacrifice of fifteen Ch'iang or one cow would be preferred (Chang 1980: 194, 228–229). Chang (1980: 124) observes that, in contrast to burials of complete bodies, which included grave goods, deposits of skulls or postcranial remains at Anyang were generally devoid of furnishings, suggesting that those who were decapitated belonged to a separate, likely inferior, social group.

These cases suggest that in some cultural contexts decapitation is associated with a particular social status that has archaeological referents. That status may be negatively valued, as with a criminal or stranger, or positively valued, as with a postmortem guardian or an honored immigrant, as in the Lapita example (Bentley et al. 2007). Those who were decapitated for sacrificial purposes are also marked in such a way as to distinguish them from other deceased individuals. Generally, individuals found in tomb contexts are laid out in patterned form. At Anyang, some sacrifices were lined up in an orderly row prone and extended, presumably after death. Similar patterning was observed at the Mississippian period Cahokia Mound 72, where four males were arranged face up, extended, and headless (Fowler et al. 1999).

Deposition and Context

Whereas death by decapitation was a preferred execution method in many ancient societies (and thus leaves its mark osteologically as well as in the form of historical documents or, occasionally, eyewitness accounts), the final disposition of the head is often undocumented (see Stojanowski and Duncan this volume for an example from Spanish Colonial Georgia). In these cases, archaeology may be the only way that a critical source of information about the past can be retrieved. Heads and skulls, and the ways in which they were treated once their use-lives ended, hold special importance for bioarchaeologists. Not only can the skull provide us with an enormous amount of information regarding the age, sex, genetic heritage, geographic origin, and health of an individual but also the context and treatment of the object can throw light on perennial concerns of social status, ethnicity, and embodiment. Though ethnographic and ethnohistoric research provides us with evidence of human skulls curated as mementos of ancestors or used to decorate or protect structures, archaeologists frequently recover heads or skulls that have been separated from their owners in three contexts: buried in caches, deposited in nonfunerary ritual contexts, or accompanying the dead in burial.

Recent excavations at the Wari site of Conchopata (AD 550–1000) in the central Peruvian Andes uncovered thirty-three trophy heads in situ, directly associated with animal bones and smashed ceramic urns depicting trophy heads (Tung 2006; see also Andrushko this volume). The combination of trophy head iconography along with the actual heads—of twenty-five adult males and eight children aged from three to six years—provides a means to reconstruct the social life of trophy heads within Wari society. Tung (2006: 137) proposes that the severed heads may be evidence of "ritual battles, secular acts of violence against enemies, ancestor veneration, or some combination thereof." Relative to this discovery, the Nasca people of the South Coast of Peru interred the heads of both men and women in caches, as many as forty-eight heads at a time (Browne et al. 1993). Given the optimal preservation conditions in some parts of Peru, many heads have survived with tissue intact, complete with cords for suspension and thorns holding the lips closed (Browne et al. 1993; Proulx 2001; Verano 1995; Williams et al. 2001; see also Forgey this volume).

Other examples of skull caching include two sets of skulls (twenty-eight skulls in one set, six in the other) cached in the Mesolithic cave site of Ofnet, Germany (Armit 2006; Frayer 1997; Orschiedt 1998, 2001, 2005), and a Late Classic Maya pit context at Colha that yielded the skulls of thirty men, women, and children (Massey 1989; Mock 1998). The Ofnet skulls had been placed in pits as fleshed heads—some with perimortem trauma as well as cuts to the vertebrae indicative of decapitation—belonging to individuals ranging in age from neonate to elderly, with a preponderance of very young children and women. The heads were treated with ochre and deposited, along with shells and tooth ornaments, in a circle facing west toward the cave entrance. Similarly, another skull nest containing the three carefully placed heads of a male, female, and disabled hydrocephalic child were found forty-nine kilometers from Ofnet. These heads also displayed perimortem injuries and cut marks to the cervical vertebrae along with an association of red ochre, similar to that found at Ofnet.

These skull caches almost certainly represent interplay between violence and ritual, with massacre suggested as a possible interpretation for both the Ofnet and Colha caches. As ethnographic studies indicate (e.g., see Bonogofsky and Graham this volume), these heads, skulls, and crania may have been used for display and then intentionally hidden from view (see also Bonogofsky 2006a, 2006b). Regardless of whether ritual, massacre, or some combination of the two processes occurred, the fact that heads, skulls, or crania (rather than some other body part) were cached is itself significant. The Ofnet and Colha cases alike represent divergences from the normative funerary practices more commonly encountered in these regions; how these examples fit into a given belief system and what heads or skulls meant to the groups that cached the objects is open to interpretation (e.g., Armit 2006).

When skulls are recovered archaeologically from a nonfunerary context, they are generally presumed to be the remains of a past ritual event. While it is possible that some of these deposits are funerary deposits, such finds may or may not stand in contrast to normative burial patterns of the culture under study. Verano and colleagues (1999) reported on the skulls of two adult males recovered from a niche in a residential context at the site of Moche in Peru. They interpreted the deposit as an offering for two reasons: first, niches are generally associated with dedicatory rituals in the Andes; and second, the normative Moche funerary practice involved inhumation burial in extended position. A second example involved Tlingit mummified or dried heads wrapped in matting and placed in boxes in caves in southeastern Alaska during the protohistoric period. One of the heads belonged to what appeared to be a high-status Tlingit adult female adorned with a labret lip ornament. De Laguna (1933: pl. 28) interpreted the deposit as storage for a set of curated trophy heads redeemed by the victims' relatives, as no other skeletal elements were present. She further noted that the preservation of human heads was not an ordinary Tlingit burial practice.

In addition to cache contexts and nonfunerary ritual deposits, skulls or their individual elements, as well as fleshed heads, may be recovered in association with a deceased individual in a burial context. In other words, a complete body may be interred with an "extra" head, either alone or in sets. The Lapita interment with three skulls, discussed above, is one example of this practice (Bentley et al. 2007). Another concerns the Neolithic site of Çatal Höyük in Anatolia. An older adult female in a flexed burial was holding to her chest the plastered skull of a younger adult female (Bonogofsky 2006a: figs. 11a, 11b; Boz and Hager 2004). The burial was inside a plaster platform over which a ritual structure had been built, leading one to wonder about a genetic relationship between the two individuals as well as their social standing within the community. In the central United States, Hopewell funerary contexts in the Ohio River valley have yielded both crania and mandibles in association with elite burials (Seeman 1988). Due to the presence of similarly modified human mandibles and predatory animal jaws, Seeman (2007) finds it likely that trophies of human body parts may link back to the more ancient practice of taking and displaying animal trophies.

During the Natufian and Early Neolithic periods in the Levant and Anatolia, however, cranial removal after decomposition of the body (Bonogofsky 2001b) became an increasingly common mortuary practice, attested first in the Natufian by isolated skulls (Goren and Bar-Yosef 1973) and headless skeletons, then in the Neolithic by caches of skulls and crania as well as headless bodies excavated from numerous settlements (see Bonogofsky 2001b). The practice of cranial removal culminated with the decoration of skulls and the use of lime plaster or marl to model facial features thereon (e.g., see Bonogofsky 2001b, 2005a, 2005b, 2006a, 2006b). Isolated postcranial remains as well as cranial fragments found with groups of skulls generally are overlooked in discussions of the skulls (Bonogofsky 2001b: 190–191), unless the skulls are found with an intact postcranial skeleton (e.g., Kenyon 1981: 78, pl. 60b) or as with the plastered skull from Çatal Höyük (see above). Examples of modeled skulls have been recovered from ten Neolithic sites, either individually or in caches containing up to fifteen skulls and crania of adults and children, males and females, usually in proximity to domestic structures (Bonogofsky 2006a: 25, 2006b; although see Goring-Morris et al. 1995 and Garfinkel 2006 for further discussion of architecture). They derive from contexts that include placement on mud-brick furniture, in graves, under plastered floors, in abandoned and built-over houses (in leveling fill), and even on floors of burned houses, along with other human—as well as faunal—remains, statuary fragments, and other cultural objects (see Bonogofsky 2001a, 2001b, 2005a, 2005b, 2006a, 2006b).

Deposits of modified and curated skulls or their components have been interpreted as grave goods, the remains of ancestors, or trophies. These categories are not mutually exclusive, as discussed in the section on social functions below.

The Head as a Social and Biological Object

The human head contains a wealth of information, both culturally and biologically, as many bioarchaeologists who have studied the head or skull highlight. Depending on the needs of a society, the body and its parts might be employed to emphasize relationships with the dead, serve as powerful ritual objects, embody a specific concept or set of qualities, or mark social status or kinship (see chapters in Bonogofsky 2006c; Chacon and Dye 2007). Although human groups share the symbolic potential of the body, most notably the head, the ways in which heads and skulls are altered, used, and displayed take culture-specific forms. So why is the head—rather than, say, the forearm or the foot—considered across cultures to be an especially noteworthy part of the body?

One reason for the prominence of the human skull in ancient societies (and in the archaeological imagination) is the way in which the head and face identify a person and communicate his or her role, status, lineage, age, sex, and gender. The distinctiveness of the head, its face, and hair are reflected in the treatment of the skull and in beliefs about the head as the seat of personhood, individuality, ancestorhood, and consciousness. Thus, the head or skull may represent or symbolize the entire body or person both before and after death. Premortem alteration and postmortem embellishments further highlight the skull as the defining bodily element and ensure its recovery, curation, and use as a potent symbol imbued with meaning at the level of the person, the lineage, or the ethnic group.

The intensive use of the skull prehistorically, when coupled with the research interests of late-nineteenth- and early-twentieth-century anthropologists, provides us with an unparalleled source of information about the past. Early anthropologists often collected only skulls and crania, viewing them as intrinsically more interesting and informative than postcranial bones (e.g., Kenyon 1961: 147). Some investigators are returning to these early collections, recovering DNA and applying a century of osteological knowledge to reanalysis. For example, Müller and colleagues (2008: fig. 4) identified plagiocephaly while restudying the cranial series from the Celtic burial ground at Münsingen-Rain, first excavated in the early 1900s. Although unable to recover ancient DNA, they attributed the marked obliqueness of the skull to a hereditary congenital condition in which the musculation of the shoulder is unilaterally shortened, causing an individual to hold his or her head at an angle. Through analysis of an existing forty-nine skulls in concert with excellent chronological control, Müller and colleagues (2008; see also Kutterer and Alt 2008) determined that the cemetery contained members of two founding lineages who were likely bound through kinship and marriage.

A similar biological association appeared at Early Neolithic Jericho. Through morphometric analyses of the skeletal material excavated in the 1950s, Kurth and Röhrer-Ertl (1981) determined that at least seven of ten skulls from a skull cache composed of five adults and five children were elongated, although the skull of a middle-aged female was shortened (due in part to in vivo cranial deformation). In addition, Kurth (in Kurth and Röhrer-Ertl 1981) diagnosed an extremely arched bony palate between a narrow parallel dental arch in all nine undamaged specimens from the skull cache. This factor, along with the segregated forms of artificial skull deformation noted above (in the section on deformation, trephination, and scalping), convinced Kurth and Röhrer-Ertl (1981: 442) that the Neolithic dead at Jericho came from three small, restricted reproductive groups that were different in morphology and behavior. Further supporting evidence for close biological relationships at Jericho arose with my assessment of six plastered skulls from an existing ten specimens—for the presence or absence of dentition—using CT scans, direct observation, and photographs (Bonogofsky 2001b, 2002). All six appear to lack third molars, thus possibly indicating genetic relatedness (see Smith 1973 for third molar agenesis at Natufian Hayonim). Only one of the plastered skulls had been modeled with its osseous mandible intact; the others consist of crania crafted to look as if the lower jaw were included (Bonogofsky 2001b: pls. 3a–3c, 2002: fig. 1; see figure 1.1).

The skull as seat of personhood, the role of the face as identifier and communicator, and the malleability of the cranial bones combine to provide archaeologists with an object laden with meaning, one that could be invested with potent symbolism or could serve as a social or biological signifier individually or collectively. Ethnographic research, historical documents, and material remains reveal patterning across cultures in the selection and use of the skulls of specific individuals, a topic I address below.

Social Functions of the Head

Anthropologists have documented a variety of functions of the human skull across cultures—for example, as a symbol of established power among the medieval Irish and British and as an object of trade and exchange in Melanesia and Polynesia. The head of an ancestor or enemy could serve as a symbol of prestige, bringing both resources and protection to a village. Family members, leaders, mourners, and victorious warriors were among those with a vested interest in how the body—and the head—was treated. The skull functioned as both a physical and a social object, and even, under certain conditions, as a subject (e.g., see O'Donnabhain this volume).

The decapitated, decorated, deformed, or otherwise modified head or skull may also be approached as an object of material culture (see Stojanowski and Duncan this volume). Below, I identify several examples of emic explanations from the point of view of insiders, involving distinctions meaningful to the culture under study, and etic interpretations of function from the perspective of outsiders, involving concepts and categories that are meaningful to Western observers. These two aspects may overlap, or they may be mutually exclusive within the same culture or ethnic group.

The archaeological contexts for such skulls and heads include trash or midden deposits; private and public spaces; funerary, ceremonial and ritual contexts; domestic areas; and areas under and within structures, including within walls and wall foundations, as well as in caves and rock shelters. In many cases, the use and function of the skull falls into several categories (see Buckberry 2006 for heads taken from individuals at both ends of the social spectrum in Anglo-Saxon England), demonstrating the skull's versatility as sign and symbol.

As noted in chapters in this volume (e.g., Bonney and Clegg), skulls, whether plain or decorated, have been used in divination and sorcery. However, skulls also figured in the avoidance of trauma. As discussed by Levene (2009), skulls inscribed with Jewish Aramaic magic incantations attest to the use of skulls by Jews during the Talmudic era in Babylonia to ward off ghosts or demons. These skulls seem to have served a purpose similar to that of the more than two thousand magic incantation bowls recovered from modern-day Iraq, dating from the third to the seventh centuries AD. Various media such as ceramic, parchment, tin, lead, copper, silver, gold, and eggs, as well as human skulls, were used as surfaces on which to inscribe protective formulas against demons thought to cause sickness, death, and other medical problems in Mesopotamia. Some of the demons being warded off (referred to as "Liliths" on the skulls studied by Levene [2009]) were thought to cause the death of infants, such as the baby snatcher Lamashtu. Skulls were used contemporaneously as well in attempts to raise the dead through necromancy (Levene 2009).

The idea that the human head or skull has the ability to ward off evil or misfortune has been documented in several contexts that are more recent. Goodale (1985: 240) recorded a practice among the Kaulong of Papua New Guinea, where the skull of the deceased is passed through a trading network and fulfils a protective function at each household along the way. Elsewhere, Williams (2006) suggests that the removal of the head, either before or after burial, may have served an apotropaic function in the case of a "bad" or "deviant" death in Anglo-Saxon England.

A related belief is that the body of the deceased might harbor dangerous forces and that the danger or threat may be averted through decapitation. Lovisek (2007) discusses how the Kwakiutl of the Northwest Coast of North America decapitated their enemies to release the soul both to obtain the soul for reincarnation and to prevent the soul from returning to the body and harming the victor.

Conversely, keeping the body intact was at times equally important, as noted for those who may have been perceived as "other" among island groups in Melanesia. For example, only two categories of people in the Trobriand Islands did not have their skulls removed after death. Weiner (1976: 69, 82) suggests that the elderly may have been excluded from skull removal because of a perceived loss of beauty and fecundity, while suspected sorcerers were buried face down to prevent the spirit's return to the village. Similarly, Bonney and Clegg (this volume), in their review of Haddon (1935), point out that although both adult males and females were mummified in the Torres Strait Islands, this treatment excluded cultural outsiders: the elderly, children, and those thought to have died of disease.

Further examples of the perceived protective powers held by skulls include their use as foundation deposits, which generally involve ritual objects placed to protect—and thus prevent—a building from falling into ruin. This may have been the intent at Early Neolithic Jericho, where isolated skulls and crania of adults and children were recovered from walls and wall foundations, from under the corner of a house, and from building fill, suggesting their placement as foundation deposits (Bonogofsky 2006a). In addition, five infant skulls severed along with their cervical vertebrae were found in the stone foundation of a plaster basin in a ceremonial building, leading their excavator to interpret them as foundation deposits (Kenyon 1981: 9, 49).

Another function of the head or skull is to represent the entire person. The trophy heads associated with the Nasca culture (100 BC–AD 700) of southern Peru may have been used this way, although Kathleen Forgey's work (this volume) indicates that the heads may not have been "trophies" after all, as the idea of the trophy head generally implies that the skull or head of the deceased was curated or displayed in order to demonstrate prowess in warfare. Another relevant example includes the Gaulish Iron Age practice of hanging the heads of defeated warriors from the necks of horses (Armit 2006).

"Trophy" heads are a symbol-laden representation of an enemy. Heads serving as trophies of war—and the motivations behind their collection—have been discussed for the New World by numerous researchers (e.g., see Chacon and Dye 2007 for Amerindian examples). Such trophy heads may be redeemed at times by the victim's relatives, as noted above in de Laguna's (1933: 32–44, pl. 28) description of three Tlingit trophy heads found in a cave in southeastern Alaska.

The head or skull of the deceased may be decorated, curated, and otherwise manipulated, by which means either the deceased as an individual or the deceased as an unnamed member of the community of ancestors is commemorated and kept as a memento. Kenyon (in Kenyon and Tushing-ham 1953) was the first to propose that the plastered skulls from the Neolithic Near East (7200–6000 BC for the Levant) served to commemorate the life of a beloved male ancestor, although my more recent research (Bonogofsky 2001a, 2001b, 2002, 2003, 2004, 2005a, 2005b, 2006a, 2006b) indicates that such skulls belonged as well to females and children (and thus not necessarily males or biological ancestors) and may have fulfilled multiple functions in ancient Near Eastern mortuary ritual, including their possible use as fertility or apotropaic devices (see also Wright 1988). Kenyon's ideas apparently origi-nated in Melanesian analogs, which are themselves problematic as examples of ancestor worship (Bonogofsky 2001b; Bonogofsky and Graham this volume).

Conversely, Oakdale (2005) discusses how dead ancestors are forgotten among the Kayabi of Amazonian Brazil through Jawosi rituals in which the Kayabi are encouraged to view their own dead as enemies and thus "other" through imagery and by the use of trophy heads and the skulls of actual en-emies. Through the rituals, the Kayabi meditate on the enemy dead, who is considered a participant in their social gathering, and whose head is meta-phorically boiled into a porridge-like liquid. Later, the house where the be-loved dead male lived and is buried is often burned down and a new one built (destruction of the house does not occur with deceased women and children), again to help remove the memory of the deceased from the community. En-emy crania were further used in boys' initiation ceremonies, in which the bones were broken and discarded and the teeth were strung onto necklaces.

The living are also encouraged to forget the beloved dead as individuals among the Ecuadorian Jivaro Achuar through funeral laments that focus on the decomposing face of the exposed male (females and children were per-ceived as easier to forget), thus allowing the man's appearance to fade from memory (Taylor 1993). In contrast, the facial features of Achuar enemies were preserved in the form of the shrunken head. The flesh of the face and head was removed from the decapitated member and preserved as a *tsantsa*, while the skull was discarded and tossed into the brush. In this context, the enemy was symbolically turned into a relative, was killed a second time, and was buried, mourned, and forgotten as one's own relative.

Disembodied Nasca heads also may have been devices used to facilitate an-cestor veneration. Forgey (this volume), as noted above, addresses this ques-tion through DNA analysis in an effort to determine whether trophy heads derived from group members or enemy outsiders. The "ancestor question" is a persistent one plaguing not only the study of the ancient Andes and the ancient Near East but also the Maya world and prehistoric Britain (Whitley

2002). The curation of the head reminded the living of the role of ancestors as lineage heads, symbols of land and resource rights, and spiritual providers, and also served as a reminder of the prowess of warriors in battle.

The various functions, then, are not mutually exclusive. Human heads may be used in multiple ways by a single cultural group or across a widespread region. The same applies to the Neolithic skulls deriving from males, females, and children, which have been excavated in isolation and from caches at numerous sites in the Middle East. The multiple contexts and diverse locations of the skulls and crania indicate that they may have functioned as mementos of the deceased, as apotropaic devices, as foundation deposits, as fertility objects, and as grave goods (Bonogofsky 2006a, 2006b), although some excavators and other discussants continue to interpret them as confirmation of ancestor worship (e.g., see Gedalyahu 2008: 1). Attention to depositional and stratigraphic context, including whether the skulls were hidden or placed on display, detailed bioarchaeological and biochemical analyses, and artifactual associations are key to unraveling the complex meanings embodied by the human head archaeologically and to identifying a particular use or meaning within a given context. Interpretation is greatly complicated, however, by the fact that archaeological signatures of the functions discussed above often overlap. Restricting our study of material culture to the identification of a single treatment, role, or function, or even age or sex category, may obscure critical phases of the life history of an object that are evident in use wear or may simplify its complex entanglements in social relations (see, e.g., Fletcher et al. 2008). Although I would maintain that studying the ways in which skulls functioned prehistorically is a valuable enterprise, pigeonholing objects only limits interpretive potential and therefore our understanding of past human societies, as I discuss later (in Bonogofsky and Graham this volume). As the section below demonstrates, in addition to their critical roles as symbols, objects of exchange, veneration, and memory, skulls represent an unparalleled source of bioarchaeological data.

The Bioarchaeology of the Skull

Twenty-first-century contextual analyses of human remains, including the chapters in this book, have their roots in the typological study of human crania, an approach championed by scientists such as Aleš Hrdlička and Georg K. Neumann (Cook 2006). For early physical anthropologists and through the mid-twentieth century, the answers to questions of the origins and diversity of the Native peoples of North America resided in the collection of skulls and the measurement of various morphological features. Although we have progressed far beyond attempts to identify racial types or to demonstrate a simple and direct relationship between intelligence and the size of the brain case, the skull remains perhaps the most informative component of the human body to modern biological anthropologists. Not only is cranial morphology critical to the accurate estimation of age and sex but also the teeth (in addition to being indicators of health, hygiene, and nutrition) can be used as sources of tissue for biochemical and isotopic analyses (see Montgomery, Knüsel, and Tucker this volume) to help determine, for example, whether an individual was a local resident, and thus presumably an "insider," or from a distant region, and thus possibly considered an "outsider."

Today, bioarchaeologists and biological anthropologists routinely exploit biochemistry, in tandem with standard osteometric and dental methods, to reconstruct ancient life histories. DNA and stable isotope analyses are increasingly employed to address questions of biological distance, diet, and even region of origin (see Forgey this volume) and are often used to test hypotheses derived from other methods. In combination with contextual analysis and a consideration of the skull as a symbolically powerful object, biochemical and osteological methods are giving us ever more detailed views of ancient lives. Several chapters in this volume (e.g., Forgey; Montgomery, Knüsel, and Tucker; Stojanowski and Duncan) demonstrate the strengths of these approaches.

In the United States, the impetus to combine the strengths of biological anthropology in skeletal analysis and archaeology in the reconstruction of ancient lifeways came with the 1977 publication of an unassuming volume by Robert L. Blakely titled *Biocultural Adaptation in Prehistoric America*. This book marked the inception of an approach to human remains that integrated the methods and insights of biological anthropologists and archaeologists. In a series of short chapters, the authors laid the foundations for an interdisciplinary approach to questions of social organization, diet, disease, and demography (e.g., Buikstra 1977; Robbins 1977) that is now commonly termed "bioarchaeology" (Buikstra 2006; Sofaer 2006).

Today, bioarchaeologists—who are generally trained both in archaeological method and in osteology, paleopathology, and population genetics—engage the human skull in myriad ways, ranging from studies of skull deformation as an indicator of social or ethnic identity (Geller this volume; Lozada this volume; Sharapova and Razhev this volume) to the implications of the plastering of the skulls of men, women, and children in the Neolithic Near East, Eurasia, North America, and Melanesia (see, e.g., Bonogofsky and Graham this volume; Bonogofsky 2006c; Fletcher et al. 2008). By combining knowledge of human biology with the social, economic, and religious context provided by archaeology, bioarchaeologists conceive of the human body as both a biological organism and a source of material culture (Sofaer 2006). The skull, with the wealth of information it provides on both the social person and the biological organism subject to various stressors, is thus an ideal subject of study.

Biological Stressors

Skeletal stress to the human head results in a number of manifestations, whether as metric variation (skeletal robustness, cranial shape) or as a process of cultural modification (cranial deformation, trephination), disease (cranial vault thickening, tuberculosis, dental caries), or violence and injury (depressed cranial fractures). Metric variation can be culturally or environmentally induced. One of the areas in which cultural context and osteology have established a most fruitful relationship is in the study of paleopathologies. The human head is a sensitive body part that expresses in skeletal form evidence of dietary stressors, violent injury, disease processes, physical activity, mechanical loading, congenital defects, and accident. In comparative studies of skeletal populations, cranial and dental differences have been observed between ethnic groups, men and women, adults and children, high- and low-status individuals (see, e.g., Geller this volume; Lozada this volume; Sharapova and Razhev this volume). Markers of health status are routinely sought in bioarchaeological studies of human remains (see, e.g., Cohen and Armelagos 1984; Cohen and Crane-Kramer 2007), often as proxies for resource access; two markers in particular (porotic hyperostosis and cribra orbitalia) are evident on the cranium. Porotic hyperostosis is expressed as lesions of the surface of the cranial vault, attributable to anemia in childhood that usually occurs on the frontal and parietals. This iron deficiency can be due to inherited anemias, such as thalassemia and sickle-cell anemia, or to a lack of absorbed iron from dietary sources (Stuart-Macadam 1991, 1992). Cribra orbitalia, which is a form of porotic hyperostosis, manifests itself in the orbital roof. Although iron deficiencies are usually considered to be the cause of cribra orbitalia, heavy parasite loads, infectious disease, and scurvy may also be implicated (Blom et al. 2005; Cook 2007; Verano 1997, 1998).

Walker (1986) found that a major contributor of childhood porotic hyperostosis in the Channel Island area of California could be a lack of sanitation with respect to water resources and garbage disposal, as well as inadvertent exposure to parasites through the consumption of marine life. These two factors would increase infection and lower the amount of iron absorbed by the body. Porotic hyperostosis began to appear during the Neolithic period and is thus usually attributed to the introduction of agriculture and a shift in diet to less meat and more foods high in carbohydrates. Alternatively, porotic hyperostosis may have appeared in the Neolithic, not because of resulting changes in diet per se but because population density increased, leading to greater exposure to pathogens (Stuart-Macadam 1991). Kent (1986) likewise found that diet mattered very little for increased porotic hyperostosis in the prehistoric Anasazi of the American Southwest. Rather, an increase in viral, bacterial, and parasitic diseases resulting from sedentism and crowding contributed to this expression of iron-deficiency anemia.

Porotic hyperostosis and cribra orbitalia can also be caused by artificial skull deformation (see Aufderheide and Rodriguez-Martin 1998: 349; Ortner and Putschar 1985). Meiklejohn and colleagues (1992) note that porotic hyperostosis is often found in crania artificially deformed in vivo from the proto-Neolithic and Neolithic Near East. More specifically, Bennike and Alexandersen (2007: 148) find that pitting reflects "processes of high vascularization attributable to growth or stress" and that mechanical loading (artificial skull deformation) may be a more plausible explanation than parasitism. They support their theory "by the fact that pitting is also seen in [southern Scandinavian] Neolithic skulls (often with a particular thickness), whereas the appearance of cribra orbitalia is almost nonexistent in any of the Mesolithic/Early Neolithic skulls" (Bennike and Alexandersen 2007: 148).

Evidence of skeletal stress has been seen as both a positive and a negative reaction to the environment. For example, most researchers agree that higher frequencies of skeletal lesions, such as evidence of porotic hyperostosis, indicate a decrease in health (Goodman 1993), yet Wood and colleagues (1992) and Cook (2007) take exception to this conclusion and propose that higher frequencies of skeletal lesions observed in early agricultural societies could be interpreted as a hardiness to survive illness and stress: in other words, "the pathological skeleton represents a survivor" (Cook 2007: 15). Skeletal evidence of stress may complement the findings of zooarchaeologists and paleoethnobotanists, who can identify potential nutritional deficiencies and differences in access to highly valued food items on the basis of faunal and plant remains. Even when these materials are unavailable, the quantity and quality of grave goods, the grave structure, and the location and disposition of the body provide broader contexts in which to consider the skeletal evidence (see, e.g., Sharapova and Razhev this volume).

Another disease related to diet is scurvy, which results from insufficient vitamin C and may produce black staining of the roots of the teeth because of hematomas, as was found among Dutch whalers buried at Spitsbergen in the seventeenth and eighteenth centuries (Maat 2004). Scurvy may also present in the form of porotic and proliferative endo- and ectocranial lesions (Brickley and Ives 2006; Mays 2008), especially among children (Ortner et al. 2001; Ortner et al. 1999). Other ailments particular to children are occipital ulcers and infections that result from cradleboarding (Holliday 1993).

In addition to its potential to express dietary deficiencies, the skull as a neurological and cognitive center is subject to violent injuries that may take several forms, including fractures and projectile point lesions. These types of trauma have been used by bioarchaeologists to gauge levels of interpersonal violence through time, between males and females, and between different ethnic or social groups. Walker (1989), for example, found significant differences in the prevalence of cranial fractures between two California populations, one of which probably experienced greater competition over resources. He also observed increasing numbers of injuries through time, suggesting that population growth and environmental instability exacerbated the situation. More than half of the injuries were on the frontal, with the left side somewhat more affected than the right side. This injury pattern indicates that the person faced a right-handed attacker, in which more middle-aged men were injured than any other age/sex category. In a study of three Peruvian populations, Tung (2007) identified an increased prevalence of cranial trauma during periods of imperial Wari rule; she also found that men and women displayed distinct patterns of head injuries, suggesting that they experienced violence in very different ways. A study from the North American Southwest also showed sex-based differences in cranial trauma (Martin 1997). Using both skeletal and archaeological evidence, Martin argued that women with multiple fractures and atypical treatment at death (i.e., burial in a prone or sprawled position) belonged to a subclass of the population that routinely endured physical abuse.

The shape of the skull, affected by artificial vault deformation (see Geller this volume; Lozada this volume; Sharapova and Razhev this volume; also see Anton 1989 for resulting facial deformation), may also be determined by additional biocultural factors such as gene flow as well as masticatory function, which influence cranial vault shortening and craniofacial morphology (Larsen 1995). There was a widespread trend toward cranial vault shortening in earlier populations, to include those in the Middle East, because of masticatory, dietary, and technological changes, especially those associated with the shift from gathering to farming and the consumption of softer foods. For example, Nubian Mesolithic foragers ca. 12,000 BP and early agriculturalists 3400–1200 BC have flat and elongated vaults with protruding supraorbital tori and occipitals, while later intensive agriculturalists AD 1500 have rounded vaults with small and more posteriorly placed faces and masticatory muscle attachment sites (Larsen 1997).

Age also influences craniofacial morphology. Craniofacial robusticity in older adult females increases with age to mimic characteristics associated with adult males. This change may be related in part to postmenopausal changes taking place in females. Cranial width increases slightly in middle-aged women and widens significantly in the vaults of old men, possibly as a result of masticatory function (Sjøvold 1995). Masticatory, dietary, and technological influences on the shape of the skull indicate that skull shape can be part of individual, not necessarily population, variation (Larsen 1997). Although brachycrania, producing short skulls, was rare among Neolithic populations in general, both brachycrania and dolichocrania, which produced elongated skulls, occurred together in the Levant as well as in the entire area of the Near East during the Early Neolithic period. According to anthropologist Gottfried Kurth's 1957 field notes from Jericho, the majority of "low stature" skulls were dolichocranic, with elongated cranial vaults and high and narrow faces. Some of these skulls, however, including the shorter, rounder skulls, had been modified in vivo, through the process of culturally induced artificial cranial deformation (see Fletcher et al. 2008; Kurth and Röhrer-Ertl 1981).

Various congenital defects may be identified on the basis of cranial remains, such as craniosynostosis (craniostenosis), that is, the premature closure of cranial sutures, a defect with a hereditary component that may present in several different forms, depending on which sutures are involved (Aufderheide and Rodriguez-Martin 1998: 52–54; Kutterer and Alt 2008; Müller et al. 2008). This genetic anomaly, which subsequently alters the shape of the skull, is referenced by Pamela Geller (this volume) to protest the application of the term *deformation* to both craniostenosis and intentional in vivo cranial modification performed for cultural reasons, as, for example, among the Maya. However, the ramifications for both are far-reaching, as demonstrated in a study of 130 Peruvian culturally altered crania examined by Anton (1989: 264), who found that "facial deformation is induced by vault deformation." Other defects, detectable through craniometrics, include hydrocephaly, which results from an accumulation of cerebral spinal fluid. Examination by Richards and Anton (1991) of a partial child's skeleton from central California, dating to the Middle Period (ca. 2500 BC–AD 500), revealed a unique craniofacial configuration and malformed postcrania as a result of this central nervous system disorder.

Dental pathologies also serve as indicators of health, social status, heredity, and physical activity. Caries and dental attrition, the latter caused by a coarse diet, are both prevalent in prehistoric skeletal samples. Dental caries is an age-progressive disease process in which organic acids ferment dietary carbohydrates to demineralize exposed tooth enamel and underlying dentin (Larsen et al. 1991). The disease process is enhanced the longer teeth are exposed to an oral environment in which bacteria and dental plaque are present and a high-carbohydrate diet is consumed.

An increase in dental caries in the New World is associated with an increase in the consumption of agricultural foods such as maize (Larsen et al. 1991). A diet high in carbohydrates like that associated with agriculture is key in the advance of dental caries. However, nonagricultural foods such as honey and sweet, sticky fruit such as dates and figs also contribute to dental caries (Larsen 1995). Larsen (1983) correlated the incidence of dental caries on the prehistoric Georgia coast in North America with diet, sex, and age to find that dental caries increased with the shift to agriculture and occurred more frequently in women than in men. This finding was echoed by Larsen and colleagues (2007) for northern Florida and upland Georgia, although adult males in central and southern Florida tended to have more caries than adult females did. Dental caries may have affected more women in coastal and upland Georgia and northern Florida because of their increased access to starchy foods such as maize (compared to men, who consumed more meat protein) and their slightly longer life exposure to the physical environment (Larsen 1983; Larsen et al. 1991; Larsen et al. 2007). However, stable isotope signatures do not fully support dietary differences as an explanation for higher caries rates in men in central and southern Florida (Larsen et al. 2007).

On the north coast of Rota, Mariana Islands, Hanson (1988) found a high rate of dental caries in deciduous teeth, while the rate of caries in adult teeth was very low. This decreased incidence was associated with the betel nut chewed by adults, as the tannins therein change the oral chemistry to inhibit cariogenic activity. Kurth and Röhrer-Ertl (1981: 441) noted extremely low rates of dental caries in the Neolithic Near Eastern population at Jericho, with only one occurrence. However, I documented caries in two deciduous molars belonging to a subadult during study of two crania recovered from a skull cache of six from this same site (Bonogofsky 1999; see Kenyon 1981: pl. VIIIa). Caries rates increased in adults in prehistoric South Asia with the introduction of agriculture although women had higher caries rates than men did (Lukacs 1996). Conversely, the teeth of young boys at Gulbarga, Karnataka, had higher rates of dental caries than did the deciduous teeth of girls (Reddy 1980). These cultural distinctions in dental health during the life span of the individual thus involve questions of age, sex, and gender as well as social status.

Ancient Near Eastern inhabitants of the early Neolithic settlement of 'Ain Ghazal, Jordan, who consumed abrasive foods high in carbohydrates, were subject to periods of nutritional stress and used their teeth as tools, as shown by Sarie (1995b) in a review of dental health. The inhabitants' diet consisted of both wild and domesticated plants and animals, which played a role in the dental wear, antemortem tooth loss, and masticatory problems. Seasonal starvation is evidenced in severe cases of enamel hypoplasia (developmental defects that represent physiological stress events) and high child mortality rates. Moreover, Sarie (1995a, 1995b) proposed that tuberculosis could have been a factor as well, finding that even though the inhabitants' diet became more varied, environmental stress was more severe (see Sharapova and Razhev this volume for hypoplasia among the Sargat in Eurasia). He further traced patterns of microstriation and dental calculus to understand mandibular function and diet patterns. Mandibles exhibited degenerative changes in the epicondyle, representing an association of arthritis with the utilization of the front teeth as tools. Degeneration of the glenoid fossa was associated with alveolar resorption and recession, severe front tooth attrition, missing teeth, and a strong muscle insertion on the ascending ramus and gonial angle. Sarie concluded that the inhabitants of 'Ain Ghazal had consumed hard, abrasive food and used their teeth as tools to cut thread and grasp basketry materials, resulting in severe tooth wear. In effect, most of the adults at 'Ain Ghazal suffered from periodontal disease, with one quarter suffering from antemortem tooth loss, possibly as a result of an agricultural diet processed using a stone pestle and mortar. Most of the wear on the anterior dentition resulted in the use of the teeth for grasping basketry material, based on the presence of striation lines and phytoliths and pollen grains of reeds and rushes in the dental calculus. An affliction of tuberculosis and the use of teeth in basket making may explain the periodontal inflammation and maxillary disease found in one female individual (Sarie 1995a; see Molnar 1972 for additional extramasticatory functions that produce grooves or faceting of teeth).

In a study of the prevalence of hypoplasias in two Alaskan populations, Keenleyside (1998) found that North Alaskan Eskimos exhibited significantly higher rates than Aleuts, in part because of differences in subsistence. Differences in dental wear patterns between males and females may indicate that tasks were divided along sex lines (Larsen 1997: 259–260). Excess wear on the labial surfaces of teeth can indicate use of labrets. Wear patterns, when combined with archaeological evidence for labrets from funerary contexts, can reveal patterns in male and female ornamentation and social signaling. For example, dental evidence of abraded canines indicates that males wore paired lateral labrets in Chile (Torres-Rouff 2003), while on the Northwest Coast free women used labrets to signal high status (Ames 1994: 221).

This short discussion of paleopathologies that produce changes in the teeth and bones of the skull is by no means exhaustive, but it does provide some indication of the breadth of information available on prehistoric health status that can be obtained from the skull. One objective of this volume is to demonstrate the sorts of insights into the past that an integrated approach to archaeological and osteological data can generate. Even when skeletal evidence is limited to the skull, identification of trauma and disease processes, as discussed above, provide critical data on research topics as diverse as social inequalities, changes in subsistence, social relations, and violence.

Joanna Sofaer, in *The Body as Material Culture* (2006), argues for greater articulation of social theory with studies of the human skeleton. In particular, she advocates an approach that emphasizes the study of the living body through the skeleton. Sofaer sees the body as the locus of biology, materiality, and representation and therefore full of interpretive potential. The skull, of all human body parts, presents the greatest prospects for the integration of the biological, physical, and material with the social, political, and representational. The chapters in this book examine the living body (through deformation of the skull), processes that convert the body from one state to another (decapitation), and postmortem actions (decoration) that, in some cases, turn the skull (or the body as a whole) into an agent of material culture (e.g., Andrushko this volume; Bonogofsky and Graham this volume; O'Donnabhain this volume). In each case, the skull is viewed as both a biological object and an object (or subject) vested with social, symbolic, or ideological meaning. The materiality of the skull permits its premortem manipulation and its deployment postmortem in a variety of ways. While bioarchaeology has perhaps not yet achieved the articulation of the physical with the social that Sofaer desires, this volume demonstrates that the study of the skull has the potential to bridge the gap between social theory and skeletal biology.

Contributions to This Volume

Chapters in this volume are organized into two parts—those that take a primarily symbolic or contextual approach to the human head and those that deal with the human skull bioarchaeologically or biochemically. Regardless of the approach that is taken, the authors all aim to address the broad question of whose heads and skulls were disembodied, decorated, deformed, or otherwise modified and/or curated and why, paying close attention to the age and sex of the individuals under study, noting that at times the deceased may be symbolically transformed to transcend one specific social category such as "ancestor" or "enemy."

Symbolic and Contextual Approaches

Heather Bonney and Margaret Clegg review ethnographic reports and other lines of evidence for the modification of skulls from the Torres Strait Islands, to determine whether one can differentiate the decorated skull of a relative from a head collected as a trophy. Ethnographic accounts of mortuary and headhunting practices, which disappeared completely from the islands during the conversion to Christianity beginning in 1871, included skulls of relatives naturally defleshed using termite mounds, as well as heads of men, women, and children severed from their bodies using bamboo knives. Heads of relatives (unspecified as to male or female) were kept as memorials and used in divination. However, heads from neighboring islanders within the Torres Strait Islands were collected during raids as trophies and status symbols, then naturally or manually defleshed and used as objects of trade between the islands.

The authors determined that skulls reported as relatives and trophies were both painted and decorated; thus, this particular criterion cannot be used to help determine from which category the skulls derived. In addition, their study of skulls from this region found no evidence for decapitation on any of the crania or mandibles (the vertebrae were not present). They did, however, find evidence of termite activity—supporting reports of termites used as natural defleshers. These types of studies are needed to help independently substantiate such cultural practices and thus move forward our understanding of whose skulls were selected and curated, as well as how and why.

In a chapter on the practice of skull modeling that combines contextual and bioarchaeological approaches, Jeffrey Graham and I review twentieth-century ethnographic evidence for all aspects of head acquisition and decoration, as well as the demographic profiles of the deceased and the uses of skulls in sorcery and divination in Melanesia. We note that perceived attractiveness and fecundity in youthful male and female individuals were determining factors in the selection of a deceased individual for special treatment of the skull. In addition, we provide an example of how slain enemies, and thus "outsiders," could be considered ancestors and thus potentially become "insiders" by contributing symbolically to the proliferation and strength of the community because of the deceased's prowess in life. Further, we observe that Kathleen Kenyon, whose work at Jericho is often cited as the example par excellence of the skull as an object of ancestor worship, used vague Melanesian analogs as the source of her interpretations of Neolithic skulls of the Near East. Strengthening our argument for the consideration of women and children in studies of skulls in archaeological and museum collections, Graham and I present a case study in nondestructive aging methods using a skull from the Sepik River region of New Guinea. We show how radiography and modern forensic methods can be applied to successfully estimate age at death from plastered or overmodeled skulls, as well as in cases when postcrania are absent and cranial remains are fragmentary. The Sepik River skull, determined to be that of a child between three and four years old, is highly unlikely to be that of a venerated ancestor of archaeological myth. This evidence provides a comparative example for recent work in the Neolithic Near East, North America, and Eurasia.

Frédérique Valentin and Noémie Rolland make a compelling case for the changing motivation behind the collection and decoration of skulls deriving from ancestors and enemies in the Marquesas Islands of French Polynesia following European contact in the eighteenth century. Based on their review of documents, illustrations, and artifacts, they determine that skulls—once curated for their soul essence after decomposition of the bodies of relatives and chiefs and worn as trophies by victorious warriors—became "made to order" curios for an expanding European market. These skulls, collected almost exclusively from the island of Nuku Hiva by nineteenth-century European explorers and mariners and described as deriving from war enemies caught outside the community, also have archaeological referents recovered from domestic as well as burial sites. This work is central to the question of whose skulls were collected and why and help to inform our understanding of past cultural practices.

In his chapter on medieval Ireland, Barra O'Donnabhain integrates three lines of evidence—archaeology, literature, and iconography—to show that the severing of heads and their collection and public display in centers of elite social and political power served to negotiate power and difference between competing groups beginning as early as the seventh century AD. He argues that decapitation was used to symbolically transform insiders, as members of a group, into social outsiders through the removal and denigration of their heads and other body parts. This concept expanded with the rise of Christianity and the notion of purgatory, denying privileged status to both the body and the soul of the social outcast.

Bioarchaeological and Biochemical Approaches

Janet Montgomery, Christopher Knüsel, and Katie Tucker analyze the remains of individuals from a Roman period cemetery (late second to early fourth centuries AD) in Yorkshire, United Kingdom, primarily comprising young to middle-aged adult males who exhibited taller than average stature for the population, as well as evidence for decapitation in forty-eight out of eighty cases (60 percent). The authors investigate the origins of six of the male adults buried at 1–3 Driffield Terrace, York (late second and early third centuries AD). Four of these six men had been decapitated, and one of the four was in leg irons. The authors' analyses of lead, strontium, and oxygen isotopes, used to explore whether these men were local or nonlocal residents, determined that the men's origins reflected the increased cosmopolitan nature of the Roman Empire; they came from mixed locations, nearby as well as very far away. Moreover, contrary to expectations that these men were social outcasts, the historical context in which these men lived indicates that they were likely Roman soldiers of higher social status, based on their burial in a prime location that was along the main approach road and on a promontory, as well as their form of death by decapitation (for the four who had been decapitated). The authors' contribution highlights the far-reaching scope of the Roman Empire and the realization that higher-status individuals who were part of this empire were allowed to choose decapitation as a more honorable form of punishment.

In a contribution from the Spanish colonial period of the southeastern United States, Christopher Stojanowski and William Duncan tackle a human calvaria attributed to a Franciscan friar killed during a rebellion by the local Guale population in the late 1500s. Using a large comparative database of cranial measurements from sites in Spain and the United States, they attempt to determine the population affinity of the individual represented by the calvaria, concluding that the remains are Iberian or even Spanish in affiliation, possibly that of the beheaded sixteenth-century priest, and thus a member of the Franciscan Order. In contrast to early-twentieth-century practices in which investigators assigned skulls to broad racial categories of "European," "African," or "Native American," Stojanowski and Duncan construct a population history of the region in order to consider all likely possibilities. They find cranial data sets comparable in both temporal and spatial terms, using, for example, sets representing late medieval Spanish and Basque populations, eighteenth- and nineteenth-century African-Americans, and seventeenth-century Euro-Americans. Instead of collapsing populations into large regional groups, this method accounts for short-term secular changes in human cranial morphology within a single population and serves as a guide for future studies.

In a contribution from an area little known to Euro-American readers, Svetlana Sharapova and Dmitry Razhev discuss the widespread practice of skull deformation among peoples of the Iron Age Sargat culture (500 BC–AD 300) living north and east of the Black and Caspian seas. Archaeological investigation of the Sargat culture has yielded numerous kurgans (burial mounds) containing the remains of males, females, and juveniles, many of whom display evidence of intentional cranial deformation. Measuring multiple cranial indices, Sharapova and Razhev interpret deformation as evidence of an emerging marker of social status. They combine the skeletal analysis with careful consideration of the context and content of each individual grave. This bioarchaeological study enables them to distinguish between sedentary peoples, who are generally thought to have constituted the local ancestral, or substratum, population, and those who pursued a nomadic lifeway on horseback as descendants of a southern aristocracy and thus belonged to the superstratum.

Maria Lozada presents a compelling case for the use of the human head as an ethnic and socioeconomic group marker in her discussion of the pre-Inca Chiribaya from southern Peru (AD 700–1359). She notes that premortem cranial modification was only one of a number of distinct cultural practices that served to reinforce and symbolize clear social and cultural differences between Chiribaya agriculturalists and fishermen. Lozada concludes that this form of group identity became widespread among the Chiribaya in response to internal sociopolitical and economic stress during the time of an encroaching colonialist state. Context is key to this nuanced interpretation of a fascinating body of evidence.

Pamela Geller draws upon skeletal remains, architectural contexts, associated artifacts, iconography, and ethnohistories to discuss Maya premortem cranial modification from northwestern Belize. Using "a life course approach informed by social theories about identity," she argues that individual heads may have been shaped in infancy to initiate a "process of becoming," perhaps indicating the eldest offspring or an intended occupation, in a sense marking the individual from infancy to ancestorhood. This Maya practice, archaeologically attested as early as the Middle Preclassic period (ca. 1200 BC), was banned after European conquest; as a result, contemporary Maya no longer mold the heads of infants. Geller's archaeological sample, which focuses on twenty-five crania that could be assessed for modification dating to the Classic period (AD 250–900) and deriving from commoner and noble classes from various sites, included both males and females—although male crania were intentionally altered more often—thus neither sex nor socioeconomic status appeared to be the impetus behind intentional cranial shaping. Geller concludes that the motivation behind this ancient practice—why intentionally mold the head of a living infant—remains unknown.

Valerie Andrushko provides a detailed description of a Wari trophy head that was fashioned for display in the Wari hinterland of Peru (AD 600–1000) during a period of impending imperial collapse. The head of a younger middle-aged male was scalped and defleshed, with nose and brain removed. Holes were punched into the skull, which was then notably decorated with a bone insert, and lifelike artificial teeth were added to replace missing dentition. Andrushko's work, heavily dependent on osteological evidence and comparative trophy heads from the Wari heartland as well as demographic data, trauma analysis, burial context, and material culture, illustrates the effort and care taken to modify human heads. Andrushko makes a strong case for the ritual importance of these heads and their use as symbols of imperial authority. Further research, such as the planned use of isotopic analysis, may help determine whether, like the trophy heads from the Wari imperial center, this trophy head from Cuzco was taken from nonlocals, which may in turn shed light on whether this head derived from an ancestor or an enemy.

Providing a roadmap for future research, Kathleen Forgey employs biochemical analysis of ancient DNA on Nasca trophy heads from the Early Nasca phases (AD 1–450) of the Nasca culture (AD 1–750), to determine biological relatedness. Using samples from trophy heads and from individuals recovered from cemetery contexts in three Peruvian valleys, Forgey was able to identify all five Amerindian haplogroups, suggesting that Nasca populations were highly diverse genetically. Further, her analysis shows that the Nazca Valley trophy heads she analyzed originated from within the Nazca Valley population. This evidence supports the assertion that, at least in the early years of trophy head use, heads may have been the curated remains of ancestors—certain individuals who were selected for special treatment after death. Forgey's study has implications for other regions of the world where archaeologists are attempting to determine whether human remains belong to local populations or to those of outsiders. Studies of ancient DNA may resolve some of the most persistent and perplexing questions in the discipline, and Forgey's important chapter highlights that potential.

Conclusions and Prospects

Archaeologists are approaching the problems presented by the ancient body and body parts through bioarchaeology and biochemical analyses, as well as through symbolic, contextual, and interpretive approaches. As the chapters in this volume demonstrate, both ways of reconstructing the past lead to ever more detailed and nuanced reconstructions of ancient lives—even those aspects of past lives formerly considered too remote, technical, or cognitive to consider. The examples presented in this volume serve as guides for dealing with some of the most contentious issues in archaeology today, such as the role of ancestors and enemies in the past; the identification of insiders and outsiders; and the ways in which elites signal their social distinctiveness and emerging power. Body parts, and human heads and skulls in particular, function as material indicators of ethnicity and status, are imbued with the power to protect and multiply, and are used to degrade, objectify, or control.

The Archaeology of Ancestors

The role of ancestors in the past—that is, as biological, lineal antecedents selected for special postmortem treatment—has received increased attention in the past decade (Whitley 2002). Biochemical approaches to this question, which use ancient DNA to determine whether an individual was a group member or an outsider, as well as whether male or female, provide new lines of evidence for dealing with this often-intractable question. The issue of ancestors can also be dealt with through the skull as material culture, as when skulls from Oceania are used for the purpose of legitimization or to emphasize descent from specific individuals or lineages (see Valentin and Rolland this volume; Stodder 2011). Additional comprehensive analyses focused on premortem treatments such as intentional cranial deformation and postmortem selections of skulls for curation and decoration—like those analyses I performed (e.g., Bonogofsky 2001b, 2005b; Bonogofsky and Malhi 2000) for the Levant and Anatolia, which combined personal examinations, photographs, x-rays, CT scans, and DNA analysis with archaeological context—will more fully address whose skulls were selected for special treatment and why. Future studies of skulls also will help archaeologists to identify the ways in which the remains of lineal ancestors functioned prehistorically. Perhaps such tangible forms of evidence will discourage further use of the term *ancestors* to explain everything from the presence of standing stones to the collection, modification, and decoration of the skulls of men, women, and children.

The Archaeology of Enemies

The study of the human head and skull can reveal the ways in which humans created cultural objects they could manipulate, degrade, or even honor. The disembodied head thus becomes a marker of the ability of the individual, group, state, or empire to control both the body and the spirit (O'Donnabhain this volume). Such heads represent rights to property and resources, representations of prowess and success in battle, or loci of spiritual power with which to manipulate or forget the dead. As a material manifestation—tangible evidence of rights, abilities, and past events—the "trophy" head is imbued with culture-specific significance. Attention to the context of the archaeological remains of skulls, to documentary and iconographic evidence, and even to subsistence data and site patterning gives us great interpretive possibilities, which I hope that future research will pursue (Bonogofsky 2001b).

The Archaeology of Emerging Elites

The rise of elites and the ways in which elites reinforce their authority are also issues having worldwide archaeological implications. In Eurasia, skull deformation served to mark out more recently arrived groups as privileged and distinct (Sharapova and Razhev this volume), while in South America, communities of occupational specialists used head imagery as a visual cue to ethnicity (Lozada this volume). Emerging chiefs among Iron Age Celts used the concept of headhunting as a form of symbolic capital to establish and consolidate power, harnessing the power of the human head in ritual and iconography (Armit 2006). Attention to the head within the context of emerging elite authority—expressed in deformation, ornamentation, and treatment after death—will help to illustrate the ways in which manipulation of the living bodies of elites and control of their material remains facilitated acquisition of social, political, and economic power.

Summary

In sum, the human skull represents a powerful symbol—one that is altered during life or death to signal ethnicity, ancestorhood, personal prowess, or political authority. As a highly salient object of material culture, the head is invested with meaning that changes depending on context—those political, social, and economic conditions that require an object with which to negotiate, manipulate, and control. Ethnographic evidence suggests that skulls have complex life histories as dynamic ritual objects, while iconography and historical documents indicate that skulls have critical roles as expressions of the power of emerging elites.

As a biological object subject to violence, disease processes, nutrient availability, cultural practices, and the vagaries of daily life, the skull is one of the most informative parts of the human body. Individual teeth and cranial bones can reveal infection, resource stress, congenital defects, and patterns in human activity. By integrating our study of the skull, employing all of the available archaeological, conceptual, and physical evidence and techniques, our reconstructions of the human past will become more complete, allowing us to better understand what life was like for individuals of both sexes and all ages and statuses—even for those most neglected in life and forgotten in death.

References Cited

Allison, Marvin J., Enrique Gerszten, Juan Munizaga, Calogero Santoro, and Guillermo Focacci. 1981. La práctica de la deformación craneana entre los pueblos Andinos. *Chungará: Revista de Antropología Chilena (Arica)* 7: 238–260.
Ames, Kenneth M. 1994. The Northwest Coast: Complex Hunter-Gatherers, Ecology, and Social Evolution. *Annual Review of Anthropology* 23: 209–229.

Andrushko, Valerie A., and John W. Verano. 2008. Prehistoric Trepanation in the Cuzco Region of Peru: A View into an Ancient Andean Practice. *American Journal of Physical Anthropology* 137: 4–13.

Anonymous. n.d. Bits and Pieces: Whatever Became of Them? *Historic UK*. Historic UK, Rugby, England. http://www.historic-uk.com/HistoryUK/England-History/BitsandPieces.htm (accessed November 15, 2009).

Anton, Susan C. 1989. Intentional Cranial Vault Deformation and Induced Changes of the Cranial Base and Face. *American Journal of Physical Anthropology* 79: 253–267.

Appadurai, Arjun. 1986. Introduction: Commodities and the Politics of Value. In *The Social Life of Things: Commodities in Cultural Perspective*, edited by A. Appadurai, 3–63. Cambridge University Press, Cambridge.

Armit, Ian. 2006. Inside Kurtz's Compound: Headhunting and the Human Body in Prehistoric Europe. In Bonogofsky 2006c, 1–14.

Arnold, Denise Y., and Christine A. Hastorf. 2008. *Heads of State: Icons, Power, and Politics in the Ancient and Modern Andes*. Left Coast Press, Walnut Creek, California.

Arnott, Robert, Stanley Finger, and C. U. M. Smith, editors. 2003. *Trepanation: History, Discovery, Theory*. Swets and Zeitlinger, Lisse, the Netherlands.

Arriaza, Bernardo T. 1995. *Beyond Death: The Chinchorro Mummies of Ancient Chile*. Smithsonian Institution Press, Washington, D.C.

Aufderheide, Arthur C. 1985. The Enigma of Ancient Cranial Trepanation. *Minnesota Medicine* 68 (2): 119–122.

———. editor. 2009. *Overmodeled Skulls*. Heide Press, Duluth, Minnesota.

Aufderheide, Arthur C., and Conrado Rodriguez-Martin. 1998. *Cambridge Encyclopedia of Paleopathology*. Cambridge University Press, Cambridge.

Bateson, Gregory. 1932. Social Structure of the Iatmül People of the Sepik River. *Oceania* 2: 245–291, 401–452.

———. 1958. *Naven: A Survey of the Problems Suggested by a Composite Picture of the Culture of a New Guinea Tribe from Three Points of View*. Stanford University Press, Stanford.

Bennike, Pia, and Verner Alexandersen. 2007. Population Plasticity in Southern Scandinavia: From Oysters and Fish to Gruel and Meat. In Cohen and Crane-Kramer 2007, 130–148.

Bentley, R. Alexander, Hallie R. Buckley, Matthew Spriggs, Stuart Bedford, Chris J. Ottley, Geoff M. Nowell, Colin G. Macpherson, and D. Graham Pearson. 2007. Lapita Migrants in the Pacific's Oldest Cemetery: Isotopic Analysis at Teouma, Vanuatu. *American Antiquity* 72 (4): 645–656.

Berryman, Carrie Ann. 2007. Captive Sacrifice and Trophy Taking among the Maya. In Chacon and Dye 2007, 377–399.

Bienert, Hans-Dieter. 1991. Skull Cult in the Prehistoric Near East. *Journal of Prehistoric Religion (Göteborg)* 5: 9–23.

Bienert, Hans-Dieter, Michelle Bonogofsky, Hans Georg K. Gebel, Ian Kuijt, and Gary Rollefson. 2004. Where Are the Dead? In *Central Settlements in Neolithic*

Jordan. Studies in Early Near Eastern Production, Subsistence, and Environment, vol. 5, edited by H. D. Bienert, H. G. K. Gebel, and R. Neef, 157–175. Ex Oriente, Berlin.

Blakely, Robert L., editor. *Biocultural Adaptation in Prehistoric America*. University of Georgia Press, Athens.

Blom, Deborah E. 2005. Embodying Borders: Human Body Modification and Diversity in Tiwanaku Society. *Journal of Anthropological Archaeology* 24: 1–24.

Blom, Deborah E., Jane E. Buikstra, Linda Keng, Paula D. Tomczak, Eleanor Shoreman, and Debbie Stevens-Tuttle. 2005. Anemia and Childhood Mortality: Latitudinal Patterning along the Coast of Pre-Columbian Peru. *American Journal of Physical Anthropology* 127 (2): 152–169.

Bonogofsky, Michelle. 1999. Bioarchaeological Snapshots: Skeletal Markers of Health and Relatedness at Early Neolithic 'Ain Ghazal and Jericho. Unpublished manuscript. Submitted to the Department of Anthropology, University of California, Berkeley.

———. 2001a. Cranial Modeling and Neolithic Bone Modification at 'Ain Ghazal: New Interpretations. *Paléorient* 27 (2): 141–146.

———. 2001b. *An Osteo-Archaeological Examination of the Ancestor Cult during the Pre-Pottery Neolithic B Period in the Levant*. Ph.D. dissertation, University of California, Berkeley. University Microfilms International, Ann Arbor, Michigan.

———. 2002. Reassessing "Dental Evulsion" in Neolithic Plastered Skulls from the Levant through the Use of Computed Tomography, Direct Observation, and Photographs. *Journal of Archaeological Science* 29: 959–964.

———. 2003. Neolithic Plastered Skulls and Railroading Epistemologies. *Bulletin of the American Schools of Oriental Research* 331: 1–10.

———. 2004. Including Women and Children: Neolithic Modeled Skulls from Jordan, Israel, Syria and Turkey. *Near Eastern Archaeology* 67 (2): 118–119.

———. 2005a. Anatolian Plastered Skulls in Context: New Discoveries and Interpretations. *Arkeometri Sonuçları Toplantısı* 20: 13–26.

———. 2005b. A Bioarchaeological Study of Plastered Skulls from Anatolia: New Discoveries and Interpretations. *International Journal of Osteoarchaeology* 15: 124–135.

———. 2006a. Complexity in Context: Plain, Painted and Modeled Skulls from the Neolithic Middle East. In Bonogofsky 2006c, 15–28.

———. 2006b. Cultural and Ritual Evidence in the Archaeological Record: Modeled Skulls from the Ancient Near East. In *The Archaeology of Cult and Death: Proceedings of the Session "The Archaeology of Cult and Death,"* edited by M. Georgiadis and C. Gallou, 45–69. Archaeolingua, Budapest.

———, editor. 2006c. *Skull Collection, Modification and Decoration*. BAR International Series 1539. Archaeopress, Oxford, U.K.

Bonogofsky, Michelle, and Ripan Malhi. 2000. A Sex-Based DNA Analysis of 8,500 Year Old "Ancestor" Skulls from the Levant. *American Journal of Physical Anthropology* Supplement 111 (30): 110.

Boylston, A., Christopher J. Knüsel, and C. A. Roberts. 2000. Investigation of a

Romano-British Rural Ritual in Bedford, England. *Journal of Archaeological Science* 27: 241–254.

Boz, Başak, and Lori D. Hager. 2004. Human Remains. *Çatal Höyük 2004 Archive Report*, vol. 2008. http://www.catalhoyuk.com/archive_reports/2004/ar04_18.html (accessed May 24, 2010).

Brickley, Megan, and Rachel Ives. 2006. Skeletal Manifestations of Infantile Scurvy. *American Journal of Physical Anthropology* 129 (2): 163–172.

Brown, James A. 2003. The Cahokia Mound 72–Sub 1 Burials as Collective Representation. *Wisconsin Archeologist* 84 (1–2): 83–99.

Browne, David M., Helaine Silverman, and Rubén García. 1993. A Cache of 48 Nasca Trophy Heads from Cerro Carapo, Peru. *Latin American Antiquity* 4 (3): 274–294.

Buckberry, Jo. 2006. Kings, Saints and Criminals: The Removal and Display of Heads in Later Anglo-Saxon England. Abstract. In *EAA 12th Annual Meeting Abstracts Book*, edited by H. Dobrzańska, B. Sz. Szmoniewski, and K. Ryba, 234. Institute of Archaeology and Ethnology, Polish Academy of Sciences, Kraków.

Buckberry, Jo L., and D. M. Hadley. 2007. An Anglo-Saxon Execution Cemetery at Walkington Wold, Yorkshire. *Oxford Journal of Archaeology* 26 (3): 309–329.

Buikstra, Jane E. 1977. Biocultural Dimensions of Archeological Study: A Regional Perspective. In Blakely 1977, 67–84.

———. 2006. Preface to *Bioarchaeology: The Contextual Analysis of Human Remains*, edited by J. E. Buikstra and L. A. Beck, xvii–xx. Elsevier, Amsterdam.

Buikstra, Jane E., Paula D. Tomczak, Maria Cecilia Lozada Cerna, and Gordon F. M. Rakita. 2005. Chiribaya Political Economy. In Rakita et al. 2005, 66–80. University Press of Florida, Gainesville.

Chacon, Richard J., and David H. Dye, editors. 2007. *The Taking and Displaying of Human Body Parts as Trophies by Amerindians*. Springer, New York.

Chang, Kwang-chih. 1980. *Shang Civilization*. Yale University Press, New Haven, Connecticut.

———. 1983. *The Archaeology of Ancient China*. 4th ed. Yale University Press, New Haven, Connecticut.

Clark, J. Desmond, Yonas Beyene, Giday WoldeGabriel, William K. Hart, Paul R. Renne, Henry Gilbert, Alban Defleur, et al. 2003. Stratigraphic, Chronological and Behavioural Contexts of Pleistocene *Homo sapiens* from Middle Awash, Ethiopia. *Nature* 423: 747–752.

Clark, John E. 1984. Late Woodland Mortuary Practices at Juntunen, Michigan. Unpublished manuscript. On file at the Museum of Anthropology, University of Michigan.

Clark, John E., and Arlene Colman. 2008. Time Reckoning and Memorials in Mesoamerica. *Cambridge Archaeological Journal* 18 (1): 93–99.

Cohen, Mark Nathan, and G. J. Armelagos, editors. 1984. *Paleopathology at the Origins of Agriculture*. Academic Press, Orlando, Florida.

Cohen, Mark Nathan, and Gillian M. M. Crane-Kramer, editors. 2007. *Ancient Health:*

Skeletal Indicators of Agricultural and Economic Intensification. University Press of Florida, Gainesville.

Conklin, Beth A. 1995. Thus Are Our Bodies, Thus Was Our Custom: Mortuary Cannibalism in an Amazonian Society. *American Ethnologist* 22 (1): 75–101.

———. 2001. *Consuming Grief: Compassionate Cannibalism in an Amazonian Society.* University of Texas Press, Austin.

Cook, Della Collins. 2006. The Old Physical Anthropology and the New World: A Look at the Accomplishments of an Antiquated Paradigm. In *Bioarchaeology: The Contextual Analysis of Human Remains,* edited by J. E. Buikstra and L. A. Beck, 27–71. Elsevier, Amsterdam.

———. 2007. Maize and Mississippians in the American Midwest: Twenty Years Later. In Cohen and Crane-Kramer 2007, 10–19.

Cordy-Collins, Alana. 2001. Decapitation in Cupisnique and Early Moche Societies. In *Ritual Sacrifice in Ancient Peru,* edited by E. P. Benson and A. G. Cook, 21–33. University of Texas Press, Austin.

Crubézy É., J. Bruzek, J. Guilaine, E. Cunha, D. Rougé, and J. Jelinek. 2001. The Antiquity of Cranial Surgery in Europe and in the Mediterranean Basin. Comptes Rendue de l'Academie des Sciences Paris. *Sciences de la Terre et des Planètes* 332: 417–423.

de Laguna, Frederica. 1933. Mummified Heads from Alaska. *American Anthropologist* 35 (4): 742–744.

DeLeonardis, Lisa. 2000. The Body Context: Interpreting Early Nasca Decapitated Burials. *Latin American Antiquity* 11 (4): 363–386.

Fletcher, A., J. Pearson, and J. Ambers. 2008. The Manipulation of Social and Physical Identity in the Pre-Pottery Neolithic: Radiographic Evidence for Cranial Modification at Jericho and its Implications for the Plastering of Skulls. *Cambridge Archaeological Journal* 18 (3): 309–325.

Forgey, Kathleen, and Sloan R. Williams. 2005. Were Nasca Trophy Heads War Trophies or Revered Ancestors? Insights from the Kroeber Collection. In Rakita et al. 2005, 251–276.

Fowler, Melvin L., Jerome Rose, Barbara Vander Leest, and Steven R. Ahler. 1999. *The Mound 72 Area: Dedicated and Sacred Space in Early Cahokia.* Reports of Investigations no. 54. Illinois State Museum, Springfield.

Frayer, David W. 1997. Ofnet: Evidence for a Mesolithic Massacre. In *Troubled Times: Violence and Warfare in the Past,* edited by D. L. Martin and D. W. Frayer, 181–216. Gordon and Breach, New York.

Garfinkel, Yosef. 2006. The Burials of Kfar HaHoresh: A Regional or Local Phenomenon? *Journal of the Israel Prehistoric Society* 36: 109–116.

Gedalyahu, Tzvi Ben. 2008. *Three 9,000-Year-Old Skulls Found in Galilee.* http://www.israelnationalnews.com/News/News.aspx/127175 (accessed July 23, 2008).

George, Kenneth M. 1996. *Showing Signs of Violence: The Cultural Politics of a Twentieth-Century Headhunting Ritual.* University of California, Berkeley.

Goodale, Jane C. 1985. Pig's Teeth and Skull Cycles: Both Sides of the Face of Humanity. *American Ethnologist* 12 (2): 228–244.

Goodman, A. H. 1993. On the Interpretation of Health from Skeletal Remains. *Current Anthropology* 34 (3): 281–288.

Goren, N., and O. Bar-Yosef. 1973. Natufian Remains in Hayonim Cave. *Paléorient* 1 (1): 49–68.

Goring-Morris, A. Nigel, Yuval Goren, Liora K. Horwitz, Daniella Bar-Yosef, and Israel Hershkovitz. 1995. Investigations at an Early Neolithic Settlement in the Lower Galilee: Results of the 1991 Season at Kefar HaHoresh. *'Atiqot* 27: 37–62.

Griffin, Patricia S., C. A. Grissom, and G. O. Rollefson. 1998. Three Late Eighth Millennium Plastered Faces from 'Ain Ghazal, Jordan. *Paléorient* 24 (1): 59–70.

Haddon, A. C. 1935. *General Ethnology.* Vol. 1 of *Reports of the Cambridge Anthropological Expedition to the Torres Straits.* Cambridge University Press, Cambridge.

Hanson, D. B. 1988. Prehistoric Mortuary Practices and Human Biology. In *Archaeological Investigations on the North Coast of Rota, Mariana Islands,* edited by B. M. Butler, 375–435. Micronesian Archaeological Survey Report 23, Occasional Paper 8. Southern Illinois University of Carbondale, Center for Archaeological Investigations.

Harman, M., T. I. Molleson, and J. L. Price. 1981. Burials, Bodies and Beheadings in Romano-British and Anglo-Saxon Cemeteries. *Bulletin of the British Museum (Natural History) Geology Series (London)* 35 (3): 145–188.

Hillman, David, and Carla Mazzio, editors. 1997. *The Body in Parts: Fantasies of Corporeality in Early Modern Europe.* Routledge, New York.

Holliday, Diane Young. 1993. Occipital Lesions: A Possible Cost of Cradleboards. *American Journal of Physical Anthropology* 90 (3): 283–290.

Hoshower, Lisa M., Jane E. Buikstra, Paul S. Goldstein, and Ann D. Webster. 1995. Artificial Cranial Deformation at the Omo M10 Site: A Tiwanaku Complex from the Moquegua Valley, Peru. *Latin American Antiquity* 6 (2): 145–164.

Hoskins, Janet, editor. 1986. *Headhunting and the Social Imagination in Southeast Asia.* Stanford University Press, Stanford.

———. 1989. On Losing and Getting a Head: Warfare, Exchange, and Alliance in a Changing Sumba, 1888–1988. *American Ethnologist* 16 (3): 419–440.

Jacobi, Keith P. 2007. Disabling the Dead: Human Trophy Taking in the Prehistoric Southeast. In Chacon and Dye 2007, 299–338.

Kaiser, Elke. 2003. *Studien zur Katakombengrabkultur zwischen Dnepr und Prut.* Von Zabern, Mainz am Rhein.

———. 2006. Plastered Skulls of the Catacomb Culture in the Northern Pontic Region. In Bonogofsky 2006c, 45–58.

Keenleyside, Anne. 1998. Skeletal Evidence of Health and Disease in Pre-Contact Alaskan Eskimos and Aleuts. *American Journal of Physical Anthropology* 107 (1): 51–70.

Keesing, Roger M. 1982. *Kwaio Religion: The Living and the Dead in a Solomon Island Society*. Columbia University Press, New York.

Kellner, Corina M. 2006. "Trophy Heads" in Prehistoric Peru: Wari Imperial Influence on Nasca Head-Taking Practices. In Bonogofsky 2006c, 101–111.

Kelly, E. P. 2006. Secrets of the Bog Bodies: The Enigma of the Iron Age Explained. *Archaeology Ireland* 20 (1): 26–30.

Kent, Susan. 1986. The Influence of Sedentism and Aggregation on Porotic Hyperostosis and Anemia: A Case Study. *Man* 21: 605–636.

Kenyon, Kathleen M. 1961. *Beginning in Archaeology*. Praeger, New York.

———. 1981. *The Architecture and Stratigraphy of the Tell*. Vol. 3 of *Excavations at Jericho*, edited by T. A. Holland. British School of Archaeology in Jerusalem, London.

Kenyon, Kathleen M., and A. Douglas Tushingham. 1953. Jericho Gives Up Its Secret. *National Geographic Magazine* 104 (6): 853–870.

Knudson, Kelly J., and Christopher M. Stojanowski, editors. 2009. *Bioarchaeology and Identity in the Americas*. University Press of Florida, Gainesville.

Kurth, Gottfried, and Olav Röhrer-Ertl. 1981. On the Anthropology of the Mesolithic to Chalcolithic Human Remains from the Tell es-Sultan in Jericho, Jordan. In vol. 3 of *Excavations at Jericho*, edited by T. A. Holland, 407–481. British School of Archaeology in Jerusalem, London.

Kutterer, A., and K. W. Alt. 2008. Cranial Deformations in an Iron Age Population from Münsingen-Rain, Switzerland. *International Journal of Osteoarchaeology* 18 (4): 392–406.

Larsen, Clark Spencer. 1983. Behavioural Implications of Temporal Change in Cariogenesis. *Journal of Archaeological Science* 10: 1–8.

———. 1995. Biological Changes in Human Populations with Agriculture. *Annual Review of Anthropology* 24: 185–213.

———. 1997. *Bioarchaeology: Interpreting Behavior from the Human Skeleton*. Cambridge University Press, Cambridge.

———. 2007. Foreword to Cohen and Crane-Kramer 2007, ix–x.

Larsen, Clark Spencer, Dale L. Hutchinson, Christopher M. Stojanowski, Matthew A. Williamson, Mark C. Griffin, Scott W. Simpson, Christopher B. Ruff, et al. 2007. Health and Lifestyle in Georgia and Florida: Agricultural Origins and Intensification in Regional Perspective. In Cohen and Crane-Kramer 2007, 20–34.

Larsen, Clark Spencer, R. Shavit, and M. C. Griffin. 1991. Dental Caries Evidence for Dietary Change: An Archaeological Context. In *Advances in Dental Anthropology*, edited by M. A. Kelley and C. S. Larsen, 179–202. John Wiley and Sons, New York.

Leach, Edmund R. 1958. Magical Hair. *Journal of the Royal Anthropological Institute* 88 (2): 147–164.

Levene, Dan. 2009. Rare Magic Inscription on Human Skull. *Biblical Archaeology Review* (Mar./Apr.): 46–50.

Lewis, Mary E. 2008. A Traitor's Death? The Identity of a Drawn, Hanged and Quartered Man from Hulton Abbey, Staffordshire. *Antiquity* 82 (315): 113–124.

Li, Chi. 1977. *Anyang*. University of Washington Press, Seattle.

Lincoln, Bruce. 1991. *Death, War, and Sacrifice: Studies in Ideology and Practice*. University of Chicago Press, Chicago.

Littleton, Judith, and Karen Frifelt. 2006. Trepanations from Oman: A Case of Diffusion? *Arabian Archaeology and Epigraphy* 17 (2): 139–151.

Lock, Margaret. 2002. *Twice Dead: Organ Transplants and the Reinvention of Death*. University of California Press, Berkeley.

Lovisek, Joan A. 2007. Human Trophy Taking on the Northwest Coast: An Ethnohistorical Perspective. In Chacon and Dye 2007, 45–64.

Lozada, Maria Cecilia, and Jane Buikstra. 2006. Emblems of Ethnic Identity: Cranial Modification Patterning among the Pre-Inka Chiribaya of Southern Peru. Abstract. In Bonogofsky 2006c, 135.

Lukacs, J. R. 1996. Sex Differences in Dental Caries Rates with the Origin of Agriculture in South Asia. *Current Anthropology* 37: 147–153.

Maat, G. J. R. 2004. Scurvy in Adults and Youngsters: The Dutch Experience. *International Journal of Osteoarchaeology* 14 (2): 77–81.

Martin, Debra L. 1997. Violence against Women in the La Plata River Valley (A.D. 1000–1300). In *Troubled Times: Violence and Warfare in the Past*, edited by D. L. Martin and D. W. Frayer, 45–75. Gordon and Breach, New York.

Massey, Virginia. 1989. *The Human Skeletal Remains from a Terminal Classic Skull Pit at Colha, Belize*. Papers of the Colha Project, vol. 3. Texas Archeological Research Laboratory, University of Texas at Austin; Texas A&M University, College Station.

Mays, S. 2008. A Likely Case of Scurvy from Early Bronze Age Britain. *International Journal of Osteoarchaeology* 18 (2): 178–187.

Mednikova, Maria B. 2002. Scalping in Eurasia. *Anthropology and Archeology of Eurasia* 41 (4): 57–67.

Meiklejohn, C., Agelarakis, P. A. Akkermans, P. E. L. Smith, and R. Solecki. 1992. Artificial Cranial Deformation in the Proto-Neolithic and Neolithic Near East and Its Possible Origin: Evidence from Four Sites. *Paléorient* 18 (2): 83–97.

Mendoza, Marcela. 2006. Skulls Collected for Scalping in the Gran Chaco. In Bonogofsky 2006c, 113–118.

Mendoza, Rubén G. 2007. The Divine Gourd Tree: Tzompantli Skull Racks, Decapitation Rituals, and Human Trophies in Ancient Mesoamerica. In Chacon and Dye 2007, 400–443.

Métraux, Alfred. 1963. Warfare, Cannibalism, and Human Trophies. In *Handbook of South American Indians*, vol. 5, edited by J. H. Steward, 383–409. Cooper Square Publishers, New York.

Miller, Virginia E. 1999. The Skull Rack in Mesoamerica. In *Mesoamerican Architecture as a Cultural Symbol*, edited by J. K. Kowalsky, 341–360. Oxford University Press, New York.

Mock, Shirley Boteler. 1998. The Defaced and the Forgotten: Decapitation and Flaying/Mutilation as a Termination Event at Colha, Belize. In *The Sowing and the Dawning: Termination, Dedication, and Transformation in the Archaeological and Ethnographic Record of Mesoamerica*, edited by S. Boteler Mock, 113–123. University of New Mexico Press, Albuquerque.

Molleson, Theya, and S. Campbell. 1995. Deformed Skulls at Tell Arpachiyah: The Social Context. In *The Archaeology of Death in the Ancient Near East*, edited by S. Campbell and A. Green, 44–55. Oxbow Books, Oxford, U.K.

Molnar, Stephen. 1972. Tooth Wear and Culture: A Survey of Tooth Functions Among Some Prehistoric Populations. *Current Anthropology* 13 (5): 511–526.

Müller, Felix, Peter Jud, and Kurt W. Alt. 2008. Artefacts, Skulls and Written Sources: The Social Ranking of a Celtic Family Buried at Münsingen-Rain. *Antiquity* 82: 462–469.

Murphy, Eileen, Ilia Gokhman, Yuri Chistov, and Ludmila Berkova. 2002. Prehistoric Old World Scalping: New Cases from the Cemetery of Aymyrlyg, South Siberia. *American Journal of Archaeology* 106 (1): 1–10.

Nystrom, Ken C. 2006. Trepanation in the Chachapoya Region of Northern Perú. *International Journal of Osteoarchaeology* 17 (1): 39–51.

Oakdale, Suzanne. 2005. Forgetting the Dead, Remembering Enemies. In Rakita et al. 2005, 107–123.

O'Flaherty, Wendy Doniger. 1988. *Other Peoples' Myths: The Cave of Echoes*. Macmillan, New York.

Orschiedt, Jörg A. 1998. Ergebnisse einer neuen Untersuchung der spätmesolithischen Kopfbestattungen aus Süddeutschland. *Urgeschichtliche Materialhefte* 12: 147–160.

———. 2001. Die Kopfbestattungen der Ofnet-Höhle: Ein Beleg für kriegerische Auseinandersetzungen im Mesolithikum. *Archäologische Informationen* 24 (2): 199–207.

———. 2005. The Head Burials from Ofnet Cave: An Example of Warlike Conflict in the Mesolithic. In *Warfare, Violence and Slavery in Prehistory*, edited by M. P. Pearson and I. J. N. Thorpe, 67–73. BAR International Series 1374. British Archaeological Reports, Oxford.

Ortner, Donald J., Whitney Butler, Jessica Cafarella, and Lauren Milligan. 2001. Evidence of Probable Scurvy in Subadults from Archeological Sites in North America. *American Journal of Physical Anthropology* 114 (4): 343–351.

Ortner, Donald J., Erin H. Kimmerle, and Melanie Diez. 1999. Probable Evidence of Scurvy in Subadults from Archeological Sites in Peru. *American Journal of Physical Anthropology* 108 (3): 321–331.

Ortner, Donald J., and W. G. J. Putschar. 1985. *Identification of Pathological Conditions in Human Skeletal Remains*. Smithsonian Institution, Washington, D.C.

Ossenberg, Nancy, S. 1964. Skeletal Remains from Hungry Hall Mound II. Unpublished manuscript prepared for the Royal Ontario Museum.

Owsley, Douglas W. 1994. Warfare in Coalescent Tradition Populations of the Northern Plains. In *Skeletal Biology in the Great Plains: Migration, Warfare, Health, and Subsistence*, edited by D. W. Owsley and R. L. Jantz, 333–343. Smithsonian Institution Press, Washington, D.C.

Özbeck, Metin. 2009. Remodeled Human Skulls in Köşk Höyük (Neolithic Age, Anatolia): A New Appraisal in View of Recent Discoveries. *Journal of Archaeological Science* 36: 379–386.

Proulx, Donald A. 2001. Ritual Uses of Trophy Heads in Ancient Nasca Society. In *Ritual Sacrifice in Ancient Peru,* edited by E. P. Benson and A. G. Cook, 119–136. University of Texas Press, Austin.

Rakita, Gordon F. M., Jane E. Buikstra, Lane A. Beck, and Sloan R. Williams, editors. 2005. *Interacting with the Dead: Perspectives on Mortuary Archaeology for the New Millennium.* University Press of Florida, Gainesville.

Reddy, V. R. 1980. Dental Caries in the Deciduous Teeth of the Children from Gulbarga, Karnataka. *Acta Anthropogenetica* 4: 201–238.

Ricci, F., C. Fornai, V. Tiesler Blos, O. Rickards, S. di Lernia, and G. Manzi. 2008. Evidence of Artificial Cranial Deformation from the Later Prehistory of the Acacus Mts. (Southwestern Libya, Central Sahara). *International Journal of Osteoarchaeology* 18 (4): 372–391.

Richards, Gary D., and Susan C. Anton. 1991. Craniofacial Configuration and Postcranial Development of a Hydrocephalic Child (ca. 2500 B.C.–500 A.D.): With a Review of Cases and Comment on Diagnostic Criteria. *American Journal of Physical Anthropology* 85 (2): 185–200.

Robbins, Louise M. 1977. The Story of Life Revealed by the Dead. In Blakely 1977, 10–26.

Rollefson, Gary O. 1983. Ritual and Ceremony at Neolithic 'Ain Ghazal (Jordan). *Paléorient* 9 (2): 29–38.

Rosaldo, Renato. 1980. *Ilongot Headhunting, 1883–1974: A Study in Society and History.* Stanford University Press, Stanford.

Sarie, Issa. 1995a. An Early Case of Tuberculosis: 'Ain Ghazal, Jordan. *Newsletter of the Institute of Archaeology and Anthropology.* Yarmouk University, Irbid, Jordan.

———. 1995b. Subsistence and Diet of 'Ain Ghazal Inhabitants as Inferred from the Analysis of Human Dentition. Master's thesis, Institute of Archaeology and Anthropology, Yarmouk University.

Scheper-Hughes, Nancy. 2001. Bodies for Sale—Whole or in Parts. *Body and Society* 7 (2–3): 1–8.

Seeman, Mark F. 1988. Ohio Hopewell Trophy-Skull Artifacts as Evidence for Competition in Middle Woodland Societies circa 50 B.C.–A.D. 350. *American Antiquity* 53 (3): 565–577.

———. 2007. Predatory War and Hopewell Trophies. In Chacon and Dye 2007, 167–189.

Sharp, Lesley A. 1994. Organ Transplantation as a Transformative Experience: Anthropological Insights into the Restructuring of the Self. *Medical Anthropology Quarterly* 9 (3): 357–389.

Shishlina, Natalia I. 2006. Decoration of Skulls: Funerary Rituals of the Yamnaya and Catacomb Cultures in the Eurasian Bronze Age. In Bonogofsky 2006c, 59–66.

Silverman, Helaine, and Donald A. Proulx. 2002. *The Nasca*. Blackwell Publishers, Malden, Massachusetts.

Sjøvold, T. 1995. Testing Assumptions for Skeletal Studies by Means of Identified Skulls from Hall Statt, Austria. In *Grave Reflections: Portraying the Past through Cemetery Studies*, edited by S. R. Saunders and A. Herring, 241–281. Canadian Scholars' Press, Toronto.

Smith, Patricia. 1973. Family Burials at Hayonim. *Paléorient* 1 (1): 69–71.

Sofaer, Joanna R. 2006. *The Body as Material Culture: A Theoretical Osteoarchaeology*. Cambridge University Press, Cambridge.

Speal, C. Scott. 2006. Postmortem Skeletal Modifications of the Pre-Columbian North American Mid-Continent. In Bonogofsky 2006c, 119–131.

Steadman, Dawnie Wolfe. 2008. Warfare Related Trauma at Orendorf, a Middle Mississippian Site in West-Central Illinois. *American Journal of Physical Anthropology* 136 (1): 51–64.

Stewart, T. D. 1958. Stone Age Skull Surgery: A General Review, with Emphasis on the New World. In *Annual Report of the Board of Regents of the Smithsonian Institution, 1957*, 469–491. U.S. Government Printing Office, Washington, D.C.

Stodder, Ann L. W. 2006. The Taphonomy of Cranial Modification in Papua New Guinea: Implications for the Archaeology of Mortuary Ritual. In Bonogofsky 2006c, 77–89.

———. 2011. Iconography and Power in Sepik Skull Art. In *Breathing New Life into the Evidence of Death: Contemporary Approaches to Mortuary Analysis*, edited by A. Baadsgaard, A. Boutin, and J. E. Buikstra. School for Advanced Research Press, Santa Fe, New Mexico. Forthcoming.

Stordeur, Danielle, and Rima Khawam. 2007. Les cránes surmodelés de Tell Aswad (PPNB, Syrie). Premier regard sur l'ensemble, premières réflexions. *Syria* 84: 5–32.

Strouhal, Eugen. 1973. Five Plastered Skulls from Pre-Pottery Neolithic B Jericho: Anthropological Study. *Paléorient* 1 (2): 231–247.

Stuart-Macadam, Patty. 1991. Porotic Hyperostosis: Changing Interpretations. In *Human Paleopathology: Current Syntheses and Future Options*, edited by D. J. Ortner and A. C. Aufderheide, 36–39. Smithsonian Institution, Washington, D.C.

———. 1992. Porotic Hyperostosis: A New Perspective. *American Journal of Physical Anthropology* 87 (1): 39–47.

Taylor, Anne Christine. 1993. Remembering to Forget: Identity, Mourning and Memory among the Jivaro. *Man*, n.s., 28 (4): 653–678.

Torres-Rouff, Christina. 2003. Oral Implications of Labret Use: A Case from Pre-Columbian Chile. *International Journal of Osteoarchaeology* 13: 247–251.

Tung, Tiffiny A. 2006. The Social Life of Wari Trophy Heads from the Ancient Andes. Abstract. In Bonogofsky 2006c, 137.

———. 2007. Trauma and Violence in the Wari Empire of the Peruvian Andes: Warfare, Raids, and Ritual Fights. *American Journal of Physical Anthropology* 133 (3): 941–956.

Vadetskaia, Elga B. 2006. The Yenisei Mummies with Modeled Skulls and Masks from Siberia. In Bonogofsky 2006c, 67–75.

Verano, John W. 1995. Where Do They Rest? The Treatment of Human Offerings and Trophies in Ancient Peru. In *Tombs for the Living: Andean Mortuary Practices,* edited by T. D. Dillehay, 189–227. Dumbarton Oaks, Washington, D.C.

———. 1997. Advances in the Paleopathology of Andean South America. *Journal of World Prehistory* 11 (2): 237–268.

———. 1998. Disease in South American Mummies. In *Mummies, Disease and Ancient Cultures,* edited by A. Cockburn, E. Cockburn, and T. A. Reyman, 215–234. 2nd ed. Cambridge University Press, Cambridge.

———. 2001. The Physical Evidence of Human Sacrifice in Ancient Peru. In *Ritual Sacrifice in Ancient Peru,* edited by E. P. Benson and A. G. Cook, 165–184. University of Texas Press, Austin.

Verano, John W., Santiago Uceda, Claude Chapdelaine, Ricardo Tello, Maria Isabel Paredes, and Victor Pimentel. 1999. Modified Human Skulls from the Urban Sector of the Pyramids of Moche, Northern Peru. *Latin American Antiquity* 10 (1): 59–70.

Walker, Phillip L. 1986. Porotic Hyperostosis in a Marine-Dependent California Indian Population. *American Journal of Physical Anthropology* 69 (3): 345–354.

———. 1989. Cranial Injuries as Evidence of Violence in Prehistoric Southern California. *American Journal of Physical Anthropology* 80 (3): 313–323.

Webb, William S., and Raymond S. Baby. 1957. *The Adena People No. 2.* Ohio State University Press for the Ohio Historical Society, Columbus.

Weber, Jochen, and Alfred Czarnetzki. 2001. Neurotraumatological Aspects of Head Injuries Resulting from Sharp and Blunt Force in the Early Medieval Period of Southwestern Germany. *American Journal of Physical Anthropology* 114: 352–356.

Weiner, Annette B. 1976. *Women of Value, Men of Renown.* University of Texas Press, Austin.

White, Tim D. 1986. Cut Marks on the Bodo Cranium: A Case of Prehistoric Defleshing. *American Journal of Physical Anthropology* 69: 503–509.

———. 1992. *Prehistoric Cannibalism at Mancos 5MTUMR-2346.* Princeton University Press, Princeton.

White, Tim D., and N. Toth. 1991. The Question of Ritual Cannibalism at Grotta Guattari. *Current Anthropology* 32: 118–138.

Whitley, James. 2002. Too Many Ancestors. *Antiquity* 76 (291): 119–126.

Williams, Howard. 2006. *Death and Memory in Early Medieval Britain.* Cambridge University Press, Cambridge.

Williams, Sloan R., Kathleen Forgey, and Elizabeth Klarich. 2001. An Osteological Study of Nasca Trophy Heads Collected by A. L. Kroeber during the Marshall Field Expeditions to Peru. *Fieldiana: Anthropology,* n.s., 33. Field Museum of Natural History, Chicago.

Williamson, Ron. 2007. "Otinontsiskiaj ondaon" ('The House of Cut-Off Heads'): The History and Archaeology of Northern Iroquoian Trophy Taking. In Chacon and Dye 2007, 190–221.

Wiltschke-Schrotta, Karin, and Peter Stadler. 2005. Beheading in Avar Times (630–800 A.D.). *Acta Medica Lituanica (Vilnius)* 12 (1): 58–64.

Wood, J. W., G. R. Milner, H. C. Harpending, and K. M. Weiss. 1992. The Osteological Paradox. *Current Anthropology* 33 (4): 343–358.

Wright, G. R. H. 1988. The Severed Head in Earliest Neolithic Times. *Journal of Prehistoric Religion (Göteborg)* 2: 51–56.

Wyckoff, Larry M. 1978. Post-Mortem Human Bone Deformation. *Wisconsin Archaeologist* 59 (4): 345–357.

PART I

Symbolic and Contextual Approaches

2

Heads as Memorials and Status Symbols

The Collection and Use of Skulls in the Torres Strait Islands

HEATHER BONNEY AND MARGARET CLEGG

This chapter deals with mortuary and headhunting practices in the Torres Strait Islands; these practices disappeared completely in the period up to and including the conversion to Christianity, beginning in 1871 with the arrival of the London Missionary Society led by the Reverend Samuel Macfarlane. This event is referred to by islanders as the "Coming of the Light." Ethnographic reports indicate that islanders from the Torres Strait practiced the removal of heads both as part of their own mortuary ritual and in the course of headhunting raids. Heads of unspecified relatives were decorated and retained, sometimes being used for divination. The heads of outsiders—including those of males, females, and children from other islands and shipwreck victims—were kept as trophies and traded between islands and with people from Papua New Guinea. Torres Strait Islanders do not appear to have engaged in the worshipping of ancestors, and heads were not retained for this purpose.

The ethnographic information presented is based on the observations of Alfred Haddon (1890, 1904, 1932, 1935), who first travelled to the islands in 1888, returning ten years later with the Cambridge Anthropological Expedition. These reports are supplemented by osteological evidence from a collection of male, female, and subadult crania and/or mandibles of 141 individuals from the region that are currently housed in the Natural History Museum in London. All 141 have been studied, but we are still in the process of collecting age, sex, and metric data.

Approximately 117 of these individuals originated from a head house on the island of Mabuiag, which was used for storing trophy heads. These were sent to the United Kingdom by Reverend Macfarlane in the late nineteenth century after the structure was destroyed (Thomas 1885). The remaining individuals were obtained from various islands in the Torres Strait by other collectors and

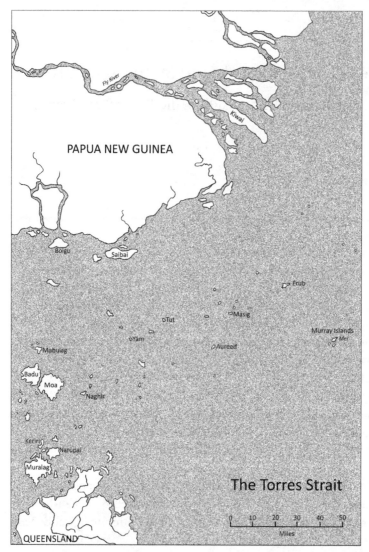

Figure 2.1. Map of the Torres Strait Islands. © Natural History Museum, London.

are believed to consist mostly of the remains of islanders. Archival and metric work is ongoing in an attempt to separate islanders from outsiders.

The Torres Strait Islands hosted a diverse array of practices in the treatment of the dead despite covering an area only two hundred kilometers across. These islands are situated in the seaway between the Cape York Peninsula of Queensland in northeastern Australia and Papua New Guinea (figure 2.1). Traditional mortuary ritual varied between the islands, but the practices could be divided into distinct east and west groupings. The eastern group comprised Uga, Erub, and the Murray Islands. The majority of the other islands within the strait, including Mabuiag, formed the western group.

Ethnographic Evidence for the Collection and Preparation of the Heads of Relatives

Skull Preparation in the Western Islands

According to Haddon (1904), the bodies of deceased, unspecified relatives in the western islands were placed on platforms supported by four posts, shortly after death. This platform was covered by a low-pitched roof made using pandanus mats. Food was left for the corpse, so that the spirit (*mari*) of the deceased would not become hungry and return to the village. Islanders believed that everyone had a mari, part of which disappeared at death, the remaining part needing to be driven away. On some of the northwestern islands, bodies were buried, instead of being placed on platforms, which seems to be a practice derived from New Guinea (see Bonogofsky and Graham this volume). Bodies were generally buried less than a foot deep, sometimes with a loop threaded through the mouth and nose and tied to a stake that was left exposed at the surface so that when the body began to decompose, the head could be pulled from the earth without disturbing the rest of the corpse.

The relatives would return five or six days later, making loud noises on the return to scare away the remaining mari before attempting to remove the head of the corpse. If the mari remained, they believed that the head would be difficult to remove. The cranium and mandible were removed by the first and second *imi*, respectively (directly translated as "brother-in-law," but this may not necessarily always reflect the actual familial link), who took the leading ceremonial role during the mourning process. The cranium and mandible were then placed in a termite mound, an earth oven, or a creek in order to clean off the soft tissue. The remainder of the corpse was covered in grass and left until skeletonized, at which point the bones were rolled in a mat and deposited in a crevice in the rocks.

After the head had been cleaned, a skull-giving ceremony was held. The imi would decorate the skull by painting it with red earth and then would place it in a basket. The facial jewelry of the deceased was placed on the basket roughly according to the position it was worn in life. On most western islands, with the exception of Mabuiag (where the same process was undertaken but without facial modeling), facial features were modeled on the skull using beeswax and clay (figure 2.2), and the mandible was sometimes lashed onto the cranium

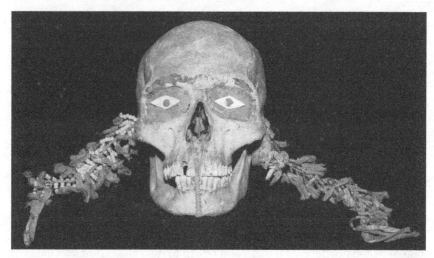

Figure 2.2. BMNHPAHR571. Skull of a young adult male with facial features modeled during the mortuary ritual. Collected on Naghir Island during the voyage of HMS *Alert* and donated to the Natural History Museum, London, in 1884 by the Lords of the Admiralty. © Natural History Museum, London.

(Haddon 1904). The decorated cranium was then presented to the widow. The skull was sometimes carried around in a bag during the period of widowhood. Skulls were then usually kept within the houses of relatives in their baskets. Occasionally they were used for divining, and eventually they were left in crevices in the rocks.

Divination Using Skulls

Heads of the unspecified deceased were often used for divining to identify the "sorcerer" responsible for the death of the individual; islanders did not believe in "natural" death, instead believing that a sorcerer was always responsible. The ritual took several forms. On Moa, after the imi collected the head on the fourth or fifth day after burial, he would go to the sea with a group of friends of the deceased to perform the divining method *mari maidelaig*: they would place the head in the sea, and (depending on the translation) it would float with the face pointing in the direction of, or float towards, the island where the sorcerer responsible resided (Haddon 1935).

Skulls of deceased family members were also used for divining while they were kept in the houses. They would be cleaned and repainted and anointed with particular leaves. Inquirers would ask the skull to speak the truth then place it on their pillow as they went to sleep. The skulls would reportedly make a "chattering noise," and the dreams of the inquirer were interpreted as the messages from the skull, upon which action would be taken (Haddon 1890). Two skulls described by Haddon as "divining skulls" (1932) actually appear to fit within the bounds of the western islands' mortuary ritual and do not necessarily appear to have been decorated specifically for the purposes of divining.

Crania were also used in divining prior to or during dugong hunts and headhunting raids. In Boigu, a Maisiri Zogo (Maisiri shrine) was made at the ceremonial spot, or *kwod*. A circle of grass in the form of a nest was laid down. The "Maisiri"—a dark stone approximately the size of a human head with eyes marked on it—was placed within the nest. A human skull was brought and the frontal bone scraped, with the scrapings placed on the Maisiri. The scrapings were mixed with leaves, flowers, and bark. After the ceremony, the Maisiri was placed in the bow of the canoe to be used in a headhunting raid (Haddon 1935). On other islands, skulls of relatives were placed in the canoes; Haddon (1890) reports that this was partly due to affection and partly for divining purposes.

Mummification in the Eastern Islands

Mummification was a common practice for male and female tribe members on the eastern islands of Erub and Mer. However, children and the elderly were usually buried and left, as were those who were believed to have died from disease (see Weiner 1976 for additional differential practices involving the heads of suspected sorcerers and the elderly). In the early twentieth century, Elliot Smith (1915) proposed that mummification methods in Melanesia, including the Torres Strait, were influenced by the "diffusion" of ancient Egyptian practices. This, of course, instigated some controversy (Pretty 1969) and was eventually refuted when anthropogenic mummies from the western coast of South America were radiocarbon dated to about two thousand years prior to the first pharaonic dynasty (Aufderheide 2003).

Mummification in the Torres Strait essentially involved the desiccation of the body to preserve it temporarily for the duration of the funerary rites, which could last up to a year after the individual died. They were also created out of affection for the deceased, to "make like photo" (Haddon 1935). The mummies were not intended to be permanent, and as such, few have survived to the present day. The following account of mummification is based on Haddon's observations (Haddon 1935).

When an individual died, if the body was to be mummified, the hair of the head and face was cut off and disposed of. A piece of wood was used to measure the length of the nose and cut to the correct size. This was preserved by a female relative for use when making a wax mask for the prepared skull. The mouth was filled with dried banana or sago palm leaves to prevent the escape of the odor of decomposition. The corpse was attached to a frame and left to dry for two to three days. When the skin became loose, the body on the frame was taken out to the reef in a canoe. The epidermis was rubbed off, and a sharp shell was used to make an incision in the side of the abdomen, through which the viscera were removed and thrown into the sea. The abdominal cavity was filled with pieces of nipa palm, and the incision was closed using fishing line. An arrow was used to remove the brain through an incision in the neck, which was used to access the foramen magnum.

The body was brought back to the island and placed in a sitting position on a stone. It was then painted with red earth and seawater. It was lashed to a new frame, and a small stick was attached to the jaw to prevent it from drooping. The frame was then fastened vertically to two posts in the rear of the deceased individual's house, and the body was screened from public view with coconut leaves. Holes were made between the first and second digits of the hands and feet, and the body was gently rubbed in order to assist the escape of decomposition fluids. These were sometimes collected in a bowl beneath the body and mixed with food and eaten. A fire was lit beneath the body, and it was left for around ten days. At this point, the hands and feet would have become partially dry. A bamboo knife was used to remove the skin of the palms and soles along with the nails. The tongue was cut out and placed in a bamboo clamp to keep it straight while it dried. These parts of the body were presented to the widow after the feast, after which she would wear them during her widowhood and on ceremonial occasions.

Four to six months later, the "dead man's likeness" ceremony was held. The body was in an advanced stage of mummification at this point. The friends met at the house of the deceased, and the mummy was taken to the beach, where a dance was held. The body was then affixed to a new bamboo frame and carried back to the hut. It was fastened to the center pole that supported the roof. The dried skin was again painted red; nautilus nacre was cemented into the orbits, with round spots of beeswax representing pupils. The body was decorated with ornaments and leaves (figure 2.3). If the skull was the only part being kept, it was decorated as described and suspended from the center of the roof. Sometimes the skin was allowed to dry on the heads of younger men (figure 2.4); older individuals would have their features modeled in wax.

Eventually the mummy would begin to fall to pieces. A feast was then held, but only if the deceased was male. The head was then removed and a wax model made, which was presented to the "brother" of the deceased. The body was moved to the beach and placed on a platform built on the trunks of four palm trees; there it was left. The head was sometimes used for divination.

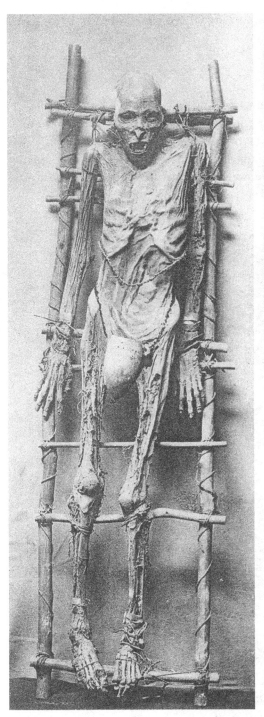

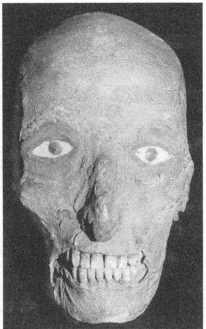

Left: Figure 2.3. Mummy collected on Darnley Island by Charles Lemaistre, captain of the French barque *Victorine* in 1872 and donated to the Royal College of Surgeons. Photographed and described before being defleshed (Flower 1879). Reproduced from Flower 1879.

Above: Figure 2.4. BMNHPAHR583. Dried head of a young adult male from the Torres Strait (island unknown) donated to the Natural History Museum, London, in 1846 by the Earl of Derby. © Natural History Museum, London.

Ethnographic Evidence for Headhunting Other Islanders and Shipwrecked Outsiders

Raids on Other Islands

Headhunting attacks on other islands were not usually due to any ill-feeling or revenge (Haddon 1890) but were purely for the purpose of obtaining heads, which would earn the men glory and status among the women of their own island. Heads were collected indiscriminately from men, women, and children. However, islanders would not take women prisoners or violate them; if any member of the attacking party did so, he would be executed.

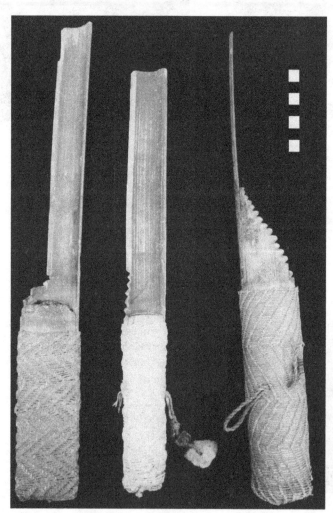

Figure 2.5. Bamboo beheading knives from the collections of the Horniman Museum, London (scale in centimeters). Photograph by Heather Bonney with permission of the Horniman Museum, London.

By the time Haddon and the Cambridge Anthropological Expedition arrived on the islands in 1898, European iron knives had replaced the traditional bamboo knives, or *upi* (western islands) and *kwoier* (eastern islands). Bamboo knives (figure 2.5) were extremely sharp, owing to the silica particles along the edge. When the knife became dulled, a notch was cut just above the handle, and the edge was split off. A shell was used to cut an edge at the opposite end, from which a layer was peeled down to the notch. A new edge was said to be good for cutting off only one head, such that a fresh edge was needed for each decapitation—leading to the assumption that the number of notches on a knife was equal to the number of heads it had taken. Haddon (1904) reported that in Mabuiag a head was removed by cutting around the neck with a bamboo knife before twisting off the head. No specific detail about the method of head removal is provided for other islands.

The bamboo knife was always paired with a head carrier, or *sungei*. This was a cane loop about the same length as the knife. The ends were lashed onto a crosspiece around fifteen centimeters long. The loop was passed in at the neck and out of the mouth of a severed head, and this was then utilized to carry the heads home (Haddon 1935).

Heads collected on raids were defleshed in the same manner as heads of deceased relatives. They were either manually stripped or placed in an oven or in a termite mound. Several crania in the Natural History Museum collection contain termite "carton" (nesting material consisting of fecal matter mixed with other local materials) within the sphenoid foramina (figure 2.6). On islands where the heads were skinned manually, the eyeballs and flesh were often fed to boys to assist them in developing "manly qualities."

The crania and mandibles were separated. The brain was broken up using a stick and shaken out through the foramen magnum. The "best" skulls were given beeswax cheeks and noses and nautilus nacre eyes and then placed in baskets in prominent positions in the Augudalkula cave on Pulu, a small island off Mabuiag, or within the head house on Mabuiag itself. The "indifferent" or less visually pleasing specimens were painted red and placed in the darkest corners of the cave. It was reportedly the last insult to tell an opponent on a raid that you kill them for *dabun kurubad*—the corner of the cave. The mandibles were painted red and retained by the headhunter as proof of valor. Crania were also kept in a head house—*kwikwi-iut*. There were probably two such head houses on Mabuiag (Haddon 1935), in which islanders kept their weapons and the trophy crania and mandibles. Head houses appear to have been confined to the western islands. The relationships between, and differing purposes of, the cave and head house on Pulu and Mabuiag are unclear.

Trophy crania and mandibles were also used as a form of currency and had

Figure 2.6. BMNHPAHR487. Evidence of termite activity in the sphenoid bone of a trophy skull from the collection at the Natural History Museum, London. © Natural History Museum, London.

a defined value. Mandibles were often purchased by men from New Guinea. According to Haddon (1935: 80), an islander told him, "Good money for buy canoe or any kind of thing, that one!—New Guinea man, when he get them jaw-bone, he say he been kill all them men, he make big talk."

Massacre of Shipwrecked Outsiders

Islanders believed that spirits of the deceased haunted the islands and visited them at night, trying to enter their huts. They referred to these spirits as *lammoor* or *lamar*, which means "a white man" (Haddon 1935). Both male and female members of the unfortunate crew of any ship wrecked in the islands were often massacred. The islanders may well have believed that those shipwrecked crews were spirits of the dead returning to haunt them and thus killed the crew members in the belief that it could prevent the reappearance of the spirits. Occasionally, members of the tribe would "recognize" victims of the wreck as resembling their deceased relatives, and these crew members would be spared. According to most accounts, these individuals were usually children or young women who posed little risk to the islanders and were then integrated into the tribe.

One of the most notorious shipwrecks in the area was that of the *Charles Eaton* in 1834. The ship was sailing from Sydney to Canton when, during a storm, it hit a reef in the Torres Strait. Some of the crew escaped and eventually made it back to England, but the rest were not so fortunate. According to the accounts of a surviving cabin boy, John Ireland (Haddon 1935), the crew were picked up by some apparently friendly islanders in a canoe and taken to one of the islands. Ireland reported that he woke up to hear the islanders beating the heads of the rest of the crew with their clubs, and then saw them eating the crew members' eyes and cheeks. Ireland and another cabin boy, John Sexton, were spared. They were taken to another island, where a raft from the ship had landed. The crew from the raft had met a similar fate, with the exception of the two sons of Captain D'Oyly. Ireland and one of the younger boys were taken to various other islands over the following months until they were purchased by a man from Murray Island. In 1836, a rescue expedition led by Captain Lewis recovered seventeen skulls from Aureed Island, which he believed belonged to the crew; these were subsequently buried in Sydney. They also rescued John Ireland and one of the D'Oyly brothers from Murray Island. The other brother was believed to have been killed, and John Sexton had fallen ill and died sometime previously (Haddon 1935).

Osteological Evidence for Decapitation and Defleshing

The head house collection from the Torres Strait at the Natural History Museum consists of a broad demographic, with roughly equal numbers of males, females, and unsexed subadults. They range in age from approximately four years old to elderly individuals; headhunting practices do not seem to have been particularly selective.

A diverse range of cut marks can be observed on 53 percent of the trophy mandibles collected from the head house on Mabuiag. Some of these cuts may be due to the defleshing process (figure 2.7). The majority of cuts are found on the posterior ramus (20 percent of the mandibles had marks in this area) and on the anterior and posterior lateral surface of the ramus. Although cuts on the posterior ramus are sometimes associated with decapitation, the marks on the trophy mandibles consist of repeated cuts down the entire length of the back of the mandible (figure 2.8). The marks are not the type normally associated with decapitation or disarticulation. Three mandibles had cut marks on the anterior mandibular body. A sample of the cut marks from the lateral

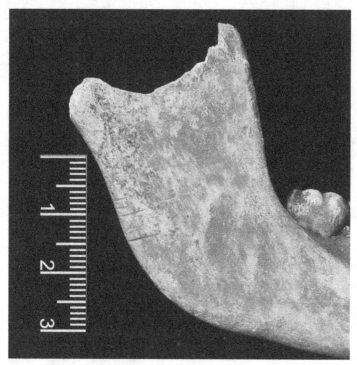

Figure 2.7. BMNHPAHR509. Cut marks on the ramus of a trophy mandible, possibly due to defleshing. Scale in centimeters. © Natural History Museum, London.

ramus of several mandibles was cast using silicone paste and examined under the Alicona infinite-focus microscope (figure 2.9). Profile analysis showed that the cuts were consistent with experimental cut marks made with a bamboo knife on animal bone in a study by West and Louys (2007).

None of the crania bears any cut marks (although see Stodder 2006 for examples from Papua New Guinea), and no evidence of frontal bone scraping for the Maisiri Zogo ceremony (see section on divination) was found. Moreover, no osteological evidence for decapitation (such as damage to the occipital condyles or cranial base) was found on any of the crania in the collection. This is the expected observation if the ethnographic information about the method of head removal is correct (see section on headhunting), such that heads were removed at the neck, with the cervical vertebrae attached to the head discarded during the defleshing process. There was no evidence for modification of skulls to enable suspension and display. No cut marks were found on any of the nontrophy crania (i.e., those reportedly of relatives). There

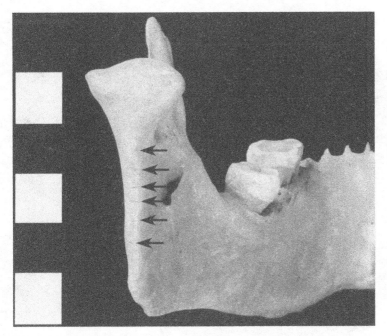

Figure 2.8. BMNHPAHR560. Cut marks on the posterior ramus of a trophy mandible. Scale in centimeters. © Natural History Museum, London.

is no mention in the ethnographic record of knives being used in the Torres Strait to remove heads during the funerary process; rather, it is specifically stated that bodies were left to decompose for several days and that the mari had to be scared away or the head would be difficult to remove, which may indicate that the head was literally pulled from the body. The heads of mummies are described as having been cut off, but with the body being completely desiccated, we find it unlikely that this would leave any marks on the cranium or mandible. One such mummified head in the collection shows no osteological damage, the head having been removed between the second and third cervical vertebrae (see Montgomery, Knüsel, and Tucker this volume for related evidence from Roman Britain).

Decoration and painting of skulls cannot be used to infer any discrimination between the heads of relatives or trophies, as the practices were seemingly applied to both. The osteological evidence demonstrates that if cut marks are found on mandibles collected from the Torres Strait Islands, then the mandible and any associated cranium were almost certainly collected as trophies. This, however, does not mean that an individual is not an islander, as heads were frequently collected from nearby islands during raids. Additional osteological

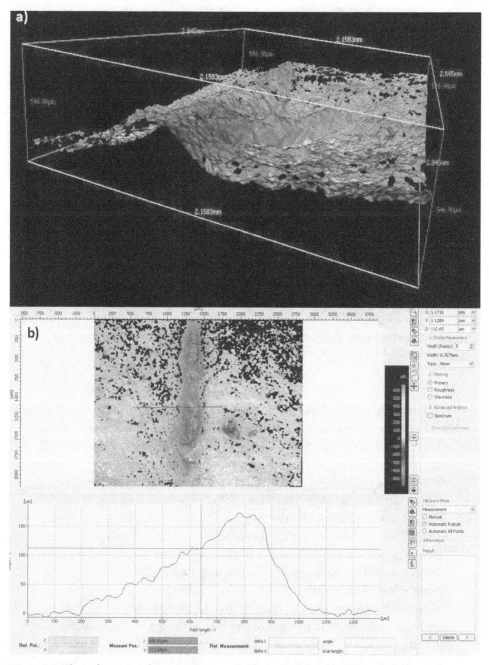

Figure 2.9. Three-dimensional reconstruction of cut mark peel, taken from the superior posterior ramus of mandible BMNHPAHR509 in figure 2.7, under (a) Alicona infinite-focus microscope and (b) profile analysis. © Natural History Museum, London.

data (such as metric data currently being collected for discriminant function analysis) is required to separate islanders from nonislanders, which is necessary for repatriation.

Conclusions

In the Torres Strait Islands, skulls of loved ones were retained as memorials, while heads of those from other islands were collected as status symbols and used for trade. In the treatment of their own dead, some Torres Strait Islanders followed the widely recurring theme that ritual treatment of remains should be undertaken in order that the spirit did not persist and cause them trouble. However, unlike other cultures holding this belief system, these islanders appear to have preserved heads and bodies purely out of affection for deceased family members and to assist during a long regimented grieving process. Torres Strait Islanders showed no evidence of worshipping ancestors or a ritual belief that spirits or a "soul substance" remained within the head (after being driven off), a belief commonly ascribed to tribes from other areas that hold similar practices (Needham 1976; see Bonogofsky and Graham this volume).

The coexistence of headhunting practices and the retention of trophy heads and those of deceased relatives appears to have no significant ritual relationship. Both practices are far more complex than may first appear, and the lack of contemporary ethnological research makes analysis extremely difficult. The accounts of Haddon and the Cambridge Anthropological Expedition, while extremely thorough, were made after the arrival of the London Missionary Society and the conversion to Christianity (see Valentin and Rolland this volume for Western impact on Marquesan society). With language barriers and individual interpretation taken into account, there is likely to be some degree of confusion within the complexity of the descriptions of mortuary and headhunting ritual. As noted above, no specific osteological evidence for decapitation was found, but there was corroboration of the ethnographic description of the practices of defleshing both manually and by using termite mounds. Moreover, both ethnographic and osteological evidence indicate that the heads of insiders and outsiders and of local and nonlocal residents alike (including those of males, females, and children) were curated by the Torres Strait Islanders.

Acknowledgments

We thank Michelle Bonogofsky for comments and suggestions. Our thanks also go to the Photographic Unit at the Natural History Museum, London.

We are grateful to Wayne Modest, keeper of anthropology at the Horniman Museum, for access to the bamboo knives.

References Cited

Aufderheide, A. C. 2003. *The Scientific Study of Mummies*. Cambridge University Press, Cambridge.

Flower, W. H. 1879. Illustrations of the Mode of Preserving the Dead in Darnley Island and in South Australia. *Journal of the Anthropological Institute of Great Britain and Ireland* 8: 389–395.

Haddon, A. C. 1890. The Ethnography of the Western Tribe of the Torres Straits. *Journal of the Anthropological Institute of Great Britain and Ireland* 19: 297–440.

———. 1904. *Sociology, Magic and Religion of the Western Islanders*. Reports of the Cambridge Anthropological Expedition to the Torres Straits, vol. 5. Cambridge University Press, Cambridge.

———. 1932. *Head-hunters: Black, White and Brown*. Abridged edition. Watts, London.

———. 1935. *General Ethnology*. Reports of the Cambridge Anthropological Expedition to the Torres Straits, vol. 1. Cambridge University Press, Cambridge.

Needham, R. 1976. Skulls and Causality. *Man* 11: 71–88.

Pretty, G. L. 1969. The Macleay Museum Mummy from Torres Straits: A Postscript to Elliot Smith and the Diffusion Controversy. *Man* 4 (1): 24–43.

Smith, E. 1915. *The Migrations of Early Culture*. Manchester University Press, Manchester.

Stodder, A. L. W. 2006. The Taphonomy of Cranial Modification in Papua New Guinea: Implications for the Archaeology of Mortuary Ritual. In *Skull Collection, Modification and Decoration*, edited by M. Bonogofsky, 77–89. BAR International Series 1539. Archaeopress, Oxford, U.K.

Thomas, O. 1885. Account of a Collection of Human Skulls from Torres Straits. *Journal of the Anthropological Institute of Great Britain and Ireland* 14: 328–343.

Weiner, A. B. 1976. *Women of Value, Men of Renown*. University of Texas Press, Austin.

West, J. A., and J. Louys. 2007. Differentiating Bamboo from Stone Tool Cut Marks in the Zooarchaeological Record, with a Discussion on the Use of Bamboo Knives. *Journal of Archaeological Science* 34: 512–518.

3

Melanesian Modeled Skulls, Mortuary Ritual, and Dental X-Rays

Ancestors, Enemies, Women, and Children

MICHELLE BONOGOFSKY AND JEREMY GRAHAM

Uncertainty regarding the identification of an object or skeletal specimen may be constructive when unresolved ambiguities "serve as stimuli for the development of research" (Winter 1999: 251). These ambiguities are dispelled with the application of a label in which objects are categorized, an owner is named, and an object's use is identified. At the same time, these identifications can be limiting and serve to discourage investigation into the true ownership, nature, and use of an object, because its meaning is already "known." This process may produce unsupported assumptions or untested hypotheses that stand as fact, preventing us from working out the methodologies necessary for further investigation (Winter 1999: 250–251). This has been particularly important in cross-cultural issues related to the interpretation of skulls.

Unsupported assumptions are a frequent occurrence with the modeled and decorated skulls from Melanesia that appear in ethnographic collections around the world. As will be apparent in the case study presented below, many skulls may spend years in collections without basic information on age, sex, or cultural context being ascertained. Because of the circumstances of original acquisition, whether the skulls represent ancestors, enemies, or some other social category remains unknown. The limited information available for these skulls perpetuates colonialist perspectives on Melanesian cultural practices and implies that native peoples live(d) in a "timeless state of primitive savagery" (Hoskins 1996c: 16–17). Critical studies of collecting (e.g., O'Hanlon and Welsch 2000; Thomas 1991) in tandem with the wealth of ethnographic research that has emerged over the past three decades (Goodale 1985; Hoskins 1989, 1996a, 1996b; Rosaldo 1980) demonstrate how skulls, as well as many other ethnographic objects, were "entangled" in complex social engagements involving both native Melanesians and nineteenth-century Euro-American collectors.

Many missionaries and other Euro-Americans of the late nineteenth and early twentieth centuries believed that ancestor worship was the reason behind the preservation and handling of human skulls. Collectors and ethnographers—most often males with their own agendas and classification schemes—focused on the role of skulls in mortuary practices pertaining to men in Melanesian societies (e.g., Rivers 1914; see also White 1992 for discussion on how cultural biases can often distort the interpretation of scientific data regarding human skeletal remains from ethnographic and archaeological contexts worldwide). Contrary to these androcentric accounts, in many Melanesian societies the skulls of deceased men, women, and children were removed from the body (and sometimes decorated) for a variety of reasons that were often unconnected with ancestors or veneration. Europeans imposed the term *ancestor worship*, often based on a misunderstanding of Melanesian funerary practices; skulls, as the ethnographic objects most closely associated with these mortuary practices, were thus interpreted as those of ancestors. The labeling, classification, and museum interpretation of the skulls reflected these biases, with far-reaching consequences.

Further, decorated skulls may be accessioned and labeled by museums as part of a larger set of ethnographic objects. As a result, a skull may be overlooked by researchers who assume that the labels accurately reflect the contents of a collection, thus preventing scholarly investigation of a skull hidden within a larger body of material. For example, the skull illustrated in figure 3.1 was donated to the Phoebe A. Hearst Museum of Anthropology as part of a collection described on the catalog card in masterful understatement as "Shells; type collection."

Simplified ethnographic labels of "ancestor" or "enemy," as applied to modeled skulls from Melanesia, were also transferred to visually parallel material from disparate regions of the world. One noteworthy example is the plastered and modeled skulls from the Neolithic Near East (Bonogofsky 2001a, 2001b, 2002a, 2003; see Bonogofsky this volume figure 1.1), which date to as early as ca. 7500 BC (*Khaleej Times* 2006; see Kaiser 2006; Shishlina 2006; Vadetskaia 2006 for examples from Eurasia). Kathleen Kenyon found the first such skulls at Jericho in 1953 and extensively discussed them as portraits of venerated male ancestors who were tribal or family elders (e.g., Kenyon and Tushingham 1953: 870). Even though there is no direct evidence linking the Neolithic skulls with Melanesian practices, Kenyon based her interpretation on vague "modern anthropological parallels" (e.g., Kenyon 1979: 35) that were largely unsubstantiated. This interpretation, put forth by an acknowledged expert,

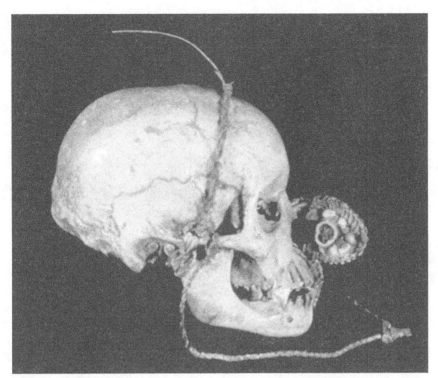

Figure 3.1. Skull decorated with a bamboo noseplug with rattan trim; four feathers hang from carrying cord. New Hebrides (Vanuatu), Melanesia, collected 1963–1964 by Dr. and Mrs. Richard Shulter Jr. Courtesy of Phoebe A. Hearst Museum of Anthropology and the Regents of the University of California; photography by Michelle Bonogofsky (catalog no. 11-38439; acc. no. 2085).

limited future inquiry into the age, sex, nature, and function of the skulls; the problem was compounded by the fact that the skulls were classified as archaeological—rather than anthropological—specimens (Kurth and Röhrer-Ertl 1981: 437), making them unavailable for study by physical anthropologists during the course of the site's excavation.

The result of this initial classification was that none of the Neolithic skulls were studied (with results published) by a physical anthropologist for another twenty years (Strouhal 1973). By then, Kenyon's interpretation had become so entrenched in the literature that it continued to be built upon and applied for the next fifty years to subsequently excavated plastered skulls from other sites in the Middle East and limited more-intensive investigation of whose skulls were modeled and why (Bonogofsky 2003). Kenyon's original interpretation and the many investigators who accepted her identification of the skulls as those of venerated male ancestors thus became fixed in Near Eastern

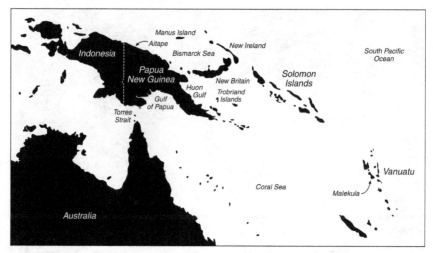

Figure 3.2. Map of Melanesia. © Ann L. W. Stodder. Used by permission.

scholarship and likely reinforced the belief that Melanesian skulls, like their Neolithic "counterparts," represented the remains of esteemed ancestors. This perception may eventually change now that earlier hypotheses concerning Neolithic skulls have been disproved, the validity of Kenyon's interpretation has been undermined, and new methods have been developed and applied to both ethnographic and archaeological specimens (e.g., Bonogofsky 2001a, 2001b, 2002a, 2002b, 2003). The case study presented below is one example of how radiographic and dental analysis of museum specimens can contribute to scholarly discussion of modeled skulls. These skulls present challenges to bioarchaeologists and museum personnel because the modeling material obscures direct observation of dentition and cranial morphology. This example demonstrates, through a nondestructive aging method, that the skulls of children, as well as adults, were extensively modified after death. The case study also provides a method for evaluating the age of modeled skulls in other museum collections, as well as those recovered from archaeological sites.

In addition to modern radiographic, skeletal, and dental analyses, ethnographic accounts of mortuary practices in Melanesia offer richer insight into the meaning and function of skulls than either their museum labels indicate or their collectors may have realized. Rather than focusing on the skulls of old men, many Sepik River groups that practiced skull decoration, such as the Iatmül (Bateson 1932, 1936), selected skulls for special treatment based on their perception of beauty, youth, and fertility. The second section of the chapter focuses on the selection, decoration, use, and function of human skulls of relatives and enemies in Melanesia (figure 3.2). Key ethnographic writings, by, among others, Bateson (1932, 1936), Landtman (1916), Seligmann (1910), and Weiner (1976) are discussed in order to delve beyond the problematic museum labels and accession records that often hinder the interpretation of old collections.

A Child's Skull from the Sepik River Valley

One challenge to the archaeological and ethnographic study of modeled skulls from Melanesia, the Near East, and Eurasia (see, e.g., chapters in Bonogofsky 2006c) is the fact that most of the skeletal and dental markers used to determine age at death are obscured by modeling material or are completely unavailable (Bonogofsky 2001a, 2001b, 2002a, 2002b, 2005a, 2005b, 2006a, 2006b, 2006c). Without data on whether and how often the skulls of subadults were modeled and decorated postmortem, it is difficult to address the issue of ancestor veneration or to understand how skulls functioned in Melanesian society in anything but the most general terms. Forensic odontology, which is applied here, is the branch of dentistry that deals with the evaluation of dental materials for the purpose of postmortem identification, usually within a law enforcement or judicial context. This sort of forensic medicine relies on detailed knowledge of dental anatomy, pathologies, and developmental abnormalities. Radiographs are routinely employed to aid in the identification process.

The case study presented below focuses on an overmodeled skull (no. 22; figures 3.3, 3.4) of unknown origin held at the Melbourne Dental School at the University of Melbourne. On the left parietal, the initials "WRS" and "2182" were found. Through consultation with Dr. Barry Craig at the South Australian Museum, Adelaide, Graham concluded that the skull was collected or owned by William Ramsay Smith (1859–1937), a Scot who became medical superintendent of Adelaide Hospital in 1896 and later served as coroner. Smith had a serious interest in anthropology and photographed and wrote extensively about Australian Aboriginal peoples. In his book *In Southern Seas— Wanderings of a Naturalist*, he described an artifact-collecting tour, which included New Guinea (now divided politically into a province of Indonesia and the independent nation of Papua New Guinea), in the early years of the twentieth century (Smith 1924). We may reasonably conclude that Smith acquired the child's modeled skull during his travels sometime prior to 1924, likely from the Sepik River region of New Guinea (Papua New Guinea; figure 3.2). The skull may have entered the Melbourne Dental School collection in

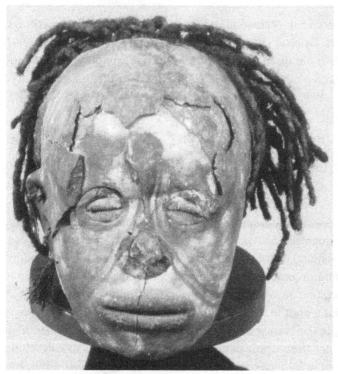

Figure 3.3. Anterior view of child's skull (no. 22) from the Sepik River region. The left modeled ear is missing, exposing a large section of the temporal bone, where the external auditory meatus is visible. Portions of unpainted modeling material containing shell grit are visible directly above the exposed temporal bone. Courtesy Melbourne Dental School, University of Melbourne.

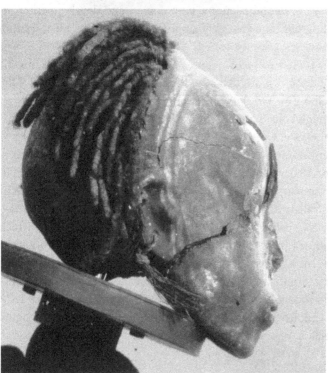

Figure 3.4. Right lateral view of child's skull (no. 22). The modeling material has pulled away from the frontal bone and is visible in cross section. Courtesy Melbourne Dental School, University of Melbourne.

the 1930s via its dean, Sir Arthur Amies, or through Thomas Draper Campbell, his counterpart at the Adelaide School of Dental Science, author of *Dentition and Palate of the Australian Aboriginal* (1925) and also an anthropologist.

The use of the developing dentition to determine the age of children has its origins in the British Factory Act of 1833; emergence of the lower incisors was the basis for determining whether a child was over age nine (Dean 2007). Major advances in the study of children's dentitions (e.g., Cohen 1928) continued into the 1940s, when Schour and Massler (1941; Massler and Schour 1941) produced their diagrams charting dental formation and emergence. The original charts have undergone revision (e.g., Buikstra and Ubelaker 1994; Ubelaker 1978) but remain a world standard. Since that time, knowledge of children's dentitions has expanded with the development of the forensic sciences, biological anthropology, and bioarchaeology. While forensic specialists and bioarchaeologists routinely age children's remains on the basis of tooth development (e.g., Halcrow et al. 2007; Scheuer 2002), museum specimens represent a relatively new application of aging methods.

In addition to the Schour and Massler (1941) diagram, Graham used three other aging methods to assess the age at death of the child represented by skull no. 22 (Moorrees et al. 1963; Gustafson and Koch 1974; and Demirjian and Goldstein 1976). Moorrees and colleagues (1963) divided the formation of children's teeth into thirteen stages that described the development of the crown (six stages), root (five stages), and apex (two stages). Using radiographs of 345 children aged between birth and twenty years of age, they determined the mean age for the attainment of each of the thirteen stages for each permanent tooth. Further, they charted boys and girls separately and reported each age to two standard deviations. Gustafson and Koch (1974) identified four significant landmarks of tooth formation: commencement of calcification, crown completion, emergence, and root completion. Their chart provides both the mean age for attainment of each landmark and an age range but does not provide separate charts for boys and girls.

Demirjian and colleagues (1973) had developed a simpler system of four stages pertaining to crown formation and four to root formation using relative proportions of each and an alphabetical identification system. In 1962, Tanner and colleagues developed and applied the concept of a "maturity score" to human skeletal maturation. This system was the basis for the revised dental aging system (e.g., Demirjian et al. 1973), which used tables of scores for each tooth, providing separate tables for boys and girls. The sum of these scores generated a maturity score with percentile spreads ranging from 10 to 90 percent. Demirjian and colleagues (1973) initially used the stages of development for seven teeth on one side of the mandible, but Demirjian and Goldstein (1976) later revised this method so that only four teeth of the mandible were required to determine the estimated age with a similar degree of precision.

The Melanesian skull at the University of Melbourne (no. 22) was sufficiently overmodeled and decorated that direct observation of the teeth was impossible without damage to the modeling materials. Graham relied instead upon radiographs to determine age. In 2000, the skull was weighed and photographed. Radiographs were taken by a dental radiographer at the Royal Dental Hospital of Melbourne. The overmodeling material rendered the orthopantomograph (OPG, a panoramic image), the lateral radiographs, and the anteroposterior radiograph useless for dental aging analysis; only the left and right lateral oblique radiographs (taken at a 45-degree angle) showed the developing teeth in sufficient detail for dental aging (figure 3.5).

Basic osteometrics of the skull are as follows: 14.5 centimeters long (from the artificial glabella to the most distal curvature of the skull); 12.2 centimeters wide (from artificial ear to artificial ear); and 11.2 centimeters high (from the anterior margin of the foramen magnum to the artificial vertex of the skull). The overall impression is of child, rather than adult, proportions. The skull weighed 670 grams, which included the modeling material. No determination of the biological sex of this child could be made, as DNA analysis was deemed too destructive for use on this specimen and osteological markers of sex are insufficiently developed in children to yield accurate results, even under the most favorable circumstances. The modeling of the skull made even the most basic observations of cranial morphology impossible; the modeling itself is quite complex and includes applied eyes and hair, as well as red and black paint.

The anterior portion of the skull is covered with a gray claylike material, which reproduces the facial features (figures 3.3, 3.4). The skull is very fragile; large fragments of the modeling material are missing, especially from the forehead. Shell grit appears to have been used as a tempering agent. The eyes are represented by cowrie shells (13×19 millimeters) and are surrounded by black paint. The nose has fractured off, exposing the clay material that served as a core. The mouth is black and cigar-shaped, disproportionately large given the dimensions of the face as a whole (external measurements: 50 millimeters long, 18 millimeters wide at midline). The left ear is missing, but the right ear is modeled with a large circular tragus; there are two holes through the earlobe and twine loops through each hole.

Running anterior to the hairline is a black band, which continues down to the right ear. Two dark crimson lines run along the forehead anterior to the black band, then down in front of the ears to the angle of the mandible. From

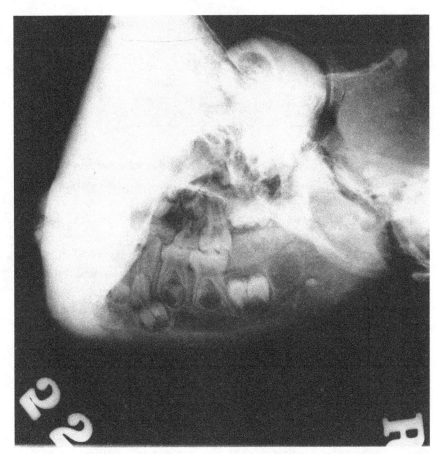

Figure 3.5. Right lateral oblique radiograph of child's skull (no. 22). Although the modeling material has obscured the face, much of the dentition is visible with this radiograph. The two lower right deciduous molars are clearly visible in occlusion with the two upper deciduous molars. Both the lower right premolars have just started to form within the mandible. The two lower right permanent molars appear as opacities within the jaw; only the crown of the first molar is complete, and that of the second molar is just starting to calcify. Courtesy Melbourne Dental School, University of Melbourne.

there they then swing upwards, to run along the sides of the nose, framing the central black line that runs along the nasal midline.

The clay material is heaped at the vertex of the skull; holes hold the hair, styled in dreadlocks approximately 80–90 millimeters long. The posterior half of the skull, which was not covered by the modeling material, is blackened, although under the hair, the bone appears dark gray. The basal aspect of the skull is completely blackened. The spheno-occipital suture is open. The clay

Table 3.1. Summary of dental aging results

Method	Estimated age
Schour and Massler 1941	3.0–4.0 years old
Moorrees et al. 1963	3.1 years old
Gustafson and Koch 1974	3.0–4.0 years old
Demirjian and Goldstein 1976	3.2 years old

completely covers the mandible, up to the gingival margins of the lower teeth, with tufts of twine emerging from the material on the lingual aspect in the midline.

In order to age the skull, Graham began with a comparison of the skull's left lateral oblique with a lateral oblique of a four-year-old boy from the University of Illinois at Chicago (UIC; www.uic.edu/classes/orla/orla312/correlated _images_skulls.htm). Gross similarities indicated that the initial impression of a relatively young child was correct. However, the radiograph of skull no. 22 showed the dentition to be slightly less developed than that of the UIC child. Graham proceeded to the application of the four dental aging methods discussed above. Using the Schour-Massler chart, the Sepik River child was determined to be more than three and less than four years of age. Moreover, all four methods yielded reasonably similar results, and Graham concluded that the child was between 3.2 and 4.0 years old at death. Results of each of the four aging methods are summarized in table 3.1.

In sum, application of these four methods enables analysts to assign an individual to a much more narrow age range than is usually possible on the basis of skeletal morphology alone. Some stages of pelvic fusion, for example, take place between ages three and ten—not very useful for either bioarchaeology or forensic work (Scheuer 2002: 303). Graham and other forensic odontologists from around the world successfully employed these dental developmental schema in the Reconciliation Section of the Thai Tsunami Victims' Identification Centre (TTVIC) in Phuket, Thailand, following the 2004 Boxing Day tsunami, demonstrating their utility to forensic work.

For the purposes of paleodemography—establishing a demographic profile for a cemetery population, for example—these methods will enable bioarchaeologists to age the remains of children to within a year when sufficient dental evidence is present. These methods are significantly more accurate than skeletal markers, such as epiphyseal fusion or long bone diaphysis length, and can be applied even when postcranial remains are fragmentary or absent. More specifically, as a case study of a modeled Melanesian skull, this example demonstrates that the skulls of children—not just adults—underwent significant postmortem manipulation. To assume, then, that modeled skulls represent biological "ancestors," at least in Melanesia, is in error and brings into question the assumed ages at death of individuals whose skulls were modeled in Eurasia and the Neolithic Near East (see Bonogofsky 2001b, 2004, 2006c, this volume). Whether Sepik River groups could consider a subadult as an ancestor in conceptual or cosmological terms is an entirely different question and deserves greater attention.

Modeled and Decorated Skulls in Melanesia

Researchers in the late nineteenth and early twentieth centuries, including the British, Germans, Americans, and Dutch, returned to their home countries with reports and examples—such as the Sepik River skull discussed above—of the skulls of both the enemies and the relatives of native Melanesians. They saw decorated skulls of children, women, and men that were reportedly kept as relics, prayed to for protection and plenty, and used as tools in sorcery, divination, and fecundity rituals.

While these early observers, who were mostly males, may have brought along biased classification systems and preconceptions, informants had their own understanding of what information was important or even possible to relate (see, e.g., chapters in Herle and Rouse 1998; O'Hanlon 2000). Although caution should be exercised in the use of these early sources, they do provide enough detail to highlight the richness and variety of mortuary practices of diverse island groups. One common denominator in the early accounts, however, seems to be the connection between the skull and the beauty, youth, and fecundity of the deceased individual (Bonogofsky 2001b: 33).

The Iatmül people of the Sepik River region of New Guinea (Papua New Guinea; figure 3.2) modeled portrait faces in clay on the skulls of dead relatives, as well as on skulls collected in warfare. The Iatmül felt that the skull had special power after it had been removed from the body. Modeled skulls of relatives and enemies included face painting and ornaments to create a somewhat realistic likeness (figure 3.6). Consequently, the modeled skulls were categorized by some researchers (e.g., Bateson 1932: 262) as decorative art, while incised skulls that are relatively undecorated—from, for example, the Lower Sepik or the Fly River—likely became part of biological collections (Stodder 2006: 83, figs. 5, 7–9, 11, 2011).

The skull was just as effective whether or not it was modeled realistically. One example that illustrates the power of a visual impression and the qualities imbued in that object is the head of Mwaim. Mwaim had been an attractive young man with a particularly fine nose from the village of Mindimbit in the

Figure 3.6. Skull of an enemy or relative overmodeled in clay with face painting and ornaments from Iatmül, Tambunum, Middle Sepik River, Papua New Guinea. Reproduced by permission of University of Cambridge Museum of Archaeology and Anthropology (Bateson Collection, acc. no. 1930-411).

Iatmül region. According to Bateson, Mwaim was murdered because he had seduced all of the married women in his small village of less than two hundred inhabitants (Bateson 1932: 406, pl. VI). The dead man's clan preserved his modeled skull, on which his distinctive nose was re-created, as a "precious relic of his clan" and kept it hidden in a basket. Women of the village would thereafter spend time near the house in which the skull was kept, due to a belief in the skull's continued erotic influence. Although no mention was made regarding the body of Mwaim, perhaps because this was not important to the storytellers, Bateson related that the face was modeled on the skull in clay and decorated with nassa (a small gastropod) shells. The clay was left unpainted and there were no eyes, but the re-created face did have a long clay nose supported by a looped piece of cane.

Skulls of Iatmül men and women might be chosen for decoration and display based simply on the good looks of the person while alive. The skull of a Kankanamun village woman, who had died three generations prior to the 1930s, had been first cleaned, modeled with clay, displayed during funeral ceremonies, and then buried. Because she was considered to be strikingly beautiful with a particularly attractive nose, the men later dug up her skull "and probably substituted another skull in the grave" (Bateson 1936: pl. 25). Since then, her modeled and painted skull had been used, presumably for three generations, as the head of a ceremonial doll that represented clan ancestral spirits associated with fertility. The re-creation of the woman was so lifelike that even her breasts were portrayed, using the halves of coconut shells. Another portrait skull, that of a dead man from the same village and similarly chosen for his handsome looks, was also lavishly ornamented. According to Bateson, it was then used as the head of a figure in a secret ceremony designed to promote the prosperity and fertility of Kankanamun (Bateson 1936: pl. 27).

Modeled skulls were sometimes placed on figures for reasons unassociated with beauty or fecundity. In one case, the modeled and decorated skull of the *laua* (a kinship term denoting clan relatives such as a sister's son or a sister's husband's father) was set on a figure on a platform. This platform was suspended from the roof of a house to represent the spirit's voyage down the Sepik River to the land of the dead (Bateson 1936: 47).

Sometimes the modeled skull and corresponding figure were displayed to honor the accomplishments of the individual, particularly if that person had been a chief. Because the skull of a chief was sacred throughout Melanesia, his skull was often preserved after death and could even be taken as a war trophy (Rivers 1914: 261–269). In Malekula, New Hebrides (Vanuatu), the chief's skull was exhumed and realistically sculpted with clay. The modeled skull was placed on a figure in human form known as a *rambaramp* (figure 3.7). Ornaments and painted body markings indicated the man's status in life. After a time of mourning, the effigy was placed upright among others in the men's ceremonial house or "the house of the chiefs." Effigies were honored at feasts although they were clearly not worshipped. Once the effigy began to fall apart, the skull was tied to the rafters of the man's house (Guiart 1963: 122).

The skulls of children were modeled as well (e.g., Bateson 1932: pl. 9), as discussed in the above case study, yet ethnographic descriptions seldom provide information on how old children were when they died, how their skulls were used, or where they were kept. Visually, the decoration of children's skulls is not significantly different from those of adults. Teeth are present in the open mouth of one child's skull whose head was covered with a few strands of hair (Kelm 1966: fig. 257). A symmetrical pattern of white and black was painted on the modeled reddish brown base. Evidence of white paint is visible inside the vault through the back of the broken skull. Another modeled child's skull has a closed mouth, with a few strands of natural hair covering the top of the head. Shells mark the eyes, and one earring adorns an ear. The modeling and

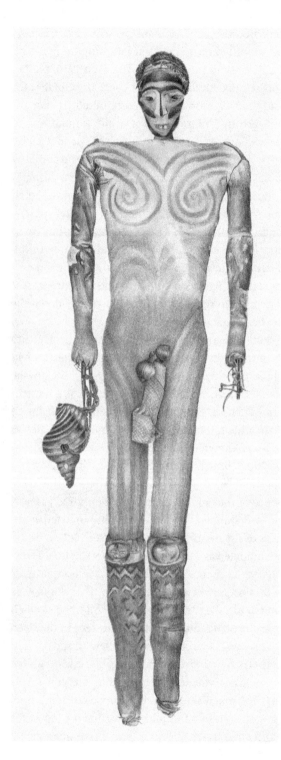

Figure 3.7. Burial effigy
(rambaramp) with human
skull and hair and decorated
with clay, bamboo, coconut
and pandanus fibers,
pigments, and shell; height
174 centimeters. Collected
from Vanuatu before 1882 by
Captain Smunsen. Courtesy
California Academy of
Sciences, San Francisco (cat.
no. CAS 0596-0001); drawing
by Rachel Diaz-Bastin.

decoration of the skulls of the deceased appear to be an attempt to capture a feature or impression (e.g., a hairstyle) associated with that individual, rather than producing a realistic portrait. Fragmentary ethnographic data suggest that skulls were eventually returned to the grave containing the postcranial remains, although how much time had passed since death is unknown.

Skulls could also be buried with the remains of another individual. In one instance among the Iatmül, the portrait skull of a dead man's brother was buried with him, for undisclosed reasons (Bateson 1936: 153–154). Because the colonial government had forbidden the indigenous practice of exposing the corpse in a canoe until the floods abated, the residents of Palimbai had to go far away to find dry land in Tshuosh country. There they buried the man with a shilling in each hand, along with his string bag and his brother's modeled skull, under a deserted house. The men oriented his grave according to the custom of the Tshuosh, with the corpse looking toward the setting sun, rather than with his feet toward the dancing ground, as they would have done in Palimbai. Whether the man's skull was later exhumed and modeled is unknown.

According to Rivers and later ethnographers, skulls of ancestors and relatives played a central role in the cult of the dead in Melanesia (Rivers 1914), while postcranial remains were modified to serve special purposes. Masks, made partly of human skulls, were used in secret society dances in southern Melanesia (Rivers 1914: 511), while preserved skulls attended and were believed to participate in ceremonial rites that took place on the same platform on which the body had decayed. The head was removed, and the rest of the bones were buried in the house that belonged to the survivors of the deceased. The dead in New Ireland were buried in a grave with a wooden roof that apparently permitted easy removal of the skull. The skull then became the object of an unspecified ceremony, after which it was again buried, during which time the arm bones were removed from the grave and made into special spears that were used only by the relatives of the deceased (Rivers 1914: 543). In the Santa Cruz Islands, the postcranial bones were recovered from their burial place within the house to make arrowheads, while the skull was kept in a chest in the house (Rivers 1914: 266).

Headhunting

Headhunting was another means of acquiring skulls in Melanesia and thereby gaining the "life-power" that was thought to be concentrated in the head. The heads of men, women, and children were taken in headhunting raids. The more prestige associated with the individual killed, the greater the reputation of the headhunter, who took the name of the one slain (Helfrich et al. 1996). Skulls in the Asmat region of Northwest (formerly Dutch) New Guinea (Indonesia) were displayed in a variety of ways. Undecorated trophy skulls of men and women were tied together in groups, so that they could be carried upside-down, or displayed in ceremonial nets in communal houses. The lower jaw and first cervical vertebrae became jewelry worn by important women. Other skulls, decorated with shells and feathers, might be hung around a man's neck, used as a headrest while sleeping, or displayed with or without the lower jaw.

Headhunting among the Asmat served as a rite of passage and a form of vengeance and enabled young men to acquire social status, prestige, and a reputation for manliness (Zegwaard 1959; see also Hoskins 1996b for examples from Sumba, Indonesia; and Valentin and Rolland this volume for motivations in the Marquesas Islands). In some contexts, headhunting served to transfer the perceived fertility and strength from the defeated enemy to the newly initiated headhunter (Hoskins 1996c: 19–20). Among some groups, the decapitated head of an enemy or unlucky guest was roasted and scalped, then the mandible was discarded. The cranium was painted and decorated before it was laid between the legs of an initiate, sometimes that of a very young boy, to allow the power residing in the skull to transfer to the boy's genitals. Afterwards, the skull was hung up in the bachelors' house, where it was kept until it was used in a dance ritual. Trophy skulls were tied together and hung on the doorpost near the fireplace as a measure of status, while possibly serving to keep away spirits who could not stand the sight of their own bones. Skulls were also hung near plants to stimulate growth (Zegwaard 1959), once again indicating a connection between skulls, fertility, and abundance.

Although missionaries and colonial officials prior to the 1930s discouraged headhunting in British New Guinea, it continued nevertheless. Male and female "homicide" victims were decapitated using special "beheading knives" (Bateson 1932: 408, 1958: 141; see Bonney and Clegg this volume figure 2.5 for an example of bamboo knives from the Torres Strait Islands); their skulls were cleaned and decorated. Enemies were not the only ones hunted; strangers, relatives, and guests also might be killed. One captured woman was tricked into thinking that she would marry into the village of her captors, who then speared her. Her skull, as with all enemy skulls, was not to be touched and was held by tongs as it was cleaned of adhering flesh. Foreigners (i.e., members of other villages) could be killed in revenge against the village from which they had come, even if they had established affinal ties. Guests were at times invited to a village only to be killed (Bateson 1936: pl. 20a). Slain enemies could be considered ancestors, possibly because they were thought to symbolically contribute to the proliferation and strength of the community due to their prowess in life. The heads of those taken were set upon *mbwan* ancestral stones, while the bodies were sometimes buried under the stones. These standing stones were phallic symbols that represented the ancestral spirits; in some cases, the mbwan ancestors were the spirits of killed enemies (Bateson 1936: 140–141).

The skulls of family members and defeated enemies were treated in similar ways in the Middle Sepik River area of British New Guinea. Both could be realistically modeled with clay and decorated with feathers, flowers, paint, and snail shells and would be kept in baskets made of palm fibers when not in use in fertility rites (Kelm 1966). The skulls, including the plastered skulls of children, varied widely in modeling, decoration, form, and expression. Some of the skulls collected in the first decades of the twentieth century were modeled to appear as if the person were in a state of sleep, while others seem to be laughing or staring off into space. Many of them were elaborately decorated with paint, shells, hair, earrings, or nose rings. Great attention was paid to an elegantly shaped nose, suggesting admiration for such a prominent feature.

In the Solomon Islands and the Torres Strait Islands (between Australia and Papua New Guinea), enemy skulls were as important as the skulls of relatives (figure 3.8). Both types of skulls were retained as permanent memorials or symbols of the dead (see Bonney and Clegg this volume for examples from the Torres Strait). In the Solomon Islands, trophy skulls of enemies could serve as offerings to propitiate and honor the ghosts of the dead, particularly those of dead ancestors, at the building of a new house or the launching of a canoe. The skulls of relatives were kept as symbols, if not the abode, of the deceased in order to honor and pacify him. The head appeared to represent the entire person, and care was taken to preserve it (Rivers 1914: 259). In the Torres Strait region, the numerous cults associated with headhunting, as observed during the period 1888–1898, incorporated human skulls or mandibles into turtle-shell masks, while others exchanged skulls throughout the islands. The skulls, including those of famous turtle hunters, were preserved in houses as keepsakes to keep alive the memory of the person, much as we treasure photos of deceased friends and relatives (Haddon 1929: 12). The skulls also enhanced the status of the headhunter.

Headhunting thus served as a means of acquiring the trophy skulls that brought prestige for the hunter, proliferation and strength to the community, and honor to the dead. The skulls and their corresponding bones were displayed, worn as ornaments, and used as pillows and strengthened social cohesion through trade.

Figure 3.8. Skull covered with putty-nut paste and inlaid with pearl shell from Rubina, New Georgia, Solomon Islands. Vegetable fiber was used for the hair and beard. The shell inlay reproduces patterns seen in facial painting. Reproduced by permission of University of Cambridge Museum of Archaeology and Anthropology (acc. no. 1916.20/Z 11208).

Manipulation of the Body and Spirit

The varied aspects of Melanesian mortuary ritual, whether involving only the skull or the entire corpse, entailed both physical and spiritual manipulation of the dead, as illustrated in numerous accounts. In the Torres Strait, the under-lying rationale for funerary rituals was to "appease the spirit of the deceased so it would not bring harm to the community, and ultimately to release it from its now useless body to depart to the isle of the dead, where it would at last be at rest" (Moore 1984: 34). Sometimes these rituals also involved mummification of the corpse by roasting on a spit over a slow fire after removal of the entrails, brain, and epidermis. The dried hands, feet, and tongue were removed and worn by the widow or widower for a year, and the skull was removed for the purpose of divination. Other bones were presented to relatives. The rest of the body was buried or put in a cave or rock niche (Moore 1984: 33). The Kwaio of the Solomon Islands exhumed the skulls of the deceased after an appropriate amount of time had passed, enacting a ritual of rebirth. Skulls were then placed in caves or fissures and maintained by a ritual specialist associated with the kin group (Keesing 1982: 156–157, 175).

When the spirit of the deceased was pacified, it was called upon to provide protection and abundance for the living. As an illustration, the chiefs on the Santa Cruz island of Vanikolo prayed to the heads of the dead for protection and abundance on a yearly basis in preparation for the digging of taro (Rivers 1914: 188, 226). The apparently undecorated skulls of the deceased were lined up in two rows of ten, and cold food offerings were placed before each skull. The cold food offerings were then passed out to the men and boys who had assembled (women were excluded), and the skulls were taken away to the houses, where they were kept in bowls. Rivers recorded no further explanation for the use of the twenty skulls or the age and sex of the skulls, nor were details provided about the houses in which the skulls were kept, yet clearly the physical and spiritual aspects of the dead were important.

Body Disposal and Preservation

Several mortuary forms could be practiced in any given area in Melanesia, as noted for the Iatmül, and could include secondary burial, mummification, and cremation, as well as a number of alternatives. Sometimes the burial form depended on the importance and marital status of the deceased. In Ambrym, New Hebrides (Vanuatu), for example, the body was interred for five months, then the skull and ribs were dug up and put under the root of a hollow tree and the long bones were put in a tree, while the body of an important man was kept in a canoe or a drum inside the house. After ten months, bones other than the skull and limbs were deposited at sea (Rivers 1914: 266).

Likewise, at Saa in the Solomon Islands, bodies of commoners were interred, while the body of an important man was hung up in the house or put in a canoe. Later, the skull was kept in the house, and the rest of the bones were buried. In contrast, the Araha of the Solomon island of San Cristoval and the islanders of the Torres Strait embalmed the dead by removing their thoracic and abdominal viscera and stuffing the cavity with wood shavings. The bodies of chiefs in San Cristoval were then placed within mastaba-like mounds with rectangular bases, sloping sides, and flat roofs (Rivers 1922: 16). In the Shortland Islands in the Bougainville Strait of the Solomon Islands, however, the bodies of chiefs and women of chiefs' rank were burnt, then collected and thrown into the water or interred, while on Eddystone Island, the bodies of the most important chiefs could be thrown into the sea at their request (Rivers 1914: 267–269).

The body of the deceased male or female continued to materially exist through the ritual transport of body parts and through caring for the grave. The social network of the deceased was also repaired through the lending of his or her body parts (Weiner 1976: 84). In Kiriwana, the largest island of the Trobriand group, the body was buried, then later inspected for sorcery (Malinowski 1929: 155) before some of the bones, hair, and fingernails were removed as relics and worn or "carried" by close family members. The skull, as the most important part, was traditionally removed only from powerful, wealthy men, from other chiefs, or from married women and men "who died while they were still young and handsome" (Weiner 1976: 82–84), emphasizing once again the importance of beauty, youth, and fecundity. The skull was decorated with paint and shells and then carried about during distributions of food and goods that accompanied the mortuary ritual before being returned to the father or son of the deceased. The skull was guarded for ten or twenty years before it was again decorated and placed on a cliff overlooking the sea. The remaining bones of all Kiriwanans, regardless of age or rank, were exhumed many years after their deaths and placed in a cave belonging to unnamed ancestral beings.

Regardless of where a man or woman in British New Guinea died, the body was brought back and buried under the dead person's house (Seligmann 1910: 726; see Bateson 1936: 153–154 for exceptions). The grave was dug up a short time later so that the skull, along with other bones, could be removed and cleaned. Some of the bones were made into spatulas or worn by the deceased's children. The lower jaw was reportedly worn either by the dead man's children or by the husband of a dead wife. The skull was regularly oiled and kept in a basket in the house during a mourning period, which lasted about twenty months. Then the skull and the rest of the skeleton were deposited in rock shelters above the cliffs. These old bones, considered highly dangerous, were avoided. The reason for an aversion to deposited bones is uncertain, but through analogy, it may have been from fear of contact with the bones of the dead of foreign clans (Seligmann 1910: 727).

Numerous modes of disposal of the dead were observed by early visitors to Melanesia, yet rare mention is made of the funerary rituals for women or children (e.g., Rivers 1914: 264, 272). The focus was on chiefs, important men, and males in general. This lack of information was partly due to access but also reflects the special interests of the male ethnographers and other primarily male observers (see chapters in Herle and Rouse 1998; O'Hanlon and Welsch 2000). Thus, we have little data available to aid us in interpreting the skulls of women and children. Given the regional, cultural, and contextual differences in mortuary practices in this region, treatment of women and children likely differed from that of men in some areas and symbolized or represented different aspects of social, ancestral, and spiritual relationships.

Wooden Figures Incorporating Skulls

Another mortuary ritual, practiced in the Geelvink Bay area of Northwest New Guinea (now Cenderawashi Bay, Irian Jaya/West Papua, Indonesia), incorporated skulls into ancestor figures known as *korwar*. These figures represented ancestors with associated cults (van Baaren 1968) and were separate from images that did not have cults connected with them, such as grave figures, memorial figures, protective figures, and symbolic representations of ancestors. The korwar were offered sacrifices, taken along in warfare (headhunting), and consulted for answers in their capacity as a medium of communication between the deceased and living relatives. Favorable outcomes were attributed to the intervention of the korwar. However, if the outcome was less than desirable, the presumably powerless korwar might be thrown against a post and broken (van Hasselt 1876, cited in van Baaren 1968: 27).

Most korwar were fashioned completely from wood, although some incorporated the human skull with the wooden image or consisted solely of the decorated skull. Each form denoted the spirit of the deceased, and the term *korwar* was used by extension for the skull and the wooden ancestor figure. Korwar belonged to individual families, but they could also represent clan ancestors venerated by the entire community. The skulls of men, women, and children could be chosen as korwar, although the criteria used in their selection were not detailed—beyond what is offered below—by the missionaries and travelers who gathered the information, as made available by van Baaren (1968: figs. 3.1–3.3, 3.5).

The heads of firstborn male and female children twelve years of age or older were allowed to naturally separate from the body (taking about twenty days) while the body lay exposed on a platform or in a small boat. The body was then covered in leaves and buried with rich gifts in a grave filled with earth. The head was taken to the parents' house while the flesh decomposed for another two or three months, after which friends and relatives assembled in the house of the bereaved family. Either the skull was inserted into a carved wooden image, which had been hollowed out to accommodate the skull at the top, or wooden ears and a nose were crafted and fastened to the skull. A small red fruit (or blue beads) simulated the eyes. Any teeth that had fallen out during the cleaning of the skull were replaced before the lower jaw and cranium were inserted into the hollow head of the korwar. A meal was held in honor of the deceased represented by the skull, which was placed in the middle of the guests. The face of the skull was painted with soot, chalk, and other substances, and a red cloth was wrapped around the head. The korwar was kept secluded afterwards in a corner of the room (Goudswaard 1863, cited in van Baaren 1968: 23).

While the skull of a dead father or mother was treated the same as the skull of a dead firstborn child in Northwest New Guinea, skulls reportedly were not removed from infants, other children, slaves, or persons not considered important. Children under two years of age were placed in a basket and hung in a tree (as a sacrifice). The other deceased were placed in a shallow grave and covered only with sticks and rocks; a few simple utensils needed for the afterlife were hung on a bamboo stake that marked the head (Goudswaard 1863, cited in van Baaren 1968: 23–24). The differential treatment between persons apparently perceived as both fertile and important and those who were not appears to be related to fear of the dead—but fear only of those who were considered powerful or otherwise respected in life, because souls of slaves in life remained slaves in death.

The korwar represented rough, yet symbolically idealized, portraits of deceased family members (Meyer 1875, cited in van Baaren 1968: 31). Each bore a representation of the hairstyle worn by the individual in life. The wooden male figures usually held an openwork shield, while the women held snakes in both hands (von Rosenberg 1878, cited in van Baaren 1968: 33). The korwar, about 45 centimeters from head to foot, lived within the household and was taken on travels as a protective power (van Balen 1886, cited in van Baaren 1968: 38). Although the number of korwar ancestor figures kept in one house at any given time is unclear, the number appears to have varied, as individuals died and new korwar were crafted and as old figures lost their usefulness and were discarded (van Baaren 1968: 85).

Sorcery and Divination

Decorated and plain skulls from both relatives and enemies were used in sorcery and divination for a variety of purposes and were obtained from deceased men, women, and children. For example, the Kiwai Papuans who lived at the mouth of the Fly River in British New Guinea hunted both sexes and all ages for skulls, which they strung on a head carrier. Skulls with a lower jaw were hung on a tree and used to divine the outcome of a headhunting party, while enemy skulls without lower jaws were hung up in the men's house or kept un-der sleeping mats and used as headrests (Landtman 1916). At times, the dried genitalia of the deceased were attached to the skull to indicate sex, perhaps an indication of the lack of sexual dimorphism apparent in the youthful cranium. Elsewhere in British New Guinea, the Roro-speaking tribes of Yule Island and the St. Joseph River used elaborately decorated skulls in sorcery. Of particular note is one case in which the skull of a young adult, believed by the observer to be a female, was used as a charm to cause the death of an enemy (Seligmann 1910: pl. 40). In the Torres Strait, skulls of prominent men, with their features restored in wood and clay, were used in divination to determine which enemy had caused a death. The head of the corpse was removed from the exposed body after one week and was consulted for evidence of sorcery. The skull was kept for about six weeks, during which time the person's features were restored on the skull using clay and wood. After six weeks, the newly modeled skull was given to the widow to carry around in a basket until her mourning period ended about one year later (Moore 1984: 33, fig. 162, 561–565).

Beauty, youth, and fecundity, along with physical accomplishments and the use of divination, as well as the fear of sorcery, appear as interrelated themes in various ethnographic accounts involving skull collection and decoration. Only two categories of people in the Trobriand Islands did not have their skulls removed after death. Suspected sorcerers were buried face down to pre-vent the spirit's return to the village, apparently out of fear that dangerous magic forces residing in the body would otherwise be freed to harm the villag-ers (Weiner 1976: 69). The other, possibly more encompassing, group was the elderly. The skulls of old people were not removed. The reasoning behind the exclusionary treatment of the aged was not explained, but it may be related to a perceived loss of beauty and fecundity (Weiner 1976: 82, 84).

Conclusions

In summary, the skulls of relatives and enemies, males and females, children and adults, commoners and chiefs, as well as the beautiful and the youth-ful were treated with great care throughout Melanesia. They were collected from the recently dead and were left plain or were modeled and/or deco-rated (see Stodder 2005, 2006, 2011 for additional skull treatments from the north coast of Papua New Guinea). Sometimes the skulls were incorporated as heads of ceremonial dolls, effigies, or wooden figures. They were used to honor the ancestors and pacify the dead and could be honored for their own accomplishments.

Skulls were kept as memorials of deceased relatives and displayed as trophies of defeated enemies. The skulls of the deceased were associated with vitality and spiritual power (Rosaldo 1977) and kept as relics and memorials and also were used in fertility rites and as tools in sorcery and divination. Collectively and individually, the skulls functioned to bring prosperity and protection to the individual and community and strengthened the social cohesion between family, community, and regional groups through their treatment, display, transport, and exchange.

Mortuary ritual in Melanesia reveals a strong link between the skulls of males and females, children and adults, and concepts of beauty and youth with fertility and abundance at the individual and community level (Bonogofsky 2001b: 33). One example that clearly combines all of these characteristics is the plastered skull of the handsome young man named Mwaim. His sexuality was thought by the village women to have been preserved in his skull. Even though his skull was kept by his family inside their house, the skull was treated as a relic by women in the village who thought Mwaim's erotic powers could somehow transfer to them where they stood outside of his family's house (Bateson 1932: 406). Consequently, this skull was important to the reproductive beliefs of the entire community. Another clear example from Melanesia that connects the skull of a beautiful, youthful individual and clan ancestral spirits associated with fecundity is the plastered skull of a young woman that was exhumed by the Iatmül and used for generations in a community-based fertility ceremony (Bateson 1936: pl. 25).

Decorated skulls generally were displayed only during specific ceremonies. The rest of the time they were kept hidden away in dwellings and shrines, in corners and inside bowls, baskets, and chests. The emphasis on beauty, youth, and fertility apparently influenced the selection of skulls for special treatment in a way that was not noted on the museum labels and accession records, nor did the early ethnographers who wrote about the skulls particularly stress it. As a result, the diverse nature and uses of skulls were masked by the limited categories of "enemy" or "ancestor," which connoted male warrior or honored (male) elder.

Skulls of youthful, beautiful people, whether they were modeled or left untreated, served as memorials that were honored through their curation and participation in fertility rites. The spirit of the dead man, woman, or child was pacified by offerings of food and through public and private displays of the skull. These processes kept alive the memory of the deceased (albeit sometimes in collective, unnamed form) and nurtured his or her spirit, just as the living hoped that the dead would provide protection and fertility. The skulls of members of society—regardless of age, sex, social status, or affiliation—potentially could be used, with emphasis placed on skulls that came from the young and physically attractive. The dead were sometimes buried under the house in which the decorated skull was later kept, further reinforcing a connection between the living and the dead.

This overview of ethnographic material illustrates the great diversity in the origins, basis for selection, and function of human skulls in Melanesia and highlights how important it is for (bio)archaeologists to look beyond standard object categories and received wisdom. Assuming that an archaeologically recovered skull or museum specimen represents an ancestor can discourage exploration of alternative interpretations and perpetuate unfounded inferences. Skulls from Melanesia, which are often presented in simple and straightforward terms as deriving from ancestors or enemies, are clearly complex objects with "entangled" life histories. The case study of a child's skull from the Sepik River region, presented above, demonstrates not only that the skulls of children received considerable elaboration but also the combined utility of radiographs and dental aging methods. These methods can be applied to museum specimens as well as to archaeologically recovered skulls; the resulting data may be significantly more accurate and precise than standard skeletal aging methods. Further, dental aging is useful even when skull remains are fragmentary and postcranial elements are absent.

Kathleen Kenyon did not have access to the forensic methods and sophisticated radiography discussed here, and she was apparently influenced not only by the museum labels but also by select ethnographic accounts that focused on men in general and chiefs in particular (e.g., Rivers 1914) for her interpretation of plastered skulls from Neolithic Jericho (e.g., Kenyon and Tushingham 1953: 870; Bonogofsky 2001a, 2001b, 2002a, 2002b, 2003). Kenyon also may have been influenced by the categorization of the Melanesian skulls as "decorative art" (e.g., Bateson 1932: 262) when she promoted the idea that "portrait skulls" from Jericho were those of venerated male ancestors, an assertion that has been disproved through extensive restudy (e.g., Bonogofsky 2001b, 2003, 2006a, 2006b).

Finally, the association in Melanesia between the skulls of young males and females and concepts of beauty and fertility, as well as the exclusion of the skulls of the elderly and the socially deviant (e.g., sorcerers), defies efforts to uncritically apply categories such as "ancestor" or "enemy." Rather, skull modeling and mortuary ritual in Melanesia represented a highly variable practice with different regional, cultural, and temporal expressions. There is no reason to think that prehistoric people of the Near East or Eurasia, who also plastered and modeled skulls and practiced complex mortuary rituals (see chapters in Bonogofsky 2006c), had a more simplistic or less diverse set of beliefs about the dead and their proper treatment. The examples from Melanesia thus serve as a cautionary tale for bioarchaeologists and curators who encounter human skulls from any world region, either in situ or in museum collections. Ancestors, enemies, women, and children were all part of Melanesian ritual practice; consideration of their roles should form a part of bioarchaeological interpretations of human remains elsewhere.

Acknowledgments

Bonogofsky: I thank Robin Boast, deputy director and curator for world archaeology, University of Cambridge Museum of Archaeology and Anthropology, for discussion of specific ethnographic sources that may have influenced Kathleen Kenyon's interpretation of Neolithic plastered skulls. I thank Ann L. W. Stodder, New Guinea Research Program, the Field Museum, for the impetus to refocus my earlier work and for her comments. I also thank Russell P. Hartman, senior collections manager, and Rachel Diaz-Bastin, illustrator, both at the California Academy of Sciences, for research access and for the drawing of the rambaramp.

Graham: I thank Mark Mountford for his fine radiography work and Barry Craig of the South Australian Museum for assistance in determining the origins of skull no. 22.

References Cited

Bateson, Gregory. 1932. Social Structure of the Iatmül People of the Sepik River. *Oceania* 2: 245–291, 401–452.

———. 1936. *Naven: A Survey of the Problems Suggested by a Composite Picture of the Culture of a New Guinea Tribe from Three Points of View.* Cambridge University Press, Cambridge.

———. 1958. *Naven: A Survey of the Problems Suggested by a Composite Picture of the Culture of a New Guinea Tribe from Three Points of View.* 2nd ed. Stanford University Press, Stanford.

Bonogofsky, Michelle. 2001a. A New Look at the "Ancestor Cult" in the Levant. *Proceedings of the Near and Middle Eastern Civilizations Graduate Students Annual Symposia 1998–2000,* 141–151. Benben Publications, Mississauga, Ontario, Canada.

———. 2001b. *An Osteo-Archaeological Examination of the Ancestor Cult during the Pre-Pottery Neolithic B Period in the Levant.* Ph.D. dissertation, University of California, Berkeley. University Microfilms International, Ann Arbor, Michigan.

———. 2002a. A Radiographic Examination of an 8,500 Year Old Plastered Skull from Jericho. *Journal of the Association of Graduates in Near Eastern Studies* 9 (1): 1–7.

———. 2002b. Reassessing "Dental Evulsion" in Neolithic Plastered Skulls from the Levant through the Use of Computed Tomography, Direct Observation, and Photographs. *Journal of Archaeological Science* 29: 959–964.

———. 2003. Neolithic Plastered Skulls and Railroading Epistemologies. *Bulletin of the American Schools of Oriental Research* 331: 1–10.

———. 2004. Including Women and Children: Neolithic Modeled Skulls from Jordan, Israel, Syria and Turkey. *Near Eastern Archaeology* 67 (2): 118–119.

———. 2005a. Anatolian Plastered Skulls in Context: New Discoveries and Interpretations. *Arkeometri Sonuçları Toplantısı* 20: 13–26.

———. 2005b. A Bioarchaeological Study of Plastered Skulls from Anatolia: New Discoveries and Interpretations. *International Journal of Osteoarchaeology* 15: 124–135.

———. 2006a. Complexity in Context: Plain, Painted and Modeled Skulls from the Neolithic Middle East. In Bonogofsky 2006c, 15–28.

———. 2006b. Cultural and Ritual Evidence in the Archaeological Record: Modeled Skulls from the Ancient Near East. In *The Archaeology of Cult and Death: Proceedings of the Session "The Archaeology of Cult and Death,"* edited by M. Georgiadis and C. Gallou, 45–69. Archaeolingua, Budapest.

———, editor. 2006c. *Skull Collection, Modification and Decoration.* BAR International Series 1539. Archaeopress, Oxford, U.K.

Buikstra, Jane E., and Douglas H. Ubelaker. 1994. *Standards for Data Collection from Human Skeletal Remains.* Research Series no. 44. Arkansas Archeological Survey, Fayetteville.

Campbell, Thomas Draper. 1925. *Dentition and Palate of the Australian Aboriginal.* Hassell Press, Adelaide, Australia.

Cohen, J. T. 1928. The Dates of Eruption of the Permanent Teeth in a Group of Minneapolis Children. *Journal of the American Dental Association* 15: 2337–2341.

Dean, Christopher. 2007. Growing Up Slowly 160,000 Years Ago. *Proceedings of the National Academy of Sciences* 104 (15): 6093–6094.

Demirjian, A., and H. Goldstein. 1976. New Systems for Dental Maturity Based on Seven and Four Teeth. *Annals of Human Biology* 3 (5): 411–421.

Demirjian, A., H. Goldstein, and J. M. Tanner. 1973. A New System of Dental Age Assessment. *Human Biology* 45 (2): 211–227.

Goodale, Jane C. 1985. Pig's Teeth and Skull Cycles: Both Sides of the Face of Humanity. *American Ethnologist* 12 (2): 228–244.

Goudswaard, A. 1863. *De Papoewa's van de Geelvinksbaai: Hoofdzakelijk naar mondelinge mededeelingen van ooggetuigen.* H. A. M. Roelants, Schiedam, the Netherlands.

Guiart, Jean. 1963. *The Arts of the South Pacific.* Translated by Anthony Christie. Thames and Hudson, London.

Gustafson, G., and G. Koch. 1974. Age Estimation up to 16 Years of Age Based on Dental Development. *Odontologisk Revy* (Lund) 25: 297–306.

Haddon, Alfred C. 1929. *The Religion of a Primitive People.* Liverpool University Press, Liverpool.

Halcrow, S. E., N. Tayles, and H. R. Buckley. 2007. Age Estimation of Children from Prehistoric Southeast Asia: Are the Dental Formation Methods Used Appropriate? *Journal of Archaeological Science* 34 (7): 1158–1168.

Helfrich, Klaus, Holger Jebens, Wolfgang Nelke, and Carolina Winkelmann. 1996. *Asmat: Mythos und Kunst im Leben mit den Ahnen*. Preussischer Kulturbesitz, Berlin.

Herle, Anita. 1998. The Life-Histories of Objects: Collections of the Cambridge Anthropological Expedition to the Torres Strait. In *Cambridge and the Torres Strait: Centenary Essays on the 1898 Anthropological Expedition*, edited by A. Herle and S. Rouse, 77–105. Cambridge University Press, Cambridge.

Herle, Anita, and Sandra Rouse, editors. 1998. *Cambridge and the Torres Strait: Centenary Essays on the 1898 Anthropological Expedition*. Cambridge University Press, Cambridge.

Hoskins, Janet. 1989. On Losing and Getting a Head: Warfare, Exchange, and Alliance in a Changing Sumba, 1888–1988. *American Ethnologist* 16 (3): 419–440.

———, editor. 1996a. *Headhunting and the Social Imagination in Southeast Asia*. Stanford University Press, Stanford.

———. 1996b. The Heritage of Headhunting: History, Ideology, and Violence on Sumba, 1890–1990. In Hoskins 1996a, 216–248.

———. 1996c. Introduction: Headhunting as Practice and as Trope. In Hoskins 1996a, 1–49.

Kaiser, Elke. 2006. Plastered Skulls of the Catacomb Culture in the Northern Pontic Region. In Bonogofsky 2006c, 45–58.

Keesing, Roger M. 1982. *Kwaio Religion: The Living and the Dead in a Solomon Island Society*. Columbia University Press, New York.

Kelm, Heinz. 1966. *Kunst vom Sepik I*. Vol. 10. Museum für Völkerkunde, Berlin.

Kenyon, Kathleen M. 1979. *Archaeology in the Holy Land*. 4th ed. Ernest Benn, London.

Kenyon, Kathleen M., and A. Douglas Tushingham. 1953. Jericho Gives Up Its Secrets. *National Geographic Magazine* 104 (6): 853–870.

Khaleej Times Online [Dubai]. 2006. 9,500-Year-Old Decorated Skulls Found in Syria. September 24. http://www.khaleejtimes.com/DisplayArticleNew.asp?xfile=data/middleeast/2006/September/middleeast_September544.xml&section=middleeast (accessed May 19, 2010).

Küchler, Susanne. 1988. Malangan: Objects, Sacrifice and the Production of Memory. *American Ethnologist* 15 (4): 625–637.

Kurth, Gottfried, and Olav Röhrer-Ertl. 1981. On the Anthropology of the Mesolithic to Chalcolithic Human Remains from the Tell es-Sultan in Jericho, Jordan. In *The Architecture and Stratigraphy of the Tell*, vol. 3 of *Excavations at Jericho*, edited by T. A. Holland, 407–481. British School of Archaeology in Jerusalem, London.

Landtman, Gunnar. 1916. The Magic of the Kiwai Papuans in Warfare. *Journal of the Royal Anthropological Institute of Great Britain and Ireland* 46: 322–333.

Malinowski, Bronislaw. 1929. *The Sexual Life of Savages in North-Western Melanesia*. Harvest, New York.

Massler, M., and I. Schour. 1941. Studies in Tooth Development: Theories of Eruption. *American Journal of Orthodontics and Oral Surgery* 27 (10): 552–576.

Meyer, A. B. 1875. *Notizen über Glauben und Sitten der Papúas des mafoor'schen Stammes auf Neu Guinea*. C. C. Meinhold and Söhne, Dresden.

Moore, David R. 1984. *The Torres Strait Collections of A. C. Haddon*. British Museum Press, London.

Moorrees, C. F. A., E. A. Fanning, and E. E. Hunt. 1963. Age Variation of Formation Stages for Ten Permanent Teeth. *Journal of Dental Research* 42: 1490–1502.

O'Hanlon, Michael. 2000. Introduction to O'Hanlon and Welsch 2000, 1–34.

O'Hanlon, Michael, and Robert L. Welsch, editors. 2000. *Hunting the Gatherers: Ethnographic Collectors, Agents and Agency in Melanesia, 1870s–1930s*. Berghahn, New York.

Rivers, W. H. R. 1914. *The History of Melanesian Society*. Cambridge University Press, Cambridge.

———. 1922. The Unity of Anthropology. *Journal of the Royal Anthropological Institute of Great Britain and Ireland* 52: 12–25.

Rosaldo, Michelle Z. 1977. Skulls and Causality. *Man* 12 (1): 168–170.

Rosaldo, Renato. 1980. *Ilongot Headhunting 1883–1974: A Study in Society and History*. Stanford University Press, Stanford.

Scheuer, Louise. 2002. Application of Osteology to Forensic Medicine. *Clinical Anatomy* 15: 297–312.

Schour, I., and M. Massler. 1941. The Development of the Human Dentition. *Journal of the American Dental Association* 28: 1153–1160.

Seligmann, C. G. 1910. *The Melanesians of British New Guinea*. Cambridge University Press, Cambridge.

Shishlina, Natalia I. 2006. Decoration of Skulls: Funerary Rituals of the Yamnaya and Catacomb Cultures in the Eurasian Bronze Age. In Bonogofsky 2006c, 59–66.

Smith, W. Ramsay. 1924. *In Southern Seas—Wanderings of a Naturalist*. John Murray, London.

Stodder, Ann L. W. 2005. The Bioarchaeology and Taphonomy of Mortuary Ritual on the Sepik Coast, Papua New Guinea. In *Interacting with the Dead: Perspectives on Mortuary Archaeology for the New Millennium*, edited by G. F. M. Rakita, J. E. Buikstra, L. A. Beck, and S. R. Williams, 228–250. University Press of Florida, Gainesville.

———. 2006. The Taphonomy of Cranial Modification in Papua New Guinea: Implications for the Archaeology of Mortuary Ritual. In Bonogofsky 2006c, 77–89.

———. 2011. Iconography and Power in Sepik Skull Art. In *Breathing New Life into the Evidence of Death: Contemporary Approaches to Mortuary Analysis*, edited by A. Baadsgaard, A. Boutin, and J. Buikstra. School for Advanced Research Press, Santa Fe, New Mexico. Forthcoming.

Strouhal, Eugen. 1973. Five Plastered Skulls from Pre-Pottery Neolithic B Jericho: Anthropological Study. *Paléorient* 1 (2): 231–247.

Tanner, J. M., R. H. Whitehouse, and M. J. R. Healy. 1962. *A New System for Estimating Skeletal Maturity from the Hand and Wrist, with Standards Derived from a Study of 2,600 Healthy British Children*. Centre International de l'Enfance, Paris.

Thomas, Nicholas. 1991. *Entangled Objects: Exchange, Material Culture, and Colonialism in the Pacific*. Harvard University Press, Cambridge, Massachusetts.

Ubelaker, Douglas H. 1978. *Human Skeletal Remains: Excavation, Analysis, Interpretation*. Aldine, Chicago.

Vadetskaia, Elga B. 2006. The Yenisei Mummies with Modeled Skulls and Masks from Siberia. In Bonogofsky 2006c, 67–75.

van Baaren, Theodorus P. 1968. *Korwars and Korwar Style: Art and Ancestor Worship in North-West New Guinea*. Mouton, Paris.

van Balen, J. A. 1886. Iets over het doodenfeest bij de Papoea's aan de Geelvinksbaai: Uittreksels uit een brief van den zendelingsleeraar J. A. van Balen te Roon. *T. Ind. Taal-, Land- en Volkenk.* 31: 556–575.

van Hasselt, J. L. 1876. Die Nuforesen. *Zeitschrift für Ethnologie* 8: 134–139, 169–202.

von Rosenberg, C. B. H. 1878. *Der Malayische Archipel: Land und Leute in Schilderungen, gesammelt während eines dreissigjährigen Aufenthaltes in den Kolonien*. G. Weigel, Leipzig.

Weiner, Annette B. 1976. *Women of Value, Men of Renown*. University of Texas Press, Austin.

White, Tim D. 1992. *Prehistoric Cannibalism at Mancos 5MTUMR-2346*. Princeton University Press, Princeton.

Winter, Irene J. 1999. Reading Ritual in the Archaeological Record: Deposition Pattern and Function of Two Artifact Types from the Royal Cemetery of Ur. In *Fluchtpunkt Uruk: Archäologische Einheit aus methodischer Vielfalt*, edited by H. Kühne, R. Bernbeck, and K. Bartl, 229–256. Vol. 6 of Internationale Archäologie Studia Honoria. Marie Leidorf, Rahden/Westfalia.

Zegwaard, Gerard A. 1959. Headhunting Practices of the Asmat of Netherlands New Guinea. *American Anthropologist* 61: 1020–1041.

4

Marquesan Trophy Skulls

Description, Osteological Analyses, and Changing Motivations in the South Pacific

FRÉDÉRIQUE VALENTIN AND NOÉMIE ROLLAND

Several museum and private collections curate decorated skulls from the Marquesas Islands, French Polynesia. Regarded as trophy skulls, these objects are composed of a human skull adorned with pig canines to which a mandible was ingeniously attached using a vegetal bond. Nineteenth-century descriptions of the Marquesas Islands indicate the presence in sacred places of decorated human skulls with artificial eyes. Associated iconography portrays such decorated skulls hanging at the neck or waist of a warrior, while archaeological evidence suggests a pre-European to early European period. Relying on written, iconographic, artifactual, and archaeological documentation, this chapter describes such objects, focusing on osteological observations that shed light on head or skull selection and preparation processes, and then analyzes the potential motives for human skull collection and modification in a changing Nuku Hiva society influenced by Western contact in the eighteenth century. These decorated skulls of males, females, and adolescents, once curated by the indigenous population as trophies or the remains of ancestors, apparently became made-to-order curios for an expanding European market.

Historical Descriptions of Trophy Skulls

The Marquesan archipelago (figure 4.1) was discovered by Europeans in 1595, when it was sighted by Alvaro de Mendaña y Neyra and Pedro Fernandez de Quirós; however, actual first contact between Westerners and indigenous people only dates back to the end of the eighteenth century (Baert 1999; Bailleul 2001). Archaeological discoveries indicate that human trophy skull production began in the pre-European period in the Marquesas Islands, with such skulls apparently associated with domestic occupation sites as well as

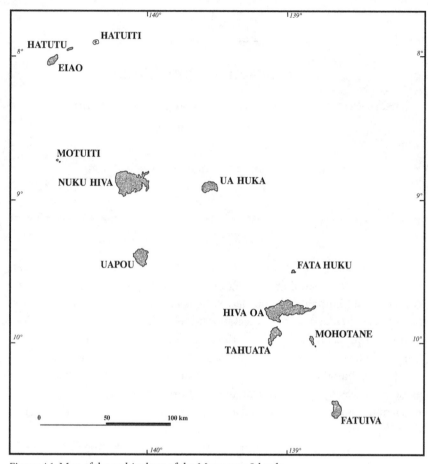

Figure 4.1. Map of the archipelago of the Marquesas Islands.

burial sites. In contrast, ethnohistorical reports suggest their use in warrior rituals during the protohistoric period. The written records indicate that the modified heads were those of war enemies, prisoners caught outside of the community.

The main sources of information on Marquesan trophy skulls are written records (Dumoutier 1843; Gracia 1843; Melville 1996 [1846]; Radiguet 2001 [1861]; Vincendon-Dumoulin and Desgraz 1843; von den Steinen 1925–1928; von Langsdorff 1812), associated iconography (Radiguet 2001 [1861]; von den Steinen 1925–1928; von Langsdorff 1812), and the objects themselves. Collected almost exclusively on Nuku Hiva—one of the main islands forming the archipelago (figure 4.1)—during the nineteenth century by European explorers and mariners, they are represented by exemplars now curated in museum and private collections (briefly described in table 4.1, below). None of the skulls in this inventory have been found in archaeological contexts; however, some Marquesan archaeological sites revealed burial practices that could be integrated into the protocol for producing these artifacts.

Nineteenth-century accounts of Marquesan trophy skulls include those from explorers such as Max Radiguet (2001 [1861]), who observed a human skull adorned with pig canines and artificial eyes on a mortuary platform on Tahuata Island. He dramatically described his discovery, made while accompanying Abel Aubert Dupetit-Thouars during the French annexation of the archipelago in 1843:

> Vaguement entrevu dans l'obscurité, il me semblait pâle et chauve; il appuyait sur la pierre deux dents canines, aiguës et disposées comme celles d'un morse; son œil large et rond, sans paupière, chatoyait dans l'ombre et me dévorait du regard. . . . C'était un crâne humain dont on avait bouché les orbites avec des rondelles en nacre de perle, plates et larges comme des pièces de cinq francs. Un trou perforé au milieu restait noir en guise de prunelle; un morceau de bois remplissait la cavité nasale; deux dents longues, menaçantes étaient fichées dans l'alvéole des canines; enfin des cordons en bourre de coco retenaient au maxillaire de nombreuses touffes de poils disposées en barbe, et aux oreilles des plaques de bois ovales blanchies à la chaux. (Radiguet 2001 [1861]: 64)

> [As I vaguely perceived him in the darkness, he seemed to me pale and bald; two of his sharp, canine teeth, placed like the fangs of a walrus, were pressed into the stone; his large, round, lidless eye shimmered in the shadow and devoured me with its gaze. . . . It was a human skull whose orbits had been plugged with slices of mother-of-pearl, flat and as wide as five-franc coins. A hole perforated in the middle remained black, representing a pupil; a piece of wood filled the nasal cavity; two long, menacing teeth were driven into the hollows of the canines; and finally, coconut-fiber cords held to the jawbone a beard made up of numerous tufts of hair, and oval plates of lime-whitened wood to the ears.]

Herman Melville, another early observer of Marquesan society, saw (hanging in a house) human skulls wrapped in bark cloth called tapa, one being decorated with eyes made of seashell in the eye sockets and human hair twisted into two buns on top of the skull. He reported,

> The skull was in a state of perfect preservation, and from the slight glimpse I had of it, seemed to have been subjected to some smoking operation which had reduced it to the dry, hard, and mummy-like appearance it presented. The two long scalp-locks were twisted up into

balls upon the crown of the head in the same way that the individual had worn them during life. The sunken cheeks were rendered yet more ghastly by the rows of glistening teeth which protruded from between the lips, while the sockets of the eyes—filled with oval bits of mother-of-pearl shell, with a black spot in the center—heightened the hideousness of its aspect. (Melville 1876: 265, cited in Handy 1923: 139)

General Characteristics

Following the first Western explorers of the archipelago, several authors (Boës and Sears 1993, 1996, 2002; Bounoure 1999; Candelot 2001; Handy 1923; Lavondès and Jacquemin 1995; Le Fur 1999; Linton 1923; Péré 1993; Rollin 1929; Suggs 1961; Valentin and Rolland 2002; Vigneron 1985) have described Marquesan trophy skulls (figure 4.2), recognizing the following common descriptive features: a vegetal braid linking the mandible to the skull; a piece of

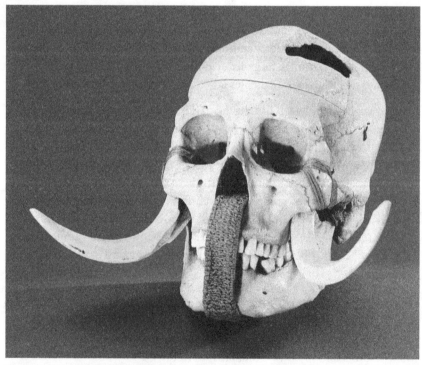

Figure 4.2. Trophy skull from Nuku Hiva, Marquesas Islands, French Polynesia. Note the two pig tusks, as well as the vegetal braid linking the mandible to the skull. Collection Musée de L'Homme, Paris (no. 294851). Photo © Musée du Quai Branly, photography by Maryse Delaplanche.

wood inserted into the nasal aperture to replace the nose; pieces of mother-of-pearl, turtle shell, seeds, and other vegetal elements placed in the orbit sockets to symmetrically or asymmetrically represent the three visible parts (cornea, iris, pupil) of the eyes; pig tusks adjusted on each side of the face; and a thickly twisted suspension rope.

Additional Elements

Certain skulls include additional elements. Some display thin vegetal braids around the teeth. Several others, although they have teeth, do not show this kind of preparation, the aesthetic and/or functional significance of which has yet to be discussed. This form of adornment was probably used as a support to fasten other components, such as a beard, described in some early accounts (e.g., Dumoutier 1843; Radiguet 2001 [1861]). On some skulls—without vegetal braids around the teeth—a strip of white tapa surrounds the skull, or sometimes human hair locks, supported by a strip of white tapa or a vegetal braid net, complete the preparation. These locks could have been twisted initially into two buns linked together with a piece of white tapa on the top of the skull, imitating the hairstyle common among the young men of Nuku Hiva in the nineteenth century (Gracia 1843; Ottino-Garanger 2002; Von Langsdorff 1812; figure 4.3).

Some preparations include European fabrics; in one case, a small piece of red cloth was used to form the cornea of one eye. In another, the whole skull is covered with worn blue and red European textiles (figure 4.4). The blue fabric covers the skull from the maxillar alveolae to the basi-occipital, maintained posteriorly by large diamond-shaped net meshing and fastened anteriorly on ligatures surrounding the teeth. The red fabric is superimposed on the blue, covering the upper part of the face and forehead. Another piece of red fabric that must have covered all or a part of the mandible (Valentin and Rolland 2002) is indicated by the presence of small red textile fibers stuck in the knots that link a thin braid to the ligatures of the lower teeth. This thin braid, running transversally from one side of the skull to the other, like the alternation of red and blue horizontal strips, recalls a Marquesan nineteenth-century facial tattoo, although tattoos were never red in the Marquesas (Ottino-Garanger and Ottino-Garanger 1998). The blue textile band covering the maxilla appears to simulate the *aha epo*, a male tattoo motif (Candelot 2001). However, on the upper lip, the textile shows thirteen buttonholes in a vertical position, symmetrically placed on both sides of the nose, that might be seen as a representation of the *koniho* motif, a motif consisting of vertical striations adorning the female lips (von den Steinen 1925–1928). The diamond-mesh vegetal

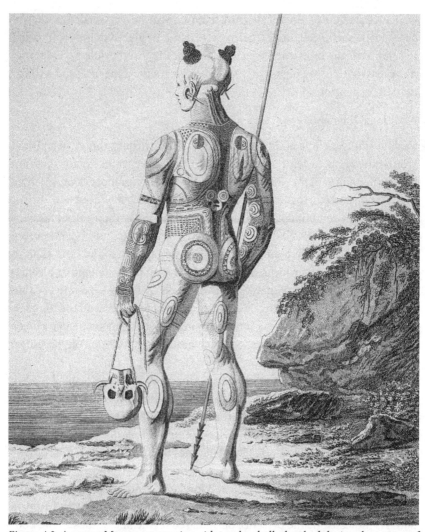

Figure 4.3. A young Marquesan warrior with trophy skull, sketched during the voyage of Krusenstern in 1804, reproduced in von Langsdorff's atlas (1812). © Bibliothèque Centrale du Muséum d'Histoire Naturelle (M.N.H.N.), Paris (France), 2009.

net covering the braincase completes this possible representation of tattooing in imitation of the Nuku Hiva male style illustrated in nineteenth-century iconography (Ottino-Garanger and Ottino-Garanger 1998).

Other skulls, completely wrapped in white tapa cloth, are generally grouped with decorated skulls. Three that are all very similar to each other are known in museum collections (Ivory 1998); these are characterized by painted designs on the cloth, representing the eyes and mouth in correct anatomical position, along with tattoos (figure 4.5). The eyes are surrounded by striated

Figure 4.4. Trophy skull from Nuku Hiva, Marquesas Islands, French Polynesia (collection of Favin Lévèque, 1845). Note the red and blue European textiles and the white tapa strip, suggesting the French tricolor national flag. Collection du Muséum d'Histoire Naturelle de La Rochelle (H.1013). Reproduced by permission, Muséum d'Histoire Naturelle de La Rochelle (France).

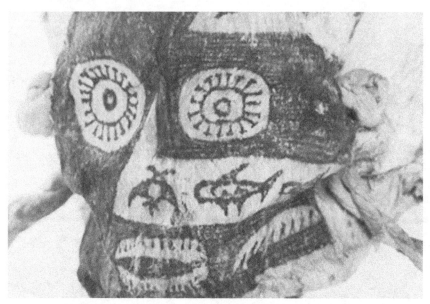

Figure 4.5. Skull wrapped in white tapa painted with tattoo motifs from Nuku Hiva (collection of J. D. Rohr, 1845). Collection Muséum d'Histoire Naturelle et d'Ethnologie de Colmar (no. 543). Courtesy Société d'Histoire Naturelle et d'Ethnologie, Colmar (France).

lines like those tattooed on the face of the Marquesan warriors (Ivory 1998), and in one case, striations surrounding the mouth suggest the feminine lip tattoo (Boës and Sears 1993). Other facial tattoos, associating geometric and naturalistic motifs of fish (shark, ray), are similar to those illustrated by Von Langsdorff (1812) in use in Nuku Hiva during the nineteenth century. In at least two cases, these modified skulls are complete with a thick rope. Other skulls, simply wrapped in white tapa but devoid of other decoration, are also known: examples have been observed in the Te Ani funerary rock shelter on Ua Huka, along with a skull wrapped in a piece of red occidental fabric (Vigneron 1984).

Analysis of Features

The above descriptions depict the repetition of features such as the association of a thick rope with both covered and uncovered skulls. Such repetition indicates standardized production of trophy skulls in the archipelago and suggests their use in a standardized or ritualized context. This rope is functional, as the iconography indicates that it was used to hang and exhibit the skull (figure 4.3).

The descriptions indicate manufacturing methods clearly oriented towards the realistic imitation of the human physiognomy. Marquesan craftsmen took pains to reproduce the sense organs with some anatomical exactness, as exemplified by the detailed treatment of the eyes, showing the distinction of their three visible components. The eyes and the nose are systematically represented, while the mouth and the skin are less frequently indicated. Ears are missing from the trophy skulls in museum collections as well as from those portrayed in iconography, but some descriptions report the presence of ear ornaments at the anatomical location of the ear (Radiguet 2001 [1861]). These male ear adornments—made of large, white, wooden plates—were used earlier than seashell, ivory, or bone earrings and were replaced by lighter items during the nineteenth century (Ivory 1995).

Trophy skulls display the same characteristics as other Marquesan representations of humans, such as the *tiki*, anthropomorphic statues (which were typically made of stone or wood) representing deified ancestors. Great importance is devoted to the eyes in these representations, as "giant eyes express the idea of knowledge and supernatural power, [and] the extended mouth, revealing the tongue, or sometimes the teeth, symbolizes challenge, a provocation of the enemy" (Ottino-Garanger 2006), while the ears and thus the sense of hearing seem less significant. The eyes (the look, or *mata*) are central notions of the Marquesan culture. They are represented and emphasized on objects as varied as stone and bone statues, war clubs, petroglyphs, wooden frames covered with painted tapa, and tattooed skin (Boës and Sears 2002; Ivory 1998; Ottino 1995; Ottino-Garanger 2002; Ottino-Garanger and Ottino-Garanger 1998), perhaps indicating an association with power, since the eyes form a link between the mana and others. Mana, as the concept of a sacred force that can reside in the head of persons as well as animals and inanimate objects or places, could be obtained through birth or through war, but it also could be lost. People or objects that possess mana are accorded "respect" because it gives authority, power, and prestige (the concept of mana is common to Melanesian, Polynesian, and Micronesian languages; see Bonogofsky and Graham this volume for examples from Melanesia).

The addition of the pig tusks, which were also used to make other Marquesan warrior ornaments (Ivory 1995; Ottino-Garanger 2002), significantly alters the humanity of the image presented by the skulls. Yet the presence of these components would not diminish the status of the skulls, as has been suggested by Delmas (1927). Pig tusks could have symbolized an interface between the worlds of the living and the dead, the intermediate nature of this animal being ascertained by its omnipresence in pre-European funerary rituals (Conte 2002; Suggs 1961).

Osteological Analysis of Five Trophy Skulls

Five of these decorated skulls, all curated in France, have been described in osteological detail (see table 4.1): the two skulls curated in the Muséum d'Histoire Naturelle et d'Ethnologie de Colmar (no. 1, no. 543), two skulls curated in the Musée de l'Homme de Paris (no. 570, no. 294853), and one skull curated in the Muséum d'Histoire Naturelle de La Rochelle (no. H.1013; Boës and Sears 1993, 1996, 2002; Valentin and Rolland 2002), revealing further information concerning the selection of specific human remains as well as the process of preparing the final products. A summary of these analyses is presented below.

Trophy skull preparation began with a complete skull, including the cranium and mandible, apart from one tapa-covered female skull for which a piece of wood replaced the mandible (no. 543; figure 4.5). In the five skulls, the reassociated bones—cranium and mandible—belong to the same skeleton. If the skull—or the head—was selected in accordance with a set of rules, they do not appear to be correlated with the biological criteria of age at death or sex. The estimated ages at death vary, with adolescents and adults of different ages and both sexes represented (Boës and Sears 1993). The cause or manner of death cannot be determined, but signs of possible perimortem violence have been identified on two individuals: Boës and Sears (1993, 1996) report a fracture on the posterior of an adult skull (table 4.1: no. 570; figure 4.6), and a fracture of the mandible on a male skull (table 4.1: no. 1).

Trophy skull processing required the removal of soft tissue, raising questions regarding the method of acquisition of the skull and the timing of preparation. None of the five skulls exhibit obvious traces of beheading (see Montgomery, Knüsel, and Tucker this volume for evidence of decapitation from Roman Britain), either on the occipital and temporal or on the mandible. Cut marks on the cranial vault, breakage of the basilar region of the occipital, and breakage of small wings of the sphenoid have been observed on one adult skull (table 4.1: no. 294853) and are interpreted as the result of defleshing, removal of the brain, and extraction of the eyes, respectively (Boës and Sears 1996, 2002; see Stodder 2006 for examples from Papua New Guinea), rather than postdepositional taphonomic damage. In this case, the use of a complete head rather than a skull is suggested, a premise that is supported by the absence of postmortem dental loss. An adolescent skull displaying an incision and cortical splitting in the vertex region, loss of bone in the basilar region, and the absence of postmortem tooth loss may reflect a similar procedure, but the covering of European fabric prevents a definitive interpretation (table 4.1: no. H.1013; figure 4.4; Valentin and Rolland 2002). Incisions on the mandible

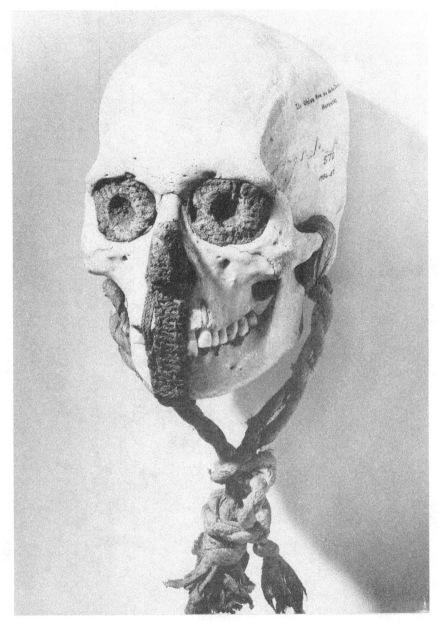

Figure 4.6. Trophy skull from Hiva Oa, Marquesas Islands, French Polynesia. A possible victim of perimortem violence, according to Boës and Sears 1996. Collection du Musée de L'Homme de Paris (France) (unidentified collection, no. 570). Photo Paris, Musée du Quai Branly. Inv. Iconothèque: PP103724, © 2009. Reproduced by permission of Musée du Quai Branly/Scala, Florence.

Table 4.1. Short inventory of Marquesan trophy skulls in museum and private collections

Museum / Reference no.	Collector / Date / Origin	Age and sex / Modifications	Ornaments	References
Muséum d'Histoire Naturelle, Lille, France No. 1135	A. Moillet Donation 1851 Nuku Hiva	Adult	Vegetal braid linking the mandible to the skull (passing under chin) Piece of wood in nasal aperture Western fabric, pearl shell disc, and vegetal fibers in eye sockets Two pig tusks Suspension rope Strip of white tapa Hair dressed in two buns linked with tapa Thin vegetal braid around upper and lower teeth	Bounoure 1999; Le Fur 1999; Candelot 2001
Muséum d'Histoire Naturelle et d'Ethnologie, Colmar, France No. 1[a]	J. D. Rohr Donation 1845 Nuku Hiva	Mature adult, male? Bone modification on mandible and mastoids, postmortem loss of lower teeth	Vegetal braid linking the mandible to the skull (passing under chin) Piece of wood in nasal aperture Suspension rope	Boës and Sears 1993, 1996; Sears 1993; Rolland 2002
Muséum d'Histoire Naturelle et d'Ethnologie, Colmar, France No. 543[a]	J. D. Rohr Donation 1845 Nuku Hiva	Mature adult, gracile, female? No bone modification, piece of wood replacing mandible	Wrapped in white tapa Painted eyes at the anatomical location and dry leaves in eye sockets Painted tattoo motifs Two ropes	Boës and Sears 1993, 1996; Sears 1993; Rolland 2002
Musée du Quai Branly, Paris, France No. 71.1887.31.7	Roland Bonaparte Donation 1887 Origin unknown		Wrapped in white tapa Painted eyes at the anatomical location Painted tattoo motifs Two ropes	Lavondès and Jacquemin 1995

Location / No.	Collector / Date / Island	Age / Modification	Features	Reference
Musée de L'Homme, Paris, France No. 570[a]	DuPetit-Thouars or Collet? 1843? Hiva Oa	Adult No bone modification, postmortem loss of lower teeth, violent death?	Piece of wood in eye sockets	Boës and Sears 1996
Musée de L'Homme, Paris, France No. 294851	Dumoutier? 1838? Nuku Hiva	Adult Trephination	Vegetal braid linking the mandible to the skull (passing under chin) Two pig tusks	Anonymous 1982
Musée de L'Homme, Paris, France No. 294852	Dumoutier 1838 Nuku Hiva		Vegetal fibers	
Musée de L'Homme, Paris, France No. 294853[a]	Dumoutier 1838 Nuku Hiva	Adult 19 cut marks on cranial vault, bone modification on mastoids, modification of occipital foramen	Vegetal braid linking the mandible to the skull (passing under chin) Piece of wood in nasal aperture Two pig tusks	Boës and Sears 1996
Musée de L'Homme, Paris, France No. 04719			Vegetal fibers Pig tusks	
Muséum d'Histoire Naturelle de La Rochelle, France No. H654	F. Gille Entry ca. 1860 Nuku Hiva	Adult	Vegetal braid linking the mandible to the skull (passing under chin) Piece of wood in nasal aperture Thin vegetal braid around upper and lower teeth	Inventory, Muséum de La Rochelle; Rolland 2002

continued

Table 4.1.—*Continued*

Museum / Reference no.	Collector / Date / Origin	Age and sex / Modifications	Ornaments	References
Muséum d'Histoire Naturelle de La Rochelle, France No. H1013[a]	Favin-Lévêque Entry ca. 1855 Nuku Hiva	Adolescent No visible bone modification, bone loss in occipital	Vegetal braid linking the mandible to the skull (passing through chin) Piece of wood in nasal aperture Reconstituted eyes with mother-of-pearl, turtle shell, and seed Thin vegetal braid around upper and lower teeth Blue and red textile covering most of the skull White tapa strip Hair dressed in two buns linked with tapa and supported by vegetal net	Gastaut 1972; Bounoure 1999; Péré 1993; Candelot 2001; Valentin and Rolland 2002
Muséum des Beaux-Arts, Dunkerque, France No. ET209/AN217	L. V. Jolly collection? 1847 Nuku Hiva		Vegetal braid linking the mandible to the skull (passing under chin) Piece of wood in nasal aperture Decoration in eye sockets Two pig tusks Two suspension ropes	Bounoure 1999; Le Fur 1999
Museum of Caen[b]	Dumont d'Urville 1838 Nuku Hiva?	Adult? Red pigment on the forehead	Vegetal braid linking the mandible to the skull (passing under chin) Piece of wood in nasal aperture Two pig tusks	Bounoure 1999

Museum für Volkerkünde, Berlin, Germany No. VI 55131	Nuku Hiva	Adult?	Wrapped in white tapa Painted eyes at the anatomical location Painted tattoo motifs	Ivory 1998
Hamburg, Germany			Vegetal braid linking the mandible to the skull (passing under chin) Piece of wood in nasal aperture? Decoration in eye sockets	Bounoure 1999
Unidentified Hamburg? Germany?		Adult	Vegetal braid linking the mandible to the skull (passing under chin) Piece of wood in eye sockets Two pig tusks	Bounoure 1999
Collection of Lord McAlpine, London, U.K.		Adult? Red pigment on forehead and eye sockets, "triangular tattoo" in left eye socket, made with pigment	Vegetal braid linking the mandible to the skull (passing under chin) Piece of wood in nasal aperture Reconstituted eyes with pearl shell and turtle shell Suspension rope	Bounoure 1999; Candelot 2001

[a] Detailed osteological description available.
[b] Formerly housed in museum but destroyed in bombardment of 1943.

of a third skull—of a male adult—and destruction of the petrous pyramid of both temporal bones are thought to result from perimortem treatment such as hanging the body with sacrificial hooks and exposure on a support (table 4.1: no. 1; Boës and Sears 1993, 1996, 2002). The two other adult skulls do not display superficial marks, but one of them (table 4.1: no. 570; figure 4.6) displays significant postmortem dental loss to the mandible, suggesting a period of time between the death of the individual and trophy preparation, with a passive defleshing of the corpse through "natural" elimination of the soft parts of the head (see Bonney and Clegg this volume and Bonogofsky and Graham this volume for related skull preparation in Melanesia).

The manufacture of the trophy skull required further bone alteration. Circular perforations in the lateral pterygoid processes and a perforation of the chin through which to pass the string linking the mandible to the cranium were observed in the European cloth-covered adolescent skull (no. H.1013; figure 4.4) but not in the other four examined here. However, the perimortem fracture observed on the anterior aspect of the mandible of one male adult (table 4.1: no. 1) might have resulted from an attempt to perform the same action rather than the supposed blow mentioned earlier. Other bone alterations include breakage of the nasal septum and vomer, observed in the nasal aperture. The breaks are from the penetration of the piece of wood simulating the nose (no. 1; Boës and Sears 1993; see Stodder 2006) and of the vegetal braid linking the calvarium with the mandible. The destruction of the palate (Vigneron 1985: 215) and extraction of the incisors (Suggs 1961: 169), supposedly caused by the introduction of this link, were not identified by the osteological analyses of the five specimens. Additionally, red pigments were applied on the forehead and the eye sockets of other skulls (Bounoure 1999: 49; Candelot 2001: 17). This practice echoes the use of red textile to cover the forehead of the adolescent specimen (no. H.1013; figure 4.4) and to fill in one of the orbit cavities of another adult skull (no. 1135).

The osteological analyses show that preparation could occur either a short or a long time after death. Indeed, postmortem dental loss could be an indicator of an exposure that was relatively long, suggesting a period of time between death and trophy preparation. The osteological study also highlights the use of skulls of both sexes and of different age categories, from adolescent to mature adult. All the investigated trophies include a cranium and a mandible belonging to a single head. This suggests the importance of the integrity of the represented face. Interestingly, in Marquesan language, there is synonymy between the designation of the face, *nutu kaha,* and the name given to the vegetal braid linking the mandible to the skull, *kaha* (Rolland 2002).

The repeated use of red pigments, or red textiles in some cases, anatomically located on the forehead and eye region seems to result from a reasoned choice. Red (and also white) is a symbolic color in the Marquesas, as it is elsewhere in Polynesia. In traditional Marquesan societies, red symbolized prestige and power, as exemplified by the caps or helmets covered with red feathers that were carried by the chiefs, while white is related to sacred concepts (Ivory 1995; Melville 1996 [1846]). With such attributes, the trophy skull appears to be a highly charged image of significant status.

Ancestors or Enemies?

The presence or absence of tapa or Western fabric wrapping the skull has been used as a criterion to distinguish two functional groups of objects. For example, Linton (1971: 59 [1925]) wrote, "It seems probable that the tapa-covered skulls preserved in some European collections [as] chief's skulls which have been used as cult objects for their decorations are quite different from those of the war trophy heads described by the early writers." Later scholars such as Boës and Sears (1993, 1996, 2002) and Le Fur (1999) have regarded tapa-wrapped skulls as both ancestral relics and war trophies. Still others challenge a strict division, based on decoration, between the skulls of ancestors and enemies (Bounoure 1999; Candelot 2001; Lavondès and Jacquemin 1995). For example, Bounoure describes examples contradicting this rigid categorization and concludes, "aucun détail d'aspect ne permet donc de distinguer aujourd'hui les crânes voués au culte de ceux offerts à la parade" ["no detail of appearance allows us to distinguish skulls intended for a religious purpose from those offered at the parade"] (Bounoure 1999: 47).

On a wider scale, the concept of a "trophy skull" (as curated in museum collections) may also be undermined by several factors, including the ancient transformation of trophies into ancestors and vice versa, as well as the general lack of accurate documentation of museum artifacts (Coiffier and Guerreiro 1999; Bonogofsky and Graham this volume; see also Oakdale 2005 for discussion of how and why enemy heads are symbolically transformed into ancestors among the Jivaro Achuar of Peru). As for other artifacts and rituals, the use of the object and associated practices may have changed over time due to circumstances discussed below.

The Trophy Skull as Part of a Complex Politico-Religious System

Despite a lack of detailed and repeated archaeological evidence for human trophy skull production in the pre-European period in the Marquesas, trophy skulls seem to be associated with pre-European activities. Possible examples have been found in domestic occupation sites in Haatuatua and Hatiheu on Nuku Hiva (Suggs 1961; Valentin 2002; Valentin and Rolland 2004), as well as burial sites in Manihina on Ua Huka (Sellier 1998). Ethnohistorical reports suggest their use in warrior rituals before the mid-nineteenth century. These written records indicate that the modified heads were those of war enemies, prisoners caught outside of the community and brought back to the *tohua*— the place for feasts and public ceremonies—with the prisoners being young or old individuals of both sexes (Dening 1974; Dumoutier 1843). After the captives had been tortured and killed, their heads were removed for preparation by the priests' assistants at the *me'ae*—the religious place. This practice is supported by sightings of decorated skulls in sacred places (Radiguet 2001 [1861]). Once completed, trophy skulls were given back to the warriors who had obtained the corpses. Other parts of the captives' bodies were also used. Hands were transformed into pendants, and bones were used in making *ivipoo*—a souvenir of an important event sometimes used as body adornment (Lavondès 1966). The decorated skulls were curated at the me'ae and at home and were used to adorn funerary canoes (Bounoure 1999; Melville 1996 [1846]) and war canoes (Crook 2007; Fanning 1833; Lavondès 1995; Rollin 1929; von den Steinen 1925–1928), but above all, trophy skulls were worn by warriors in ceremonial dress (Gracia 1843) and at war (Handy 1923) as symbols of their power and efficacy, promoting their personhood and status.

The foregoing treatment—methods of acquisition, preparation, use, and exhibition of the trophy head—is reminiscent of the widely described but still poorly understood institution of headhunting, which is distributed from Assam in India to Oceania, including Polynesia (Coiffier and Guerreiro 1999; see Bonney and Clegg this volume and Bonogofsky and Graham this volume for examples from Melanesia). In the Austronesian society of Roviana, Solomon Islands, headhunting is considered part of a complex sociopolitical system aiming to construct power and authority for political actors (Sheppard et al. 2000; see O'Donnabhain this volume for the establishment of power and authority related to the decapitation and display of enemies in medieval Ireland). This complex system intimately associates the worlds of the living and dead and includes an ancestor cult from which authority and power ultimately derive. In this system, trophy skulls serve as symbols of chiefs' and warriors' efficacy, whereas chiefs' skulls provide symbolic connections with ancestral power. Such a model, although not clearly described in the archipelago's ethnohistorical reports, may apply to the Marquesan politico-religious system, which seems to include human sacrifice motivating intervalley raids and conflicts, along with a form of ancestor cult. Several facts, noted below, suggest the existence of a Marquesan ancestor cult that included specific treatment of a chief's skull, because the chief, by his ancestral lineage and its alliances and authority over the land, held a very importance place in the community. The chief spoke and acted on behalf of the gods (Ottino-Garanger 2006); because the head is the seat of mana, the heads of chiefs, by their divine lineage, were the most coveted.

Archaeological studies reveal specific skull treatments. At the Haatuatua site on Nuku Hiva, Suggs (1961) excavated inhumations without skulls. At the Manihina site on Ua Huka, Sellier (1998) demonstrated skull removal (sometimes including the mandible) after skeletonization of the corpse, via the presence of teeth but the absence of the first cervical vertebrae. This particular treatment seems to have been applied in both cases to selected individuals, mainly male adults. There is also evidence of secondary deposits of human remains. Skulls, separated from other bones, are often present in domestic occupation sites, in tohua, and in me'ae, with a preference for the latter, based on Suggs's (1961) survey on Nuku Hiva, which indicates that among eight me'ae, six contained human remains, while among six tohua, only three contained human remains.

Ethnohistorical records mention the widespread practice of separating and wrapping bones in tapa after exposure and mummification of the deceased, then curating them in various places, including banian trees, caves, exposure platforms, habitations, and me'ae (Linton 1971 [1925]), while the skull was sometimes treated separately (Handy 1923; Linton 1971 [1925]). Wrapped in plain white tapa or red Western fabric (Ivory 1998; Vigneron 1985: 461), these "naturally" acquired skulls were neither prepared nor decorated. As a mark of their high status, authority, and power, chiefs' skulls were purposely conserved at the me'ae, venerated and used by priests in rituals (Handy 1923; Lavondès 1995), thus providing a material manifestation of the spiritual power of ancestors.

The trophy skulls symbolize one of the wheels of the system of creating and adjusting social balance by regulating and activating pre-European societies, meaning that chiefs (*papa hakaiki*), priests (*tau'a*), warriors (*toa*), and craftsmen (*tuhuna*) were the backbone of Marquesan pre-European societies. They held determinant roles and were protected by numerous *tapu* (for-bidden, sacred); this concept applies to the head, the most sacred part of the corpse, but also to places, objects, and so forth (Ottino-Garanger 2006). This fragile social equilibrium was disrupted during the nineteenth century after a major depopulation of the archipelago owing mainly to two factors: a famine caused by drought, which provoked an important emigration; and the introduction of European diseases, which generated high mortality rates (Rallu 1990).

Temporal Variations of Trophy Skull Manufacture

Archaeological research on the Marquesas Islands suggests some antiquity for the practice of human skull collection and handling (Conte 2002; Maureille and Sellier 1996; Ottino-Garanger 2006; Sellier 1998; Suggs 1961; Valentin 2002; Valentin and Rolland 2004; Vigneron 1985; for a revision of the prehistoric sequence, see Allen 2004). The two practices seem to be related: for example, skeletons without skulls were uncovered in the Haatuatua site on Nuku Hiva (Suggs 1961), and collections of skulls were excavated from a stone-faced pit in a tohua as well as from me'ae in the Hatiheu Valley on Nuku Hiva (Valentin 2002; Valentin and Rolland 2004). These may have been trophy skulls, since the cranial remains uncovered in the stone-faced pit in Hatiheu were associated with two pig canines (Valentin 2002; Valentin and Rolland 2004) and an isolated skull with the mandible in perfect articulation was found face down at the Manihina site on Ua Huka (Sellier 1998). The latter is reminiscent of the trophy skull that Suggs (1961: 169) recovered and illustrated, with the strip linking the two bones still preserved, from a *paepae* (megalithic base or platform in elevated habitations; Ottino-Garanger 2006) at the Haatuatua site.

Accounts of early Western explorers indicate production at least during the pre-European period if not earlier. For example, Georg Heinrich von Langsdorff (1812), who stayed in the Marquesas for about ten days in 1804 while associated with the Adam Johann Krusenstern and Yuri F. Lisianski Russian circumnavigation expedition (Krusenstern 1810–1812), illustrated a trophy skull in his atlas. P. Dumoutier (1843), who accompanied Dumont D'Urville, collected several trophy skulls in 1838. The use of Western fabrics in the preparation of some of skulls clearly indicates that production continued after European contact. It seems to have stopped only after massive European settlement and Christianization in the second half of the nineteenth century on Nuku Hiva, which permanently modified traditional Marquesan cultural practices (Bailleul 2001).

Wide variability has been observed among the Marquesan trophy skull samples. Some of these variations could indicate manufacturing change over time. Despite possible destruction owing to passing time, the skulls more recently introduced into museum and private collections exhibit more elaborate manufacture than do earlier ones. These more recent artifacts display characteristics such as the inclusion of Western materials and thin sinnet ligatures around the teeth that do not exist on earlier skulls. The early illustration by Von Langsdorff (1812) supports this hypothesis. It shows a simple composition made of a skull and mandible linked together by a vegetal strip, with a piece of wood replacing the nose and an associated suspension rope. The fabrication process appears to have changed over time with the integration of materials brought by the new settlers but also through innovation consisting of the addition of new ornaments.

From Headhunting to Curios

Procedural changes to the production of trophy skulls suggest that an ancient practice was diverted to a new interest. A similar remark has been evoked regarding the evolution of the use of ornaments: "On perçoit ici une évolution probable des Marquisiens vers un détachement de ce qui autrefois avait eu un sens et un pouvoir et n'en possédant plus depuis l'installation des nouveaux-venus" ["Here we perceive a probable evolution of the Marquesans toward a detachment from that which once had a meaning and a power, and which no longer does since the arrival and settlement of the newcomers"] (Ottino-Garanger 2002: 64). From this perspective, the production of trophy skulls was initially religious or politico-religious in nature, as noticed by the first Western explorers; it did not stop but instead revived in response to the settlement of newcomers in the islands. The changes in trophy skull manufacture might have emerged from the demand of Westerners eager to obtain such a curiosity for various reasons stemming from the mentality of Europeans during the second part of the nineteenth century, for they were keen to demonstrate Marquesan savagery and to collect exotic objects to enrich ethnographic museums.

Indeed, one may wonder whether the more recent skulls made with Western materials might not be curios made to order. They do show outstanding features of traditional Marquesan culture such as tattoos, a hairstyle with locks twisted into two hair buns, and tapa headbands. But such exotic images may also include ironical features, clearly showing, as Thomas (1995: 158) states, "la capacité des indigènes à intégrer et à manipuler les icones du pouvoir colonial qui venait de débarquer sur leurs plages" ["the ability of indigenous people to integrate and manipulate the icons of the colonial power that had just landed on their shores"]. This is exemplified by the skull fully covered with Western textiles (figure 4.4), which exhibits the stunning double alternation of three colors, blue-white-red, suggesting a double evocation of the French national flag.

Conclusions

The handling of human skulls in the prehistoric and protohistoric Marquesas Islands took different expressions. One of these was the elaboration of trophy skulls, which were used in the context of politico-religious activities, being worn and exhibited during various rituals. Initially prestigious objects, these trophy skulls lost their original meaning and value when they became curios, objects of trade, between the natives (whose ancient religion had started to disappear with forceful Christianization) and Westerners (who were eager to obtain representative images of ancestral Marquesan culture). As noted by Dening (1980), a Marquesan ethnography describing the full process of religious change and symbol transfer needs to be written. Further bioarchaeological and iconographic research, combined with the careful ethnographic review advocated by Dening, has the potential to increase our understanding and appreciation for the changing meaning of these objects and the transformation of the culture from which they derived. Continued excavation of archaeological sites—such as tohua, me'ae, and other sacred places—should also increase our knowledge of the transformation of the skulls of the ancestors and enemies of the indigenous population into curios purchased by Western outsiders.

Acknowledgments

We thank Michelle Bonogofsky for her comments and suggestions and Ian Lilley for commenting on an earlier draft.

References Cited

Allen, M. S. 2004. Revisiting and Revising Marquesan Culture History: New Archaeological Investigations at Anaho Bay, Nuku Hiva Island. *Journal of the Polynesian Society* 113 (2): 143–196.

Anonymous. 1982. *Le Musée de l'Homme, Anthropologie, Ethnologie, Préhistoire.* Ouest-France, Rennes, France.

Baert, A. 1999. *Le Paradis Terrestre, un mythe espagnol en Océanie: Les voyages de Mendaña et de Quirós, 1567–1606.* L'Harmattan, Paris.

Bailleul, M. 2001. *Les îles Marquises: Histoire de la Terre des Hommes du XVIIIème à nos jours.* Cahier du Patrimoine (Histoire) 3. Ministère de la Culture de Polynésie Française, Papeete, French Polynesia.

Boës, E., and S. Sears. 1993. Crânes ancestraux, crânes trophées des Marquises. *Bulletin de la Société d'Histoire Naturelle de Colmar* 62: 97–108.

———. 1996. Les crânes trophées Marquisiens (XVIIIème, XIXème siècles): Interprétation des interventions anthropiques. *Bulletins et Mémoires de la Société d'Anthropologie de Paris* 8 (3–4): 275–288.

———. 2002. Archéologie, ostéologie, ethnologie et région oculaire: État de la question autour des îles Marquises. In *Autour de l'oeil dans l'Antiquité, approche pluridisciplinaire*, edited by J. Royer, M.-J. Roulière-Lambert, and A.-S. Cohën, 19–27. Le Centre Jurassien du Patrimoine, Lons-le-Saunier, France.

Bounoure, G. 1999. Les crânes des Iles Marquises. *Arts d'Afrique Noire* 109: 42–51.

Candelot, J.-L. 2001. Crânes-trophée des Iles Marquises. *Tahiti-Pacifique Magazine* 123: 15–20.

Coiffier, C., and A. Guerreiro. 1999. La chasse aux têtes: Une dette de vie? In *La mort n'en saura rien*, edited by Y. Le Fur, 31–45. Musée National des Arts d'Afrique et d'Océanie, Réunion des Musées Nationaux, Paris.

Conte, E. 2002. Current Research on the Island of Ua Huka, Marquesas Archipelago, French Polynesia. *Asian Perspectives* 41 (2): 258–268.

Crook, W. P. 2007. *Récit aux îles Marquises, 1797–1799*. Haere Po, Papeete, French Polynesia.

Delmas, S. 1927. *La religion ou le paganisme des Marquisiens*. G. Beauchesne, Paris.

Dening, G., editor. 1974. *The Marquesan Journal of Edwards Robarts, 1797–1824*. Pacific History Series 6. Australian National University Press, Canberra.

———. 1980. *Island and Beaches, Discourse on a Silent Land, Marquesas, 1774–1880*. University Press of Hawaii, Honolulu.

Dumoutier, P. 1843. Notice phrénologique et ethnologique sur les naturels de l'archipel Nouka-Hiva par M. Dumoutier. In *Iles Marquises ou Nouka-Hiva: Histoire, géographie, mœurs*, edited by C. Vincendon-Dumoulin and C. Desgraz, 292–304. Arthus Bertrand, Paris.

Fanning, E. 1833. *Voyages Round the World; with Selected Sketches of Voyages to the South Seas, North and South Pacific Ocean, China, etc [. . .] Between the Years 1792 and 1832*. Collins and Hannay, New York.

Gastaut, H. 1972. *Le crâne, objet de culte, objet d'art*. Musée Cantini, Marseille.

Gracia, M. 1843. *Lettres sur les Iles Marquises, ou mémoires pour servir à l'étude religieuse, morale, politique et statistique des Iles Marquises et de l'Océanie orientale*. Gaume Frères, Paris.

Handy, E. S. C. 1923. *The Native Culture in the Marquesas*. Bernice P. Bishop Museum Bulletin 9. Bishop Museum, Honolulu, Hawaii. Bayard Dominick Expedition Publication, reprint 1971. Kraus, New York.

Ivory, C. 1995. Le rôle de la parure personnelle aux Iles Marquises au cours de la première période du contact, 1774–1821. *Bulletin de la Société des Etudes Océaniennes* 268: 63–73.

———. 1998. Painted Tapa from the Marquesas Islands. In *Easter Island in Pacific Context: South Sea Symposium*, edited by C. Stevenson, G. Lee, and F. J. Morin, 51–54. Easter Island Foundation, Los Osos, Chile.

Krusenstern, A. J. 1810–1812. *Reise um die Welt in den Jahren 1803, 1804, 1805 und 1806, auf Befehl seiner K. M. Alexander des Ersten auf den Schiffen Nadeshda und Newa unter dem Commando des Capitains von der Kaiserlichen Marine*. Der Verfasser, St. Petersburg, Russia.

Lavondès, A. 1966. *Musée de Papeete: Catalogue des collections ethnographiques et archéologiques*. ORSTOM, multigraphié, Papeete, French Polynesia.

———. 1995. La société traditionnelle. In *Trésors des îles Marquises*, edited by M. Panoff, 31–39. Réunion des Musées Nationaux, Paris.

Lavondès, A., and S. Jacquemin. 1995. Des premiers écrits aux collections d'objets. In *Trésors des îles Marquises*, edited by M. Panoff, 26–30. Réunion des Musées Nationaux, Paris.

Le Fur, Y., editor. 1999. Notices 13, 14, 15. In *La mort n'en saura rien, reliques d'Europe et d'Océanie*. Réunion de Musées Nationaux, Paris.

Linton, R. 1923. *The Material Culture of the Marquesas Islands*. Bernice P. Bishop Museum Memoirs, vol. 8, no. 5. Bayard Dominick Expedition Publication no. 5. Bishop Museum, Honolulu, Hawaii.

———. 1971 [1925]. *Archaeology of the Marquesas Islands*. Bernice P. Bishop Museum Bulletin 23. Bishop Museum, Honolulu, Hawaii. Bayard Dominick Expedition Publication no. 10, reprint 1971. Kraus, New York.

Maureille, B., and P. Sellier. 1996. Dislocation en ordre paradoxal, momification et decomposition: Observations et hypotheses. *Bulletins et Mémoires de la Société d'Anthropologie de Paris* 8 (3–4): 313–327.

Melville, H. 1846. *Typee—A Peep at Polynesian Life during a Four-months' Residence in a Valley of the Marquesas*. New York.

———. 1996 [1846]. *Taïpi*. Translated by Théo Varlet and Francis Ledoux. Gallimard, Paris.

Oakdale, Suzanne. 2005. Forgetting the Dead, Remembering Enemies. In *Interacting with the Dead: Perspectives on Mortuary Archaeology for the New Millennium*, edited by G. F. M. Rakita, J. E. Buikstra, L. A. Beck, and S. R. Williams, 106–123. University Press of Florida, Gainesville.

Ottino, P. 1995. Les bambous pyrogravés marquisiens. *Bulletin de la Société des Etudes Océaniennes* 268: 44–54.

Ottino-Garanger, M.-N. 2002. Etre avant que de paraître, l'art de la parure dans un archipel océanien: Les Marquises. In *Kannibals et Vahinés: Les sources de l'imaginaire*, edited by C. Stéfani, 49–73. Musée des Beaux-Arts de Chartres, Chartres, France.

Ottino-Garanger, P. 2006. *Archéologie chez les Taïpi: Hatiheu, un projet partagé aux Marquises*. IRD Editions. Au vent des îles, Singapore.

Ottino-Garanger, P., and M.-N. Ottino-Garanger. 1998. *Le tatouage aux Iles Marquises*. Editions Gleizal, Papeete, French Polynesia.

Péré, J. 1993. Présence d'un espace esthétique et culturel marquisien au Muséum de La Rochelle. In *Créer en Afrique*, 79–85. Deuxième colloque européen sur les arts d'Afrique noire, collection Arts d'Afrique Noire. Collectif, Arnouville, France.

Radiguet, M. 2001 [1861]. *Les derniers sauvages: Aux Iles Marquises, 1842–1859*. Editions Phébus, Paris.

Rallu, J.-L. 1990. *Les populations océaniennes aux XIXè et XXè*. INED-PUF, Paris.

Rolland, N. 2002. *La Place du crâne dans les sociétés marquisiennes anciennes*. Master's thesis, Department of Histoire de l'Art et Archéologie, Université Paris I, Panthéon-Sorbonne, France.

Rollin, L. 1929. *Les îles Marquises: Géographie, ethnographie, histoire, colonisation et mise en valeur*. Société d'Editions géographiques, maritimes et coloniales, Paris.

Sears, S. 1993. *Catalogue de la collection des Iles Marquises ramenées par Jean-Daniel Rohr en 1845*. Muséum d'Histoire Naturelle de Colmar, Colmar, France.

Sellier, P. 1998. *Manihina, Ua Huka, archipel des Marquises, Polynésie française— Archéologie funéraire, campagne 1998*. Gouvernement territorial, Ministère de la culture, de l'enseignement supérieur et de la vie associative, Papeete, French Polynesia.

Sheppard, P. J., R. Walter, and T. Nagaoka. 2000. The Archaeology of Head-Hunting in Roviana Lagoon, New Georgia. *Journal of the Polynesian Society* 109 (1): 9–37.

Stodder, A. L. W. 2006. The Taphonomy of Cranial Modification in Papua New Guinea: Implications for the Archaeology of Mortuary Ritual. In *Skull Collection, Modification and Decoration*, edited by M. Bonogofsky, 77–89. BAR International Series 1539. Archaeopress, Oxford, U.K.

Suggs, R. C. 1961. *The Archaeology of Nuku Hiva*. Anthropological Papers no. 49. American Museum of Natural History, New York.

Thomas, N. 1995. *L'art de l'Océanie*. Thames and Hudson, Paris.

Valentin, F. 2002. Hatiheu, Nuku Hiva, îles Marquises, Fouille du pakeho du paepae 15, tohua Teiipoka, résultats préliminaires. CNRS-UMR 7041. Unpublished report, Paris.

Valentin, F., and N. Rolland. 2002. Rapport sur le crâne trophée marquisien (H1013) du Muséum d'Histoire Naturelle de La Rochelle. CNRS-UMR 7041. Unpublished report, Paris.

———. 2004. Rapport sur les restes humains découverts lors de la fouille 2003 dans le pakeho 15 du tohua de Teiipoka (Hatiheu, Nuku Hiva, Marquises): Disposition et caractéristiques paléobiologiques. CNRS-UMR 7041. Unpublished report, Paris.

Vigneron, E. 1984. Recherches archéologiques à Ua Huka, Iles Marquises—rites funéraires et croyances. Notes et Documents 11. ORSTOM, Papeete, French Polynesia.

———. 1985. Recherches sur l'histoire des attitudes devant la mort en Polynésie Française. Ph.D. dissertation (doctorat de troisième cycle), EHESS Toulouse, France.

Vincendon-Dumoulin, C., and C. Desgraz. 1843. *Iles Marquises ou Nouka-Hiva: Histoire, géographie, mœurs*. Arthus Bertrand, Paris.

von den Steinen, K. 1925–1928. *Die Marquesaner und ihre Kunst*. Reimer, Berlin.

von Langsdorff, G. H. 1812. *Bemerkungen auf einer Reise um die Welt, in den Jahren 1803 bis 1807*. Friedrich Wilmans, Frankfurt-am-Main.

5

The Social Lives of Severed Heads

Skull Collection and Display in Medieval and Early Modern Ireland

BARRA O'DONNABHAIN

Archaeological and historical data suggest that the collection and display of skulls and other body parts were among the many strategies used in the ne-gotiation of power and difference between competing groups in medieval and early modern Ireland. This chapter explores the roles played by decapitation and dismemberment across a number of cultural and temporal contexts in Ireland in which the bodies of individuals, of both group insiders and outsid-ers, who were perceived as a threat to established political and social power were demolished physically and symbolically. Evidence for these practices is found in archaeologically retrieved human skeletal remains as well as in con-temporary literary and artistic depictions. The contextual analysis of cranial and postcranial remains suggests that the collection and display of heads and other body parts underwent various transformations over time that reflect changing political and social circumstances but also perhaps changing under-standings of the body and the soul (see also chapters in this volume by Forgey; Stojanowski and Duncan; Valentin and Rolland).

Early Medieval Period (AD 450–1170)

The population of Ireland has been culturally and biologically diverse through-out most of the historic period, that is, post–fifth century AD. The arrival of Viking groups beginning at the end of the eighth century, followed by more-sustained immigration from Britain beginning in the twelfth century, resulted in the presence of a plurality of ethnic and cultural identities that resulted in interactions that were often antagonistic but were also characterized by pro-cesses of hybridity and syncretism (Graham 1997).

Archaeological evidence for skull collection and display in Ireland is relatively sparse in the Early Medieval period prior to the arrival of the Vikings
at the end of the eighth century AD. Many excavations have occurred at the
enclosed rural farmsteads that form the typical settlements of the Irish AD
500–1000, but human remains have not been a common find at these sites.
In contrast, a number of contemporary elite-level sites, whose architecture
tends to be of a more strategic nature, have produced skeletal remains with
evidence of trauma. The human remains from the seventh-century levels of
the high-status lake dwelling at Lagore, County Meath (figure 5.1), included
fourteen skulls with evidence of decapitation (Hencken 1950; O'Sullivan 1998:
116). Most of the human remains were found scattered about the edge of the
site, which may have been surrounded by a palisade, where the remains could
possibly have been displayed. The presence of two iron collars with chains and
a possible leg iron has been interpreted as a means of restraining prisoners or
slaves, but these could have also functioned in the display of living individuals. Human skulls were also found at two other high-status lake dwellings, at
Ballinderry 1 (Hencken 1936) and Ballinderry 2 (Hencken 1942). Of the three
skulls from the second of these sites, two had cut marks. At the stone fortress
at Cahercommaun, County Clare (figure 5.1), human remains were concentrated just inside the innermost of three concentric ramparts (Hencken 1938).
When these elite sites were excavated in the 1930s, the excavator made passing
references to the possible use of the skulls for display. However, little attention
has been paid to this suggestion since then.

More-secure evidence for early medieval skull collection and display was
found at the Viking enclave at Dublin, which was established by Scandinavian
groups in the early tenth century. Extensive excavations of tenth- to twelfth-
century levels of the settlement were carried out at a number of sites at Wood
Quay, Dublin, in the 1970s and early 1980s (figure 5.2). Though the cemeteries
used at that time were not identified, human remains were a relatively common occurrence in the settlement and these could be divided on stratigraphic
grounds into two temporal groups. The earlier of these dated to the tenth/
eleventh centuries and was dominated by seventeen isolated skulls. These were
found adjacent to a series of earth and gravel banks that were built around the
settlement. Of the seventeen skulls, fifteen belonged to adult males, and six of
these have evidence of injury that includes both blade wounds and blunt-force
trauma. There is evidence of decapitation in four of these skulls, and one of
the four has damage to the base and top of the head that is consistent with a
pointed object being forced through it (figure 5.3). This is the only one of the
seventeen with osteological evidence that correlates with the display of the

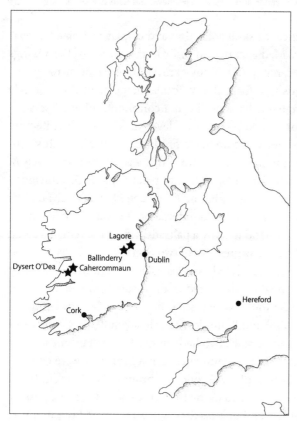

Figure 5.1. Map of Ireland
and Britain showing
locations mentioned in
the text.

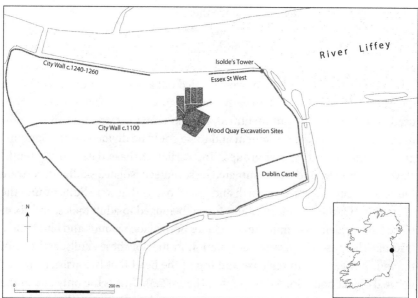

Figure 5.2. Plan of medieval Dublin showing lines of city walls and locations mentioned
in the text.

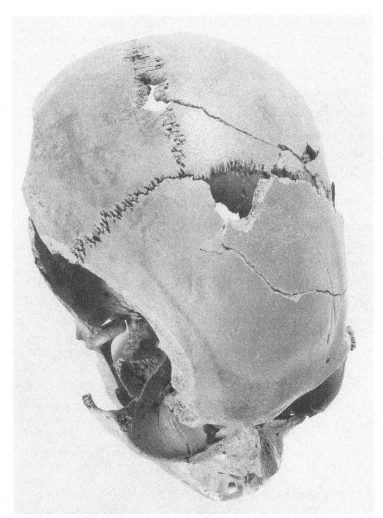

Figure 5.3. Skull from Viking-age levels of Dublin with multiple perimortem cutting wounds and damage consistent with display on a pointed object. Photograph: National Museum of Ireland.

head. However, as this action does not always leave traces detectable in bone (see Stojanowski and Duncan this volume), the contexts in which the skulls were found are significant: they were found at or near the succession of banks topped by palisades that enclosed the town. The concentration of skulls along the perimeter of the settlement may indicate that these heads were taken there for the purpose of display.

These skulls from Viking Dublin—as well as those recovered from archaeological excavations at the indigenous sites mentioned above—are very similar to the descriptions of decapitations and trophy heads in literature of the period. This collection of annals and heroic tales was written down by Irish clerics from the sixth century onwards, and the heroic tales may be based on an older oral tradition (Mac Niocaill 1975; Radner 1978). The annalistic literature contains accounts of heads being taken as trophies and of enemies thereby being dishonored by this act:

> And the youth returned to Condail with the head, . . . "Have you brought a trophy with you?" asked Murchad. "I have," said the warrior: "the head of Donn Bó." *Fragmentary Annals of Ireland*, AD 722 (FA178) (Radner 1978)

> The burning of Dún Amhlaeibh at Cluain Dolcáin, by the son of Gaithen and the son of Ciarán, son of Ronán; and one hundred of the heads of the foreigners [Vikings] were exhibited by the chieftains in that slaughter at Cluain Dolcáin. *Annals of the Four Masters*, AD 865 (M865.12) (Connellan 1846)

> Aed son of Niall plundered all the strongholds of the foreigners i.e., in the territory of the North, both in Cenél Eógain and Dál Araidi, and took away their heads, their flocks, and their herds from camp by battle (?). A victory was gained over them at Loch Febail and twelve score heads taken thereby. *Annals of Ulster*, AD 866 (AU866.4) (Mac Airt and Mac Niocaill 1983)

Enemies were further dishonored when the victors placed the severed head under or between their thighs and crushed it:

> Then a group came before Flann, and they had the head of Cormac the king; they said to Flann, "Life and health, triumphant powerful king: we have the head of Cormac for you; and as is the custom with kings, raise your thigh, and put this head under it, and crush it with your thigh." *Fragmentary Annals of Ireland*, AD 908 (FA423) (Radner 1978)

However, there are also references to severed heads of elite individuals being treated with considerable respect and even affection, as in this further reference to the treatment of the head of Cormac, king of Munster (a province in the south of Ireland) by Flann, king of Ireland:

> Flann took the head in his hands, and kissed it, and he carried the consecrated head and the true martyr around him three times. After that the head was honourably brought from him to the body, . . . and

it was greatly honoured there, where it produces omens and miracles. *Fragmentary Annals of Ireland*, AD 908 (FA423) (Radner 1978)

The annals even contain tales in which disembodied heads speak and sing:

Then the warrior heard mournful piping and song; and he heard then in the clump of rushes next to him a war chanting that was sweeter than any music. The youth went towards it. "Do not come to me," said the head to him. *Fragmentary Annals of Ireland*, AD 722 (FA178) (Radner 1978)

The annalistic references to decapitation increase in frequency beginning in the ninth century and are specifically mentioned in descriptions of hostilities between the Christian Irish and the pagan Viking groups, such as in the account of this battle in AD 864:

Victory was gained over the foreigners [Vikings], and a slaughter was made of them. Their heads were collected to one place, in the presence of the king. *Annals of the Four Masters*, AD 864 (M864.3) (Connellan 1846)

Viking groups were also recorded to have taken heads. However, as this record from AD 869 may suggest, the chauvinistic Irish annalists described the Vikings' behavior in such detail as to suggest that they regarded it as unorthodox:

His head was later brought to the Norwegians, and they stuck it on a pole, and took turns shooting at it, and afterwards they threw it into the sea. *Fragmentary Annals of Ireland*, AD 869 (FA377) (Radner 1978)

Late Medieval Period (AD 1170–1600)

Dublin was captured by knights of the English king Henry II in 1171 and was to remain under English control for the rest of the Middle Ages and beyond. Human remains were used to powerful effect from the beginning of the English presence, as the Irish annals described in 1172:

Tigernan Ua Ruairc, king of Breifni . . . was killed by the . . . Saxons. He was beheaded also by them and . . . the head was raised over the door of the fortress, a sore, miserable sight for the Irish. The body was hung in another place, with its feet upwards. *Annals of Ulster* (AU1172.2) (Mac Airt and Mac Niocaill 1983)

The Justiciary Rolls, which contain accounts of court rulings of the medieval English colony in Ireland, listed hanging as the standard punishment for

Figure 5.4. The execution by hanging, drawing, and quartering of Hugh Despencer in Hereford (England), 1326. Bibliothèque National de France.

crimes that ranged from stealing to murder (Mills 1905). Offences against the Crown were considered to be more serious and had to have an appropriately worse penalty. Throughout the Middle Ages and indeed up until the early nineteenth century, those convicted of treason were sentenced to be hanged, drawn, and quartered. Contemporary depictions of this act do not survive from Ireland, but a fourteenth-century manuscript by the French artist Jean Froissart contains an image (figure 5.4) of the execution by hanging, drawing, and quartering of Hugh Despencer in Hereford (England) in 1326. This mode of execution followed a standard procedure, and as was the case with most executions, this vivisection was carried out in public. Once the victim was hanged for a short while but not dead, he was castrated, disembowelled ("drawn," contrary to Lewis 2008: 117), and decapitated, and the torso with attached limbs was cut into four portions, with one limb per portion. The head and the quarters were mounted on the city walls.

Excavations along the lines of the medieval walls of Dublin at a number of sites have produced portions of skulls and other human remains that may once have hung on the walls, gates, and towers. Isolde's Tower was located at the northeast corner of the town (figure 5.2). It overlooked the seaward approaches to Dublin and would have been the first portion of the city defenses encountered by anyone approaching the town from the sea. Excavations at the foot of the tower and the adjacent town wall at Essex Street West (figure 5.2) resulted in the recovery of the remains of up to seven adult males. These included portions of at least five skulls as well as portions of a right and left arm. None of the limb bones had any cut marks, but three of the crania had injuries consistent with decapitation. Another cranium bore evidence of a cutting wound but no direct evidence of decapitation. The single cranium from Essex Street West had a blade wound to the right mastoid process as well as blade injuries to the first and fourth vertebrae (see Montgomery, Knüsel, and Tucker this volume for decapitation in Roman Britain). The three injuries to the fourth cervical vertebra indicate that the head was not removed by a single blow, while a small nick on the medial surface of the left lamina of the first cervical vertebra may have been produced by a sharp blade that was pushed up through the vertebral foramen (O'Donnabhain 1995a, 1995b; O'Donnabhain and Cosgrave 1994). The combination of the nature of the injuries to some of these remains and their archaeological context suggests that these represent body parts that were once displayed on the walls of Dublin, the latter skull on a sharp instrument of some kind. Pictorial evidence of this practice survives from the period of the English colony. One of a series of woodcuts published in 1581 shows the Lord Deputy Henry Sidney leaving Dublin Castle in the 1570s to campaign against the rebel Irish (figure 5.5). This work of propaganda depicts the heads of three men mounted on spikes over the gate of the castle. All of the woodcuts in the series were accompanied by verse, and the one that accompanied this particular image states, "There trunckles heddes do plainly showe, each rebels fatall end, And what a haynous crime it is, the Queene for to offend" (Derricke 1883 [1581]: pl. VI).

Figure 5.5. Sir Henry Sidney, Lord Deputy of Ireland, leaves Dublin Castle to campaign against Irish rebels, some of whose heads are displayed above the gate of the castle. Reproduced from Derricke 1883 [1581]: pl. VI.

Early Modern Period (Seventeenth to Nineteenth Centuries)

The penalty of hanging, drawing, and quartering remained on the Statute Books in Ireland and Britain until 1870. However, in practice, the public display of body parts of those accused of serious crime metamorphosed during the eighteenth and nineteenth centuries. While old practices of placing heads on spikes at the city gates survived, bodies of some malefactors were given over to medical schools for public dissection. The bodies of executed criminals were the only legal source of cadavers for dissection prior to the Anatomy Act of 1832, which made the bodies of the poor and destitute available to science (Richardson 1987, 2006). Of over four hundred executions by hanging that were recorded in contemporary newspapers to have taken place in Cork (figure 5.1) between 1712 and 1831, no one was recorded to have been drawn (disembowelled), while in seventeen cases, the body was decapitated after execution. In five of these latter cases, the head was displayed at the city jail. The same newspaper records mention that in twelve cases, bodies were given over to local hospitals for dissection (O'Mahony 1997). This was clearly not intended to offer the prisoner the chance of redemption through a contribution to knowledge, however: the cases that merited dissection involved murders that were obviously perceived to be worse than the usual, as they involved cases of fratricide, uxoricide, murder of a social superior (including a servant who killed his master), and rebellion. An English engraving (figure 5.6) by William Hogarth from 1751 illustrates the practice of public dissection as part

Figure 5.6. Public dissection from Hogarth, *The Four Stages of Cruelty* (1751). Reproduced from Shesgreen 1973: fig. 80.

of the penalty for murder (Shesgreen 1973: fig. 80). Hogarth made a clear analogy between dissection and the practice of hanging, drawing, and quartering, as the image shows the cadaver being disembowelled while the noose is still present around the neck. Hogarth's *Reward of Cruelty* (Shesgreen 1973: fig. 80) was accompanied by the following verses:

> Behold the Villain's dire disgrace,
> Not Death itself can end,
> He finds no peaceful burial place
> His breathless Corpse no friend.
>
> His heart exposed to prying eyes
> To pity has no claim
> But dreadful; from his bones shall rise
> His Monument of Shame.

Discussion

Various commonalities in the examples above can be read as representing similar behaviors regarding the human head in different cultural and temporal contexts. The physical act of cutting off the head and impaling it for display can be attested in each of the different settings. In the three medieval cultural contexts (Irish, Viking, and the English colony), the archaeological evidence for dismembering and decapitation occurs in locations that were centers of social and political power, indicating that the public display of body parts was one means by which such power was exercised and maintained. It also suggests something of the identity of the beheaded: people who were perceived as a threat to that power. This may have taken many forms, but whether criminal, enemy, or traitor, the individual received postmortem treatment suggestive of an identification as "other" (see also Stojanowski and Duncan this volume). There is also a patterning to the location of remains within the centers of power: the heads and body parts tend to occur at the boundaries of the medieval sites. Placing the remains in liminal locations would have amplified the visual messages sent to those both inside and outside the settlement while also reinforcing the symbolic exclusion of those whose body parts were treated in this manner. The display of skulls and quartered bodies resulted in the executed individual continuing to have a strong social presence long after the spectacle of his execution, extending the symbolic resonance of his corporal destruction and thereby amplifying the power of political elites.

Apart from these commonalities, nuanced differences can be discerned between the differing cultural contexts. The early Irish literature clearly indicates that the severed head was taken as a trophy and that this act dishonored one's enemies and provided a means of gaining power over them. The dishonor was further emphasized to the early medieval Irish by actions such as kings placing a severed head under their thighs. However, there is some ambiguity in the contemporary references to the taking of heads, and there are indications of a diversity of cultural understandings. The taker of the skull was occasionally depicted as having a respectful attitude towards the head. Furthermore, tales such as those quoted above of disembodied heads singing and talking and of the head as a source of hidden knowledge suggest that a severed head could be perceived in some circumstances as a potential source of power in itself (see also Bonogofsky and Graham this volume for examples from Melanesia). This theme of the severed head that speaks represents an oblique acknowledgement of the continued social presence of those whose remains were displayed postmortem. It is tempting to relate the idea of severed heads having an intrinsic power to Irish church architecture of the twelfth century; the disembodied human head is an important motif on these churches, almost always occurring at liminal locations such as doorways (figure 5.7). These sculptures may reflect the contemporary Christian understanding of the head as the seat of the soul (Carruthers and Ziolkowski 2002). The theme of the talking severed head suggests that for the early medieval Irish, the separation between the realms of the living and the dead was not clear-cut and that there was a degree of elision between body and soul. In the seventh and eighth centuries, while clerics were writing about the powers of disembodied heads, the death rituals of the early Irish church were spreading to Britain and continental Europe, making an important contribution to the development of the concept of purgatory, where most of the dead wait for admission to heaven (Paxton 1990). This marked a fundamental shift in the relationship between the living and the dead in that the actions of the living in the form of prayer played an essential role in the fate of the souls of the dead. It seems likely that the corollary of this was that the actions of the living in dishonoring the dead could also have a negative influence on the ultimate fate of a soul.

The evidence for trophy heads in Viking Dublin may have had other impetuses. During the tenth century, Dublin changed from being an independent Scandinavian enclave to become dependent on local Irish kings, for whom it was an important source of mercenaries. It was an important player in a fragmented political landscape of ever-shifting alliances and ongoing struggles for dominance. In these circumstances, the display of skulls on the boundaries

Figure 5.7. Detail from a twelfth-century church doorway, Dysert O'Dea, County Clare, Ireland. Photograph by the author.

of the settlement could have been intended to send multiple signals: a visual warning to potential enemies outside the town ramparts but also a powerful indicator to potential allies of the military prowess of the inhabitants of Dublin, a corporate muscle-flexing combined with a pragmatic advertising of martial skills. Although the town remained an important part of the Norse world throughout the tenth century and into the eleventh, there is considerable archaeological evidence for acculturation and hybridization between the Vikings and the Irish in Dublin (O'Donnabhain and Hallgrímsson 2001). When the Norse sagas were written in Iceland in the thirteenth century, the motif of severed heads that talk reappeared (e.g., the head of Mím in the Sigrdrífumál; Hollander 1962). This may reflect the borrowing from the early medieval Irish of cultural understandings of skull collection and display and, maybe more important, of concepts of bodies and souls.

The late medieval practice of hanging, drawing, and quartering was a punishment for offenses against the Crown, and the display of the head and body parts was a message addressed to enemies both within and without. This butchery incorporated features that were designed to intimidate and terrorize both the victim and the broader society with messages of disgrace and damnation, in this world and the next. In common with the other archaeological assemblages detailed here, the late medieval examples discussed above are unlikely to represent random acts; rather, their form and contexts indicate that they represent the product of ritualized, extended executions. Michel Foucault (1975) took an example of this kind of brutality as the starting point for his discussion of the development of the modern prison system, and his perspective provides an interesting lens through which to view the exercise of state power. For Foucault, the principal aim of such ritualized violence was the punishment of the body. In public executions, the body was acted upon and then displayed in a horrific manner. Displaying heads and body parts was just the culmination of a process of torture, public degradation, and vivisection that involved a strong element of public performance in which the triangular relationship of executioner/victim/audience was a crucial component. In the case of hanging, drawing, and quartering for treason, the performance involved the transformation of the body of an insider, a member of the group, to that of an outsider, something that was physically, socially, and spiritually dead (see Stojanowski and Duncan this volume for an inverse process). The transformation from insider to outsider literally involved taking the insides out in a manner designed to cause the greatest horror. Furthermore, the castration of the victim, while being part of the physical destruction of the living person, also symbolized that the traitor's lineage was damned (families of those convicted of treason were often dispossessed of their lands). In an era when most people would have accepted the concept of a corporeal resurrection, the physical separation of the body parts also brought the risk of eternal damnation for the executed individual and a further level of anguish.

The public torture and decapitation of prisoners diminished during the eighteenth and nineteenth centuries throughout Europe; Foucault (1975) argued that this was due to a fundamental change in attitudes towards punishment that involved a shift away from the idea of punishment-as-performance. He linked this to a change in attitudes towards the body and the soul. The physical dismemberment of the human body was central to early performative executions, while in the eighteenth and nineteenth centuries, there was a move away from the demolition of the body. The shift from public torture and death to long-term incarceration in prison meant that the body was acted upon in a fundamentally different manner. Physical torture was replaced by a system in which the body was subjected instead to surveillance and regulation, or as Hogarth put it in 1751, living bodies were "exposed to prying eyes" (Shesgreen 1973: fig. 80). While the body was still central to punishment, the overall aim changed to the reform of the soul. Foucault argued that the conceptualization of the soul changed in the eighteenth century and that this was related to the development of the human sciences, the rational and systematic investigation of the nature of human life that arose out of the Enlightenment. For Foucault (1975), the modern concept of soul is a product of the human sciences, the associated methods of examination and observation, and the particular regime of power and knowledge they produced. This incorporated the Cartesian notion of dualism that, in contrast to the elision suggested by the medieval literature, promoted a greater distinction between body and soul.

Foucault (1975) was not alone in arguing that in the post-Enlightenment era, the ritualized decapitation of enemies, coercion, religion, and other traditional means of maintaining power were gradually replaced by the new agencies of rationalism: science and medicine. In common with other areas of life such as health care and death, punishment was appropriated by science as a form of social control. Punishment moved from the public gaze to something regulated by experts within prison walls. This move out of the public view was related to the ambiguity of the role of observers in the triangle of executioner/ victim/audience at public executions. The crowd was often recorded to have sympathy for the victim (Henry 1994), and this was a potential problem for political elites. Manipulating the composition of the audience was a means of removing this problem. For some crimes that were regarded as particularly heinous, judges included a stipulation that an execution was followed by anatomical dissection. As strategies of control through knowledge and power changed, the bodies of the executed became available for intimate scrutiny and destruction, not by the traditional executioner (whom Foucault [1975: 11] referred to as the "anatomist of pain") but by the new guardians of the political order: men of science.

Decapitation and the violent destruction of bodies probably always have been an integral part of human affairs, and many societies attempt to solve their perceived problems through physical violence (Carman 1997; Walker 2001). Brutal regimes of punishment and dishonor that focus on the physical destruction of the body have been and continue to be features of many political settings. These are culturally determined acts that have motivations and intent beyond the destruction of individuals; even as they reveal socially constructed attitudes towards bodies and souls, they are ultimately about the extension and maintenance of power.

Acknowledgments

I would like to thank the following: John O'Connell for bringing the Cork data to my attention; Nick Hogan for his help with figures 5.1 and 5.2; and Tomás Ó Carragáin for reading and commenting on an earlier draft of this chapter.

References Cited

Carman, J. 1997. Approaches to Violence. In *Material Harm: Archaeological Studies of War and Violence*, edited by J. Carman, 1–23. Cruithne Press, Glasgow.

Carruthers, M. J., and J. M. Ziolkowski. 2002. *The Medieval Craft of Memory: An Anthology of Texts and Pictures*. University of Pennsylvania Press, Philadelphia.

Connellan, O. 1846. *The Annals of Ireland: Translated from the Original Irish of the Four Masters*. Geraghty, Dublin.

Derricke, J. 1883 [1581]. *The Image of Ireland, with a Discoverie of Woodkarne*. Adam and Charles Black, Edinburgh.

Foucault, M. 1975. *Discipline and Punish: The Birth of the Prison*. Penguin, London.

Graham, B. 1997. Ireland and Irishness: Place, Culture and Identity. In *In Search of Ireland: A Cultural Geography*, edited by B. Graham, 1–15. Routledge, London.

Hencken, H. 1936. Ballinderry Crannog, No. 1. *Proceedings of the Royal Irish Academy* 43C: 103–239.

———. 1938. *Cahercommaun, A Stone Fort in Co. Clare, Dublin*. Royal Society of Antiquaries of Ireland, Dublin.

———. 1942. Ballinderry Crannog, No. 2. *Proceedings of the Royal Irish Academy* 47C: 1–76.

———. 1950. Lagore Crannog: An Irish Royal Residence of the 7th to 10th Centuries AD. *Proceedings of the Royal Irish Academy* 53C: 1–247.

Henry, B. 1994. *Dublin Hanged: Crime, Law Enforcement and Punishment in Late Eighteenth Century Dublin*. Irish Academic Press, Dublin.

Hollander, L. M. 1962. *The Poetic Edda*. University of Texas Press, Austin.

Lewis, M. 2008. A Traitor's Death? The Identity of a Drawn, Hanged and Quartered Man from Hulton Abbey, Staffordshire. *Antiquity* 82: 113–124.

Mac Airt, S., and G. Mac Niocaill. 1983. *The Annals of Ulster (to AD1131)*. Dublin Institute for Advanced Studies, Dublin.

Mac Niocaill, G. 1975. *The Medieval Irish Annals*. Dublin Historical Association, Dublin.

Mills, J. 1905. Calendar of the Justiciary Rolls. Proceedings in the Court of the Justiciar of Ireland Preserved in the Public Record Office of Ireland. Public Record Office, Dublin.

O'Donnabhain, B. 1995a. The Human Remains. In *Excavations at Essex Street West, Dublin*, edited by L. Simpson, 117–120. Temple Bar Archaeological Reports 2. Temple Bar Properties, Dublin.

———. 1995b. Monuments of Shame: Some Probable Trophy Heads from Medieval Dublin. *Archaeology Ireland* 9 (4): 12–15.

O'Donnabhain, B., and U. Cosgrave. 1994. The Human Remains. In *Excavations at Isolde's Tower*, edited by L. Simpson, 97–100. Temple Bar Archaeological Reports 1. Temple Bar Properties, Dublin.

O'Donnabhain, B., and B. Hallgrímsson. 2001. Dublin: The Biological Identity of the Hiberno-Norse Town. In *Medieval Dublin II*, edited by S. Duffy, 65–87. Four Courts Press, Dublin.

O'Mahony, C. 1997. *In The Shadows: Life in Cork, 1750–1930*. Tower Books, Cork, Ireland.

O'Sullivan, A. 1998. *The Archaeology of Lake Settlement in Ireland*. Royal Irish Academy, Dublin.

Paxton, F. S. 1990. *Christianizing Death: The Creation of a Ritual Process in Early Medieval Europe*. Cornell University Press, Ithaca, New York.

Radner, J. N. 1978. *Fragmentary Annals of Ireland*. Dublin Institute for Advanced Studies, Dublin.

Richardson, R. 1987. *Death, Dissection and the Destitute*. Routledge and Kegan Paul, London.

———. 2006. Human Dissection and Organ Donation: A Historical and Social Background. *Mortality* 11 (2): 151–165.

Shesgreen, S. 1973. *Engravings by Hogarth*. Dover, New York.

Walker, P. L. 2001. A Bioarchaeological Perspective on the History of Violence. *Annual Review of Anthropology* 30: 573–596.

PART II

Bioarchaeological and Biochemical Approaches

6

Identifying the Origins of Decapitated Male Skeletons from 3 Driffield Terrace, York, through Isotope Analysis

Reflections of the Cosmopolitan Nature of Roman York in the Time of Caracalla

JANET MONTGOMERY, CHRISTOPHER J. KNÜSEL, AND KATIE TUCKER

In August 2004, beneath the former gardens of an eighteenth-century mansion on Driffield Terrace, in the city of York, United Kingdom, the York Archaeological Trust revealed part of a large, highly unusual nonattritional Roman period cemetery population comprising eighty individuals, forty-eight (60 percent) of whom had been decapitated from behind with a very fine, sharp blade; the heads were placed in the graves with the rest of the body but not in anatomical position. Investigators recognized very early that this was an extremely unusual, if not unique, finding because of the very high proportion of decapitated adult males, a practice that had been encountered previously only sporadically in contemporary cemeteries. The cemetery is located southwest of the city walls, near the main Leeds-to-York road at the Mount, which is the highest point in the area and on the edge of the largest glacial moraine in Britain (Clark et al. 2004).

To investigate whether the origins of the decapitated individuals were as unusual as the cemetery population profile, investigators selected six adult male individuals for lead, strontium, and oxygen isotope analysis. Isotope analysis of archaeological human remains has been used for over twenty years to provide evidence for geographical origins using these three systems (Molleson et al. 1986; Sealy et al. 1995; White et al. 1998; Price et al. 2006). Elements present in ingested food and water are incorporated into teeth and bones. Because isotope ratios of some elements vary geographically, and on the assumption that ancient people sourced the bulk of their diet locally, these differences can be used as proxy indicators to draw conclusions about whether individuals were of local or nonlocal origin (see Forgey this volume for an exploration of Nasca trophy head origins using ancient DNA). Tooth enamel, a skeletal tissue that is highly resistant to alteration during life and after burial (Ericson 1993; Wang and Cerling 1994; Hoppe et al. 2003; Trickett et al. 2003; Montgomery, Evans, and Cooper 2007), represents childhood origins and diet and is, therefore, a useful tissue for investigations of whether early-life residency is consistent with the place of burial.

Strontium derives from rocks, and its isotope ratios are indicative of the surface geology or, in some regions, unconsolidated drift (such as loess) of the home region (Bentley 2006). Oxygen isotope ratios of rainfall vary geographically with latitude, altitude, and distance from the sea; because the ratio of biogenic phosphate is related to that of drinking water, oxygen ratios provide an indication of the climatic regime prevailing in the home region (Dansgaard et al. 1975; Longinelli 1984; Fricke et al. 1995). The oxygen isotope ratios measured in either the phosphate (used in this study) or carbonate fraction of tooth enamel can be converted to precipitation and thus compared to contour maps of $\delta^{18}O$ values of precipitation such as those for Britain produced by Darling and colleagues (Darling et al. 2003; Darling and Talbot 2003). There are several published calibration equations (Longinelli 1984; Luz et al. 1984; Levinson et al. 1987; D'Angela and Longinelli 1991; Iacumin et al. 1996; Evans, Chenery, and Fitzpatrick 2006; Hoppe et al. 2006; Daux et al. 2008; Chenery et al. 2010) but no consensus as to which is the "right" one. All will provide slightly different results, and even the most accurate equation may change with location, climate, culture, and time period. Given this current uncertainty, and because we do not always know where people were sourcing their water (e.g., wells, springs, rivers, lakes) or whether they modified it subsequently through boiling or brewing, all of which could affect the local oxygen isotope ratio considerably (Darling et al. 2003; Brettell 2008; Daux et al. 2008), allowing for a larger margin of error than simply the analytical uncertainty when interpreting oxygen isotope ratios is probably wise. This approach has been used in this chapter.

As outlined for strontium, lead isotopes record the geological origin of the lead and enter the food chain through soils, water, plants, and animals. Prior to the large-scale metal production and transport that occurred during the Roman period (Hong et al. 1994; Rosman et al. 1997), lead may thus provide similar information to that associated with strontium. However, following the widespread extraction and use of lead ore for metal products, which in England occurred during the Roman period (Tylecote 1992; Montgomery 2002; Budd et al. 2004), the natural lead compositions of humans are frequently swamped by anthropogenic lead and provide evidence of the cultural sphere they inhabited rather than geographical origin. In conjunction with the levels of lead present, the lead isotope ratio can, therefore, provide information about an individual's exposure to anthropogenic metals and pollution and may be able to discriminate between urban and rural populations (Montgomery 2002; Montgomery et al. 2005).

The Geological Setting

The Vale of York is an extensive, low-lying, alluvial basin that was once a large glacial lake but is now a rolling landscape of glacial deposits and flat floodplains. The bedrock geology of the vale (figure 6.1) and of the wider Yorkshire region comprises a sedimentary sequence of silicate and marine carbonates that increase with age from east to west (British Geological Survey 2001). The

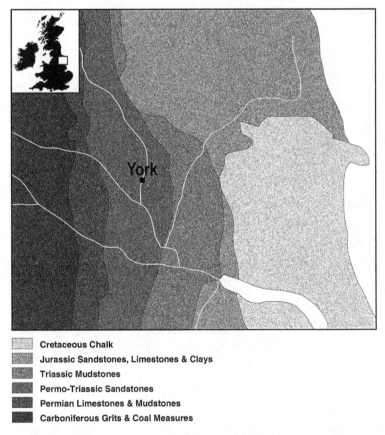

Cretaceous Chalk
Jurassic Sandstones, Limestones & Clays
Triassic Mudstones
Permo-Triassic Sandstones
Permian Limestones & Mudstones
Carboniferous Grits & Coal Measures

Figure 6.1. Simplified geological sketch map of the Yorkshire region of the British Isles, centered on the city of York. The map shows the sequence of sedimentary rocks of increasing age from east to west. Unconsolidated drift deposits in the Vale of York are not shown.

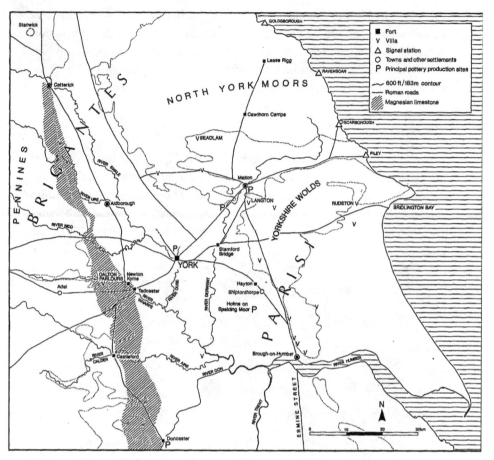

Figure 6.2. Roman York in regional context. Courtesy Patrick Ottaway.

Permo-Triassic sandstones and marls that crop out in the York region are largely concealed by Quaternary sediments, principally of glacial, lacustrine, aeolian, and riverine origin (British Geological Survey 1977). The city of York, and Driffield Terrace in particular (Ottaway 2005), is located on the largest glacial moraine in Britain (Clark et al. 2004), which stands above the marshy lowland of the valley of the Ouse. The North York Moors, Hambleton Hills, and Howardian Hills, which are formed mainly of Jurassic sandstones, clays, and limestones, form the eastern boundary along with the Yorkshire Wolds, which largely consist of Cretaceous Chalk. On its western side, the vale is flanked by low foothills of Permian Magnesian limestones, beyond which are the Carboniferous uplands of the Pennines.

The Site

Graced with the social amenities familiar to the Roman world—baths, temples, and other public and private buildings—York (Eboracum; figure 6.2), founded by the Romans in AD 71, was the site of a legionary fortress and colonia (settlement of Roman citizens) and was an imperial residence on two occasions: during the reign of Septimius Severus (AD 193–211) and that of Constantine the Great (ca. AD 274–337). The Mount was the area through which the road to Tadcaster (Roman Calcaria) ran. It was lined with tombstones and *mausolea*, some of which were recovered during building works in the eighteenth through early twentieth centuries (Ottaway 1993). A large cemetery was also excavated in the 1950s at Trentholme Drive (Wenham 1968), and a few burials from the Mount have been excavated since, but the present sample of eighty burials is the largest found since the 1950s. The area of the cemetery from which the burials were recovered was located at the highest point in the local landscape, on a small, steep glacial moraine, as noted above. The Trentholme Drive cemetery, which apparently did not contain any decapitated burials, was at the foot of, rather than on, this prominent landscape feature (figure 6.3).

In total, eighty skeletons were recovered from two separate excavations conducted between 2004 and 2005 (Hunter-Mann 2005; Ottaway 2005) on the properties of 1–3 and 6 Driffield Terrace, less than 50 meters apart (this number includes a single inhumation excavated during building work at 129 The Mount). They were subjected to full osteological analysis, including the compilation of a skeletal inventory, assessment of age and sex, collection of metric and nonmetric data, and recording and photographing of pathological conditions.

The burials on both sites appeared to follow no specific alignment, and there was some intercutting of graves, indicating that the burials had occurred over a period of time (figure 6.4). Four individuals from 1–3 Driffield Terrace were interred as double burials (Ottaway 2005; figure 6.5 [SK15, SK16]), with individual skeletons placed directly on top of one another, while 6 Driffield Terrace had one double burial, one triple burial, and one burial with four individuals (Hunter-Mann 2005). The evidence indicates contemporaneous burial of multiple individuals within single graves. Only four individuals out of the fifty-six excavated from 1–3 Driffield Terrace had been buried in coffins (Ottaway 2005), while nearly all of the graves excavated from 6 Driffield Terrace contained evidence for coffins (Hunter-Mann 2005). Evidence for grave goods, shoes, and clothing was limited. Two individuals had pottery vessels,

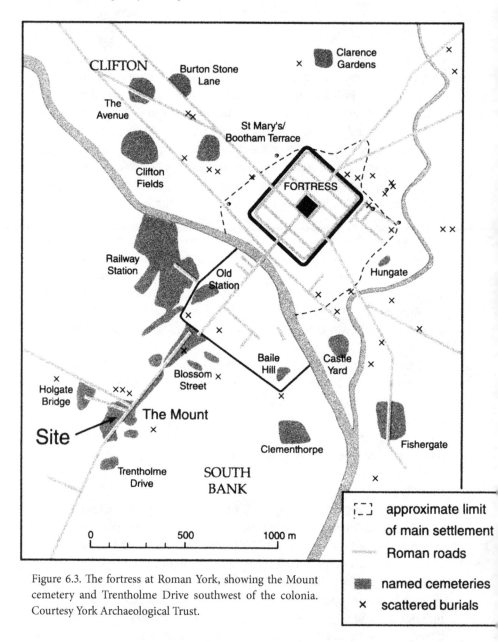

Figure 6.3. The fortress at Roman York, showing the Mount cemetery and Trentholme Drive southwest of the colonia. Courtesy York Archaeological Trust.

and two were buried with the partial skeletons of chickens (Ottaway 2005), while five individuals from the site were buried with hobnail boots (*calcei*). The presence of hobnail boots in the grave of one individual from 6 Driffield Terrace was the only evidence for shoes or clothing from any of the graves at this site (Hunter-Mann 2005).

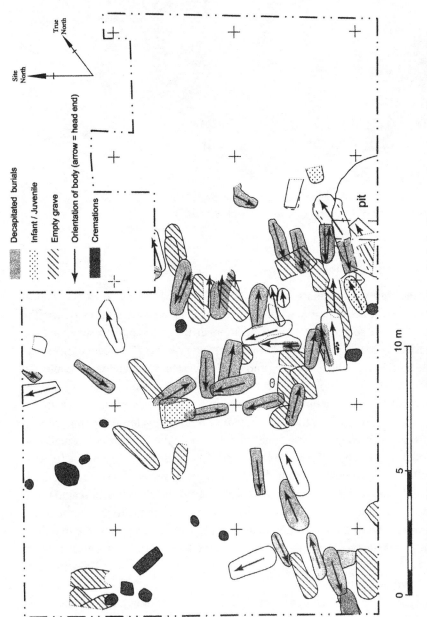

Figure 6.4. Plan view of the cemetery at 3 Driffield Terrace, showing the lack of any consistent grave alignment and the intercutting of burials. Courtesy York Archaeological Trust.

Figure 6.5. Double burial of decapitated individuals SK15 (4146) and SK16 (4147) from 3 Driffield Terrace. Courtesy York Archaeological Trust.

The Decapitations

Of the eighty individuals from Driffield Terrace, forty-five had osteological evidence for decapitation, with another three having contextual evidence (the head not in correct anatomical position in the grave but no surviving cut marks due to loss of relevant elements); this represents 79 percent of the sixty-one individuals who had crania and cervical vertebrae surviving. Cuts affected vertebrae from the uppermost cervical (C-1) to the second thoracic (T-2) (figures 6.6, 6.7), and the number of cuts on individual skeletons ranged from one or two cuts, which was the most common finding, to eleven separate cuts on six of the cervical vertebrae from the same individual. Seven individuals also had cuts to the mandible, and three had cuts to the mastoid process (usually associated with cuts through the upper cervical vertebrae), while one individual had a cut to the clavicle, one had cuts to the clavicle and scapula, and one had cuts to the first rib; all of these were associated with cuts through the thoracic vertebrae. Two individuals also had numerous cuts to the mandible with large parts of the bone missing (figure 6.8 [SK33]). Decapitation alone is unlikely to have produced such cuts, and they may represent deliberate acts of facial disfigurement.

Where the cuts through the vertebrae could be assigned a direction, the vast majority came from the posterior (see figure 6.7). Where cuts originated anteriorly, the individual also had cuts from the posterior. The nature of the cut marks suggests that a very fine and sharp blade was used to chop through the neck, as the majority of the vertebrae were sliced through their full

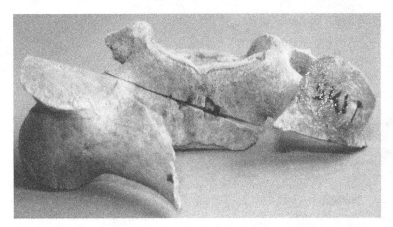

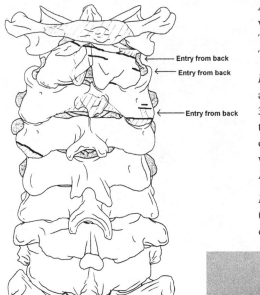

Entry from back

Entry from back

Entry from back

Above: Figure 6.6. Cleanly bisected cervical vertebra from SK17 (4130), 3 Driffield Terrace. Courtesy York Archaeological Trust.

Left: Figure 6.7. Posterior view of cervical and upper thoracic vertebrae of SK47 (4471), 3 Driffield Terrace, showing multiple cuts to the posterior of the vertebrae. Original diagram produced by Caroline Needham with additions by authors. Courtesy York Archaeological Trust.

Below: Figure 6.8. Mandible from SK33 (4253), 3 Driffield Terrace, showing multiple cuts. Courtesy York Archaeological Trust.

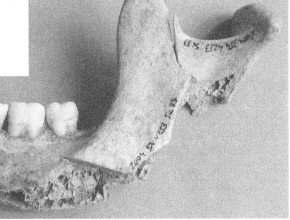

Figure 6.9. Decapitated individual SK37 (4344) from 3 Driffield Terrace, buried wearing heavy iron rings around his ankles. Courtesy York Archaeological Trust.

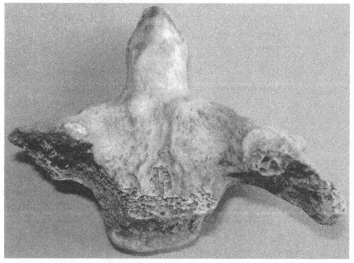

Figure 6.10. Second cervical vertebra of decapitated individual SK37 (4344) from 3 Driffield Terrace, depicting rougher cut to the inferior arch and body. Courtesy York Archaeological Trust.

thickness from a single blow with very little fracturing and fragmentation of the bones, although there was some splitting of the laminae. The only exception to this was, perhaps significantly, the individual buried with the iron rings around his ankles (figure 6.9 [SK37]), whose second cervical vertebra was cut and fractured (figure 6.10), which may suggest that a different type of weapon or a different method was used to perform this decapitation. The polishing (smoothness) of the cut surfaces indicates that the cuts were perimortem and that the bone contained the same amount of collagen as it did in life (Wenham 1989). The splitting of the laminae indicates that the musculature and ligaments were present and intact when the decapitation took place (Boylston et al. 2000: 246).

Decapitations have been found during previous excavations of a number of Romano-British cemeteries. Philpott (1991: 79–80) notes ninety-eight examples of decapitated burials with a frequency of 6.1 percent of all inhumations from cemeteries where decapitation was found. Roberts and Cox's (2003: 158) study, which includes information from sites discovered after the publication of Philpott's survey, reports fifty-eight decapitations (5.5 percent of the total number of inhumations from relevant cemeteries). The largest number of affected individuals from any one site was fifteen out of ninety-four burials (16 percent) from Cassington, Oxfordshire (Clarke 1979: 373), followed by twelve out of eighty-eight burials (14 percent) from Kempston, Bedfordshire (Boylston et al. 2000). The percentage of affected individuals from Driffield Terrace, using the ratio of decapitated individuals to the total number of inhumations, is therefore nearly four times higher than that recorded for any other Romano-British cemetery. Philpott (1991: 79) notes all ages and both sexes among the decapitated individuals, with a large number of older women represented, while Boylston (2000: 368) notes that a small number of children and infants also were decapitated. All of the cemeteries where decapitation has been found appear to be normal attritional cemeteries with both sexes and a full range of ages represented among both the decapitated individuals and the cemetery population as a whole. This is not the case for the Driffield Terrace cemetery.

Various authors have noted that the most common method of decapitation was from the front of the body, with precise, incised cuts (e.g., Harman et al. 1981: 165; Philpott 1991: 80; Boylston 2000: 368). This observation has led many writers to interpret the decapitations as some form of postmortem burial rite (Clarke 1979; Harman et al. 1981; Philpott 1991). One of the few previously recorded exceptions to this pattern is the set of six decapitated individuals from Cirencester, Gloucestershire, in which five of the decapitations were performed from behind (four males and one female) with an extremely sharp blade. Wells (1982: 194) interpreted these decapitated individuals as victims of penal execution. Execution is also the preferred explanation for decapitations from the Anglo-Saxon period; decapitations occurred from behind, and individuals were often buried in awkward positions with the hands positioned as though tied (Reynolds 1997; Hayman and Reynolds 2005).

In addition to the decapitations, five individuals, four of whom had been decapitated (SK3, SK8, SK16, SK45), had other perimortem blade injuries. Two of these (SK8, SK16) were stabbing wounds that would have penetrated the soft tissues of the lower abdomen, and one (SK45) was a cut to the distal femur that would have sliced through the muscles of the thigh. These injuries may represent attempts to incapacitate the individual. The other two (SK3, SK15) perimortem blade injuries are "parry"-type fractures to the forearm and hand, which often occur when an individual attempts to defend the face and head from attack. Sixteen individuals (ten of whom were decapitated; one nondecapitation was a six- to seven-year-old child) had evidence for perimortem cranial trauma, the majority of which were blunt force. Out of the total of eighty inhumations, fifty-five were decapitated or had perimortem blade injuries or cranial trauma (68.7 percent, or 90.1 percent of the sixty-one individuals who had crania and cervical vertebrae). The patterns seen in this population are different from nearly all of the Romano-British cemeteries where decapitations have been recorded. One interpretation is that the Driffield Terrace decapitations represent some form of execution of the sort suggested for Cirencester and the Anglo-Saxon period.

Demographic Profile

The population from Driffield Terrace comprises mostly young- to middle-adult males with an average stature 3.5 centimeters above the average for males from Roman Britain (see Werner 1998: 39; Conheeney 2000: 286; Roberts and Cox 2003: 142). Of the eighty individuals, only six (7.5 percent) were under the age of 18 at the time of death: two fetuses/neonates (up to one month old), one young child (1–6 years), one older child (7–12 years), and two adolescents (13–18 years). An additional three individuals (3.8 percent) were either adolescents or young adults (around 16–25 years). Of the adult individuals, ten (12.5 percent) could not be assigned to a more precise age cohort. Of the remaining sixty-one adults, the majority (*n*=45, or 56.3 percent of the eighty individuals) died between the ages of 26 and 45; fourteen died as young adults (19–25 years); only two individuals lived past age 45. This age structure does not reflect the expected pattern for preindustrial populations, in which the youngest age classes experience very high mortality, with a decline toward adolescence (figure 6.11); mortality rates rise again in young adulthood, but the majority of individuals survive into mature adulthood (Chamberlain 2000: 106). This profile, which describes an attritional cemetery population, is better seen in the Roman cemetery in eastern London, where 25 percent of the individuals were 18 years old or younger at the time of death, 31 percent of deaths occurred

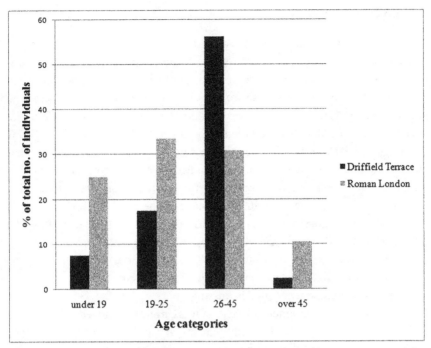

Figure 6.11. Differences in age structure in the populations from Driffield Terrace and the eastern cemetery of Roman London.

between the ages of 26 and 45, and 10.5 percent of individuals survived past the age of 45 (Werner 1998).

At York, 88.8 percent of the population (*n*=71) were adults, not counting those three individuals who were either adolescents or young adults; only 7.5 percent of the York cemetery population was 18 years or younger. Compared with the pattern seen in London, the York sample has double the number of individuals dying between the ages of 26 and 45 and far too few subadults and mature adults. This would suggest that the population from York does not represent a normal attritional cemetery population (see Gowland and Chamberlain 2005). The fracture profile of the population seems to relate to interpersonal violence, with the majority killed by decapitation (i.e., decapitation is the mode of death) or after having sustained blows to the head or postcranial blade injuries. The age profile of the cemetery, with all individuals being male or probable male, suggests a military context, a premise that is supported by the taller-than-average stature for the population, since the Roman army had height standards for recruits (Friedl 1992: 35).

Methods and Samples

Six of the adult male skeletons excavated from 3 Driffield Terrace were selected by one of us (Tucker) for isotope analysis (table 6.1). The individuals included two nondecapitated skeletons (SK10 and SK35) representative of
other nondecapitated individuals from the site; one double decapitation burial
(SK15 and SK16; their heads were switched at the time of burial [see figure
6.5]); and two decapitated individuals (SK33 and SK37), one of whom (SK37
[see figure 6.9]) was wearing heavy iron rings on each ankle, which appear
to have been cold-forged onto his legs some considerable time prior to death
(Rogers 2005), based on infections of the tibiae and fibulae. The head of SK37
(see figure 6.9) was found by his left tibia, and the head of SK33 (mandible
depicted in figure 6.8) was found beyond his feet. As is typical for this site,
the latter four individuals had been decapitated by cuts through the cervical
vertebrae: SK15, by cuts to C-3 to C-4; SK16, by cuts to C-6; SK33, by cuts to
C-1 to C-5; and SK37, by cuts to C-2, with additional cuts to the parietals and
left temporal, while the occipital is missing.

A small sample of enamel and dentine was carefully removed with a dental
saw from a second or third mandibular molar from the six male skeletons
(table 6.1) and cleaned of all surface tissue using tungsten carbide dental burrs.
Although the recently excavated teeth had not been glued into the alveolar
bone, they were found to be stuck fast, probably as a result of the clay burial
soil, and this made the teeth extremely difficult to remove without damaging the surrounding alveolar bone. Because of the importance of undertak-
ing this work with minimal destruction, the enamel was removed while the
teeth remained in situ in the mandible. Consequently, and as a result of tooth

Table 6.1. Sample details of individuals examined by isotope analysis

Context no.	Skeleton	Sex	Age (years)	Tooth sampled	Notes
4089	SK10	Male	36–45	M2 lower left	Nondecapitated control
4146	SK15	Male	26–35	M3 lower right	Decapitated double burial—skull found with SK16's postcranial skeleton
4147	SK16	Male	36–45	M3 lower right	Decapitated double burial—skull found with SK15's postcranial skeleton
4253	SK33	Male	26–35	M2 lower right	Decapitated
4263	SK35	Male	36–45	M2 lower right	Nondecapitated control
4344	SK37	Male	36–45	M2 lower right	Decapitated, shackled

morphology and alignment, for two individuals (the double burial of SK15 and SK16) the enamel could not be removed from the second molars without the risk of damaging the teeth on either side, so the third molar was sampled. Second mandibular molar tooth crowns mineralize between the ages of 2.5 and 8 years (Gustafson and Koch 1974), while the timing of enamel formation in third molars can be assumed to derive from the period of life from approximately 10 to 16 years of age, although the development and age of eruption of this tooth is the most variable of all the permanent teeth (Hillson 1996). Enamel preservation for all teeth was graded as good following the methods of Montgomery (2002).

The enamel samples were removed and sealed in containers and transferred to the clean laboratories at the Natural Environment Research Council (NERC) Isotope Geosciences Laboratory (NIGL), Nottingham, United Kingdom. The isotope compositions of strontium and lead were obtained using a Finnigan MAT262 thermal ionization multicollector mass spectrometer. The reproducibility of the international strontium standard, NBS987, during a period of analysis did not exceed ±0.000030 (2σ), or ±0.004 percent (2σ). All samples were corrected to the accepted value of $^{87}Sr/^{86}Sr=0.710250$ to ensure that there was no induced bias through mass spectrometer drift. Strontium isotope data are presented as $^{87}Sr/^{86}Sr$ ratios. Lead isotope fractionation was monitored with suitable-sized (20ng) runs using NBS981, and data were corrected for fractionation using the associated standards run. Reproducibility of the isotope ratios, based on repeated determinations of the NBS981 standard (2σ, $n=19$), are as follows: ±0.15 percent for $^{208}Pb/^{204}Pb$; ±0.11 percent for $^{207}Pb/^{204}Pb$; ±0.07 percent for $^{206}Pb/^{204}Pb$; ±0.04 percent for $^{207}Pb/^{206}Pb$; and ±0.08 percent for $^{208}Pb/^{206}Pb$. Laboratory contamination, monitored by procedural blanks for both lead and strontium, was negligible.

The oxygen isotope ratios of silver phosphate obtained from enamel using a modified method of O'Neil and colleagues (1994) were measured by continuous-flow isotope ratio mass spectrometry (CFIRMS) using a TC/EA (high-temperature-conversion elemental analyzer) coupled to a Thermo Finnigan Delta Plus XL isotope ratio mass spectrometer via a ConFlo III interface. Samples were analyzed in triplicate, corrected, and converted to the Standard Mean Ocean Water (SMOW) scale against NBS120C in-house reference material. The reproducibility over the analytical period for NBS120C and "batch control" ACC1 were ±0.18‰ and ±0.15‰, respectively. The measured ratios were converted to drinking-water values using the equation of Levinson and colleagues (1987) after a correction of +1.4‰:

$$\delta^{18}O_{\text{Drinking Water}} = (\delta^{18}O_{\text{Phosphate Oxygen}} -19.4) / 0.46$$

Table 6.2. Isotope data

Sample no.	Tissue	$\delta^{18}O\ PO_4$ [a]	$\delta^{18}O_{dw}$ [b]	$\delta^{18}O_{dw}$ [c]	Sr ppm	$^{87}Sr/^{86}Sr$ [d]	Pb ppm	$^{206}Pb/^{204}Pb$ [e]	$^{207}Pb/^{204}Pb$	$^{208}Pb/^{204}Pb$	$^{207}Pb/^{206}Pb$	$^{208}Pb/^{206}Pb$
DRIF-10	Enamel	15.0	-12.6	-11.3	67	0.709563	1.1	18.42	15.54	38.21	0.844	2.076
DRIF-10	Dentine				153	0.709077						
DRIF-15	Enamel	18.9	-4.1	-4.5	73	0.714202	1.8	18.37	15.58	38.23	0.848	2.081
DRIF-15	Dentine				216	0.711442						
DRIF-16	Enamel	17.7	-6.8	-6.7	71	0.709407	0.4	18.39	15.55	38.24	0.846	2.079
DRIF-16	Dentine				177	0.710044						
DRIF-33	Enamel	17.4	-7.4	-7.1	131	0.708920	0.7	18.46	15.57	38.31	0.843	2.075
DRIF-35	Enamel	17.4	-7.3	-7.1	67	0.709401	2.4	18.50	15.58	38.33	0.842	2.072
DRIF-37	Enamel	18.2	-5.7	-5.8	42	0.708924	0.7	Pb isotope sample failed				

[a] Mean enamel phosphate. External and sample reproducibility was estimated at ±0.18‰ (1σ).
[b] Calculated using Levinson's equation (Levinson et al. 1987) after correction for the difference between the average published values for NBS120C and NBS120B used by Levinson.
[c] Calculated using Daux et al. 2008: Equation 4.
[d] External reproducibility was estimated at ±0.004% (2σ).
[e] External reproducibility was estimated at ±0.15% for $^{208}Pb/^{204}Pb$; ±0.11% for $^{207}Pb/^{204}Pb$; ±0.07% for $^{206}Pb/^{204}Pb$; ±0.04% for $^{207}Pb/^{206}Pb$; and ±0.08% for $^{208}Pb/^{206}Pb$ (2σ, n=19).

The correction accounts for the difference between the best estimate (+20.0±0.5‰) for NBS120B, applicable to Levinson's calibration data, with the NIGL value for NBS120B of +21.4‰ (Chenery et al. 2010). This latter value is the equivalent of the modern standard (NBS120C) value at NIGL of $\delta^{18}O$=21.71±0.35‰ (1σ, n=11). The NIGL value for NBS120C is in agreement with the international recognized value for NBS120C (Chenery et al. 2010). Drinking-water values were also calibrated using Equation 4 of Daux and colleagues (2008); this equation produces comparable $\delta^{18}O$‰ values, which, given analytical reproducibility and the difficulties in accounting for seasonal variation or the cultural modification of drinking water, would not significantly alter the interpretation of the values presented here (table 6.2).

Results and Discussion

Lead Isotope Analysis

The enamel lead concentrations for the six individuals range from 0.4 to 2.4 parts per million (ppm). When compared to data for archaeological British populations, these are not unusually high concentrations (figure 6.12) and reflect a childhood snapshot of exposure rather than the long-term accumulation in adult tissues. To put this in a modern context, a study of living children at the Broken Hill lead-mining community in Australia by Gulson and colleagues (Gulson, Howarth, et al. 1994; Gulson, Mizon, et al. 1994; Gulson and Wilson 1994; Gulson et al. 1996) concluded that low exposure resulted in enamel-lead concentrations of <2 ppm, whereas high exposure produced enamel-lead concentrations of ~2–10 ppm. In Britain, pre-Roman populations usually have enamel lead levels of <1 ppm (figure 6.12), and the lead tends to have variable isotope ratios that reflect the composition of local rocks (and therefore geographic origins) rather than exposure to anthropogenic pollution such as water from lead pipes, food and drink produced in lead cooking pots, food additives, medicaments, inhalation of airborne pollutants, or accidental ingestion of lead in the environment via dust from dirty hands (Montgomery et al. forthcoming).

From the Roman period onwards, lead concentrations tend to rise, and this is coupled with a "cultural focusing" (Montgomery et al. 2005) of the $^{207}Pb/^{206}Pb$ ratio to ~0.846, which is characteristic of English ore lead (Rohl 1996). The lead isotope sample for SK37 failed. SK35 is therefore unusual in that the concentration indicates exposure to anthropogenic ore sources but the source of the lead does not seem to be solely from English deposits. This may also apply to SK10 and SK33, whose lead isotope ratios differ from those

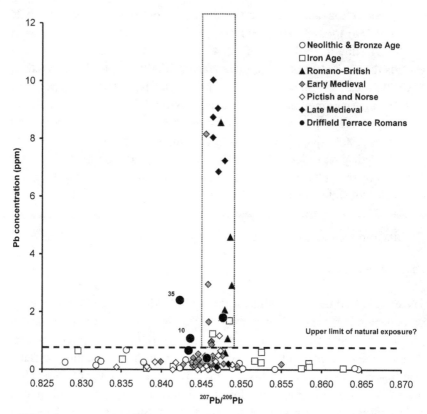

Figure 6.12. Plot of enamel lead concentrations against lead isotope ratio for the Driffield Terrace individuals in comparison with data for British individuals since the Neolithic. The plot illustrates the "cultural focusing" of lead isotope signatures as a result of anthropogenic extraction and use of metals: individuals with high levels of lead all have $^{207}Pb/^{206}Pb$ ratios ~0.846. SK35 and SK10 display unusual lead compositions for pre-nineteenth-century British individuals. Data sources: Montgomery 2002; Montgomery et al. 2005; Montgomery 2009; Montgomery et al. forthcoming.

obtained from other late-Roman period individuals excavated in England (figure 6.13). In contrast, SK15 and SK16 both have lead isotope compositions that are entirely consistent with exposure to English ore lead sources. Such lead ratios indicate exposure to sources of younger lead such as the Mesozoic ore deposits of the Mediterranean region (Stos-Gale et al. 1997; Boni et al. 2000; Sayre et al. 2001). Unfortunately, as a consequence of the extensive mining and transport to continental Europe of metal resources during the Roman period, exposure to English ore lead (or other ore sources with similar isotope ratios) could have occurred anywhere in the Roman Empire where such lead was exported and used (Boni et al. 2000). The lead data can thus provide no

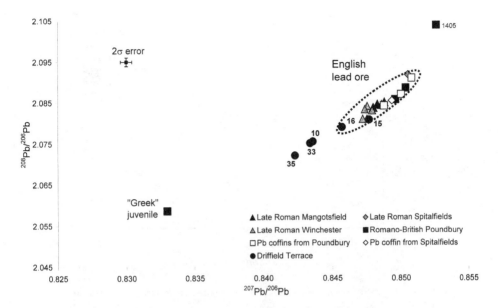

Figure 6.13. Plot of enamel lead isotope ratios of the Driffield Terrace individuals (SK37 missing) with other data from contemporary burials from England. The vast majority of individuals with a lead concentration >1 ppm fall within the field of English ore lead (denoted by the dashed oval), as do all the lead coffins. The "Greek" juvenile from Poundbury has a very different ratio, but this is consistent with the English Chalk from which it was excavated. SK35, SK33, and SK10 fall outside the English ore lead field. Data sources: Montgomery 2002; Montgomery et al. forthcoming; for Poundbury, Molleson et al. 1986.

evidence for specific origins but do indicate that SK35 and possibly SK10 and SK33 are inconsistent with cultural exposure to solely English lead pollution and may be explained by exposure to pollution of a different origin during the first sixteen years of life.

Strontium Isotope Analysis

The enamel strontium isotope ratios and compositions of the six individuals range from 0.70892 to 0.71420. The range of published ratios for human tooth enamel from England is not much larger than this: most tend to fall within 0.707 and 0.714 (Montgomery 2002; Evans and Tatham 2004; Montgomery et al. 2005; Evans, Chenery, and Fitzpatrick 2006; Evans, Stoodley, and Chenery 2006; Montgomery, Cooper, and Evans 2007). Similarly, the range of strontium concentrations is 42–131 ppm, which is consistent with values obtained from modern and archaeological humans in England, where concentrations of ~50–150 ppm are usually found (Montgomery 2002; Brown et al. 2004;

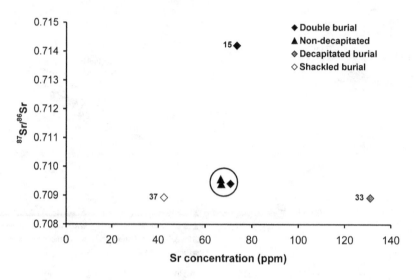

Figure 6.14. Plot of strontium isotope ratios against strontium concentrations of the Driffield Terrace individuals. The circle encloses a cluster of three individuals (SK10, SK16, SK35) who have very similar strontium compositions. 2σ errors for the strontium isotope ratios are contained within the symbols.

Evans and Tatham 2004; Montgomery et al. 2005; Evans, Chenery, and Fitzpatrick 2006; Evans, Stoodley, and Chenery 2006; Montgomery, Cooper, and Evans 2007). Figure 6.14 shows that three individuals cluster together (SK10, SK16, SK35) and the remaining three are separated on the basis of their isotope ratio or their strontium concentration.

For three of the teeth analyzed, a sample of the crown dentine was also processed. In modern individuals, these two co-genetic tissues have the same strontium isotope ratio, and because neither subsequently remodels, they retain these values until burial (Montgomery 2002). Although enamel is highly resistant to postmortem diagenesis, buried dentine, particularly in the case of its strontium composition, tends to equilibrate with the soil (Budd et al. 2000; Hoppe et al. 2003; Trickett et al. 2003), and a change in strontium isotope ratio towards that of the soil pore fluid is usually present, coupled with an increase in strontium concentration (Montgomery 2002). Diagenetic mixing vectors between enamel and crown dentine from the same tooth can, therefore, in the absence of environmental samples, be used to provide an estimate of the local soil strontium values rather than providing information from the individual's lifetime (Montgomery, Evans, and Cooper 2007). This is illustrated in figure 6.15, and while none of the three samples is likely to have entirely

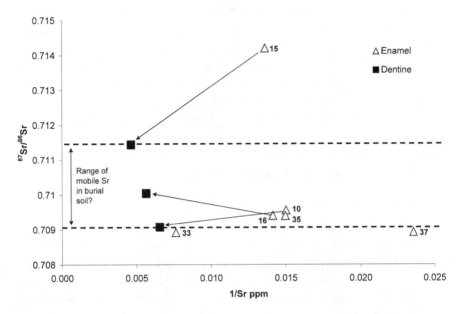

Figure 6.15. A plot of strontium isotope ratios against the inverse strontium concentration for enamel and, for three teeth, crown dentine of Driffield Terrace individuals. Diagenetic vectors for enamel-dentine pairs are shown and used to estimate the possible range of strontium present at the site. The cluster of three individuals (SK10, SK16, SK35) that fall within this range indicates that these three have a strontium composition consistent with local values.

equilibrated with the mobile strontium in the burial soil, the mobile strontium in the glacial drift overlying the Permo-Triassic bedrock of York is likely to have a ^{87}Sr/^{86}Sr ratio somewhere between 0.7090 and 0.7115. This is a wider range than the 0.7096 to 0.7105 previously suggested for Triassic biospheres (Montgomery et al. 2009).

The range illustrated in figure 6.15 is likely to be too wide (given that it is produced from only three incompletely equilibrated dentine samples) but may simply reflect the heterogeneity of the minerals and source rocks within the glacial till. Biosphere ratios between 0.7090 and 0.7105 would be consistent with Jurassic and Triassic sedimentary silicate rocks in England (Montgomery 2002; Evans and Tatham 2004; Montgomery et al. 2006; Montgomery et al. 2009), and these rocks may all have contributed to the glacial till in the area (Clark et al. 2004). The cluster of three individuals—SK10, SK16, and SK35—falls within this 0.7090–0.7105 range, which adds weight to the suggestion that these individuals were local residents. In contrast, SK33 and SK37 have lower strontium isotope ratios (<0.709) that are indicative of origins in regions of marine carbonates such as chalk and limestones (Montgomery et al. 2000; Evans and Tatham 2004; Evans, Chenery, and Fitzpatrick 2006; Evans, Stoodley, and Chenery 2006; Montgomery, Cooper, and Evans 2007). Such rocks are present in the Cretaceous, Jurassic, and Permian terrains that form the higher ground surrounding the Vale of York basin and may provide local places of origin for these two individuals. SK15 has a radiogenic isotope ratio that is rarely found in English burials and suggests origins in regions of Paleozoic, possibly granitic, rocks that are not found in Yorkshire or, indeed, most of central and eastern England; the main outcrops in Britain are to the west in the Lake District or Wales or to the north in Scotland.

Oxygen Isotope Analysis

The measured enamel phosphate $\delta^{18}O$ ranges from 15.0‰ to 18.9‰. This is a wide range of values for indigenous Britons and, when calibrated to drinking-water values, produces a $\delta^{18}O$ range of -4.1‰ to -12.6‰. The modern-day range for mean annual precipitation (the source of drinking water) in Britain is -4‰ to -9‰, as indicated in figure 6.16; however, values above -6‰ are only found in the extreme west of Britain and those above -5‰ occur only in the Outer Hebrides (Darling et al. 2003; Darling and Talbot 2003). Three of the individuals (SK16, SK35, SK33) have oxygen isotope ratios that are consistent with eastern England, in general, and York, in particular, and their strontium compositions would not contradict this conclusion. However, this group is not entirely composed of the same three individuals who formed the cluster of strontium compositions in figure 6.14: one individual (SK10) in this strontium cluster has an unusually low $\delta^{18}O$ ratio, which is inconsistent with any location in the British Isles and is indicative of high latitude, high altitude, or inland continental European regions. Such enamel phosphate $\delta^{18}O$ ratios have, for example, been obtained from Inuit in medieval Greenland (Fricke et al. 1995). The strontium isotope ratio would, however, suggest that this would be a region of young Mesozoic rocks rather than granitic or older Paleozoic terrains. SK15 and SK37 have oxygen isotope ratios above -6‰, and these are indicative of origins in western England, although SK15's ratio would only be consistent with the Outer Hebrides.

There are two complicating factors to consider before an interpretation can be made. First, how valid is it to compare oxygen isotope ratios obtained from archaeological enamel to maps of modern precipitation? And second, although the isotope ratios obtained for four of the individuals are consistent with origins in England—and Occam's razor would suggest that this is the most parsimonious explanation—isotope analysis is an exclusive technique that can rule out places of origin but cannot discriminate among the many

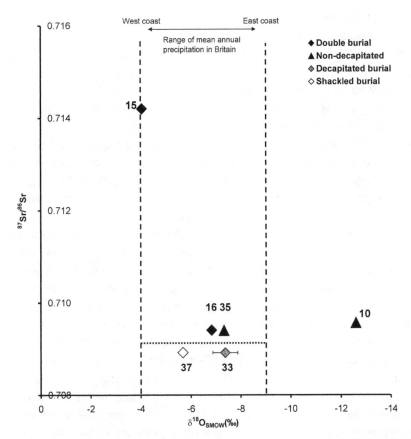

Figure 6.16. Plot of strontium isotope ratio against oxygen isotope ratio for Driffield Terrace individuals. The dashed vertical lines represent the extent of mean annual oxygen isotope ratios in the modern British precipitation. Oxygen isotope ratios above -6‰ occur solely down the extreme west coast of Britain. Samples falling below the horizontal dotted line are consistent with regions of marine carbonates such as chalk and limestone. Errors are within the symbol for strontium (2σ) and shown at ±0.5‰ for oxygen, which takes into account the additional error associated with the conversion of measured phosphate values to precipitation.

possible places throughout the world that may also be characterized by a similar isotope profile to that of eastern England. Archaeological knowledge may suggest that many of these places make little or no sense in the time period under investigation, and for reasons of space and lack of available data, listing them all may be impossible, but it should always be borne in mind that only in very rare instances may a truly unique profile be found.

Is it valid to assume that the climate difference between Britain in the second century AD and today is negligible? The individuals in our study were living in what is known as the Roman Warm Period, when grape cultivation was widespread in Britain and average temperatures were thought to be ~2°C warmer than those of today (Lamb 1977, 1995). Temperature can affect both weather and patterns of rainfall in complex ways that may vary considerably depending on topography and latitude, even in a relatively small island such as Britain (Lamb 1981). Moreover, individual teeth record seasonality on far smaller time scales than the majority of climatic proxies can hope to do, and differences between two individuals may be due to a single anomalously warm or cold year. Nonetheless, there is mounting evidence from current research across Europe for cultivation taking place much farther north and on higher ground, slightly lower sea levels (due to steric effects), and raised temperatures in the proxy records in the Roman Warm Period (Swindles, personal communication 2009). For example, a shift to notably warmer and drier summers resulting in water deficits in Britain and Ireland has been documented in the first few centuries AD (Swindles et al. 2010), along with upland clearances on the English Pennines to create fields that are today no longer suitable for agriculture (Bartley and Chambers 1992), and in continental Europe there is evidence that some of the Alpine passes were also ice free in winter between 2.25 and 1.7 kyr BP—the Roman Warm Period (Vollweiler et al. 2006). Increased aridity and temperature can certainly affect the $\delta^{18}O$ ratios of groundwaters through increased evaporation (Darling et al. 2003; Leng and Anderson 2003; Gazis and Feng 2004; Hoppe et al. 2004); the result is that the waters become enriched in the heavier ^{18}O isotope and thus the $\delta^{18}O$ ratios shift towards ratios indicative of warmer climates. All these considerations indicate that if there was a difference between the $\delta^{18}O$ ratios of modern-day precipitation and that of Britain in the Roman Warm Period, it would result in enamel phosphate ratios that are shifted towards less negative ratios, that is, the oxygen isotope range for Britain in figure 6.16 would move to the left. However, given published estimates that a 2°C temperature rise would produce a shift of only 1‰ in mean annual $\delta^{18}O$ ratios of rainfall (Rozanski et al. 1992, 1993), based on current evidence, any systematic shift in population $\delta^{18}O$ enamel ratios during this period is not likely to exceed 1‰. This would clearly have no effect on the conclusion of non-British origins for SK10, as this individual would move farther away from the British field. Neither would this difference be sufficient to make SK16, SK33, SK35, or SK37 inconsistent with an origin in Britain. It would, however, bring SK15 into the range for the west coast of Britain.

Comparative data from other Romano-British skeletons from Winchester and the Lankhills Roman cemetery of Winchester, which are located on the Cretaceous Chalk of the South Downs in southwestern England, are shown

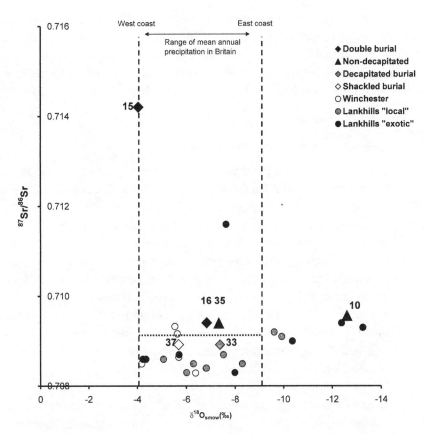

Figure 6.17. Plot of strontium isotope ratios against oxygen isotope ratios for the Driffield Terrace skeletons and comparative contemporary Romano-British burials from Winchester (Montgomery et al. 2008) and the Lankhills Roman cemetery of Winchester (Evans, Stoodley, and Chenery 2006) in southern England. The dashed vertical lines represent the extent of the oxygen isotope ratios in British precipitation. Individuals falling below the horizontal dotted line have strontium isotope values consistent with marine carbonates such as chalks and limestones and are probably too low for the Vale of York. Individuals SK16 and SK35 are consistent with the Vale of York for both strontium and oxygen isotope ratios.

in figure 6.17. The majority of these data are consistent with origins on the Cretaceous Chalk (they fall below the horizontal dotted line), but several individuals from both the archaeologically defined "local" and "exotic" (see Evans, Stoodley, and Chenery 2006) groups have oxygen isotope ratios that are inconsistent with an origin in Britain. Of particular note are the two "exotic" individuals from the Lankhills cemetery—Lankhills 81, a possible male of 30–35 years of age at death, and Lankhills 426, a possible male of 25–35 years of age at death—that have the same isotope profile as SK10, a result that strongly suggests similar origins outside Britain for these three individuals. Several individuals from the Winchester and Lankhills sites have strontium and oxygen ratios that would indicate they had local origins on the Cretaceous Chalk of southern England; such a profile is also shared by SK37.

Summary of Composite Isotopic Results

To summarize the individual results obtained:

- SK10—The oxygen ratio is too low for this nondecapitated individual to have originated in Britain or most of northern Europe and indicates that he originated somewhere extremely cold or at a high altitude. The lead isotope composition would support a non-English origin. The Alps and possibly the Italian Apennines are possibilities and would also be consistent with the strontium results. Alternatively, the origin could be somewhere far inland and continental with young Mesozoic rocks, such as eastern central Europe. The observation that this individual has a highly unusual $\delta^{13}C$ ratio indicative of consumption of C4 plants such as millet (G. Müldner, personal communication 2009) strongly supports a non-British origin and may indicate an origin in eastern central Europe (see Le Huray and Schutkowski 2005; Le Huray 2006).
- SK15—The oxygen isotope ratio is consistent with only the extreme west coast of Britain (e.g., the Outer Hebrides) and is too high for most of northern Europe. The radiogenic strontium isotope ratio indicates origins in Paleozoic or granitic terrains. Therefore, this decapitated individual may have originated somewhere warm with old rocks such as Sardinia, Corsica, the southernmost tip of Italy, or North Africa around the Red Sea region but not Mediterranean Africa, which is unlikely to provide such radiogenic strontium values.

Table 6.3. Summary of isotope results

Skeleton	Lead	Oxygen	Strontium	Overall
SK10	Nonlocal?	Nonlocal	Local	Nonlocal
SK15	Local	Nonlocal	Nonlocal	Nonlocal
SK16	Local	Local	Local	Local
SK33	Nonlocal?	Local	Local	Local?
SK35	Nonlocal	Local	Local	Nonlocal?
SK37	NA	Nonlocal	Local	Nonlocal

- SK16, SK33, and SK35—The oxygen and strontium results are consistent with origins in the north/east Yorkshire region. However, they are also consistent with much of present-day France, Germany, Holland, Denmark, and southern Norway. The lead compositions of SK35 and SK33 are unusual for English burials and suggest exposure during childhood to non-English ore lead from Mesozoic ores such as those found in the Mediterranean region (Boni et al. 2000).
- SK37—This shackled and decapitated individual has an isotope profile that indicates origins in western Britain in regions of chalk or basalt. There, rocks are restricted in their outcrop: basalt is principally found in Scotland and chalk in southern England. As figure 6.17 shows, the results for SK37 would be entirely consistent with Cretaceous Chalk in southern England. Alternatively, if this individual did not originate in Britain, there are many places around the Mediterranean Sea that would be suitable places of origin.

In summary (table 6.3), oxygen and strontium isotope ratios suggest that two decapitated individuals (SK16, SK33) may be of local origin and one decapitated individual (SK37) may have originated in the southwest of Britain or the Mediterranean region—these three individuals have low levels of lead that suggest little childhood exposure to anthropogenic sources. There are hints, however, from the lead isotope ratio that SK33 was not exposed to English ore lead as a child. More work is needed to clarify this. Two individuals (SK10, nondecapitated; SK15, decapitated) are unlikely to have originated in Britain, and one nondecapitated individual (SK35) has a lead composition that is highly unusual for English ore lead or archaeological skeletons—these three have the highest enamel-lead concentrations, which are highly likely to derive from childhood exposure to pollutant, anthropogenic lead such as from lead piping, lead vessels, and food additives.

Conclusions

The Location of Roman Cemeteries

Roman cemeteries occur along the approach roads to urban centers. These cemeteries form a repeated though not exclusive pattern (see Pearce 2000) throughout the Roman Empire, whether along the Via Appia in Rome (Patterson 2008) or along the road from London to Colchester, which passed through Aldgate in Roman London (Barber and Bowsher 2000). Other examples are

found along the major approaches to the more completely investigated Verulamium, Roman St. Albans (Hertfordshire, United Kingdom), which include
large concentrations of burials along Watling Street, the major route to the
north in the Roman period; the Folly Lane site, along the route to Colchester
(Niblett 1999); the King Harry Lane site to the southwest and Winchester;
and the St. Stephen's cemetery site, south towards London (see Niblett 2000:
97, fig. 10.1). The Roman elites, especially, chose to be buried along the major
approach roads, often on high points overlooking the urban center; this is
the case for the still-extant tomb of Caelia Metella, the wife of the Triumvir
Crassus, which is situated at a high point along the Via Appia, the main route
from Rome to the southeast and the port at Roman Brindisium (modern Brin-
disi, Puglia, Italy; Toynbee 1971: 155).

The burials at Driffield Terrace, York, are located along the main approach
road from the south, the former Via Praetoria (Hutchinson and Palliser 1980),
on a promontory, so such a prime location might be expected to be reserved
for people of high status. Given that decapitations are often associated with
individuals considered to have been social outcasts in the Roman period
(Boylston et al. 2000; Philpott 1991: 84–85, 232), as well as in the post-Ro-
man period (Harman et al. 1981; Buckberry 2008; Reynolds 2008), this prime
location might seem a contradiction. Importantly, Reynolds (2008) argues
that the increasingly formalized nature of decapitated burials in the seventh
and eighth centuries AD reflects the rise and increasing political and social
control exerted during early medieval state formation in England (see also
O'Donnabhain this volume for medieval Ireland). These might include criminals and social outcasts, but this category need not imply that decapitated
individuals were of lower social status.

In the Roman world, the demise of the condemned was determined by
social status. Those of lowly status might be meted death in a myriad of ways,
including by crucifixion, being burned alive, or being thrown to beasts. Those
of higher social status, however, had more control over the form of their fate.
Such individuals might be offered exile, suicide, or beheading, a rapid but
honorable form of execution (Hope 2000: 112). Thus, the burials at Driffield
Terrace are unlikely to be those of common criminals; a far more likely explanation is that they were men of higher status whose mode and manner of
death merited burial in a location befitting their status. This would suggest
that such individuals were of higher social status (as indicated by their relative
stature; see Floud et al. 1990; Steckel 1995; Bogin 1999: 303ff.), and that, despite
the pattern in which their severed heads were deposited in the graves, would
indicate not only a pattern to their manner of death but also that their bodies
were recovered for organized and otherwise normative burial. The controlled

and repeated manner of their decapitation, the paucity of other weapon-related traumatic injuries, and the relatively lengthy time span covered by these burials would seem to exclude death in battle.

Although a number of healed fractures were observed, along with evidence for perimortem cranial blunt-force trauma caused by blows of significant force, there was little evidence for unhealed postcranial fractures, and those that do occur suggest that they may have been received in the course of an attempt to disable or subdue the victim in the perimortem interval (i.e., injuries to the axial skeleton occurred about the same time as other postcranial injuries), for the majority of perimortem injuries are directed at the neck. The unhealed blunt-force cranial injuries may have come with these attempts to subdue the individual or from after-death treatment of the severed heads.

Historical Context

The period from which these inhumations date, stretching from the late second to the early third century AD, marks a tumultuous period within the Roman Empire and one that affected and was influenced by events in York. In the first chapter of his *Ecclesiastical History of the English Church and People*, Bede (1968) relates that in AD 189 the Roman emperor Septimius Severus, an African from Lepcis Magna in North Africa, came to Britain when nearly all the tribes allied to Rome deserted under the imperial pretender Albinus. Albinus would eventually be defeated by Septimius Severus at a battle fought at Lugdunum in Gaul (modern-day Lyon, France). Severus's seventeen-year reign was marked by violent civil wars and punitive raids into present-day Scotland, perhaps as far north as the Moray Firth, north of modern Aberdeen. In the closing years of the second century, Caledonians and an allied group called the Maeatae made forays into the north of present-day England, capturing and holding Eboracum (York) for a period of time (Cary and Scullard 1975). These incursions, brought about by the vacuum left by Albinus's withdrawal of the Roman soldiery from Britain in his bid for the imperial purple, made the most northern border of the empire so unstable as to demand the presence of the emperor to restore political order.

Under Septimius Severus, York became capital of Britannia Inferior, and the emperor took up residence there for periods of time in the early decades of the third century. The Severan dynasty saw the final demise of the Roman Senate's authority over the selection of the emperor and the emergence of what Cary and Scullard (1975: 499) refer to as a "military monarchy" centered on the emperor himself. Pogrom-like killings and executions were a common feature of politics during this period. The two individuals who were not decapitated (SK10 and SK35) do not appear to have originated in Britain and may thereby support the notion that there was an ethnic component to those treated in this manner. Emperor Antoninus, an "irredeemable lunatic" (Girling 2006) otherwise known as Caracalla, the eldest son of Septimius Severus, who came to York in AD 208, was a chief protagonist in such killings. Among others, Caracalla assassinated his brother and co-ruler Geta and the praetorian prefect and his father-in-law Gaius Fulvius Plautianus and family, including Caracalla's wife, Fulvia Plautilla (Grant 1985: 110, 122), the latter after being denounced for an alleged plot against his father, Septimius Severus. An example of the fate that befell those who opposed these military monarchs comes with the demise of Albinus, who either stabbed himself or was stabbed to death during or shortly after the battle at Lyon. The pretender's head was sent to Rome as a grisly warning, and his sons, who at first had been granted pardons, were later beheaded, along with their mother (Grant 1985: 117).

An enduring legacy of the Severan dynasty was the increased cosmopolitan nature of the empire that came with the origins of the emperor and his sons. As noted above, Septimius Severus came from Tripolitana (modern-day Libya). His wife, the redoubtable Julia Domna, who variously bore the nickname the "Philosopher" and the title "Mother of the Camp and the Senate," was of Syrian origin and gathered in her intellectual circle the philosopher Philostratus and the physician Galen (Grant 1985: 111). The praetorian prefect, Plautianus, although of the *gens* Fulvii (an old Roman patrician family), also hailed from North Africa and was a fellow-townsman of Septimius Severus from Lepcis Magna. These far-flung and mixed origins provide textual indications that accords well with the disparate origins attested by the isotopic results of this study. The diverse origins of these men—from what were the Roman provinces of Britannia Inferior, Britannia Superior, Gaul, eastern European provinces of the Roman Empire, and Syria/Judea, as well as from the Italian peninsula and North Africa—contrast with their apparently similar fate as casualties of state-sponsored Roman proscription.

Acknowledgments

Montgomery and Knüsel: We thank Patrick Ottaway and Christine McDonnell of the York Archaeological Trust for granting permission for us to analyze the skeletons from Driffield Terrace. We also extend our thanks to Graeme Swindles (Geography, University of Leeds), who provided insights into climatic conditions during the Roman period and drew our attention to his paper on this topic. The isotope analyses presented in this paper were commissioned by Ian Potts, the producer, and funded by the British Broadcasting Corporation (BBC) for the *Timewatch* program "The Mystery of the Headless

Romans," http://www.bbc.co.uk/history/programmes/timewatch/article_romans_01.shtml. The isotope measurements were made at the Natural Environment Research Council (NERC) Isotope Geosciences Laboratory, Keyworth, Nottingham, United Kingdom, by Carolyn Chenery and Dr. Jane Evans.

Knüsel's participation in this project was funded by a Leverhulme Research Fellowship (RF/6/RFG/2008/0253).

Tucker: The osteological portion of this chapter draws on an original skeletal analysis report that I conducted for the York Archaeological Trust. I thank Caroline Needham, Centre for Anatomy and Human Identification, College of Life Sciences, University of Dundee, Scotland, for producing the vertebrae illustration and Simon Cleggett for hours of discussion on decapitations and Roman cemeteries.

References Cited

Barber, B., and D. Bowsher. 2000. *The Eastern Cemetery of Roman London: Excavations 1983–1990*. Museum of London Archaeological Service Monograph 4. Museum of London, London.

Bartley, D. D., and C. Chambers. 1992. A Pollen Diagram, Radiocarbon Ages and Evidence of Agriculture on Extwistle Moor, Lancashire. *New Phytologist* 121 (2): 311–320.

Bede, The Venerable. 1968. *History of the English Church and People*. Translated by Leo Sherley-Price. Penguin Books, Harmondsworth, U.K.

Bentley, R. A. 2006. Strontium Isotopes from the Earth to the Archaeological Skeleton: A Review. *Journal of Archaeological Method and Theory* 13 (3): 135–187.

Bogin, B. 1999. *Patterns of Human Growth*. 2nd ed. Cambridge University Press, Cambridge.

Boni, M., G. Di Maio, R. Frei, and I. M. Villa. 2000. Lead Isotopic Evidence for a Mixed Provenance for Roman Water Pipes from Pompeii. *Archaeometry* 42 (1): 201–208.

Boylston, A. 2000. Evidence for Weapon-Related Trauma in British Archaeological Samples. In *Human Osteology in Archaeology and Forensic Science*, edited by M. Cox and S. Mays, 357–380. Greenwich Medical Media, London.

Boylston, A., C. J. Knüsel, C. A. Roberts, and M. Dawson. 2000. Investigation of a Romano-British Rural Ritual in Bedford, England. *Journal of Archaeological Science* 27: 241–254.

Brettell, R. 2008. "Impious Easterners": Oxygen and Strontium Isotopes as Indicators of Provenance in "Migration Period" Cemetery Populations. Unpublished MSc. thesis, Division of Archaeological, Geographical and Environmental Sciences, University of Bradford, U.K.

British Geological Survey. 1977. *Quaternary Map of the United Kingdom South*. Ordnance Survey/NERC, Southampton, U.K.

———. 2001. *Solid Geology Map UK South Sheet*. Ordnance Survey/NERC, Southampton, U.K.

Brown, C. J., S. R. N. Chenery, B. Smith, C. Mason, A. Tomkins, G. J. Roberts, L. Serunjogi, and J. V. Tiberindwa. 2004. Environmental Influences on the Trace Element Content of Teeth—Implications for Disease and Nutritional Status. *Archives of Oral Biology* 49 (9): 705–717.

Buckberry, J. 2008. Off With Their Heads: The Anglo-Saxon Execution Cemetery at Walkington Wold, East Yorkshire. In *Deviant Burial in the Archaeological Record*, edited by E. Murphy, 148–168. Studies in Funerary Archaeology 2. Oxbow Books, Oxford, U.K.

Budd, P., J. Montgomery, B. Barreiro, and R. G. Thomas. 2000. Differential Diagenesis of Strontium in Archaeological Human Dental Tissues. *Applied Geochemistry* 15 (5): 687–694.

Budd, P., J. Montgomery, J. Evans, and M. Trickett. 2004. Human Lead Exposure in England from Approximately 5500 BP to the 16th Century AD. *Science of the Total Environment* 318 (1–3): 45–58.

Cary, M., and H. H. Scullard. 1975. *A History of Rome: Down to the Reign of Constantine*. 3rd ed. St. Martin's Press, New York.

Chamberlain, A. 2000. Problems and Prospects in Palaeodemography. In *Human Osteology in Archaeology and Forensic Science*, edited by M. Cox and S. Mays, 101–115. Greenwich Medical Media, London.

Chenery, C., G. Müldner, J. Evans, H. Eckardt, and M. Lewis. 2010. Strontium and Stable Isotope Evidence for Diet and Mobility in Roman Gloucester, UK. *Journal of Archaeological Science* 37: 150–163.

Clark, C. D., P. L. Gibbard, and J. Rose. 2004. Pleistocene Glacial Limits in England, Scotland and Wales. In *Quaternary Glaciations—Extent and Chronology*. Part I of *Europe*, edited by J. Ehlers and P. L. Gibbard, 47–82. Developments in Quaternary Science 2. Elsevier, Amsterdam.

Clarke, G. 1979. *The Roman Cemetery at Lankhills*. Winchester Studies 3, Part II, Pre-Roman and Roman Winchester. Clarendon Press, Oxford, U.K.

Conheeney, J. 2000. Inhumation Burials. In *The Eastern Cemetery of Roman London: Excavations 1983–1990*, edited by B. Barber and D. Bowsher, 277–296. Museum of London, London.

D'Angela, D., and A. Longinelli. 1991. Oxygen Isotopes in Living Mammal's Bone Phosphate: Further Results. *Chemical Geology* 86: 75–82.

Dansgaard, W., S. J. Johnsen, N. Reeh, N. Gundestrup, H. B. Clausen, and C. U. Hammer. 1975. Climatic Changes, Norsemen and Modern Man. *Nature* 255: 24–28.

Darling, W. G., A. H. Bath, and J. C. Talbot. 2003. The O and H Stable Isotopic Composition of Fresh Waters in the British Isles, part 2, Surface Waters and Groundwater. *Hydrology and Earth System Sciences* 7 (2): 183–195.

Darling, W. G., and J. C. Talbot. 2003. The O and H Stable Isotopic Composition of Fresh Waters in the British Isles, part 1, Rainfall. *Hydrology and Earth System Sciences* 7 (2): 163–181.

Daux, V., C. Lécuyer, M.-A. Héran, R. Amiot, L. Simon, F. Fourel, F. Martineau, N. Lynnerup, H. Reychler, and G. Escarguel. 2008. Oxygen Isotope Fractionation between Human Phosphate and Water, Revisited. *Journal of Human Evolution* 55 (6): 1138–1147.

Ericson, J. E. 1993. Ba/Ca as a Diagenetic Indicator for Evaluating Buried Bone Tissues: Advances in Tissue Selection, Reducing Contamination and Data Evaluation. In *Prehistoric Human Bone: Archaeology at the Molecular Level*, edited by J. B. Lambert and G. Grupe, 157–171. 1st ed. Springer, Berlin.

Evans, J. A., C. A. Chenery, and A. P. Fitzpatrick. 2006. Bronze Age Childhood Migration of Individuals near Stonehenge, Revealed by Strontium and Oxygen Isotope Tooth Enamel Analysis. *Archaeometry* 48: 309–321.

Evans, J., N. Stoodley, and C. Chenery. 2006. A Strontium and Oxygen Isotope Assessment of a Possible Fourth Century Immigrant Population in a Hampshire Cemetery, Southern England. *Journal of Archaeological Science* 33 (2): 265–272.

Evans, J. A., and S. Tatham. 2004. Defining "Local Signature" in Terms of Sr Isotope Composition Using a Tenth–Twelfth Century Anglo-Saxon Population Living on a Jurassic Clay-Carbonate Terrain, Rutland, UK. In *Forensic Geoscience: Principles, Techniques and Applications*, edited by K. Pye and D. J. Croft, 237–248. Geological Society of London Special Publication. London.

Floud, R., K. Wachter, and A. Gregory. 1990. *Height, Health, and History: Nutritional Status in the United Kingdom, 1750–1980*. Cambridge University Press, Cambridge.

Fricke, H. C., J. R. O'Neil, and N. Lynnerup. 1995. Oxygen Isotope Composition of Human Tooth Enamel from Medieval Greenland: Linking Climate and Society. *Geology* 23 (10): 869–872.

Friedl, K. E. 1992. Body Composition and Military Performance: Origins of the Army Standards. In *Body Composition and Physical Performance*, edited by B. M. Marriot and J. Grumstrup-Scott, 31–55. National Academies Press, Washington, D.C.

Gazis, C., and X. H. Feng. 2004. A Stable Isotope Study of Soil Water: Evidence for Mixing and Preferential Flow Paths. *Geoderma* 119 (1–2): 97–111.

Girling, R. 2006. A Cemetery of Secrets. *Sunday Times* (London), March 26.

Gowland, R. L., and A. T. Chamberlain. 2005. Detecting Plague: Palaeodemographic Characterisation of a Catastrophic Death Assemblage. *Antiquity* 79: 146–157.

Grant, M. 1985. *The Roman Emperors: A Biographical Guide to the Rulers of Imperial Rome, 31 BC–AD 1476*. Charles Scribner's Sons, New York.

Gulson, B. L., D. Howarth, K. J. Mizon, M. J. Korsch, and J. J. Davis. 1994. The Source of Lead in Humans from Broken Hill Mining Community. *Environmental Geochemistry and Health* 16: 19–25.

Gulson, B. L., K. J. Mizon, M. J. Korsch, and D. Howarth. 1996. Importance of Monitoring Family Members in Establishing Sources and Pathways of Lead in Blood. *Science of the Total Environment* 188: 173–182.

Gulson, B. L., K. J. Mizon, A. J. Law, M. J. Korsch, J. J. Davis, and D. Howarth. 1994. Source and Pathways of Lead in Humans from the Broken Hill Mining Community—An Alternative Use of Exploration Methods. *Economic Geology* 89: 889–908.

Gulson, B. L., and D. Wilson. 1994. History of Lead Exposure in Children Revealed from Isotopic Analyses of Teeth. *Archives of Environmental Health* 49: 279–283.

Gustafson, G., and G. Koch. 1974. Age Estimation Up to 16 Years of Age Based on Dental Development. *Odontologisk Revy* 25: 297–306.

Harman, M., T. I. Molleson, and J. L. Price. 1981. Burials, Bodies and Beheadings in Romano-British and Anglo-Saxon Cemeteries. *Bulletin of the Natural History Museum (Geology)* 35 (3): 145–188.

Hayman, G., and A. Reynolds. 2005. A Saxon and Saxo-Norman Execution Cemetery at 42–54 London Road, Staines. *Archaeological Journal* 162: 215–255.

Hillson, S. 1996. *Dental Anthropology.* 1st ed. Cambridge University Press, Cambridge.

Hong, S., J.-P. Candelone, C. C. Patterson, and C. F. Boutron. 1994. Greenland Ice Evidence of Hemispheric Lead Pollution Two Millennia Ago by Greek and Roman Civilizations. *Science* 265: 1841–1843.

Hope, V. M. 2000. The Treatment of the Corpse in Ancient Rome. In *Death and Disease in the Ancient City*, edited by V. M. Hope and E. Marshall, 104–127. Routledge, London.

Hoppe, K. A., R. Amundson, M. Vavra, M. P. McClaran, and D. L. Anderson. 2004. Isotopic Analysis of Tooth Enamel Carbonate from Modern North American Feral Horses: Implications for Paleoenvironmental Reconstructions. *Palaeogeography, Palaeoclimatology, Palaeoecology* 203 (3–4): 299–311.

Hoppe, K. A., P. L. Koch, and T. T. Furutani. 2003. Assessing the Preservation of Biogenic Strontium in Fossil Bones and Tooth Enamel. *International Journal of Osteoarchaeology* 13: 20–28.

Hoppe, K. A., A. Paytan, and P. Chamberlain. 2006. Reconstructing Grassland Vegetation and Paleotemperatures Using Carbon Isotope Ratios of Bison Tooth Enamel. *Geology* 34 (8): 649–652.

Hunter-Mann, K. 2005. 6 Driffield Terrace, York. Assessment Report on an Archaeological Excavation, 2005/55 (unpublished). York Archaeological Trust for Excavation and Research, York, U.K.

Hutchinson, J., and D. M. Palliser. 1980. *Bartholomew City Guide: York.* John Bartholomew and Son, Edinburgh.

Iacumin, P., H. Bocherens, A. Mariotti, and A. Longinelli. 1996. Oxygen Isotope Analyses of Co-existing Carbonate and Phosphate in Biogenic Apatite: A Way to Monitor Diagenetic Alteration of Bone Phosphate. *Earth and Planetary Science Letters* 142: 1–6.

Lamb, H. H. 1977. *Climatic History and the Future.* Vol. 2 of *Climate—Present, Past and Future.* Methuen, London.

———. 1981. Climate from 1000 BC to 1000 AD. In *The Environment of Man: The Iron Age to the Anglo-Saxon Period*, edited by M. Jones and G. Dimbleby, 53–65. British Archaeological Reports British Series 87. BAR, Oxford.

———. 1995. *Climate, History and the Modern World.* 2nd ed. Routledge, London.

Le Huray, J. D. 2006. La Tène Dietary Variation in Central Europe: A Stable Isotope Study of Human Skeletal Remains from Bohemia. In *Social Archaeology of*

Funerary Remains, edited by R. Gowland and C. J. Knüsel, 99–121. Oxbow Books, Oxford, U.K.

Le Huray, J. D., and H. Schutkowski. Diet and Social Status during the La Tène Period in Bohemia—Carbon and Nitrogen Stable Isotope Analysis of Bone Collagen from Kutná Hora-Karlov and Radovesice. *Journal of Anthropological Archaeology* 24: 135–147.

Leng, M. J., and N. J. Anderson. 2003. Isotopic Variation in Modern Lake Waters from Western Greenland. *Holocene* 13 (4): 605–611.

Levinson, A. A., B. Luz, and Y. Kolodny. 1987. Variations in Oxygen Isotope Compositions of Human Teeth and Urinary Stones. *Applied Geochemistry* 2: 367–371.

Longinelli, A. 1984. Oxygen Isotopes in Mammal Bone Phosphate: A New Tool for Paleohydrological and Paleoclimatological Research? *Geochimica et Cosmochimica Acta* 48: 385–390.

Luz, B., Y. Kolodny, and M. Horowitz. 1984. Fractionation of Oxygen Isotopes between Mammalian Bone-Phosphate and Environmental Drinking Water. *Geochimica et Cosmochimica Acta* 48: 1689–1693.

Molleson, T., D. Eldridge, and N. H. Gale. 1986. Identification of Lead Sources by Stable Isotope Ratios in Bones and Lead from Poundbury Camp, Dorset. *Oxford Journal of Archaeology* 5 (2): 249–253.

Montgomery, J. 2002. Lead and Strontium Isotope Compositions of Human Dental Tissues as an Indicator of Ancient Exposure and Population Dynamics. Unpublished Ph.D. dissertation, Department of Archaeological Sciences, University of Bradford, U.K.

Montgomery, J., P. Budd, and J. Evans. 2000. Reconstructing the Lifetime Movements of Ancient People: A Neolithic Case Study from Southern England. *European Journal of Archaeology* 3 (3): 407–422.

Montgomery, J., R. E. Cooper, and J. A. Evans. 2007. Foragers, Farmers or Foreigners? An Assessment of Dietary Strontium Isotope Variation in Middle Neolithic and Early Bronze Age East Yorkshire. In *From Stonehenge to the Baltic: Living with Cultural Diversity in the Third Millennium BC*, edited by M. Larsson and M. Parker Pearson, 65–75. Archaeopress, Oxford, U.K.

Montgomery, J., J. A. Evans, and C. A. Chenery. 2008. Report on the Isotope Analysis of Four Late Roman Individuals from the Eagle Hotel, Winchester. Unpublished report, Winchester Archaeology Unit, Winchester, U.K.

Montgomery, J., J. A. Evans, C. A. Chenery, and G. Müldner. 2009. Stable Isotope Analysis of Bone. In *Wasperton: A Roman, British and Anglo-Saxon Community in Central England*, edited by M. O. H. Carver, C. Hills, and J. Scheschkewitz, 48–49. Boydell and Brewer, Woodbridge, U.K.

Montgomery, J., J. A. Evans, S. R. Chenery, V. Pashley, and K. Killgrove. 2010. "Gleaming, White and Deadly": The Use of Lead to Track Human Exposure and Geographic Origins in the Roman Period in Britain. In *Roman Diasporas: Archaeological Approaches to Mobility and Diversity in the Roman Empire*, edited by H. Eckardt. *Journal of Roman Archaeology*. Forthcoming.

Montgomery, J., J. A. Evans, and R. E. Cooper. 2007. Resolving Archaeological Populations with Sr-Isotope Mixing Models. *Applied Geochemistry* 22 (7): 1502–1514.

Montgomery, J., J. A. Evans, D. Powlesland, and C. A. Roberts. 2005. Continuity or Colonization in Anglo-Saxon England? Isotope Evidence for Mobility, Subsistence Practice, and Status at West Heslerton. *American Journal of Physical Anthropology* 126 (2): 123–138.

Montgomery, J., J. A. Evans, and G. Wildman. 2006. ^{87}Sr/^{86}Sr Isotope Composition of Bottled British Mineral Waters for Environmental and Forensic Purposes. *Applied Geochemistry* 21 (10): 1626–1634.

Niblett, R. 1999. *The Excavation of a Ceremonial Site at Folly Lane, Verulamium.* Britannia Monograph Series 14. Society for the Promotion of Roman Studies, London.

———. 2000. Burial, Society and Context in the Provincial Roman World. In *Burial, Society and Context in the Roman World*, edited by J. Pearce, M. Millett, and M. Struck, 97–104. Oxbow Books, Oxford, U.K.

O'Neil, J. R., L. J. Roe, E. Reinhard, and R. E. Blake. 1994. A Rapid and Precise Method of Oxygen Isotope Analysis of Biogenic Phosphate. *Israel Journal of Earth Sciences* 43: 203–212.

Ottaway, P. 1993. *English Heritage Book of Roman York.* Batsford, London.

———. 2005. 1–3 Driffield Terrace, York. Assessment Report on an Archaeological Excavation, 2005/27 (unpublished). York Archaeological Trust for Excavation and Research, York, U.K.

Patterson, J. R. 2008. On the Margins of the City of Rome. In *Death and Disease in the Ancient City*, edited by V. M. Hope and E. Marshall, 85–103. Routledge, London.

Pearce, J. 2000. Funerary Rites in Verulamium during the Early Roman Period. In *Burial, Society and Context in the Roman World*, edited by J. Pearce, M. Millett, and M. Struck, 1–12. Oxbow Books, Oxford, U.K.

Philpott, R. 1991. *Burial Practices in Roman Britain: A Survey of Grave Treatment and Furnishing, a.d. 43–410.* British Archaeological Reports (British Series) 219. Tempus Reparatum, Oxford, U.K.

Price, T. D., V. Tiesler, and J. H. Burton. 2006. Early African Diaspora in Colonial Campeche, Mexico: Strontium Isotopic Evidence. *American Journal of Physical Anthropology* 130 (4): 485–490.

Reynolds, A. J. 1997. The Definition and Ideology of Anglo-Saxon Execution Sites and Cemeteries. In Death and Burial in Medieval Europe, edited by G. De Boe and F. Verhaeghe, 33–41. Papers of the Medieval Europe Brugge 1997 Conference, vol. 2. Instituut voor het Archeologisch Patrimonium, Zellik, Belgium.

———. 2008. *Anglo-Saxon Deviant Burial Customs.* Oxford University Press, Oxford.

Roberts, C., and M. Cox. 2003. *Health and Disease in Britain from Prehistory to the Present Day.* Sutton Publishing, Stroud, U.K.

Rogers, N. 2005. Small Finds. In 1–3 Driffield Terrace, York: Assessment Report on an

Archaeological Excavation, edited by P. Ottaway, 4–57. York Archaeological Trust for Excavation and Research, York, U.K.

Rohl, B. 1996. Lead Isotope Data from the Isotrace Laboratory, Oxford: Archaeometry Data Base 2, Galena from Britain and Ireland. *Archaeometry* 38: 165–180.

Rosman, K. J. R., W. Chisholm, S. Hong, J.-P. Candelone, and C. F. Boutron. 1997. Lead from Carthaginian and Roman Spanish Mines Isotopically Identified in Greenland Ice Dated from 600 BC to 300 AD. *Environmental Science and Technology* 31: 3413–3416.

Rozanski, K., L. Araguds-Araguds, and R. Gonfiantini. 1992. Relation between Long-term Trends of ^{18}O Isotope Composition of Precipitation and Climate. *Science* 258: 981–985.

———. 1993. Isotopic Patterns in Modern Global Precipitation. In *Climate Change in Continental Isotopic Records*, 1–37. Geophysical Monograph 78. American Geophysical Union, Washington, D.C.

Sayre, E. V., E. C. Joel, M. J. Blackman, K. A. Yener, and H. Özbal. 2001. Stable Lead Isotope Studies of Black Sea Anatolian Ore Sources and Related Bronze Age and Phrygian Artefacts from Nearby Archaeological Sites. Appendix: New Central Taurus Ore Data. *Archaeometry* 43 (1): 7–115.

Sealy, J. C., R. Armstrong, and C. Schrire. 1995. Beyond Lifetime Averages: Tracing Life Histories through Isotopic Analysis of Different Calcified Tissues from Archaeological Skeletons. *Antiquity* 69: 290–300.

Steckel, R. H. 1995. Stature and the Standard of Living. *Journal of Economic Literature* 33: 1903–1940.

Stos-Gale, Z. A., G. Maliotis, N. H. Gale, and N. Annetts. 1997. Lead Isotope Characteristics of the Cyprus Copper Ore Deposits Applied to Provenance Studies of Copper Oxhide Ingots. *Archaeometry* 39 (1): 83–123.

Swindles, G. T., A. Blundell, H. M. Roe, and V. A. Hall. 2010. A 4500-Year Proxy Climate Record from Peatlands in the North of Ireland: The Identification of Widespread Summer "Drought Phases"? *Quaternary Science Reviews* 29 (13–14): 1577–1589.

Toynbee, J. M. C. 1971. *Death and Burial in the Roman World.* Cornell University Press, Ithaca, New York.

Trickett, M. A., P. Budd, J. Montgomery, and J. Evans. 2003. An Assessment of Solubility Profiling as a Decontamination Procedure for the Sr-87/Sr-86 Analysis of Archaeological Human Skeletal Tissue. *Applied Geochemistry* 18 (5): 653–658.

Tylecote, R. F. 1992. *A History of Metallurgy.* Institute of Materials, London.

Vollweiler, N., D. Scholz, C. Mühlinghaus, A. Mangini, and C. Spötl. 2006. A Precisely Dated Climate Record for the Last 9 kyr from Three High Alpine Stalagmites, Spannagel Cave, Austria. *Geophysical Research Letters* 33: L20703.

Wang, Y., and T. E. Cerling. 1994. A Model of Fossil Tooth and Bone Diagenesis: Implications for Paleodiet Reconstruction from Stable Isotopes. *Palaeogeography, Palaeoclimatology, Palaeoecology* 107 (3–4): 281–289.

Wells, C. 1982. The Human Burials. In *Romano-British Cemeteries at Cirencester*, edited by A. McWhirr, L. Viner, and C. Wells, 135–202. Cirencester Excavation Committee, Cirencester, U.K.

Wenham, L. P. 1968. *The Romano-British Cemetery at Trentholme Drive, York*. Ministry of Public Buildings and Works Archaeological Report 5. Ministry of Public Buildings and Works, London.

Wenham, S. J. 1989. Anatomical Interpretations of Anglo-Saxon Weapon Injuries. In *Weapons and Warfare in Anglo-Saxon England*, edited by S. C. Hawkes, 123–139. Oxford University Committee for Archaeology, Oxford.

Werner, A. 1998. *London Bodies: The Changing Shape of Londoners from Prehistoric Times to the Present Day*. Museum of London, London.

White, C. D., M. W. Spence, H. L. Q. Stuart-Williams, and H. P. Schwarcz. 1998. Oxygen Isotopes and the Identification of Geographical Origins: The Valley of Oaxaca versus the Valley of Mexico. *Journal of Archaeological Science* 25: 643–655.

7

Biohistory and Cranial Morphology

A Forensic Case from Spanish Colonial Georgia

CHRISTOPHER M. STOJANOWSKI AND WILLIAM N. DUNCAN

As several chapters in this volume have shown, skulls are collected from ancestors and enemies, insiders and outsiders, men, women, and children, and
used for an array of purposes with numerous connotations (see also chapters
in Bonogofsky 2006). Thus, it is not surprising that forensic anthropologists
and bioarchaeologists frequently encounter isolated examples in a variety of
contexts other than criminal investigations and archaeological sites.

Skulls are found in homes (as family heirlooms), in museums, in pawn-
shops, and on eBay (Huxley and Finnegan 2004; Murad and Murad 2000;
Steadman 2003; Willey and Leach 2003). They are collected as war trophies
(Sledzik and Ousley 1991), traded as curiosities and as art, and sold for class-
room instruction. This ephemeral, symbolic valuation directly translates into
the unfortunate commercial value of human remains; skulls are always the
most expensive element of the human body. While the people collecting human skulls may do so for a variety of reasons, ranging from ritual purposes
to morbid novelty, the skulls are also significant to the societies from which
they were taken because they often reflect acts of violence. Sometimes the
destruction of an object can give it additional meaning and even sacred status. Taussig (1999) calls this type of violence defacement. It may occur to a
variety of objects, but humans and human remains are common targets. For
example, Geronimo's remains would have been sacred to his descendants under any circumstances, but the rumor that they were taken and held by the
Skull and Bones fraternity turns their potential sacrality into a kinetic one.
The point is that isolated skulls are by definition divorced from their original
contexts, and that divorce oftentimes animates the latent symbolic potency
of such skulls for the relatives of the deceased. Thus, returning the remains
to the nearest kin or native culture is one of the basic goals for anthropologists in such cases. As a result, one of the fundamental questions we must

address when presented with isolated skulls is one of population affinity. By this we mean affinity in both its broadest (temporal and geographical affinity to specific biological populations) and its narrowest (positive identification of an individual) senses. How, then, can we identify the population to which a recovered skull is most similar so that we might return it to the appropriate descendant community? This is a particularly important question when the deceased are far removed in time or when circumstances make individuation impossible, and it is an extremely difficult one to answer.

Because of this articulation with descendant communities, returning remains to the appropriate interest group is one of the most important and rewarding aspects of forensic practice. One common way of dealing with isolated skulls is to compare them to a preexisting data framework, such as the Howells database (Howells 1989, 1995), or to use Fordisc (Jantz and Moore-Jansen 1988; Ousley and Jantz 1996, 1998), a program that applies multivariate statistical analysis to allocate unknown crania to predetermined comparative population samples. The shortcomings of such analyses have been documented and debated (Belcher et al. 2002; Campbell and Armelagos 2007; Freid et al. 2005; Naar et al. 2006; Williams et al. 2005), but no alternatives have been proposed. The impasse seems to focus on the use of the program itself and how best to interpret its results rather than advancing the method in a manner that considers the recent evolutionary history of craniofacial form. Human crania have demonstrated significant change within populations in as little as a single generation (Gravlee et al. 2003a, 2003b), such that collapsing time periods may not provide the most accurate results. Similarly, substituting one sample for another within a folk taxonomy of "social races" is problematic, for various methodological and theoretical reasons, as opponents of forensic anthropology have been quick to point out (Armelagos and Van Gerven 2003; Goodman 1997; Goodman and Armelagos 1996; Smay and Armelagos 2000).

In this chapter, we describe our attempt to assess population affinity of a calvaria (Fort King George 121) that has been attributed to a sixteenth-century priest killed and beheaded in coastal Georgia during Spanish occupation of the region (figure 7.1). This individual, Fray Pedro de Corpa, along with four other priests killed during the same rebellion, is being considered for canonization by the Catholic Church (Harkins 1990), and our efforts at population affinity assessment speak directly to the issue of cultural patrimony. Our participation was initiated at the request of the Franciscan Order so that some closure to this local legend could be obtained. Our contribution to this volume is how we construct a comparative data matrix in an attempt to avoid reifying folk taxonomies of social races and ignoring the now well-documented reality

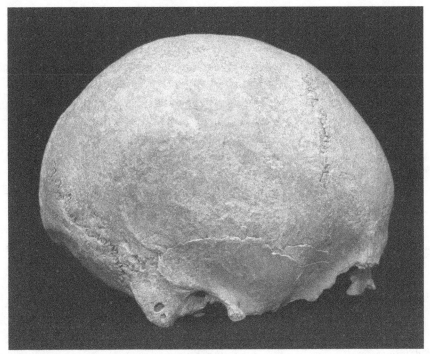

Figure 7.1. Right lateral view of the Fort King George (FKG-121) calvaria.

of short-term secular change in craniofacial form. We do so by using historical and archaeological data to reconstruct the occupation history of the archaeological site complex at which the Fort King George calvaria (hereafter FKG-121) was recovered, an approach advocated by Brues (1992) but infrequently used in practice.

Methodological Context

To fully explain the rationale behind our approach, a brief review of previous cranial allocation studies is warranted. Comparative craniometry proceeds under a rather standardized approach. An individual cranium is allocated to one of a number of comparative populations based on multivariate analysis of craniofacial dimensions. It is important to note that the researcher is the one defining the sampling universe by selecting which populations should be used in the comparison. The theoretical basis of this approach is that the population to which the cranium is most similar is the most likely source population. The entire process proceeds under the assumption that there is geographical patterning to human craniofacial form. The ability to accurately assess population affinity depends on the distance between the comparative population means (the more distinct the means, the better), the degree of variability within each comparative population (the lower the variability, the better), and the ability of the researcher to capture this degree of variability in his or her data analysis (usually the more variables, the better) and interpret the results accordingly. This last point is critical because often the analysis suggests a nonresult but the researcher may not recognize it as such. If the measurement set produces poor separation between comparative populations, or if the selected comparative samples are poor representatives of the population to which the isolated skull actually belongs, there is little hope for an accurate allocation.

The dissemination of Fordisc (Jantz and Moore-Jansen 1988; Ousley and Jantz 1996, 1998) and, in its later versions, the inclusion of craniometric data from the W. W. Howells data set, had a tremendous influence on the practice of comparative craniometry. The ability to analyze data from individual skulls using a prepackaged program was invaluable for assessment of population affinity, and its use has become widespread in numerous formal and informal forensic settings. Unfortunately, as the authors of that software note, the data sets included do not necessarily represent a majority of human craniometric variation (Ousley and Jantz 1996, 1998). The uninformed use of these existing databases may be problematic for four reasons.

First is the assumption that different geographical populations of humans are sufficiently distinct craniometrically from one another as well as suffi-ciently homogenous intrapopulationally that they can be distinguished. "Suf-ficiently" is defined in terms of whether or not distances between popula-tions exceed the degree of overlap in phenotypic variability. In other words, researchers must be able to distinguish between cranial variations that exist within a population from variation between populations. A major criticism levied against forensic anthropology is that variation is ultimately continu-ous, rather than discrete (Armelagos and Van Gerven 2003; Goodman and Armelagos 1996; Williams et al. 2005), and this drawback is surmountable only if the measurements are capable of the required level of group separation (itself determined by the degree of intrapopulation variability). As a criticism, this applies not only to Fordisc but also to all attempts at craniometric affinity assessment.

Second, the comparative samples included in Fordisc are not time sensitive, which is problematic given known secular changes in craniofacial form (An-gel 1976; Jantz 2001; Jantz and Meadows-Jantz 2000; Sparks and Jantz 2002; Wescott and Jantz 2005), which have most prominently been discussed in the context of the Boas immigrant data set (Gravlee et al. 2003a, 2003b; Sparks and Jantz 2002). Eighteenth-century Euro-American crania may be quite distinct from modern Euro-American crania, although such secular changes may not significantly blur existing geographically based craniofacial diversity. Again, the effects of microevolutionary change on the success of an allocation analysis depend on the degree of separation between the comparative populations.

Third, because of the ever-changing landscape of craniofacial diversity, an unknown specimen is unlikely to be well represented by the samples included in either the Forensic Data Bank (FDB) or Howells data set, a fact supported by low typicality probabilities (i.e., the probability that an unknown individual belongs to a specific group) reported when using these databases (see also Ross et al. 2004; Ubelaker et al. 2002). A low typicality probability indicates that the unknown skull is an outlier in reference to the comparative populations and should be interpreted as a nonresult.

Fourth, there is a tendency to reify racial types and collapse time. For example, in one of the most frequently cited craniometric allocation methods (Giles and Elliot 1962), all Native Americans (15,000+ years across two continents) are represented by the Archaic period Indian Knoll cemetery from Kentucky. Given the range of phenotypic variability within the Americas (Ross et al. 2002), such an approach is essentialist and typological because it assumes that every Native American in the Western hemisphere is more similar to all other Native Americans than to anyone who originated on another continent.

Historical and Archaeological Context

The Fort King George "skull" was reportedly found during excavations along the banks of the Darien River in Georgia by Sheila Caldwell in the 1950s (figure 7.2). The bluff had been the location of the British Fort King George during the 1720s and prior to that had been the site of two consecutive Spanish missions dating from the late sixteenth through late seventeenth centuries (Caldwell 1953, 1954). Native Americans had inhabited the bluff for as long as three thousand years prior to the establishment of the European context (Caldwell 1943) and during historic times were associated with the Guale polity. The Guale were missionized by the Spanish beginning in the late sixteenth century (Jones 1978; Worth 1995), and it was during this initial Spanish occupation of the area that the story of Pedro de Corpa emerged.

Pedro de Corpa was one of a half-dozen Franciscan friars serving mission communities along the Georgia coast during the last quarter of the sixteenth century. Because of political turmoil, disease, demographic collapse, and general resistance to the Spanish presence, revolts were a common feature of the earliest phases of conversion to Catholicism. In 1597, a large rebellion

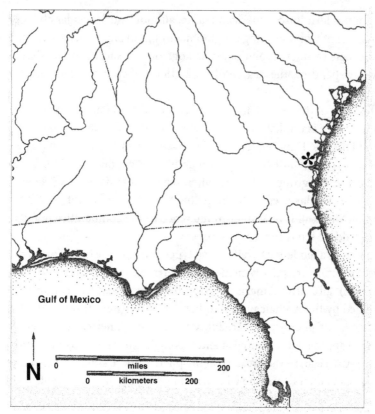

Figure 7.2. Map of northern Florida and southern Georgia with the Fort King George site location indicated by the asterisk.

occurred among the Guale, which resulted in the killing of five Franciscans (Pedro de Corpa at Tolomato, Blas de Rodriguez and Miguel de Auñón on the island of Guale, Antonio de Badajoz at Tupiqui, and Francisco de Veráscola at Asao) and the detainment and torment of a sixth (Francisco de Avila). Although internal politics surely played some role in this rebellion, received wisdom suggests that the violence erupted because of the enforcement of a strict ban on polygamy and the punishment of a youth named Juanillo, the heir to an esteemed political office, for taking a second wife (Geiger 1937; Lanning 1935; Oré 1936). In the weeks of violence that followed, which included heavy-handed Spanish reprisals, the missions were destroyed and missionary efforts were stalled for nearly a decade. Three of the friars' bodies were located and recovered (Barcia 1951 [1723]: 188–189; Geiger 1937: 92, 94n77, 112; Harkins 1990: 471; Lanning 1935: 87, 89, 96; Omaechevarría 1955: 310); however, the bodies of Pedro de Corpa and Francisco de Veráscola were never found and presumably remain buried somewhere along the Georgia coast to this day (Lanning 1935).

Based on a limited historical record, the following can be ascertained about the two missing Georgia martyrs. Both Pedro de Corpa and Francisco de Veráscola were killed via blunt-force trauma using wooden weapons called macanas (Brooks 1906: 41, 43, 45; Lanning 1935: 89–90). Pedro de Corpa was beheaded, and his head was then impaled and displayed at the village he served (Barcia 1951 [1723]: 182; Lanning 1935: 86; Oré 1936: 73–74), but the skull was either moved or hidden shortly after his death, because it was not observed when the Spanish governor visited the Tolomato mission some weeks after the rebellion began (see note 46, chapter 8 in Oré 1936).

Both friars may have been scalped, as this was common practice at the time and documented during the revolt (Lanning 1935: 95). The Spanish retaliatory force found scalps, but it is not known to whom they belonged. The final critical detail is the physical location of the mission each friar served: de Corpa served the Tolomato community, while Francisco de Veráscola served the Asao community. Considerable debate exists about the locations of these missions and villages (see Jones 1978; Worth 1995, 2004). Initial historical opinion placed Tolomato near the Darien River (Lanning 1935), and this assumption, combined with the report of finding a broken human cranium with no associated remains, led to the original attribution to Pedro de Corpa. However, more-recent analysis of historical texts suggests that the Darien bluffs were the location of the village of Asao during the sixteenth century (Jones 1978; Worth 1995, 2004). In either case, a Spanish priest is known to have been killed during the sixteenth century along the banks of the Darien River, where the English would eventually establish Fort King George.

Previous Analyses

Previous analysis of the calvaria (Stojanowski and Duncan 2008, 2009) indicates that the individual was male and between thirty and fifty years old at the time of death, which is consistent with what is known about both Pedro de Corpa and Francisco de Veráscola (Harkins n.d.). The pattern of fractures is consistent with, but not diagnostic of, the story of Pedro de Corpa's murder. A possible Lefort III fracture—the complete detachment of the face from the cranial vault—was documented. The cranial base was damaged, which is possibly consistent with decapitation and subsequent impalement of the severed skull (figure 7.3; see Montgomery, Knüsel, and Tucker this volume; O'Donnabhain this volume). No evidence of scalping was observed, a detail

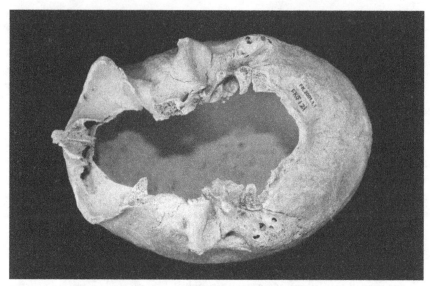

Figure 7.3. Inferior view of the Fort King George calvaria, demonstrating damage to the cranial base consistent with impalement of the skull.

mitigated by the degree of cortical exfoliation and the possibility that the Guale did not use steel tools to scalp their victims.

Initial comparative craniometric analysis suggested a non–Native American affinity when compared to samples within the FDB and Howells data set (Stojanowski and Duncan 2008). Based on vault shape, FKG-121 was allocated to the Egyptian (presumed "Caucasoid"; see Howells 1989, 1995) series in the Howells data set with typicality probabilities ranging from approximately .20 to .001 depending on which suite of measurements was used (Stojanowski and Duncan 2008). Comparison with data from the FDB produced an allocation to the European sample with a low typicality probability (.072) (Stojanowski and Duncan 2008). The low typicality probability indicates one problem with current approaches to craniometric affinity assessment using published software (Fordisc) and data sets (FDB and the Howells data set); simply put, these data sets are incomplete representations of global human craniofacial form, as the authors of the software take pains to note.

A Different Approach to Population Affinity Assessment

Given the low typicality probabilities often reported in forensic cranial allocation studies, documented changes in craniofacial form through time, and well-founded critiques of typological approaches to ancestry assessment that reify gross morphological types, we developed a different approach for this analysis of FKG-121. The method we use is simple and designed to address a specific hypothesis: Is it possible to exclude the possibility that FKG-121 belonged to one of the missing Georgia martyrs based on craniometric form?

The most appropriate comparative framework is one that is constructed using samples of the appropriate age (roughly sixteenth through nineteenth century) incorporating samples from populations that could actually be represented by the specimen in question. For example, rather than using a sample of Native Americans from the southwestern United States (included in Fordisc 2.0), seventeenth-century Arikara from North Dakota, pene-contemporary Chumash of California, or a sample of ancient Peruvian skulls (all of which are included in the Howells data set) to evaluate whether the Fort King George calvaria could be "Native American," the approach advocated here uses indigenous Guale crania from the Georgia coast for comparison. Likewise, there is little a priori reason to presume, unless one assumes a racial approach to human variation, that medieval Norse or pene-contemporary Hungarian populations are representative of seventeenth-century Spain or that twentieth-century African-American populations are reflective of the earliest West African slaves imported to the New World. Therefore, in an effort to anchor our analyses within a local population using a nonracial approach to human variation, we begin with a brief discussion of the historical and archaeological setting of this part of Georgia, focusing on the archaeological history of the Darien bluffs, in particular.

Human Occupation at the Fort King George Site

Joseph Caldwell's excavation along the Darien bluffs found evidence for Native American occupation dating to three thousand years ago (Caldwell 1943). Sheila Caldwell conducted an extensive excavation along the bluff and identified two distinct periods of Guale-Spanish occupation, the first dating from the time of the Georgia martyrs (1570–1597) and the second representing a seventeenth-century mission later located there (Caldwell 1953, 1954), both of which likely had associated burials. The latter mission was abandoned in 1686 when the Guale retreated south in the wake of English encroachment, slave raids by the Westo, and assaults on the Georgia coast by pirates (Worth 1995). From 1686 until 1721, the area was devoid of permanent occupation, although there was likely an itinerant Native American presence. In 1721, John Barnwell constructed Fort King George (in service until 1727), which housed several hundred English soldiers (Lewis 1967: 24), many of whom were buried in a formal cemetery near the fort (Caldwell 1943). A company of Swiss deserters from French Louisiana also made an appearance at the fort (Cook 1990: 49), and Barnwell's journal indicates the presence of African slaves (1926: 198), who were brought to North America during the earliest colonization efforts by the Spanish. After the fort burned in 1727, the area was reoccupied under direction from John Oglethorpe by 177 Scottish Highlanders who would go on to found the town of New Inverness, which became modern-day Darien. A tabby house (built of shell-based concrete) was constructed on the site in 1803 (Cook 1990: xvi). The later history of the site was dominated by lumber operations, beginning in 1806 with the Eastern Saw Mill Company (Kelso 1968), which maintained a presence until the Civil War. In 1878 the Hilton Timber and Lumber Company established another milling operation that seemed to have been in service until 1914, when the area was abandoned once again (Kelso 1968).

Constructing a Comparative Database

Given this site's occupational history, the Fort King George calvaria could represent one of many different populations: a precontact or colonial period Native American from the local Guale who lived along the Darien bluffs during two phases of Spanish occupation; an African slave, likely from a West African country, or a colonial period African-American; a Euro-American from the seventeenth, eighteenth, or nineteenth century or, more specifically, an eighteenth-century English soldier or Scottish Highlander; or a Spaniard from the sixteenth or seventeenth century (if Pedro de Corpa) or a Basque of similar age (if Francisco de Veráscola). None of these specific populations is represented in the Howells data set. However, we were able to extract published data for many of these populations from the literature (table 7.1). Published raw data were available for the Scottish, English, West African, and Guale population samples, while colonial period Euro-American and African-American population samples were copied from the archives at the Smithsonian Institution, where they were included in the papers of J. Lawrence Angel. However, only published means were available for the critical samples from late medieval Spanish and Basque populations. Therefore, a more informal, phenetic approach was used for this analysis in recognition of the limitations of this methodology.

One of the more difficult issues was defining the list of data variables. FKG-121 is an incomplete specimen preserving only the braincase and lacking the anterior portion of the foramen magnum. This latter point means that estimates of cranial vault height and base length cannot be measured on FKG-121. In addition, the splanchnocranium is entirely absent and the critical features of facial geometry, which demonstrate geographical patterning in humans (nasal and cheek shape), are not preserved. When this physical limitation is combined with the vagaries of publication trends by time and by country, the available list of measurement variables that were both present on FKG-121 and available in the literature diminished. In the final analysis, we used only six variables that capture aspects of cranial vault length and breadth: maximum cranial length (GOL), frontal chord (FRC), parietal chord (PAC), occipital chord (OCC), frontal arc (FAC), and maximum cranial breadth (XCB). Measurements for biasterionic breadth (ASB) and biauricular breadth (AUB) were recordable for FKG-121 but not consistently reported in the literature.

Means were generated by national or ethnic group for each population sample for broad time periods that correspond with the colonial period in North America (AD 1600–1800s), as summarized in table 7.1. Because of our certainty that FKG-121 is male based on the robusticity of key features of cranial morphology (mastoid process, nuchal crest, glabella projection), we only included data for male individuals. The resulting matrix of population means was then subjected to principal components analysis to extract common size- and shape-based components among variable means. These components were then plotted along with the FKG-121 calvaria to determine the most similar source population.

Results

The principal components analysis produced three components with eigenvalues greater than one, representing 85 percent of the original variation among sample means. Variable loadings indicate that factor 1 represents a contrast between cranial length and breadth; factor 2 is more difficult to interpret but seems to contrast the length of the parietal bone in relationship to the other variables; while factor 3 represents a contrast between the shape and size of the frontal bone relative to the occipital bone. The bivariate plot for principal components 1 and 2 is presented in figure 7.4. Several observations are noteworthy. First, despite the use of sample means for only six craniometric variables, geographic divisions are well represented in this figure: the two Native American samples are isolated in the upper left corner of the plot, the West African sample is more isolated in the lower left corner of the plot, the two African-American colonial period samples are closer to the West African sample than they are to contemporary Euro-American colonial samples, and the samples from European populations form a cluster in the middle of the figure. Second, eighteenth-, nineteenth-, and twentieth-century Euro-American samples plot very closely to the contemporary seventeenth-century and

Table 7.1. Comparative populations used for comparison of FKG-121

Population	References	Time period
Spanish: Santa María de Hito	Galera and Garralda 1992	AD 800–1100
Spanish: Linares	Ruiz et al. 1995	AD 1900–1950
Spanish: Tarragona Spanish	Pons Rosell 1949	AD 200–400
Visigoths: Iberian Spanish	Varela 1974–75	AD 500–600
Jewish Montiuich	Prevosti and Prevosti 1951	AD 1000–1300
Spanish: Palacios de la Sierra (Burgos)	Souich et al. 1990	AD 900–1200
Spanish: Villanueva de Soportilla	Souich et al. 1991	AD 800–1100
Cataluna central (medieval Christian)	Vives 1987	AD 800–1100
Spanish: Monasterio de Suso (San Millán de la Cogolla)	Martín Rivas and Souich 1981	AD 900–1050
Spanish: Santa María de la Piscina (San Vicente de la Sonsierra)	Souich and Martín Rivas 1982	AD 1000–1200
Spanish: Terrassa, Necrópolis de la Placa Vella	Jordana and Malgosa 2002	AD 1500–1600
Basque: Modern	Rúa 1985	AD 900
Basque: Guipuzcoa, Urtiaga, Zaraus	Aranzadi 1914; Morant 1929	AD 1900?
Basque: Necrópolis de Santa Eulalia	Rodriguez 1981	AD 800–900
Basque: Necrópolis de Ordoñana	Fernandez de Prado 1978	Medieval
Basque: Necrópolis de Castros de Lastra	Arenal and Rúa 1987	AD 800
Basque: San Juan de Momoitio	Arenal and Rúa 1987	AD 1000
English: 17th century (Moorfields, Whitechapel, Faningdon)	Hooke 1926; MacDonnell 1904, 1906	AD 1600–1700
English: Anglo-Saxon period (Bidford-on-Avon, Burwell)	Brash and Young 1935; Layard and Young 1935; Morant 1926	AD 1000
Scottish (various proveniences)	Reid 1926; Turner 1901	AD 1800–1900
West Scottish Lowlands (various proveniences)	Young 1931	AD 1850–1900
Euro-American 17th century*	Angel collection, Smithsonian Archives;[a] King and Ubelaker 1996; Ubelaker n.d.	AD 1600–1700

Euro-American 18th century*	Angel collection, Smithsonian Archives;[a] Carter et al. 2004	AD 1700–1800
Euro-American 19th century*	Angel collection, Smithsonian Archives;[a] Dailey et al. 1972	AD 1800–1900
African-American 18th century*	Angel collection, Smithsonian Archives[a]	AD 1700–1800
African-American 19th century*	Angel collection, Smithsonian Archives;[a] Beck 1980; Mann and Krakker 1989; Rose 1985; Thomas et al. 1977	AD 1800–1900
American 20th century*	Angel collection, Smithsonian Archives[a]	AD 1900–1950
Guale late precontact	La Florida Bioarchaeology Project	AD 1200–1500
Guale postcontact	La Florida Bioarchaeology Project	AD 1600–1700
West Africa*	Benington and Pearson 1912; Howells data set;[b] Keith 1911; Malcolm 1920; Shrubsall 1899; von Luschan collection,[c] AMNH	AD 1850–1925

[a] J. L. Angel data copied from original data cards on file at the Smithsonian Institution Archives.

[b] Downloaded from http://konig.la.utk.edu/howells.htm.

[c] Data measured by authors; African crania part of the von Luschan collection at the American Museum of Natural History.

* See appendix for further provenience information.

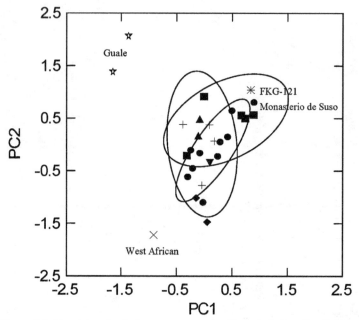

Figure 7.4. Bivariate principal components plot for population distributions in Spanish colonial Georgia. Asterisk = FKG-121; solid black circle = medieval Spanish; solid black square = Basque; plus sign = colonial Euro-American; upward-pointing triangle = English; downward-pointing triangle = Scottish; solid black diamond = colonial African-American; star = Native American Guale; × = West African. Two standard deviation confidence intervals are drawn around the Basque, Spanish, and Euro-American colonial population distributions.

Anglo-Saxon period English samples, as one might expect. Third, despite the geographical congruencies, there is considerable overlap among the Euro-American, English, Spanish, Basque, and Scottish samples. This is not unexpected given the small number of variables used.

In terms of the identity of the FKG-121 calvaria, this analysis does little to exclude the possibility that one of the Georgia martyrs is represented here. In fact, this result is about as confirmatory as one could expect given the data and analytical limitations. FKG-121 (indicated by an asterisk in figure 7.4) is most phenotypically similar to the Spanish population from the Monasterio de Suso (San Millán de la Cogolla) that dates to approximately AD 1000. FKG-121 is also similar to the three medieval Basque samples (San Juan de Momoitio, Necrópolis de Castros de Lastra, Necrópolis de Ordoñana) and to the medieval Spanish sample from Santa María de Hito. Although FKG-121 falls outside the two standard deviation confidence interval for the series of

Spanish samples (possibly reflecting the inclusion of older Spanish samples), it does fall within the confidence interval for the Basque samples. Therefore, while this analysis lacks enough specificity to distinguish Basque from Spanish samples craniometrically, the five samples to which FKG-121 is most similar are, intriguingly, all from the Iberian Peninsula. This analysis, using site occupational history to construct a more suitable comparative data universe, confirms the distinction between FKG-121 and Native American crania and also suggests that FKG-121 is not an individual of African ancestry. So we can conclude not only that FKG-121 appears "European" but also that it appears Iberian or even Spanish in affiliation.

Discussion

In 1992, Alice Brues emphasized the dichotomy between "general race vs. specific population" in forensic assessment of population affinity. Although this article is well known, we are unaware whether other scholars have followed her advice. As an alternative to current practices, however, the methodology we adopted here does allay some of the more severe criticisms of forensic anthropology within the discipline. In particular, the construction of a regionally defined comparative population database based on archaeological and historical reconstruction of site occupational histories does not fall into the trap of race science, which collapses human variation into "European," "African," or "Native American" types without distinguishing between them temporally or considering secular trends that may occur even in spatially proximate populations. In addition, the approach described above obviates concerns about microevolutionary changes within a population by using samples of the appropriate age for comparison. Therefore, several of the major criticisms of population affinity assessment using craniometric analysis are addressed by an approach based on local population history. Simply put, we ask not merely whether FKG-121 could be European but, more precisely, whether FKG-121 could be a sixteenth-century Spaniard or Basque.

The method used here is not without limitations. Most evident is the reliance on published data sets, the vagaries of variable reporting, interobserver error, and the subsequent need to use a more phenetic approach based on comparisons among sample means rather than individuals. While unavoidable at this point in our analysis of FKG-121 because of the lack of published raw data for Medieval period Spanish crania, the use of sample means in the principal components analysis removes any consideration of the sample variances. Generating statistical probabilities of membership in each population is therefore impossible. As reported above, we can make informed statements about overall similarity; based on this analysis, FKG-121 could very well be Pedro de Corpa or Francisco de Veráscola. However, there is no way to assess the degree of overlap among the comparative samples.

Future analysis of FKG-121 would be advanced if Spanish cranial data of the appropriate age were available. Similar analyses of biohistorical interest would also benefit from a much broader culture of data dissemination within forensic anthropology and bioarchaeology. Some archaeologists have been increasingly vocal in advocating for open source publishing, and such mechanisms of data exchange already exist in anthropological genetics. There is no reason why similar forums should be lacking in skeletal biology. The existence of extensive databases of regional populations would allow the use of the "local population" approach in numerous consultation venues, from formal medico-legal forensic investigations to informal case reports generated in the context of NAGPRA (Native American Graves Protection and Repatriation Act) inventorying. And it is this point that brings this chapter full circle.

Anthropologists commonly encounter isolated skulls because such skulls have been involved in or are the product of a violent act of defacement (in the sense of Taussig 1999). Their normal cultural meanings, whatever those may be in a given context, have changed to include elevated symbolic power by virtue of that defacement, and as a result the public is oftentimes more invested in those remains than they might otherwise be. This elevated interest can and should be a point of engagement between anthropology and the public. When encountering isolated skulls, anthropologists do more than simply take what people bring us, apply calipers and software to make bivariate plots, and allocate remains. The anthropologist interacts with an individual whose remains have accrued additional meaning and symbolism through the process of defacement. Although forensic assessment does not necessarily ameliorate or undo the defacement, the analysis itself becomes another part in an ongoing process that is ultimately one of social reproduction.

Anthropologists contribute by bringing closure; we help give certainty about the past to survivors. Instead of focusing on an act of violence, group members are able to acknowledge the violence suffered by the individual and ritually return that individual to the collective, which has survived. In this case, the Franciscans seek to identify and honor one of their own, bringing the life and death of a martyred fellow into the fold of Catholic veneration. From this perspective, the forensic anthropologist does not simply repatriate remains to grateful survivors but in some ways becomes a footnote incorporated into how groups create and re-create their identity in a fashion similar to that experienced by anthropologists in other subfields (see Monaghan 1995). In this case, a man whose head was severed and displayed as a trophy may now have special, spiritual status conferred upon him (see O'Donnabhain this volume for an inverse transformation).

The collection and dissemination of descriptive data relevant to population affinity assessment would allow future researchers to contribute even more, as only forensic anthropologists can, to critical questions of identity and heritage. At the same time, it would advance public discourse, moving away from race-based approaches to a more regional and contextualized understanding of human biological variation.

Appendix: Provenience Information for Table 7.1

Seventeenth-century Euro-American: Carter's Grove, Flowerdew Hundred, Gloucester Point, Martins Hundred, Shenandoah County (Va.), Patuxent Point, Site PG3.

Eighteenth-century Euro-American: Gloucester Point, Rae Burial Ground, St. Anne's Church, Moran Gallery, Fort King George, Stratford (Va.), plus miscellaneous proveniences from the J. L. Angel archives.

Nineteenth-century Euro-American: St. Marks cemetery, plus miscellaneous proveniences from the J. L. Angel archives.

Eighteenth-century African-American: Catoctin Furnace, College Landing, Deep River, First African Baptist Church, plus miscellaneous proveniences from the J. L. Angel archives.

Nineteenth-century African-American: Oakland Cemetery, First African Baptist Church, Governor's Bridge, Ocean City, Cunningham Mound D, unmarked slave cemetery in Washington (D.C.), Cedar Grove, Virgin Islands, St. Thomas, plus miscellaneous proveniences from the J. L. Angel archives.

Modern American: Miscellaneous proveniences from the J. L. Angel archives, approximately 171 FBI case files from around the United States.

West African: Agande; Agane; Aksim, Gold Coast; Ashanti; Babula; Babwe; Bakongo; Balisi; Baluba; Bangala; Bangelima; Bapoto; Bashongo; Basoko, Congo Free State; Batanga; Boki; Bushongo—Congo Free State; Calabar; Cameroon; Coffin Island, River Cess, Liberia; Congo; Creektown, Calabar; Dagomba; Djago—Gold Coast; Dogon; Efek; Ekoi—Nigeria; Ewe-Mishohe—Togo; Fan—Ogave River; Freetown, Sierra Leone; French Congo (Fernand

Vaz); Gabon; Gaboon (Fernand Vaz [1864 Series]); Gaboon (Fernand Vaz [1880 Series]); Gambe; Ghana; Guaja—French Guinea; Ibi, Benue River, Nigeria; Ibibio; Ibo; Kabila; Kamerun; Korawp; Kumabembe; Likwangulo; Mabea; Mandingo; Momou; Mongala; Mongwi; Nambetu; Nanga; Niger Delta; Oban—British Nigeria; Republic of Congo; Salago—Volta River, Gold Coast; Sango—Congo Free State; Senegal; Topoke; Vai—Liberia; West Bassai—Togo; Yendi—Togo.

References Cited

Angel, J. Lawrence. 1976. Colonial to Modern Skeletal Change in the U.S.A. *American Journal of Physical Anthropology* 45: 723–736.

Aranzadi, T. de. 1914. Sur quelques corrélations du trou occipital des crânes Basques. *Bulletin et Mémoires Société d'Anthropologie de Paris* 5: 325–382.

Arenal, Isabel, and Concepcíon de la Rúa. 1987. *Antropología de una poblacion medieval Vizcaina: San Juan de Momoitio, Garai*. Eusko Ikaskuntza, Sociedad de Estudios Vascos, San Sebastián, Spain.

Armelagos, George J., and Dennis P. Van Gerven. 2003. A Century of Skeletal Biology and Paleopathology: Contrasts, Contradictions, and Conflicts. *American Anthropologist* 105: 53–64.

Barcia, Andres de. 1951 [1723]. *Ensayo cronológico para la historia general de la Florida*. Translated by A. Kerrigan. University of Florida Press, Gainesville.

Barnwell, John W. 1926. Journal of Col. John Barnwell (Tuscarora) in the Construction of the Fort on the Altamaha in 1721. *South Carolina Historical and Genealogical Magazine* 27: 189–203.

Beck, Lane A. 1980. Physical Anthropology of Skeletal Remains from Oakland Cemetery, Atlanta, Georgia. Honors thesis, Department of Anthropology, Georgia State University, Atlanta.

Belcher, R., F. L'Engle Williams, and G. J. Armelagos. 2002. Misidentification of Meroitic Nubians Using Fordisc 2.0. *American Journal of Physical Anthropology Supplement* 34: 42.

Benington, R. Crewdson, and Karl Pearson. 1912. A Study of the Negro Skull with Special Reference to the Congo and Gaboon Crania. *Biometrika* 8: 292–339.

Bonogofsky, Michelle, editor. 2006. *Skull Collection, Modification and Decoration*. BAR International Series 1539. Archaeopress, Oxford, U.K.

Brash, J. C., and Matthew Young. 1935. The Bidford-on-Avon Skulls. *Biometrika* 27: 373–387.

Brooks, A. M. 1906. *The Unwritten History of Old St. Augustine*. The Record, Saint Augustine, Florida.

Brues, Alice M. 1992. Forensic Diagnosis of Race—General Race vs. Specific Populations. *Social Science and Medicine* 34: 125–128.

Caldwell, Joseph. 1943. Cultural Relations of Four Indian Sites of the Georgia Coast. Master's thesis, Department of Anthropology, University of Chicago.

Caldwell, Sheila K. 1953. Excavations at a Spanish Mission Site in Georgia. *Southeastern Archaeological Conference Newsletter* 31–32.

———. 1954. A Spanish Mission Site near Darien. *Early Georgia* 1: 13–17.

Campbell, A. R., and G. J. Armelagos. 2007. Assessment of FORDISC 3.0's Accuracy in Classifying Individuals from WW Howell's Populations and the Forensic Data Bank. *American Journal of Physical Anthropology Supplement* 44: 83–84.

Carter, Cindy P., Ashley Seidell, Donald P. Craig, Edmond Boudreaux, Krista L. Burleigh, Jason A. Gardner, Stacey A. Young, and Marie E. Danforth. 2004. A Bioarcheological Analysis of the French Colonial Burials at the Moran Gallery, Biloxi, MS. *Mississippi Archaeology* 39: 39–68.

Cook, Jeannette. 1990. *Fort King George: Step One to Statehood.* Darien News, Darien, Georgia.

Dailey, Robert C., L. Ross Morrell, and W. A. Cockrell. 1972. *The St. Marks Military Cemetery (8WA108).* Bureau of Historic Sites and Properties Bulletin 2. Florida Department of State, Tallahassee.

Fernandez de Prado, I. 1978. Antropología de los restos humanos medievales en la País Vasco. Tesis de licenciatura, Universidad del País Vasco, Bilbao, Spain.

Freid, D., M. K. Spradley, R. L. Jantz, and S. D. Ousley. 2005. The Truth Is Out There: How Not to Use FORDISC. *American Journal of Physical Anthropology Supplement* 40: 103.

Galera, V., and M. D. Garralda. 1992. La población medieval Cántabra de Santa María de Hito: Aspectos morfológicos y etnohistóricos. *Boletín Sociedad de España Antropología Biológica* 13: 69–87.

Geiger, Maynard. 1937. The Franciscan Conquest of Florida (1573–1618). Ph.D. dissertation, Catholic University of America, Washington, D.C.

Giles, Eugene, and Orville Elliot. 1962. Race Identification from Cranial Measurements. *Journal of Forensic Sciences* 7: 147–157.

Goodman, Alan H. 1997. Bred in the Bone? *Sciences* (March/April): 20–25.

Goodman, Alan H., and George J. Armelagos. 1996. The Resurrection of Race: The Concept of Race in Physical Anthropology in the 1990s. In *Race and Other Misadventures: Essays in Honor of Ashley Montagu in His Ninetieth Year*, edited by L. T. Reynolds and L. Lieberman, 174–186. General Hall, New York.

Gravlee, Clarence C., H. Russell Bernard, and William R. Leonard. 2003a. Heredity, Environment, and Cranial Form: A Re-analysis of Boas's Immigrant Data. *American Anthropologist* 105: 125–138.

———. 2003b. Boas's Changes in Bodily Form: The Immigrant Study, Cranial Plasticity, and Boas's Physical Anthropology. *American Anthropologist* 105: 326–332.

Harkins, Conrad. 1990. On Franciscans, Archaeology, and Old Missions. In *Columbian Consequences*, vol. 2, *Archaeological and Historical Perspectives on the Spanish Borderlands East*, edited by D. H. Thomas, 459–473. Smithsonian Institution Press, Washington, D.C.

————. n.d. The Five Franciscan Martyrs of Georgia. Postulator of the Cause. 1235 University Boulevard, Franciscan University of Steubenville. Ms. in possession of the authors.

Hooke, Beatrix G. E. 1926. A Third Study of the English Skull with Special Reference to the Farringdon Street Crania. *Biometrika* 18: 1–55.

Howells, William W. 1989. *Skull Shapes and the Map: Craniometric Analyses in the Dispersion of Modern* Homo. Papers of the Peabody Museum of Archaeology and Ethnology, vol. 79. Harvard University, Cambridge, Massachusetts.

————. 1995. *Who's Who in Skulls: Ethnic Identification of Crania from Measurements.* Papers of the Peabody Museum of Archaeology and Ethnology, vol. 82. Harvard University, Cambridge, Massachusetts.

Huxley, Angie K., and Michael Finnegan. 2004. Human Remains Sold to the Highest Bidder! A Snapshot of the Buying and Selling of Human Skeletal Remains on eBay, an Internet Auction Site. *Journal of Forensic Sciences* 49: 17–20.

Jantz, Richard L. 2001. Cranial Change in Americans, 1850–1975. *Journal of Forensic Sciences* 46: 784–787.

Jantz, Richard L., and L. Meadows-Jantz. 2000. Secular Change in Craniofacial Morphology. *American Journal of Human Biology* 12: 327–338.

Jantz, Richard L., and Peer H. Moore-Jansen. 1988. *A Database for Forensic Anthropology: Structure, Content and Analysis.* Report of Investigations 47. Department of Anthropology, University of Tennessee, Knoxville.

Jones, Grant D. 1978. The Ethnohistory of the Guale Coast through 1684. In *The Anthropology of St. Catherines Island*, vol. 1, *Natural and Cultural History*, edited by D. H. Thomas, G. D. Jones, R. S. Durham, and C. S. Larsen, 178–210. Anthropological Papers of the American Museum of Natural History, vol. 55, part 2. American Museum of Natural History, New York.

Jordana X. Y., and A. Malgosa. 2002. Terrassa, una villa medieval en transición a la época moderna: Estudio bioantropológico de la necrópolis de la Plaça Vella. *Revista España Antropología Biológica* 23: 1–25.

Keith, Arthur. 1911. On Certain Physical Characters of the Negroes of the Congo Free State and Nigeria. *Journal of the Royal Anthropological Institute of Great Britain and Ireland* 41: 40–71.

Kelso, William M. 1968. *Excavations at the Fort King George Historical Site, Darien, Georgia: The 1967 Survey.* Georgia Historical Commission Archaeological Research Series 1. Georgia Historical Commission, Darien.

King, Julia A., and Douglas H. Ubelaker. 1996. *Living and Dying on the 17th Century Patuxent Frontier.* Maryland Historical Trust Press, Crownsville.

Lanning, John T. 1935. *The Spanish Missions of Georgia.* University of North Carolina Press, Chapel Hill.

Layard, Doris, and Matthew Young. 1935. The Burwell Skulls, Including a Comparison with Those of Certain Other Anglo-Saxon Series. *Biometrika* 27: 388–408.

Lewis, Bessie. 1967. Fort King George. *Georgia Magazine* (November): 22–24.

MacDonnell, W. R. 1904. A Study of the Variation and Correlation of the Human Skull, with Special Reference to English Crania. *Biometrika* 3: 191–244.

———. 1906. A Second Study of the English Skull, with Special Reference to Moorfields Crania. *Biometrika* 5: 86–104.

Malcolm, L. W. G. 1920. Notes on the Physical Anthropology of Certain West African Tribes. *Man* 20: 116–121.

Mann, Robert W., and James J. Krakker. 1989. A Black Skeletal Sample from a Washington, D.C. Cemetery in the Context of Nineteenth Century Urban Growth. *Tennessee Anthropologist* 14: 1–32.

Martín Rivas, Encarnacion, and Philippe du Souich. 1981. Estudio antropologico de la necropolis altomedieval del Monasterio de Suso (San Millan de la Cogolla, Logroño). *Trabajos de Antropología Fisica* 2: 3–20.

Monaghan, John. 1995. *The Covenants with Earth and Rain: Exchange, Sacrifice, and Revelation in Mixtec Society.* University of Oklahoma Press, Norman.

Morant, G. M. 1926. A First Study of the Craniology of England and Scotland from Neolithic to Early Historic Times, with Special Reference to the Anglo-Saxon Skulls in London Museums. *Biometrika* 18: 56–98.

———. 1929. A Contribution to Basque Craniometry. *Biometrika* 21: 67–84.

Murad, Turhon A., and Todd D. Murad. 2000. The Postmortem Fate of Pat Gregory: A Disinterred Native American. *Journal of Forensic Sciences* 45: 488–494.

Naar, N. A., D. Hilgenberg, and G. J. Armelagos. 2006. Fordisc 2.0, the Ultimate Test: What Is the Truth? *American Journal of Physical Anthropology Supplement* 42: 136.

Omaechevarría, Ignacio. 1955. Mártires Franciscanos de Georgia. *Missionalia Hispánica* 12: 12–35, 291–370.

Oré, Luis G. 1936. *The Martyrs of Florida (1513–1616).* Joseph F. Wagner, New York.

Ousley, Stephen D., and Richard L. Jantz. 1996. *FORDISC 2.0: Personal Computer Forensic Discriminant Functions.* University of Tennessee, Knoxville.

———. 1998. The Forensic Data Bank: Documenting Skeletal Trends in the United States. In *Forensic Osteology: Advances in the Identification of Human Remains*, edited by K. J. Reichs, 441–458. 2nd ed. Charles C. Thomas, Springfield, Illinois.

Pons Rosell, José. 1949. Restos humanos procedentes de la necrópolis de época romana de Tarragona y Ampurias (Gerona). *Trabajos de Instituto "Bernardino de Sahagun" de Antropologia y Etnologia* 7: 19–206.

Prevosti, M., and A. Prevosti. 1951. Restos humanos procedentes de una necropolis judaica de Montjuich (Barcelona). *Trabajos de Instituto "Bernardino de Sahagun" de Antropologia y Etnologia* (Madrid) 12: 69–148.

Reid, R. W. 1926. Remains of Saint Magnus and Saint Rognvald, Entombed in Saint Magnus Cathedral, Kirkwall, Orkney. *Biometrika* 18: 118–150.

Rodriguez, A. 1981. Estudio antropologico de los restos humanos de la necropolis de Sta. Eulalia (Labastida, Alava). Tesis de licenciatura, Universitat Politecnica de Valencia, Spain.

Rose, Jerome C. 1985. *Gone to a Better Land: A Biohistory of a Rural Black Cemetery in the Post-Reconstruction South.* Arkansas Archeological Survey Research Series 25. Fayetteville.

Ross, Ann H., Dennis E. Slice, Douglas H. Ubelaker, and Anthony B. Falsetti. 2004. Population Affinities of 19th Century Cuban Crania: Implications for Identification Criteria in South Florida Cuban Americans. *Journal of Forensic Sciences* 49: 11–16.

Ross, Ann H., Douglas H. Ubelaker, and Anthony B. Falsetti. 2002. Craniometric Variation in the Americas. *Human Biology* 74: 807–818.

Rúa, Concepcíon de la. 1985. *El cráneo Vasco: Morfología y factores craneofaciales.* Servicio de Publicaciones de la Diputación Foral de Vizcaya, Zamudio, Spain.

Ruiz, Luis, Philippe du Souich, and Ma. L. Lara. 1995. Estudio antropológico de una coleccíon de cráneos modernos Andaluces. *Revista España Antropología Biológica* 16: 5–17.

Shrubsall, F. 1899. Notes on Ashanti Skulls and Crania. *Journal of the Anthropological Institute of Great Britain and Ireland* 28: 95–103.

Sledzik, Paul S., and Stephen Ousley. 1991. Analysis of Six Vietnamese Trophy Skulls. *Journal of Forensic Sciences* 36: 520–530.

Smay, Diana, and George Armelagos. 2000. Galileo Wept: A Critical Assessment of the Use of Race in Forensic Anthropology. *Transforming Anthropology* 9: 19–29.

Souich, Philippe du, Miguel C. Botella Lopez, and Luis Ruiz Rodriguez. 1990. Antropología de la població medieval de Palacios de la Sierra (Burgos). *Boletín Sociedad España Antropología Biológica* 11: 117–146.

———. 1991. Antropologia de la poblacion medieval de Villanueva de Soportilla (Burgos). *Anthropología y Paleoecología Humana* 6: 57–77.

Souich, Philippe du, and Encarnacion Martín Rivas. 1982. Los restos antropologicos de la necropolis medieval de Santa Maria de la Piscina (San Vicente de la Sonsiera, Logroño). *Trabajos de Antropología Fisica* 5: 30–41.

Sparks, Corey S., and Richard L. Jantz. 2002. A Reassessment of Human Cranial Plasticity: Boas Revisited. *Proceedings of the National Academy of Sciences* 99: 14636–14639.

Steadman, Dawnie Wolfe. 2003. The Pawn Shop Mummified Head: Discriminating among Forensic, Historic, and Ancient Contexts. In *Hard Evidence: Case Studies in Forensic Anthropology*, edited by D. W. Steadman, 212–226. Pearson Education, Upper Saddle River, New Jersey.

Stojanowski, Christopher M., and William N. Duncan. 2008. *Anthropological Contributions to the Cause of the Georgia Martyrs.* Occasional Papers of the Georgia Southern Museum. Georgia Southern Museum, Statesboro.

———. 2009. Historiography and Forensic Analysis of the Fort King George "Skull": Craniometric Assessment Using the Specific Population Approach. *American Journal of Physical Anthropology* 140: 275–289.

Taussig, Michael. 1999. *Defacement: Public Secrecy and the Labor of the Negative.* Stanford University Press, Stanford.

Thomas, David H., Stanley South, and Clark S. Larsen. 1977. *Rich Man, Poor Men: Observations on Three Antebellum Burials from the Georgia Coast.* Anthropological Papers of the American Museum of Natural History, vol. 54, part 3. American Museum of Natural History, New York.

Turner, William. 1901. A Contribution to the Craniology of the People of Scotland, Part I: Anatomical. *Transactions of the Royal Society of Edinburgh* 40: 547–613.

Ubelaker, Douglas H. n.d. PG3 Site Report. Ms. on file at the Smithsonian Institution Archives, Washington, D.C.

Ubelaker, Douglas H., Ann H. Ross, and Sally M. Graver. 2002. Application of Forensic Discriminant Functions to a Spanish Cranial Sample. *Forensic Science Communications* 4(3). http://www.fbi.gov/hq/lab/fsclbackissu/iuly2002/ubelakerl.htm (accessed September 6, 2008).

Varela, Tito A. 1974–1975. Estudio antropológico de los restos óseos procedentes de necrópolis Visigodas de la península Ibérica. *Trabajos de Antropología* 17: 7–157.

Vives, Elisenda. 1987. Contribució al coneixement dels enterraments medievals a Catalunya i regions limítrofes. Tesis doctoral, Universidad Autónoma de Barcelona, Spain.

Wescott, Daniel J., and Richard L. Jantz. 2005. Assessing Craniofacial Secular Change in American Blacks and Whites Using Geometric Morphometry. In *Modern Morphometries in Physical Anthropology*, edited by D. E. Slice, 231–245. Kluwer, New York.

Willey, P., and Paulette Leach. 2003. The Skull on the Lawn: Trophies, Taphonomy and Forensic Anthropology. In *Hard Evidence: Case Studies in Forensic Anthropology*, edited by D. W. Steadman, 176–188. Pearson Education, Upper Saddle River, New Jersey.

Williams, Frank L., Robert L. Belcher, and George J. Armelagos. 2005. Forensic Misclassification of Ancient Nubian Crania: Implications for Assumptions about Human Variation. *Current Anthropology* 46: 340–346.

Worth, John E. 1995. *The Struggle for the Georgia Coast: An Eighteenth-Century Spanish Retrospective on Guale and Mocama.* Anthropological Papers of the American Museum of Natural History 75. American Museum of Natural History, New York.

———. 2004. Evidence for the Locations of Guale Missions in 1597 (with Notes on Possible Locations for Physical Remains of the Martyrs). Report submitted to Fr. Conrad Harkins, vice postulator for the cause of the Georgia martyrs. Ms. in possession of the authors.

Young, Matthew. 1931. The West Scottish Skull and Its Affinities. *Biometrika* 23: 10–22.

8

Skull Deformation during the Iron Age in the Trans-Urals and Western Siberia

SVETLANA SHARAPOVA AND DMITRY RAZHEV

The practice of skull deformation is geographically widespread and exhibits considerable time-depth in Eurasia among the regions of central Europe, the Crimea, the lower Volga basin, the Cis-Urals, Central Asia, and western Siberia (Tur 1996: 237). In the Trans-Urals—the region comprising the eastern slope of the Urals—and westernmost Siberia (Dobrovol'sky 1977: 40–64) there is archaeological evidence for skull deformation from the Iron Age (Bagashev 2000; Razhev 2009; Sharapova 2007), which is the topic of this chapter. However, the earliest evidence for this practice comes from Iraq, dating to 45,000 BC (Gerszten and Gerszten 1995: 374).

Skull deformation among the Iron Age Sargat culture in the Trans-Urals and western Siberia served as a marker of social status, signaling membership in a privileged group that likely held greater social and/or political power than the majority of the population. Thus, intentional modification of the human skull represents a dramatic visual marker of social status, fulfilling a role similar to that of other forms of body modification such as piercing, tattooing, and foot binding. In contrast to clothing or more-superficial types and forms of body art and ornamentation, skull modification is an irreversible process, the skeletal embodiment of a social role.

Because early examples of intentional cranial deformation predate written history, modern investigators cannot ascertain conclusively why the shape of a child's head was modified initially (Mednikova 2006; Sharapova 2007). Some scholars, such as Fóthi (2000), suggest that it was performed to impart a more ferocious and terrifying image of a warrior, a practice similar to that of the Huns of Mongolia. By understanding the reasons for skull deformation among the Sargat, archaeologists elsewhere, such as in the ancient Near East (see Bonogofsky this volume), may better interpret their own evidence for intentional cranial modification. This practice serves many purposes, ranging from status marker (as among the Sargat) to ethnic identifier (as among the

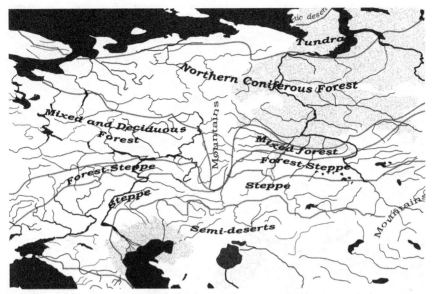

Figure 8.1. Map of the landscape zones of Eurasia. After Koryakova and Epimakhov 2007: fig. 0.2.

pre-Inca Chiribaya in southern Peru [see Lozada this volume]; see also Geller this volume for Maya examples from Mesoamerica) to purely aesthetic.

Sargat cattle and horse breeders inhabited the northern periphery of the "nomadic world" of Eurasia, a contact zone between forest, steppe, and mountain areas (figure 8.1), commonly characterized by its ecological instability. The forest-steppe of the Trans-Urals and western Siberia—a region covering 400,000 square kilometers dominated by birch-aspen coppices and biologically diverse grassy meadows—transitions into the steppe zone to the north. The forest-steppe occupied an intermediate geographical position, characterized by intense interactions between forest and steppe cultural traditions. On the whole, the forest-steppe landscapes exhibit geographic zonality and cultural diversity. Starting from the beginning of the first millennium BC, the forest-steppe was occupied by various cultures that were closely connected with the nomadic world but distinct in their economic orientation. The most significant of these was the Sargat culture (500 BC–AD 300), comprising horse and cattle breeders and well represented by both settlements and burial mounds known as kurgans. Sargat social organization demonstrates characteristics of a chiefdom, albeit in an early primitive state (Koryakova 1996, 2003; Matveeva 2000). The scholarly consensus is that the Sargat culture was a multicomponent social system. As Koryakova (2003: 283–284) noted, "Its sub-stratum was the local ancestral population; the super-stratum was presumably composed

Figure 8.2. Map of culture-group distributions in central Eurasia at the beginning of the Iron Age. After Koryakova 2003: fig. 17.6.

of nomadic and semi-nomadic clans." These clans were not large but were more active and militant than the aboriginal population. Furthermore, Sargat culture possessed a powerful ideology in which the rising aristocracy played a consolidating role. Nomads who traveled across pastures between central Asia and the Urals usually migrated to the southern forest-steppe in the summer (Tairov 1991). After 500 BC, the forest-steppe was directly impacted by the arrival of nomads—first the Saka, then the Sarmatians (Koryakova 2003: 289–290). The direction, form, and expression of such interactions with the Sargat appear in mortuary practices, evidence of trade and exchange, probable intermarriage, and skull deformation (figure 8.2).

Materials and Methods

Archaeological investigations of the Iron Age kurgans (burial mounds) in the forest-steppe zone of the Trans-Urals and western Siberia have yielded small numbers of deliberately deformed human skulls from the Sargat culture. Most Sargat kurgans were robbed by treasure hunters in the seventeenth and eighteenth centuries during Russian colonization of Siberia; some artifacts—but not the human skeletal remains—became part of the famous Siberian Collection of Peter the Great curated at the State Hermitage Museum in St. Petersburg, while the remaining contents were dispersed. Agricultural plowing through the 1900s also complicates the study of Sargat prehistory. Additionally, although Bagashev's monograph (2000) provides data on 397 Sargat skulls, most of the data on all skulls including the ones in this monograph remain unpublished and are therefore unavailable. Regardless of the poor preservation and association between the grave and cranial samples, and limited access to existing crania, our study contributes to general scholarship concerning the Sargat and cranial deformation in various geographic regions by providing new bioarchaeological, symbolic, and contextual information.

In this chapter, we present our analysis of a series of crania, rather than a general sample of Sargat interments, which in most cases exist only as incomplete skeletons separated (by grave robbers) from their respective crania. We analyze a total of sixty-five crania (table 8.1; curated by D. Razhev at the Institute of History and Archaeology, Urals Branch of the Russian Academy of Sciences and by M. Rykun at the Tomsk State University); of these, fifteen individuals from seven cemeteries displayed evidence of deformation—nine males, five females, and one juvenile.

Individuals were sexed and aged on the basis of available cranial and postcranial morphology. Sexing was based on measurements obtained from the pelvis, cranium, and mandible (Alexeev 1966; Alexeev and Debets 1964; Bass 1987); when those skeletal elements were unavailable, sexing was based on long-bone measurements. Aging was based on changes to the pubis (Brooks and Suchey 1990), auricular surface (Lovejoy et al. 1985), dentition (Ubelaker 1978) including eruption of the first and second molars (Gerasimov 1955), suture closure (Meindl and Lovejoy 1985), and epiphyseal fusion (Bass 1987; Rokhlin 1965).

Archaeological Evidence

The majority of the male crania that exhibited evidence of deformation were recorded in interments located on the periphery of the kurgan funerary area with the exception of Grave 3 from Kurgan 1 at the Ipkul'sky cemetery (table 8.2). The grave goods generally indicated a mounted warrior's social status (iron sword and dagger, iron- and bone-tanged arrowheads, bone shoulder plates, and pottery). Weaponry, as well as elements of horse-harness and ritual objects, may be considered markers of general adulthood. Most known child burials are rather modest in terms of grave goods and construction; although child burials contain objects, several types—primarily weapons—are

Table 8.1. Cranial sample by cemetery

Cemetery	Dates	No. of burial mounds	No. of excavated mounds	No. of graves	No. of individuals	No. of deformed skulls	No. of examined skulls
Gaevsky 1	400 BC–AD 300	10 plowed mounds	5	21	23 (24?)	2	8
Ipkul'sky	AD 200–400	50	8	11	5 securely documented	1	2
Karasie 9	100 BC–AD 200	11 plowed mounds	1	2	3	1	1
Murzinsky 1	400 BC–AD 200	14	9	19	17	1	4
Abatsky 1	100 BC–AD 300	5 plowed mounds	3	27	28	3	11
Abatsky 3	300 BC–AD 300	8	6	45	50	5	30
Isakovka 3	200 BC–AD 300	3 plowed mounds	3	19	21	2	9
Total		101	35	144	147 (148?)	15	65

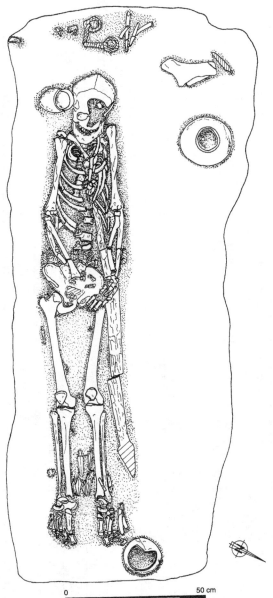

Figure 8.3. Plan view of burial containing an adult male from the Gaevsky 1 cemetery, Kurgan 6, Grave 2, with ceramics, an iron knife and sword, food remains, and horse-harness. After Koryakova et al. 1997: fig. 17.4.

0   50 cm

completely absent. Arrowheads and parts of composite bows occur most frequently in adult graves, with swords, daggers, and protective armor less often (Berseneva 2005: 11); Grave 2 from Kurgan 6 at the Gaevsky 1 cemetery is a notable exception (figures 8.3–8.6).

Within the burial grounds in this sample (i.e., synchronous and intact interments of male individuals with normal head shapes), animal bones were

Table 8.2. Male cranial sample displaying evidence of cranial deformation

Location	Sex and age	Grave goods	Comments
ISET RIVER			
Gaevsky 1, Kurgan 6, Grave 2	Male, 20–25 years old	Objects of horse-harness, iron knife and sword, composite bow, iron and bone arrowheads, bronze earring, 3 ceramic pots, remains of food offerings and clothes (leather belt fragments, pendants)	Peripheral, intact
Gaevsky 1, Kurgan 3, Grave 4	Male, 35–40 years old	Bone arrowheads, ceramic pot, fragment of stone tool	Peripheral, disturbed
Murzinsky 1, Kurgan 6, Grave 4	Male, 20–25 years old	Iron and bone arrowheads, fragments of iron knives and sword(?), glass bead, 1 imported vessel, 2 ceramic pots (one contained animal bones as remains of food offerings)	Peripheral, disturbed
TOBOL RIVER			
Ipkul'sky, Kurgan 1, Grave 3	Male, adult	Iron knife and sword, bone arrowheads, spike of a belt, iron buckles, bronze plaques, ceramic pot, horse bone	Intact, may be the central grave in this kurgan. Rhomboid-shaped hole on left side of cranial vault.
ISHIM RIVER			
Abatsky 1, Kurgan 3, Grave 4: skull 1	Male, 30–35 years old	3 ceramic pots, remains of food offerings, objects of horse harness, iron sword and dagger, iron and bone arrowheads, 2 iron plaques, iron rivet	Peripheral, intact

Abatsky 1, Kurgan 5, Grave 6	Male, 25–30 years old	Iron sword and dagger in scabbard with remains of red lacquer, fragments of quiver hook and bone plates of composite bow, iron and bone arrowheads, leather remains of bridle and iron bits with cheekpieces, bronze plaques, remains of food offerings	Peripheral, disturbed
Abatsky 1, Kurgan 5, Grave 8	Male, 50–60 years old	Iron and bone arrowheads, bone shoulder plates from composite bow, ceramic pot, animal bones as remains of food offerings	Peripheral, disturbed
Abatsky 3, Kurgan 2, Grave 7: skull 1	Male, 30–35 years old	Bronze cauldron	Collective interment (5 skeletons) in external ditch
IRTYSH RIVER			
Isakovka 3, Kurgan 2, Grave 6	Male, 20–30 years old	Bronze buckle and rivet, fragment of bone shoulder plate from composite bow, iron and bone arrowheads, fragment of iron knife, animal bones, remains of iron bits(?), skeletal elements impregnated with bronze oxide	Peripheral, within ditch

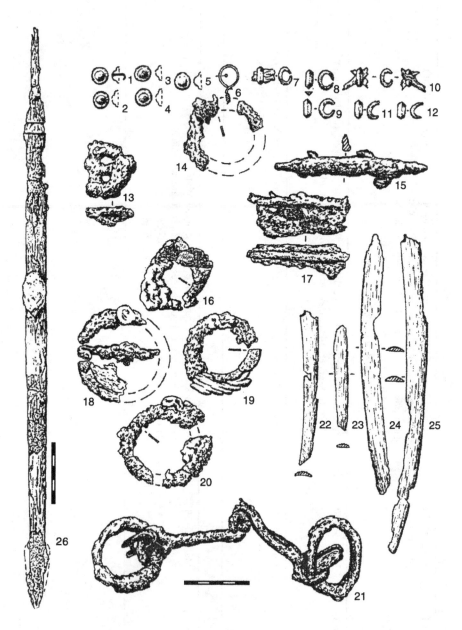

Figure 8.4. Grave goods from the Gaevsky 1 cemetery, Kurgan 6, Grave 2. Bronze objects are numbered 1–5, 7, 11, and 12. Object 6 is bronze and silver; objects 8–10 are bronze and leather; objects 13–21 and 26 are iron; and objects 22–25 are bone. Authors' collage, after Koryakova et al. 1997: figs. 19, 21.

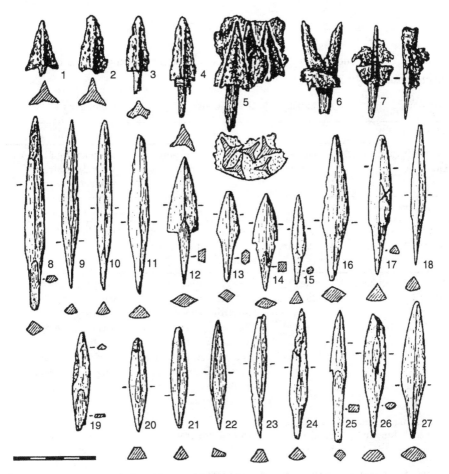

Figure 8.5. Arrowheads from the Gaevsky 1 cemetery, Kurgan 6, Grave 2. Objects 1–7 are iron; the remainder are bone. After Koryakova et al. 1997: fig. 20.

Figure 8.6. Pottery from the Gaevsky 1 cemetery, Kurgan 6, Grave 2. Authors' collage, after Koryakova et al. 1997: fig. 25: 1–2, 4.

Table 8.3. Female and subadult cranial samples displaying evidence of cranial deformation

Location	Sex and age	Grave goods	Comments
TOBOL RIVER			
Karasie 9, Kurgan 11, Grave 2	Female, 40–50 years old	2 nomadic-style pots, remains of food offerings	Peripheral, entire, secondary burial practice
ISHIM RIVER			
Abatsky 3, Kurgan 1, Grave 6	Female, 18–20 years old	Iron knife, ceramic pot, bronze fragment, horse scapula	Peripheral, disturbed
Abatsky 3, Kurgan 2, Grave 5	Female, 20–25 years old	4 ceramic pots (two contained animal bones, the remains of food offerings), gold earrings, various glass and gold beads, bronze pendant and mirror, iron finger ring, spindle whorl, iron bits with cheekpieces	Peripheral, entire, paired with girl ~7 years old, accompanied by beads, bronze earrings, iron finger ring, spindle whorl (sex of child assumed on basis of grave goods)
Abatsky 3, Kurgan 2, Grave 7: skull 3[a]	Subadult, 8–9 years old	Ceramic pot, iron knife	Collective interment (5 skeletons) in external ditch
Abatsky 3, Kurgan 2, Grave 10: skull 3	Female, 20 years old	Glass beads, iron knife	Collective interment (4 skeletons) in external ditch
IRTYSH RIVER			
Isakovka 3, Kurgan 3, Grave 8	Female, 30–40 years old	Ceramic spindle whorl, iron knife, 2 ceramic pots	Peripheral, entire

[a] This is the lone subadult in the table.

found both in vessels and within grave structures; food offerings included plenty of meat. For the Sargat, valuable imported arms—especially heavy armaments such as lacquered scabbards and precious silver and bronze wares—as well as artificial skull deformation symbolized the high social status of the deceased. There are comparatively few less-well-furnished graves—for example, a dagger instead of a sword at Gaevsky 1 (Kurgan 6, Grave 1) and the absence of horse-harnesses at Abatsky 3 (Kurgan 4, Grave 7 and Kurgan 5, Grave 3). In other words, the majority of the graves appear to represent high-status individuals. In contrast, the sample of females with deformed skulls appears to have been socially heterogeneous (table 8.3). Their graves also were in the peripheral areas of the cemeteries but contained both luxurious (bronze mirror, gold plaques, glass beads) and more-mundane (ceramic vessels, an iron knife) grave goods (see figure 8.7 for some of the luxury items).

Pottery vessels were found in many of the female graves. For example, in the secondary burial of a mature female at the cemetery of Karasie 9 (Kurgan 11, Grave 2), only pottery and food remains were recovered (figures 8.8, 8.9). Even this woman, however, with her sparsely furnished grave, could be considered a relatively privileged—and most likely nomadic—member of Sargat society given the grave construction, pottery style, and evidence of burial internment.

We did not find heavy armaments—usually associated with males—in the graves of females, although some forms of weaponry, such as arrowheads and daggers, are consistently found in graves of women (Berseneva 2005: 12). We did not identify any artifact class that accompanied only females. To our knowledge, there are no objects of Sargat material culture that are exclusively associated with one sex or the other. In some cemeteries in the Irtysh River basin, for example, spindle whorls were associated with both males and females (see Berseneva 2005: 10–14). The single child was accompanied by a sex-neutral set of grave goods (an iron knife and ceramic vessel) and was interred with four other individuals.

The relative proportion of males ($n=9$), females ($n=5$), and children ($n=1$) with deformed skulls is broadly comparable to what is known about Sargat society (Koryakova et al. 1997; Matveeva 2000), with consistently more deformed heads of males than of females or children interred throughout this vast territory (i.e., more burials throughout this vast territory consistently contain the deformed heads of males than the deformed heads of females or children). The reasons for this disparity are unknown, although we suggest that the individuals interred in kurgans were deliberately chosen and represent members of the Sargat elite.

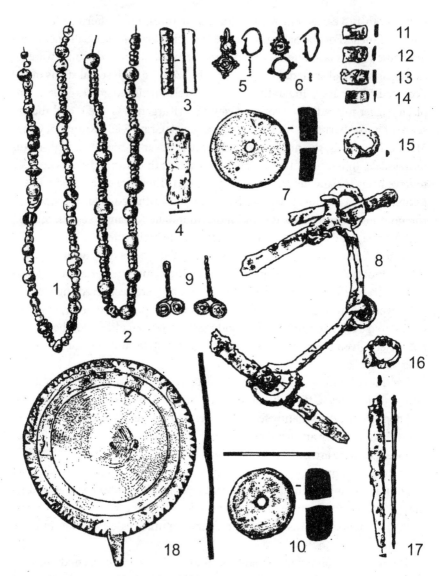

Figure 8.7. Luxury goods found with a young woman 20–25 years old from the Abatsky 3 cemetery, Kurgan 2, Grave 5. Goods include glass beads (1, 2); bronze objects (3, 4, 9), including a mirror (18); gold earrings (5, 6); clay spindle whorls (7, 10); and an iron ring (15) and several other iron objects (8, 11–14, 16, 17), including pieces of horse-harness. After Matveeva 1994: fig. 36.

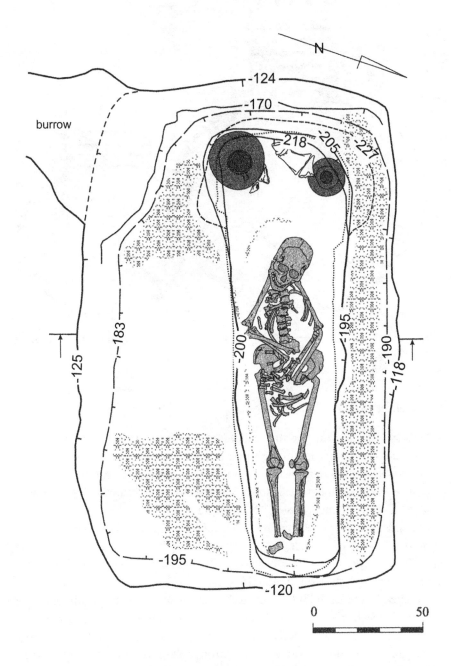

Figure 8.8. Plan view of burial of a woman 40–50 years old at Karasie 9, Kurgan 11, Grave 2, with pottery and food remains. Authors' creation, after Kovrigin et al. 2006: fig. 4.

Figure 8.9. Pottery from Karasie 9, Kurgan 11, Grave 2. Authors' creation, after Kovrigin et al. 2006: fig. 5.

Skeletal Evidence

Skeletal analyses indicate that deliberate deformation of the intravital skull was relatively common among the seven Sargat cemeteries studied here. As tables 8.4 and 8.5 demonstrate, some cranial measurements (according to Martin 1988) exhibit significant differences between deformed and nondeformed skulls (items 1, 8, 8(1), 32): longitudinal diameter, cross diameter, cranial index, and angle of frontal bone from nasion. Differences were generally more pronounced in males.

The majority of the sixty-five crania that we analyzed exhibited minor deformation, with the frontal canted posteriorly, the parietal and occipital bones flattened in the lambdoidal area, and the parietal eminence prominent. As a result, the sagittal contour of the cranial vault was amplified and became pentangular in shape (figure 8.10). Significant and pronounced skull deformation, though less common, was achieved through elongation of the cranial vault to create a wide and slightly flattened forehead and occiput (figure 8.11). All examples indicate that deformation resulted from a circular bandage placed around the cranium, with a fixed, hard construction of small boards or plates

Table 8.4. Measurements of deformed and nondeformed skulls of Sargat males

Cranial measurements	Deformed skulls			Nondeformed skulls			t
	n	x(mm)	s	n	x(mm)	s	
1. Longitudinal diameter*	10	181.4	5.0	86	185.1	7.9	-2.06
8. Cross diameter*	10	147.9	8.4	82	145.6	5.5	0.85
17. Height diameter from b	7	139.7	6.5	57	134.6	5.5	2.01
20. Height diameter from po	7	119.3	4.9	71	116.3	4.4	1.55
8(1). Cranial index*	10	81.5	4.0	80	78.8	4.2	2.03
5. Length of skull basis	5	105.6	2.9	54	104.1	3.9	1.06
32. Angle of frontal bone from nasion*	5	86.0	4.2	62	80.3	4.6	2.88
40. Length of face basis	6	100.2	4.4	51	100.7	4.3	-0.26
45. Malar diameter	8	141.3	4.6	76	138.7	5.9	1.48
48. Upper height of face	6	70.8	1.7	78	70.5	4.8	0.39
72. General angle of face profile	6	87.0	2.0	59	86.4	3.9	0.60
77. Naso-malar angle	6	144.1	1.8	84	142.7	5.7	1.47
Zm. Zygo-maxillar angle	6	133.3	6.6	59	131.9	5.1	0.52
51. Breadth of orbit from mf	9	46.8	2.0	83	45.4	2.5	2.01
52. Height of orbit	9	33.4	2.0	84	32.8	2.1	0.86
55. Height of nose	6	50.7	1.9	79	51.3	2.8	-0.71
54. Breadth of nose	8	25.4	1.8	82	25.4	1.7	0.06
75(1). Angle of bulge of nose	6	30.0	4.5	62	26.4	5.0	1.84
SC. Symotical breadth	6	7.2	0.6	69	8.2	1.9	2.98
SS. Symotical height	6	4.4	1.3	70	4.4	1.0	-0.06

Source: Cranial measurements following Martin 1988.

Abbreviations: n = number of skulls measured; x = mean measurement; s = standard deviation = v1/$(n-1)*\Sigma(x-xi)2$; t = 5% Student's t-distribution.

* Features that were significantly altered by deformation.

placed on the frontal and occipital areas. Such head deformation is referred to as the circular type (Daire et al. 2002; Zhirov 1940). This form of deformation exhibited among the Sargat crania distinguishes these skulls from other circularly deformed crania recorded from medieval funerary sites in western Siberia, where we note a pronounced deformation of the cranial vault that excludes the use of flat plates. Among the Sargat, significant differences in cranial morphology were obtained only for male individuals (see tables 8.4, 8.5), suggesting different types of practice. There is no evidence for racial differences between the examined individuals.

Almost all of the skeletons we studied are well developed, appearing to have led healthy lives since childhood. The presence of relatively few enamel hypoplasias indicates a sufficient diet with the rare occurrence of food shortages that is characteristic of hereditary aristocracy (Razhev 2001). These

Table 8.5. Measurements of deformed and nondeformed skulls of Sargat females

Cranial measurements	Deformed skulls			Nondeformed skulls			t
	n	x(mm)	s	n	x(mm)	s	
1. Longitudinal diameter*	7	173.1	9.4	40	173.0	8.6	0.02
8. Cross diameter*	7	142.7	7.4	42	140.7	5.2	0.67
17. Height diameter from b	6	136.2	8.3	27	129.9	4.9	1.80
20. Height diameter from po	7	116.1	6.6	32	112.8	4.2	1.25
8(1). Cranial index*	7	82.6	5.7	37	81.7	4.0	0.42
5. Length of skull basis	5	97.8	11.0	23	97.3	6.3	0.10
32. Angle of frontal bone from nasion	6	83.5	4.7	26	82.5	4.3	0.46
40. Length of face basis	4	93.0	11.4	20	94.2	5.8	-0.21
45. Malar diameter	8	132.9	6.1	34	128.4	6.2	1.86
48. Upper height of face	7	67.4	2.8	40	67.0	4.8	0.31
72. General angle of face profile	6	85.3	2.7	24	85.5	2.6	-0.20
77. Naso-malar angle	8	145.9	2.5	53	143.7	5.1	1.95
Zm. Zygo-maxillar angle	5	136.5	7.2	35	133.0	4.6	1.07
51. Breadth of orbit from mf	8	44.3	2.2	42	43.1	2.1	1.39
52. Height of orbit	8	32.6	1.9	43	32.8	2.0	-0.23
55. Height of nose	7	47.6	3.4	40	48.6	3.2	-0.74
54. Breadth of nose	5	24.2	2.5	44	24.3	1.8	-0.11
75(1). Angle of bulge of nose	6	22.8	4.2	30	24.0	5.5	-0.59
SC. Symotical breadth	8	9.0	2.1	42	7.8	1.6	1.51
SS. Symotical height	8	3.7	0.7	42	3.5	0.8	0.85

Source: Cranial measurements following Martin 1988.
Abbreviations: n = number of skulls measured; x = mean measurement in mm; s = standard deviation = v1/(n-1)*Σ(x-xi)2; t = 5% Student's t-distribution.
* Features that were significantly altered by deformation.

individuals were likely riders and spent a great deal of time on horseback, based on osteological markers (see Koryakova et al. 1997: 86–113; Daire et al. 2002: 13–15) in male and some female skeletons that include hypertrophied muscles (*maximus adductoris femoralis*) and numerous spinal pathologies such as Schmorl's nodes and beak-shaped osteophytes resulting in fused vertebrae. This reconstruction supports the hypothesis that the Sargat elites maintained a more mobile or nomadic economy than the majority of the Sargat population. Based on ethnographic studies, we know that among cattle pastoralists, nomadism is considered a privileged lifestyle compared to sedentism (Khazanov 1975, 2002).

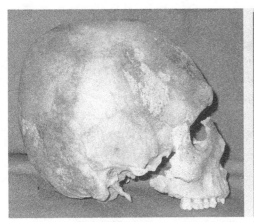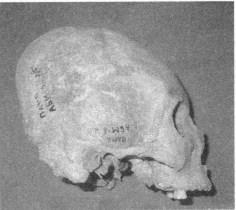

Figure 8.10. Skulls exhibiting relatively minor deformation. Note amplification of sagittal contour. *Left*, female from Abatsky 3, Kurgan 2, Grave 5; *right*, male from Abatsky 1, Kurgan 5, Grave 8. Photographs by the authors.

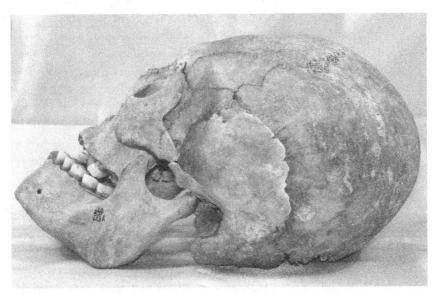

Figure 8.11. Skull of a female 40–50 years old from Karasie 9, Kurgan 11, Grave 2. Note frontal and occipital flattening. Reproduced from Kovrigin et al. 2006: fig. 6.

Iron Age Skull Deformation

Hippocrates (1881: 41) observed that ancient populations who practiced artificial skull deformation were long-headed, or dolichocephalic (Hippocrates actually used the term *macrocephalic,* as did other ancient writers [cited in Balabanova 2004], who mentioned "macrocephalic" deformation among inhabitants around the Black Sea, that is, neighbors of the Trans-Caucasian tribes). We can infer from Hippocrates that the custom of skull deformation had a symbolic function: "they account the most noble those who have the longest head" (Hippocrates 1881: 21).

The populations of the southern Asiatic steppe practiced skull deformation (and other forms of skull treatment) long before the Hunnic invasion of the region in the second century AD, a time when this tradition became widespread. In chronological terms, these populations represent Bronze Age cultures such as the Katakombnaya (2300–1850 cal BC) of the Volga and Don River basins and the Okunevskaya (1800–1300/1100 BC) of the Yenisei River basin (for regional postmortem and intravital skull treatments, see Kaiser 2006; Shishlina 2006; Vadetskaia 2006). Thereafter we do not know of any archaeological evidence of this practice for about a thousand years.

The reappearance and development of circular skull deformation can be traced to the middle of the first millennium BC (Dremov 1977; Ginzburg and Trofimova 1972; Khodjaiov 1966, 2000; Tur 1996). The earliest evidence of deliberate circular deformation was found in southern Turkmenistan at Yaz-Tepe near the ancient settlement of Merv, circa 500–400 BC, and at a few cemeteries in the Ferghana Valley in eastern central Asia. The Saka burials of the eastern territories of the Aral Sea (Chirik-Rabat cemetery) and central Kazakhstan (Egiz-Koitas funerary site) provide data on skull deformation as early as 300–200 BC.

The above evidence allows us to infer that intravital circular skull deformation took place in Eurasia during two time periods. For the first period (200 BC–AD 200), we note an increase in archaeological sites that produced deformed skulls. At the same time, deformed skulls were found in relatively small numbers (30 percent) in central Asia, the Trans-Urals, and western Siberia. Moreover, all known cases are associated with both sedentary and nomadic populations (Khodjaiov 2000). The earliest examples of deformation from the Sargat population observed in this study were the male crania from the Murzinsky 1 and Gaevsky 1 cemeteries, dating to the beginning of the first millennium AD. Radiocarbon analysis provides dates for male burials from the Murzinsky 1 cemetery as 210 BC–AD 130 and the Gaevsky 1 cemetery as

50 BC–AD 80 (Kovrigin et al. 2006: 201; Sharapova 2007: 64). Other cases, as deduced from analyses of grave goods, cannot be dated later than the first few centuries AD.

In the second period, AD 300–500, the character and spread of this phenomenon changed, with the occurrence of circular deformation reaching 80–100 percent among the late Sarmatians (Balabanova 2004: 182; Moshkova 1995: 150–163) and the Huns (Bernshtam 1940; Fedorova and Zykov 2001: 10–30). Many of these cemeteries were used by broadly dispersed, mobile societies engaged in stock breeding (Khodjaiov 2000).

The tradition of circular skull deformation in the Iron Age covered almost all of central Asia and the steppe zones of Kazakhstan and the Aral Sea. To the west, it was popular in the Sarmatian area between the Ural and the lower Don Rivers (Balabanova 2004: 172). This kind of head deformation was practiced among the inhabitants of settlements along the Sea of Azov and the Black Sea and farther west into Europe (Zhirov 1940). The eastern border of this tradition was the western slopes of the Tien Shan (Khodjaiov 2000) and Altai piedmonts (Dremov 1977; Tur 1996). In the east, we are not aware of any crania displaying circular deformation, but the Tagar culture (800 BC–AD 100) did practice a form of occipital-sincipital deformation (Gromov 2004), which is similar to the lambdoidal deformation practiced by American Indians (Buikstra and Ubelaker 1994: 162, fig. 117.1); such deformation, which need not be deliberate, is characterized by visibly flattened frontal and parietal bones. The spread of the practice of deliberate circular deformation among the Sargat population of the Trans-Urals and western Siberia allows us to identify a northern boundary for this custom. Quite likely, nomadic populations ancestral to the eastern Sakas from the Aral Sea region introduced it into the forest-steppe.

Skull Deformation in the Context of Visual Symbolism

Skeletal evidence of deliberate manipulation raises questions involving its meaning, function, symbolism, and taphonomy. Social change involves the differentiation of social groups and consolidation of membership, using a variety of signs or symbols to identify individuals (Kradin 2001: 110–116). How much of this evidence can be "excavated" from archaeological materials? The work of Polish archaeologist Zbigniew Kobylinski (1989), who suggested that symbolic thought probably dominated societies of the past, sheds light on this question. Kobylinski suggested that the material record of a culture retains the "memory" of that sociocultural system. Symbols were not only tools of differentiation but also provided social stability as abstract thinking evolved through the functional asymmetry of the two hemispheres of the brain (Koby-linski 1989: 126–127). With Kobylinski's perspective in mind, we can view the practice of skull deformation as a significant cultural symbol reflecting social relations and structure.

Skull deformation occurred rarely at first but eventually developed into a cultural tradition, according to Tur's (1996: 241) study of the origin of skull deformation, which assumed that head deformation first occurred during care of the newborn. Once it appeared in one local group, as a result of even cur-sory contact, deliberate skull deformation began to appear in many groups, including those that were ethnically distinct. The effectiveness of the skull as symbol may be one explanation for the spread of this phenomenon, and we can presume that as religious and mythological ideas changed through time, so too did the meaning of the deformed head. Eventually, deformation could have become directly associated with military, political, or other leadership roles (Sharapova 2007: 58), with a formative influence on ranked society. The display of symbols became more blatant the more hierarchical and stratified a society became, that is, changing from an association with age and sex in egalitarian societies to becoming a forcibly imposed marker in complex ones (Renfrew and Bahn 2004: 412–422).

For the successful diffusion of skull deformation, two functions are of great importance: utilitarian and prestigious (or symbolic). Many cultural innova-tions that are primarily utilitarian later acquire prestige associations or sym-bolic meaning that partly eclipses the original meaning once an innovation becomes associated with elites (Kradin 2001: 110–116; Sharapova 2007: 57–58; Tur 1996: 242). Altering the natural head form by application of various ap-pliances is of no direct utility; however, there are other known traditions that have appeared in societies despite the complete absence of practical physical value: bodily mutilation of the ears, lips, and so forth. Symbolic innovations have their roots in socially privileged groups (Arutiunov 1989: 187; Sharapova 2007: 57–58), which traditionally distinguish themselves from other members of society through outward attributes that may include clothing, headdresses, hairstyle, gesture and movement, and, in the case of the Sargat, skull deforma-tion. Even though the number of archaeological sites where we can identify skull deformation among the Sargat increased through time, the percentage of such skulls within these craniological series did not.

By the second half of the first millennium BC, the Sargat had limited the practice of skull deformation to elites. This phenomenon originated as the product of outside factors but served an internal cultural logic as a symbol of prestige. Ethnographic evidence provides data indicating that for certain political reasons, and during certain historical periods, nomadic culture was seen as prestigious by various strata of sedentary society (Arutiunov 1989: 186–198). Skull deformation emphasized this difference between nomads and sedentary peoples and signaled elite status to other nomads.

Circular skull deformation in the Trans-Ural region had a southern origin. Deformation among the Sargat population spread due to the influence of the nomadic Saka. Skull deformation must be regarded as an innovation for prestige, which primarily penetrated the elite (Arutiunov 1989: 177; Masson 1989: 25), became rooted, and spread throughout the privileged group (Kradin 2001: 110–116; Tur 1996: 242). We suggest that the group of males with deformed skulls discussed above were warriors (Koryakova 1996) or military aristocracy (Matveeva 2000) or were closely connected with defense roles in society (Berseneva 2005). Furthermore, all of the males and most females were probably descendants of a southern aristocracy. The elderly female individual from the modest burial (Karasie 9, Kurgan 11, Grave 2) belonged to the privileged, most likely nomadic, group of Sargat society rather than to the less prestigious sedentary group. The Sargat aristocracy may have been supplemented by absorption of members of stock-farming groups as kin. To maintain peaceful relationships between nomads and the outside world, so-called matrimonial diplomacy (along with other factors) likely had great importance.

The dynamics of skull deformation within the Trans-Urals during the Iron Age match the general model of development among other populations in northern Eurasia. All the above material supports the hypothesis that Sargat society, which we have reconstructed based on archaeological and anthropological data, was highly stratified and militant and consisted of select groups who practiced cattle breeding and were horseback riders. This study of the skulls of male and female Iron Age inhabitants of the Trans-Ural region and western Siberia demonstrates that deformation was used as an elite symbol of prestige to differentiate between groups in society. Skull deformation likely also functioned as an ethnic identifier at certain points in time.

This chapter has demonstrated how analyses of craniometric traits and the sex and age of the grave occupant in concert with the study of archaeological context—particularly spatial organization of kurgans and the analysis of grave goods—yield a better understanding of how certain physical traits functioned within society. As in other regions of the world, the skull was also a powerful sociopolitical tool that could, as in the case of Sargat deformation, signal status in a permanent way, making class divisions within society appear natural and immutable.

Acknowledgments

The authors are very grateful to Michelle Bonogofsky for her kind invitation to publish in this volume. We would particularly like to thank all those whose archived anthropological collections were used in this study. We thank our friend and colleague Andrey Kovrigin for his intellectual support during the early stages of our work. Our gratitude also goes to Ludmila Koryakova and Natalia Matveeva, who kindly granted us permission to reproduce their illustrations in this chapter. Our special thanks to Bryan Hanks for providing us with foreign publications on pediatric neurosurgery.

References Cited

Alexeev, V. P. 1966. *Osteometria: Metodika antropologicheskikh issledovanij* [Osteometry: Methods of anthropological analyses]. Nauka, Moscow.

Alexeev, V. P., and G. F. Debets. 1964. *Kraniometria: Metodika antropologicheskikh issledovanij* [Craniometry: Methods of anthropological investigations]. Nauka, Moscow.

Arutiunov, S. A. 1989. *Narody i kultury: Razvitie i vzaimodeistvie* [Peoples and cultures: Development and interactions]. Nauka, Moscow.

Bagashev, A. N. 2000. *Paleoantropologiya Zapadnoj Sibiri: Lesostep' v epokhy rannego zheleza* [Paleoanthropology of western Siberia: The forest-steppe in the Iron Age]. Nauka, Novosibirsk.

Balabanova, M. A. 2004. O drevnikh macrocefalakh Vostochnoj Evropy [Concerning ancient macrocephales in Eastern Europe]. In *OPUS: Interdisciplinary Investigation in Archaeology*, vol. 3, edited by M. Mednikova, 171–187. Institute of Archaeology of the Russian Academy of Sciences, Moscow.

Bass, W. M. 1987. *Human Osteology: A Laboratory and Field Manual.* 3rd ed. Missouri Archaeological Society, Columbia.

Bernshtam, A. N. 1940. *Kenkolskij mogilnik* [The Kenkolsky cemetery]. Nauka, Leningrad.

Berseneva, N. A. 2005. *Pogrebalnaya obryadnost naselenija srednego Priirtyshja v epokhy rannego zheleza: Sotsialnyje aspekty po materialam sargatskoj kultury* [Mortuary rituals of the population of the middle Irtysh river basin during the Iron Age: Social aspects based on materials of the Sargat culture]. Institute of History and Archaeology of the Russian Academy of Sciences, Ekaterinburg.

Brooks, S., and J. M. Suchey. 1990. Skeletal Age Determination Based on Os Pubis: A Comparison of the Acsadi-Nemeskeri and Suchey-Brooks Methods. *Journal of Human Evolution* 5: 227–238.

Buikstra, J., and D. Ubelaker, editors. 1994. *Standards for Data Collection from Human Skeletal Remains.* Research Series 44. Arkansas Archaeological Survey, Fayetteville.

Daire, M. Y., L. Koryakova, V. Buldashov, P. Courtaud, A. Epimajov, E. Gonzalez,

A. Kovrigin, et al. 2002. Habitats et nécropoles de l'âge du Fer au Carrefourde l'Eurasie. In *Les fouilles de 1993 à 1997*, vol. 1, edited by M.-Y. Daire and L. Koryakova, 1–291. De Broccard, Paris.

Dobrovol'sky, G. V., editor. 1977. *Prirodnye usloviya tsentral'noj chasti Zapadno-Sibirskoj ravniny* [Climate conditions of the central part of the western Siberian plain]. Moscow State University, Moscow.

Dremov, V. A. 1977. Obychai iskusstvennogo deformirovaniya golovy u drevnikh plemen Zapadnoi Sibiri [The Custom of artificial head deformation among the ancient tribes of western Siberia]. In *Problemy arkheologii i etnografii*, vol. 1, edited by M. F. Artamonov and R. F. Its, 99–110. Nauka, Leningrad.

Fedorova, N. V., and A. P. Zykov. 2001. *Kholmogorsky klad* [The Kholmogorsky hoard]. Sokrat, Ekaterinburg.

Fóthi, E. 2000. Anthropological Conclusions of the Study of Roman and Migration Periods. *Acta Biologica Szegediensis* 44: 87–94.

Gerasimov, M. M. 1955. Vosstanovlenie litsa po cherepu [Face reconstruction based on the cranium]. In *Trudy Instituta Etnografii* (no editor, special issue), 1–585. Izdatel'stvo AN SSSR, Moscow.

Gerszten, P. C., and E. Gerszten. 1995. Intentional Cranial Deformation: A Disappearing Form of Self-Mutilation. *Neurosurgery* 3: 374–382.

Ginzburg, V. V., and T. A. Trofimova. 1972. *Paleoantropologiya Srednei Asii* [Paleoanthropology of Central Asia]. Nauka, Moscow.

Gromov, A. V. 2004. Temennaya i zatylochnaya deformatsiya u drevnego naseleniya Sredneeniseiskikh stepei: Morphologiya i obychay [Sincipital and occipital deformation among the ancient population of the middle Enisei steppes: Morphology and rite]. In *OPUS: Interdisciplinary Investigation in Archaeology*, vol. 3, edited by M. Mednikova, 162–170. Institute of Archaeology of the Russian Academy of Sciences, Moscow.

Hippocrates. 1881. *Hippocrates on Airs, Waters, and Places*. Wyman and Sons, London.

Kaiser, E. 2006. Plastered Skulls of the Catacomb Culture in the Northern Pontic Region. In *Skull Collection, Modification and Decoration*, edited by M. Bonogofsky, 45–58. BAR International Series 1539. Archaeopress, Oxford, U.K.

Khazanov, A. M. 1975. *Sotsialnaya istoriya skifov* [Social history of the Scythians]. Nauka, Moscow.

———. 2002. *Kochevniki i vneshnij mir* [Nomads and the outside world]. Daik-Press, Almaty, Kazakhstan.

Khodjaiov, T. K. 1966. O prednamerennoi deformatsii golovy u narodov Srednei Asii [About deliberate head deformation among the population of Central Asia]. In *Vestnik karakalpakskogo filiala AN UzSSR*, vol. 4 (no editor), 56–60. Izdatel'stvo AN UzSSR, Nukus, Uzbekistan.

———. 2000. Obychai prednamerennoi deformatsii golovy v Srednei Asii [The custom of deliberate head deformation in Central Asia]. In *Antropologicheskie i etnograficheskie svedeniya o naselenii Srednei Asii*, edited by G. V. Rykushina and N. A. Dubova, 22–46. Stary Sad, Moscow.

Kobylinski, Z. 1989. Ethno-archaeological Cognition and Cognitive Ethno-archaeology. In *The Meaning of Things: Material Culture and Its Symbolic Expression*, edited by I. Hodder, 123–129. Harper Collins, London.

Koryakova, L. N. 1996. Social Trends in Temperate Eurasia during the Second and First Millennia BC. *Journal of European Archaeology* 4: 243–280.

———. 2003. Between Steppe and Forest: Iron Age Societies of the Urals. In *Ancient Interactions: East and West in Eurasia*, edited by K. Boyle, C. Renfrew, and M. Levine, 265–292. McDonald Institute for Archaeological Research, Cambridge, U.K.

Koryakova, L. N., V. A. Buldhashev, A. A. Kovrigin, P. A. Kosintsev, P. Courtaud, G. I. Makhonina, D. I. Razhev, J. P. Pautreau, and S. V. Sharapova. 1997. *Kul'tura zaural'skikh skotovodov na rubezhe er: Gaevskij mogilnik sargatskoi obshchnosti: Antropologicheskoje issledovanie* [Culture of Trans-Uralian cattle and horse breeders at the turn of the era: The Gaevo burial ground of the Sargat community: Anthropological research]. Ekaterinburg Press, Ekaterinburg, Russia.

Koryakova, L. N., and A. Epimakhov. 2007. *The Urals and Western Siberia in the Bronze and Iron Ages*. Cambridge University Press, New York.

Kovrigin, A. A., L. N. Koryakova, P. Courtaud, D. I. Razhev, and S. V. Sharapova. 2006. Aristokraticheskie pogrebeniya mogilnika Karasie 9 [Aristocratic interments of the Karasie 9 cemetery]. In *Yuzhnij Ural i sopredelnie territorii v skifo-sarmatskoje vremya*, edited by G. Obydennova and N. Saveliev, 188–203. Gilem, Ufa, Russia.

Kradin, N. N. 2001. *Politicheskaya antropologiya* [Political anthropology]. Ladomir, Moscow.

Lovejoy, C. O., R. S. Meindl, T. R Pryzbeck, and R. P. Mensforth. 1985. Chronological Metamorphosis of the Auricular Surface of the Ilium: A New Method for the Determination of Adult Skeletal Age at Death. *American Journal of Physical Anthropology* 68 (1): 15–28.

Martin, R. 1988. Handbuch der vergleichenden Biologie des Menschen. In *Wesen und Methoden der Anthropologie*, vol. 1, edited by R. Knussmann, 160–192. 4th ed. Gustav Fischer, Stuttgart.

Masson, V. M. 1989. *Pervye tsivilizatsii* [Early civilization]. Nauka, Moscow.

Matveeva, N. P. 1994. *Ranny zhelezny vek Priishimia* [Early Iron Age of the Ishim River basin]. Nauka, Novosibirsk, Russia.

———. 2000. *Socialno-ekonomicheskie struktury naselenija zapadnoi Sibiri v rannem zheleznom veke* [Social and economic structures of the west Siberian population in the Early Iron Age]. Nauka, Novosibirsk, Russia.

Mednikova, M. B. 2006. Fenomen kul'turnoj deformatsii golovy: Evrazijskij kontekst [Phenomenon of cultural deformation of the head: Eurasian context]. In *OPUS: Interdisciplinary Investigations in Archaeology*, vol. 5, edited by M. Mednikova, 206–229. Institute of Archaeology of the Russian Academy of Sciences, Moscow.

Meindl, R. S., and C. O. Lovejoy. 1985. Ectocranial Suture Closure: A Revised Method for the Determination of Skeletal Age at Death Based on the Lateral-Anterior Sutures. *American Journal of Physical Anthropology* 68 (1): 57–66.

Moshkova, M. G. 1995. Late Sarmatian Culture. In *Nomads of the Eurasian Steppes in the Early Iron Age*, edited by J. Davis-Kimball, V. Bashilov, and L. Yablonsky, 149–163. Zinat Press, Berkeley, California.

Razhev, D. I. 2001. *Naselenie lesostepi zapadnoi Sibiri rannego zheleznogo veka: Reconstructsija antropologicheskikh osobennostei* [Population of the forest-steppe of western Siberia in the Early Iron Age]. Institute of History and Archaeology of the Russian Academy of Sciences, Ekaterinburg.

———. 2009. *Bioantropologiya naseleniya sargatskoj obschnosti* [Bioanthropology of the Sargat entity]. Institute of History and Archaeology of the Russian Academy of Sciences, Ekaterinburg.

Renfrew, C., and P. Bahn. 2004. *Archaeology: Theories, Methods and Practice.* Thames and Hudson, London.

Rokhlin, D. G. 1965. *Bolezni drevnikh ludej* [Diseases of the ancient population]. Nauka, Moscow.

Sharapova, S. V. 2007. Simvolika prestizha v sargatskoj kul'ture: Na primere fenomena kol'tsevoj deformatsii cherepa [Symbolism of prestige in Sargat culture: Phenomenon of circular skull deformation]. In *Mif, obryad i ritual'ny predmet v dervnosti*, edited by S. Arutiunov, 57–69. Magellan, Ekaterinburg-Surgut, Russia.

Shishlina, N. I. 2006. Decoration of Skulls: Funerary Rituals of the Yamnaya and Catacomb Cultures in the Eurasian Bronze Age. In *Skull Collection, Modification and Decoration*, edited by M. Bonogofsky, 59–66. BAR International Series 1539. Archaeopress, Oxford, U.K.

Tairov, A. D. 1991. *Ranniye kochevniki yuzhnogo Zauralya v VII–II vekakh do novoi ery* [Early nomads of the southern Trans-Urals in the seventh to second centuries BC]. Institut Arkheologii RAN, Moscow.

Tur, S. S. 1996. K voprosu o proiskhozhdenii i funktsiyakh obychaya koltsevoi deformatsii golovy [On the issue of origin and function of the tradition of circular head deformation]. In *Arkheologiya, antropologiya i etnografiya Sibiri*, edited by Yu. F. Kirjushin, 237–249. Altai State University, Barnaul, Russia.

Ubelaker, D. H. 1978. *Human Skeletal Remains: Excavation, Analysis, Interpretation.* Taraxacum, Washington, D.C.

Vadetskaia, E. B. 2006. The Yenisei Mummies with Modeled Skulls and Masks from Siberia. In *Skull Collection, Modification and Decoration*, edited by M. Bonogofsky, 67–75. BAR International Series 1539. Archaeopress, Oxford, U.K.

Zhirov, E. Y. 1940. Ob iskusstvennoi deformatsii [On artificial deformation]. *Kratkie soobshcheniya o polevykh issleodovaniyakh institute istorii materialnoi kultury* (Izdatel'stvo AN SSSR [Academy of Sciences of the USSR], Moscow-Leningrad) 8: 88–95.

9

Marking Ethnicity through Premortem Cranial Modification among the Pre-Inca Chiribaya, Peru

MARÍA CECILIA LOZADA

Human cranial modification represents an extremely labor-intensive process that requires sustained molding of the cranium for long periods of time during infancy—a time when the bones of the cranial vault are relatively plastic. Given the considerable investment of time and energy required to produce permanent alterations in head shape, as well as the considerable risks of injury associated with this practice (Lekovic et al. 2007), it is natural to ask which groups of people would engage in this practice and why, and what served as the inspiration for specific head shapes.

Since cranial modification depicts identity at different levels, I examine how an analysis of cranial modification can be used to complement other forms of research to reconstruct and assess group differentiation among the pre-Inca Chiribaya of southern Peru. In particular, I focus on the use of head form as a visual cue to ethnicity, differentiating one group of "insiders" from another, as well as differentiating "insiders" collectively from "outsiders." I also explore the sociopolitical environment that may have promoted the use of symbols of group membership such as cranial modification among the Chiribaya.

Given that cranial modification is performed during infancy, it represents an irreversible symbol of ascribed corporate membership that would have accompanied a person throughout life. Although clothing, body adornment, and other material accessories could also be used to symbolize group membership, these practices are generally self-selected and, by their very nature, subject to change. By contrast, families and/or corporate groups imposed cranial modification on individuals at birth. It could not be altered later in life, and as such, head shape served as an easily visible symbol of ascribed identity, as the very location of the human head is ideal for displaying cues to an individual's identity (Croucher 2008).

Bioarchaeological studies of premortem cranial modification in prehistoric populations throughout the world have become increasingly more common, with considerable differences in methodological approaches. As a result, interpretation of this custom includes themes such as identity and gender construction, body transformation, social permeability, power relationships, social status, and group membership (Andrushko 2007; Blom 2005; Croucher 2008; Hoshower et al. 1995; Lorenz 2008; Lozada and Buikstra 2002; Tiesler 1998; Torres-Rouff 2002; see also Bonogofsky this volume, Geller this volume, and Sharapova and Razhev this volume for examples from the Neolithic Near East, New World Maya, and Iron Age Eurasia, respectively). In the Andes, researchers have moved away from the very traditional typological classification of modified skulls to a more contextualized analysis. In these studies, cranial modification is distinct from most categories of material culture that are commonly used to distinguish among different sociocultural, political, and economic groups. From case studies in the Andes, it is clear that in pre-Hispanic societies, head shape was mostly used as an emblem of personal identity or group membership. In their seminal study, Hoshower and colleagues (1995: 146) state that in the Andes, "proper interpretation of deformation patterning is not intuitively obvious because differences in head shape may signal group membership at any one of a number of levels: regional, community, and/or lineage."

The Chiribaya consolidated their power in the coastal portion of the Osmore Drainage in southern Peru (AD 700–1359; figure 9.1). Following a similar pattern to that described in colonial ethnohistorical accounts, the Chiribaya culture was made up of distinct communities of specialists such as fishermen (*pescadores*) and agriculturalists (*labradores*). Differences between these two economic groups cut across nearly every category of cultural production, from ceramic and spoon styles to mortuary patterning, and suggest a fundamental cultural divide within Chiribaya society (Lozada and Buikstra 2002; Nigra 2008). Furthermore, dietary analysis conducted by Tomczak (2003) indicates that food consumption differed between these groups. Agriculturalists consumed the greatest amount of terrestrial resources, while the diet of fishermen was based primarily on marine items. Collectively, these data provide compelling evidence that the Chiribaya culture was organized as a coastal *señorío*, which is defined as a large sociopolitical unit made up of groups of specialists under the power of lords (Rostworowski 1970). In this study, as stated above, I determine whether the *pescadores* and the *labradores* of Chiribaya also inferred ethnic distinctions through premortem cranial modification styles, and

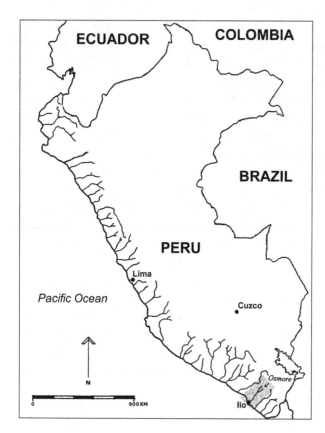

Figure 9.1. Map of Peru with study area (shown in figure 9.2) shaded. Reproduced from Lozada and Buikstra 2002.

I propose factors that may have encouraged the use of these highly visible emblems of ethnic identity.

Materials and Methods

This study includes a total of 224 skulls from three main Chiribaya sites: El Yaral (n=47), Chiribaya Alta (CHA; n=147), and San Gerónimo (n=30; figure 9.2). This collection represents an unselected series of all skulls from well-documented contexts. These sites were excavated under the direction of Jane E. Buikstra and the author during 1989 and 1990. El Yaral is a small Chiribaya settlement located about fifty kilometers from the coast. It is composed of residential areas, terraces, and two cemeteries. In contrast, Chiribaya Alta occupies a major promontory overlooking the Pacific Ocean. This site has been characterized as the capital of Chiribaya and a major site of political control (Lozada and Buikstra 2002); nine discrete cemeteries were excavated there. Finally, the site of San Gerónimo is only one hundred meters from the shore, with ninety-two tombs. The individuals buried in San Gerónimo represented

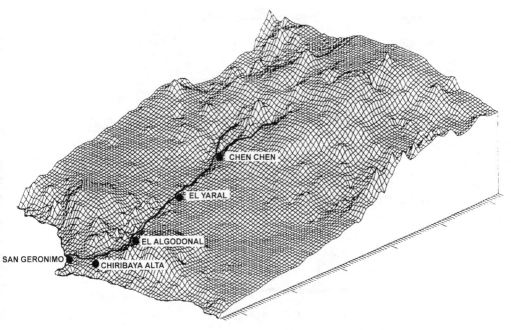

Figure 9.2. Location of sites of study. Reproduced from Lozada and Buikstra 2002.

a community of *pescadores*, while the individuals buried in the two cemeteries at El Yaral represented *labradores*. As the center of Chiribaya political control, the cemeteries of Chiribaya Alta exhibit a large degree of cultural heterogeneity reflecting ethnic affiliations with both groups of specialists.

Each skull was scored according to shape and modification technique (Lozada and Buikstra 2002). Sex of the skeletons was determined following the standards of Buikstra and Ubelaker (1994). Age at death was not considered in this study, since shape from intentional cranial molding does not change throughout life. Finally, to interpret the cranial modification styles of each individual in their appropriate context, I examined tomb location and type, as well as all associated ceramics.

The skulls used in this study were first separated into modified and non-modified, based on evidence of artificial compression of the skull. Two broad groups were distinguished. The first type was the *tabula obliqua*, characterized by fronto-occipital compression (figure 9.3). The second group consists of the circumferential type, or *annular obliqua*, characterized by an elongated and tubular vault (figure 9.4). Of the sample skulls, 40 percent were not intentionally deformed; the remaining 60 percent were deformed, with 20 percent annular and 40 percent fronto-occipital.

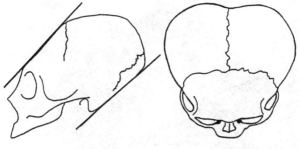

Anton (1989: 256)

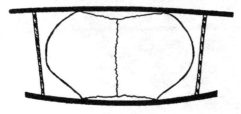

Dembo & Imbellioni (1938: 280)

Figure 9.3. Fronto-occipital type of cranial modification. Reproduced from Lozada and Buikstra 2002.

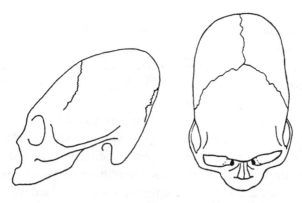

Anton (1989: 256)

Dembo & Imbellioni (1938: 280)

Figure 9.4. Annular type of cranial modification. Reproduced from Lozada and Buikstra 2002.

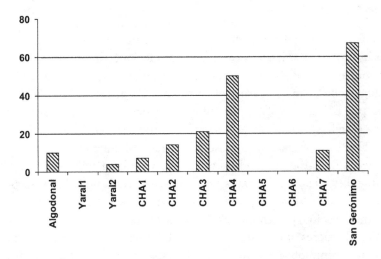

Figure 9.5. Graph of distribution of annular type of cranial modification at study sites. Reproduced from Lozada and Buikstra 2002.

I statistically tested for association between sex and cranial modification types using chi-square analysis. This test did not demonstrate a statistically significant association between sex and cranial modification. This suggests that cranial modification was not used to display or symbolize sex but instead was determined by other cultural and biological variables.

I next studied the relationship between cranial deformation types and either ceramics or cemeteries using chi-square analysis. An inspection of the cranial modification styles in relation to cemetery demonstrates that this practice served as a symbol of corporate membership within economically specialized groups. The annular style of modification, for example, is closely associated with the sites of San Gerónimo and CHA 4, both of which are closely associated with marine exploitation and consumption (figure 9.5). The individuals from San Gerónimo and CHA 4 have a specific ceramic type in common, which, like the annular form of cranial modification, is uncommon in other mortuary contexts. Interestingly, the prevalence of annular modification progressively diminishes as one moves inland, to the point that none are found in cemetery 1 at El Yaral. This distinct distribution, combined with the close association between annular modification and individuals with archaeological and dietary evidence of maritime ties, strongly suggests that this head shape was used principally by the pescadores.

Symbolic Analysis

Ethnohistorically, pescadores symbolized their separation from other communities in ways such as language and religious ideology; I propose that premortem cranial modification was yet another means by which pescadores visibly distinguished themselves from other groups. Cranial modification was, therefore, part of a cluster of distinct cultural practices including subsistence behavior, ceramic/spoon styles, and burial program that served to reinforce and symbolize clear social and cultural differences. Although genetic differences between this group and others within the Chiribaya could not be detected using skeletal nonmetric traits, pescadores nevertheless could have represented a separate ethnic group within the Chiribaya (see Barth 1969: 9–38).

In a similar fashion, the fronto-occipital style of cranial modification symbolized the labradores of Chiribaya; this type is absent at San Gerónimo but becomes more common as one moves up the valley, in reverse of the pattern found with the annular style (figure 9.6). Skulls flattened in the fronto-occipital style are most prevalent within CHA 7 and cemetery 2 at El Yaral, both of which are characterized by increasing dependence on terrestrial resources for subsistence. Burials associated with this type of cranial modification were also highly correlated with Algarrobal ceramics and burial offerings of camelid remains. These features contrast with those identified with the pescadores (summarized above) and suggest that a very different set of symbols was utilized by the labradores to identify and separate themselves from the fisher folk.

In summary, the correlation between cranial modification styles and the socioeconomic division between pescadores and labradores within the Chiribaya indicates that modification types served as an important symbol of membership within economically specialized groups. The fact that the practice of head molding had to be performed during infancy suggests that children were born into economic communities and usually were expected to remain within them. The fairly exclusive use of cemeteries devoted to the burial of individuals adhering to these lifestyles attests to the strong sociocultural imprinting that occurred with this practice. In this sense, this form of extreme body alteration served as a statement on how the Chiribaya organized their world, a view materially evident in the shape of their heads even after death.

In other contexts in the Andes, cranial modification appears to have been used as *ayllu* markers. Hoshower and colleagues' (1995) study of Tiwanaku crania in Moquegua, southern Peru, demonstrates that head form was shared among members of an extended social unit or Andean ayllu. Furthermore, subsequent Tiwanaku research by Blom (2005), both in the capital site of Tiwanaku in modern Bolivia and in peripheral territories such as the Katari Valley

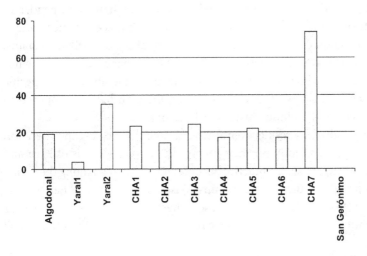

Figure 9.6. Graph of distribution of fronto-occipital type of cranial modification at study sites. Reproduced from Lozada and Buikstra 2002.

and Tiwanaku colonies in Moquegua, indicates that head form was used as a regional identifier. Tiwanaku residents in the highland plateau usually shared the annular type, while lowlanders exhibited fronto-occipital modification. Because these forms identify regional affiliation, Blom also traced population movement from the periphery to the Tiwanaku capital in the highlands. In particular, cranial types are quite heterogeneous in the capital, suggesting that its population drew upon ethnic/regional groups throughout the Tiwanaku state.

In northern Chile, Torres-Rouff (2002) uses cranial modification patterns along with funerary accoutrements to assess the impact of Tiwanaku influence in the oases of San Pedro de Atacama. Although indirect evidence of Tiwanaku highland expansion exists, her study of head shapes shows that strong local identity was maintained. In fact, local styles reflect social cohesion of the inhabitants of the Atacama desert (*atacameños*) and maintenance of ethnic boundaries against the imperial highland expansion. Although Tiwanaku presence outside the highlands has been recognized, these bioarchaeological studies indicate that the social and political interaction between Tiwanaku and colonized groups was extremely variable. Collectively, cranial modification during this period appears to have been used to distinguish membership at different levels, including residential groups (i.e., ayllus; Hoshower et al. 1995), local groups (cohesive as a result of Tiwanaku expansion; Torres-Rouff 2002), or regions (e.g., lowland vs. highland; Blom 2005).

Although head shape has been used to symbolize status and gender in other contexts (Croucher 2008; Lorenz 2008), there is no detectable relationship between cranial vault shape and either skeletal sex or individual status, as determined by artifact assemblages. This adds further credence to the notion that such bodily practices were used to delineate membership in specific *parcialidades,* or groups of specialists among the Chiribaya, as opposed to other dimensions of an individual's social persona.

To contextualize my results even further, I note that head shape alteration was not always a common practice among the coastal societies of Peru and Chile. Why, then, did such a practice become so widespread among the Chiribaya as opposed to other coastal groups? Based on his study in East Africa, Ian Hodder (1978) proposes that in cases where material culture is used for ethnic identity, boundary maintenance responds to economic or other social pressures.

Contextualized Results

The Chiribaya flourished on the coast of the Osmore Drainage at the same time that the expanding and powerful highland Tiwanaku state was establishing numerous colonies along the western slopes of the Andes (Goldstein 1993, 2005). The largest Tiwanaku midvalley settlement identified to date was located only two hundred kilometers from Chiribaya Alta, the center of Chiribaya political power (Lozada and Buikstra 2002). The relationship between the Tiwanaku highlanders and the contemporaneous coastal Chiribaya is not well understood and remains the subject of ongoing investigation; however, the archaeological record makes clear that Tiwanaku influence along the coast was extremely limited. In fact, my study of the region suggests that there was a biological and sociocultural barrier between the midvalley Tiwanaku settlers and the coastal Chiribaya peoples. During its florescence, the Chiribaya was a powerful señorío that appears to have resisted being subjugated by this expanding highland state.

Against the backdrop of rivalry between Chiribaya and midvalley Tiwanaku settlements, internal sociopolitical and economic tensions may have reached their peak among the Chiribaya. As a consequence, an increasingly complex and rigid sociopolitical order may have developed among the Chiribaya, distinguishing them from their predecessors, none of whom faced such direct competition. Such pressure for a more regimented social order may have accentuated the need for highly overt, and unalterable, symbols of group membership, with cranial modification being the most extreme example. In this respect, the highly unstable and tense political environment within the

Osmore Drainage during the Middle Horizon may have led to the increasing use of overt signs of coastal group identity among the Chiribaya. This theory will require further evaluation through a comprehensive comparison of head shapes throughout the Osmore Drainage both before and after Tiwanaku occupation. Still, my findings echo that of Torres-Rouff (2002) in northern Chile, where (as stated earlier) cranial modification patterns among the atacameños show continuity and unification in response to the threat of an expanding Tiwanaku political network.

Although numerous studies have been published recently regarding cranial modification (Blom 2005; Lorenz 2008; Torres-Rouff 2002), the inspiration for specific head shapes remains unclear. Although there are no historical records from this time period, some information can be gleaned from ethnohistorical documents and modern practices among other midvalley Andean groups. For example, Ulloa Mogollón (1965 [1557–1586]) provides a specific example of two ethnic groups inhabiting the Colca Valley prior to the Inca expansion—the Collaguas and the Cabanas—and indicates that the Collaguas associated themselves with their tutelary volcano, Sabancaya, which has high peaks. The Collaguas selected a type of cranial form that most closely resembles the high peaks of this volcano, in deference to their patron deity, or *apu*. In contrast, the Cabanas molded their heads to appear squat and wide, similar to their patron volcano Hualca-Hualca, which is much lower than the Sabancaya volcano.

Shortly after the arrival of the Spanish in the Andes, the religious authorities outlawed the ancient practice of head shaping, which had began as early as 6000–4000 BP in northern Chile (Santoro 1989). The Spaniards found this custom to be immoral and a threat to public health (Bartra 1982). In spite of this edict, this tradition survived for many years, although Andean inhabitants were forced to hide their altered head shapes under hats; consequently, this practice seems to have evolved such that hat type eventually supplanted head shape as a symbol of ethnic difference between groups (Arriaga 1968 [1621]; Capoche 1959 [1585]).

The two groups that Ulloa Mogollón discusses still inhabit the Colca Valley, and although they no longer practice this form of body modification, they have selected hat forms that continue to symbolize their spiritual link with their patron apus. Specifically, the Collaguas wear a tall, white hat with a peaked top, which recalls the tall peaks associated with the Sabancaya volcano. The white color may reflect the snow-capped peak. In contrast, the Cabanas wear a heavily embroidered dark hat that is shorter, reflecting the naturally lower height of their apu. These descriptions indicate that sacred landscapes were the inspiration for ethnic symbols among both the pre-Hispanic and modern Collaguas and Cabanas. With respect to the Chiribaya peoples, we cannot determine the precise inspiration for their cranial style; however, the experience from Colca Canyon suggests that the natural landscape was an important source of symbols used to distinguish between and among groups; in other words, head and hat shape distinguished between and among insiders and outsiders.

Conclusion

My study of cranial modification among the Chiribaya highlights both the remarkable strengths and the limitations of bioarchaeology. Through a systematic and comprehensive analysis of mortuary contexts, it is possible to conclude that cranial modification was used to reflect ethnic differences among the Chiribaya. Ethnic groups were defined primarily by economic activity, following the pattern of coastal señoríos described by the Peruvian historian María Rostworowski (1970). Other questions regarding cranial shaping are more difficult to answer. I propose several hypotheses that warrant further investigation. Specifically, the practice of cranial modification may have increased in frequency and become more standardized with the arrival of Tiwanaku settlers in the midvalley, because of a perceived cultural, economic, and/or political threat, thus further differentiating insiders from Tiwanaku outsiders. In fact, this may have led to the emergence of the Chiribaya, a more complex and rigidly structured señorío than previous coastal polities. In this context, body alterations may represent a reflection of this new social order of insiders and the more stringent boundaries between parcialidades, or groups of specialists. However, precisely what any specific head shape was meant to represent is impossible to determine. Given the uniformity of the final head shape and the considerable expertise and time required to create head forms, I propose that selection of a specific head shape was not an arbitrary process but was instead imbued with deeply symbolic meaning. The inhabitants of the Colca Canyon are the closest modern equivalents of the Chiribaya. As mentioned above, these Andean ethnic groups drew their inspiration from the surrounding mountains, divine apus from whom they believed they descended. Through a more detailed analysis of Chiribaya iconography and the correlation between head shapes and specific symbols or motifs, investigators may be able to identify parts of the Chiribaya natural landscape that inspired the fronto-occipital and annular styles of cranial modification.

References Cited

Andrushko, Valerie Anne. 2007. The Bioarchaeology of Inca Imperialism in the Heartland: An Analysis of Prehistoric Burials from the Cuzco Region of Peru. Ph.D. dissertation, Department of Anthropology, University of California, Santa Barbara.

Anton, Susan C. 1989. Intentional Cranial Vault Deformation and Induced Changes of the Cranial Base and Face. *American Journal of Physical Anthropology* 79: 253–267.

Arriaga, Pablo José de. 1968 [1621]. La extirpación de la idolatría en el Perú. In *Crónicas Peruanas de Interés Indigena,* edited by F. E. Barba, Vol. 209: 192–277. Biblioteca de Autores Españoles, Ediciones Atlas, Madrid.

Barth, Frederick. 1969. *Ethnic Groups and Boundaries: The Social Organization of Culture Difference.* Little, Brown, Boston.

Bartra, Enrique, editor. 1982. *Tercer Concilio Limense, 1582–1583, versión castellana original de los decretos con el sumario del Segundo Concilio Limense.* Publicaciones de la Facultad Pontificia y Civil de Teología de Lima, Lima.

Blom, Deborah. 2005. Embodying Borders: Human Body Modification and Diversity in Tiwanaku Society. *Journal of Anthropological Archaeology* 24: 1–24.

Buikstra, Jane, and Douglas Ubelaker, editors. 1994. *Standards for Data Collection from Human Skeletal Remains.* Research Series 44. Arkansas Archaeological Survey, Fayetteville.

Capoche, Luis de. 1959 [1585]. *Relación general del asiento y villa imperial de Potosí.* Edición y estudio preliminar por Lewis Hanke. El lazarillo de ciegos caminante [por] Concolorcorvo [pseud], vol. 122: 69–189. Biblioteca de Autores Españoles, Ediciones Atlas, Madrid.

Croucher, Karina. 2008. Ambiguous Genders? Alternative Interpretations. In *Gender through Time in the Ancient Near East,* edited by D. Bolger, 21–51. Altamira Press, Lanham, Maryland.

Dembo, Adolfo, and José Imbellioni. 1938. *Deformaciones intencionales del cuerpo humano de caracter étnico.* Humanior: Biblioteca del Americanista Moderno dirigida por el Dr. Imbellioni José Anesi, Buenos Aires.

Goldstein, Paul. 1993. Tiwanaku Temples and State Expansion: A Tiwanaku Sunken-Court Temple in Moquegua, Peru. *Latin American Antiquity* 4: 22–47.

———. 2005. *Andean Diaspora: The Tiwanaku Colonies and the Origins of South American Empire.* University Press of Florida, Gainesville.

Hodder, Ian. 1978. Economic and Social Stress and Material Culture Patterning. *American Antiquity* 44 (3): 446–454.

Hoshower, Lisa M., Jane E. Buikstra, Paul S. Goldstein, and Anne D. Webster. 1995. Artificial Cranial Deformation at the Omo M10 site, a Tiwanaku Complex from the Moquegua Valley, Peru. *Latin American Antiquity* 6 (2): 145–164.

Lekovic, Gregory P., Brenda Baker, Jill Lekovic, and Mark Preul. 2007. New World Cranial Deformation Practices: Historical Implications for Pathophysiology of Cognitive Impairment in Deformational Plagiocephaly. *Neurosurgery* 60 (6): 1137–1147.

Lorenz, Kirsi. 2008. Headshaping as Gendered Capital. In *Gender through Time in the Ancient Near East*, edited by D. Bolger, 281–311. Altamira Press, Lanham, Maryland.

Lozada, María Cecilia, and Jane E. Buikstra. 2002. *El Señorío de Chiribaya en la Costa Sur del Perú*. Instituto de Estudios Peruanos, Lima.

Nigra, Benjamin. 2008. The "Cucharas" of the Chiribaya: New Vectors for Investigating Socioeconomic Subsistence Identities, Social Boundaries and the Use of Wooden Spoons as Diagnostic Tools. B.A. thesis, Department of Anthropology, University of Chicago, Chicago.

Rostworowski de Diez Canseco, María. 1970. Mercaderes del Valle de Chincha en la epoca prehispánica: Un documento y unos comentarios. *Revista Española de Antropología Americana* 5: 135–177.

Santoro, Calógero. 1989. Antiguos Cazadores de la Puna (9,000–6,000 a.C.). In *Culturas de Chile, Prehistoria*, edited by J. Hidalgo, V. Shiappacasse, H. Niemeyer, and C. Adulnate, 57–80. Editorial Andrés Bello, Santiago.

Tiesler, Vera. 1998. *La costumbre de la deformación cefálica entre los antiguos Mayas: Aspectos morfológicos y culturales*. Instituto Nacional de Antropología e Historia, Mexico City.

Tomczak, Paula. 2003. Prehistoric Diet and Socio-Economic Relationships within the Osmore Valley of Southern Peru. *Journal of Anthropological Archaeology* 22 (3): 262–278.

Torres-Rouff, Cristina. 2002. Cranial Vault Modification and Ethnicity in Middle Horizon San Pedro de Atacama, Chile. *Current Anthropology* 43: 163–171.

Ulloa Mogollón, Juan de. 1965 [1557–1586]. Relación de la provincia de los Collaguas para la discrepción de las Indias que su magestad manda hacer. In *Relaciones geograficas de Indias, Perú*, vol. 1, edited by M. Jiménez de la Espada, 326–333. Biblioteca de Autores Españoles, Madrid.

10

Getting a Head Start in Life

Pre-Columbian Maya Cranial Modification from Infancy to Ancestorhood

PAMELA L. GELLER

The pre-Columbian Maya possessed a penchant for irreversible alteration of their bodies—filing or inlaying teeth, piercing, and tattooing skin. These morphologically varied types of modifications communicated distinct messages, producing culturally potent and widely understood symbols during painful alterations and ritually sanctioned events (Geller 2006a). Cranial modification, however, presents a marked contrast to dental alteration, piercing, and tattooing, because intentional shaping of a skull can only occur during infancy, when cranial bones are neither fully formed nor fused; for this reason, modification of crania has been described as painless (Blackwood and Danby 1955).

Ethnographic analogy yields few salient clues about ancient motivations and meanings among the pre-Columbian Maya, because contemporary Maya no longer mold their crania. In the wake of conquest, Christianization and colonialism effectively eradicated cranial modification, and sadly the social significance of these marks was lost. Repudiation of this indigenous practice finds parallels in other parts of the world where Western influence passively or forcibly infiltrated, as with the Arawe of New Britain, Melanesia (Blackwood and Danby 1955).

Fortunately, Maya scholars have a plethora of other sources from which to draw—skeletal remains, architectural context, associated artifacts, artistic images, and critically utilized ethnohistories. For example, excavators have exhumed intentionally shaped crania from Middle Preclassic graves, circa 1200 BC in Cuello, Belize (Saul and Saul 1997). Artistic portraiture of the divine and noble from disparate regions in the Classic Maya world underscores the pervasiveness of this practice, and, some 2,700 years after the initiation of cranial alteration, European chroniclers verified the continuance (and their abhorrence) of such practices. Although source materials are rich and varied, the focus of skeletal analysis is often on the documentation of stylistic differences, as opposed to interpretations about the significance of cranial shaping (although see Duncan 2009; Romano Pacheco 1987; Tiesler Blos 1998; Tiesler Blos and Romano Pacheco 2008).

To this end, I consider the shaped crania of individuals who occupied various sites—house ruins, minor centers, major centers—in the Río Bravo region of northwestern Belize. Although 132 individuals, representing both commoner and noble classes, were excavated, only 25 of these decedents, who lived and died during the Classic period (AD 250–900), could be analyzed for the presence or absence of in vivo modification. Using a life-course approach informed by social theories about identity, I argue that occupants of northwestern Belize modified infant crania to instigate a *process of becoming*. In support of this assertion, I scale down from the larger population to the community and the individual, expanding on the interments of three commoners from the minor center Dos Barbaras, finding that shaped heads may have marked a special status connected to familial position and/or occupational activities.

Marking Identity

Ethnohistoric Accounts

Chronicles of sixteenth-century Maya practices indicate that cranial modification was born of ritual circumstances associated with birth. Spanish friar Diego de Landa recognized that after binding the head of their child, the parents took him or her to a priest for naming (in Tozzer 1941: 129). No prescribed length of time or degree of pressure is recorded, and Landa is similarly silent about the sex of the infant. The friar did remark upon the role of the mother in cranial molding, as the decision to modify or not to modify lay literally and figuratively in her hands (in Tozzer 1941: 125). Yet Landa's impartiality is compromised by his declaration that molding a head caused pain and jeopardized the life of a newborn. As we know this not to be the case ethnographically (Blackwood and Danby 1955), his characterization of cranial modification as agonizing and at times fatal perhaps supplied the church with added rationale for the banning of transformative practices.

The Maya perceived such modification as ennobling and functional, rather than deforming, as implied by Juan de Torquemada's accounts: "When the children are very young, their heads are soft and can be moulded in the shape that you see ours to be, by using two pieces of wood hollowed out in the middle. This custom, given to our ancestors by the gods, gives us a noble air, and our heads are thus better adapted to carry loads" (in Tozzer 1941: 88n372). Ultimately, when we utilize ethnohistoric documents cautiously and with critical reflection, there is much to learn about cranial shaping. For instance, the Maya possessed a sophisticated working knowledge of body physiology and anatomy. Technique seems fairly uniform, though the degree of shaping appears to have been contingent on the personal predilection of those who initiated manipulation. Alteration did not require luxurious materials or laborious processes, thereby making it accessible to members from different social groups. Sexual differences did not seem to determine who did or did not have their crania shaped. With this information in hand, we may ascertain whether bioarchaeological data support historic accounts or call them into question.

Bioarchaeological Data

Dembo and Imbelloni's (1938) seminal work is a touchstone for standard classification of the forms that intentionally shaped crania take in the pre-Columbian Americas. Briefly, the two primary types—tabular or annular (or orbicular)—were contingent on the technique or apparatus used. Tabular refers to tablets secured anteriorly and/or posteriorly to the head, while an annular style resulted when bands were wrapped around the head. These types can be further subdivided into oblique (tilted posteriorly) or erect (vertical), which were produced by placing pressure on the frontal or occipital regions, respectively.

Table 10.1 summarizes the absence and presence of shaping in the twenty-five crania from the Río Bravo Conservation Area (figure 10.1), as well as the type of shaping, when present. Four of the twenty-five individuals did not exhibit cranial shaping, while five crania displayed the marks of inadvertent modification attributable to the repetition of specific practices. Distinguishing quotidian existence from ritual intent is challenging, but there are some telltale signatures. Cradleboard usage during infancy appears to have exerted pressure on the lambdoidal area (Saul 1972: 10), and four individuals from the Río Bravo region display flattened occiputs. Saul and Saul (1991: 154) also argue that repeated use of tumplines to transport heavy burdens may have produced postcoronal depressions on adult crania. In the sample from northwestern Belize, the cranium of Individual 35 from Dos Barbaras displays this suggestive groove. Interestingly, this cranium was intentionally modified in a tabular erect style (see below for further discussion).

Individuals who displayed intentional cranial modification (see table 10.1) were far more prevalent in the Río Bravo sample. More than half of all individuals (n=13; 52 percent) displayed conventional shaping of some sort. No skulls

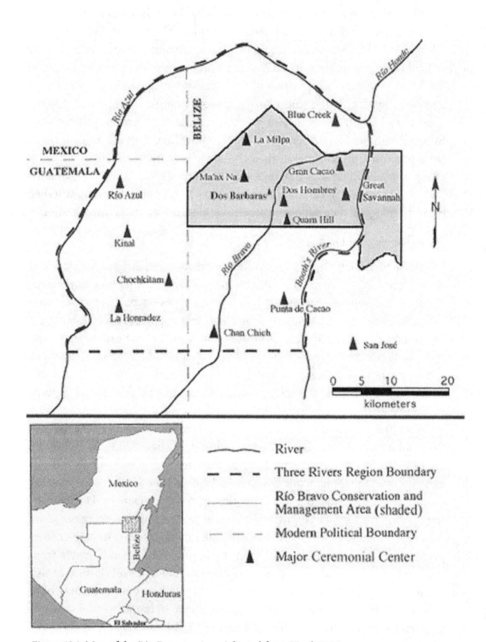

Figure 10.1. Map of the Río Bravo region. Adapted from Houk 1996.

Table 10.1. Occurrence of shaped crania at centers from the Río Bravo region

Type of cranial shaping	Total (N=25)	% of total
Absent	4	16.0
Present		
Unintentional occipital flattening	4	16.0
Unintentional postcoronal depression	1	4.0
Tabular erect	5	20.0
Possible tabular erect	1	4.0
Tabular oblique	2	8.0
Possible tabular oblique	0	0.0
Possible tabular	5	20.0
Possible cranial shaping	3	12.0

were shaped in an annular style. Tabular erect and possible tabular erect (*n*=6; 24 percent) occur more frequently in the sample than tabular oblique (*n*=2; 8 percent). Degree of shaping ranged from slight to extreme. In the case of those individuals with tabular erect modification, there were three instances of extreme, one moderate, and one slight. One individual with tabular oblique modification exhibited moderate shaping, and one individual exhibited extreme shaping. Flattened cranial fragments also pointed to the presence of possible cranial shaping for an additional three individuals in the sample.

Correlation of this information with other data may illumine which individuals were more likely to be selected for shaping, particularly with regard to sex, social position, and ethnicity. Table 10.2 summarizes the presence and absence of intentional shaping in the sample based on sex. Also included in table 10.2 are the three individuals whose flattened frontal bones suggest possible cranial shaping. From this small sample, male crania displayed shaping more often than females. Nonetheless, both sexes had their crania modified as infants.

Individuals with intentionally shaped crania were recovered from a range of grave types—from humble pit graves to grand, labor-intensive tombs—with no established assemblage of grave goods. Decedents with intentional cranial modification were found both with and without grave goods. Hence,

Table 10.2. Intentional tabular cranial shaping by sex in the Río Bravo sample

	M	M?	M + M?	% of total (N=25)	F	F?	F + F?	% of total (N=25)
Cranial shaping +	3	5	8	32.0	1	0	1	4.0
Possible cranial shaping	0	0	0	0	1	1	2	8.0
Cranial shaping –	2	1	3	12.0	1	0	1	4.0

contingent on grave types and grave goods, a specific and ascribed socioeconomic status did not appear to be a prerequisite for cranial shaping (although see Sharapova and Razhev this volume for examples from Eurasia). The stylistic distinction between erect and oblique, however, is discussed below.

Of the sixteen individuals with intentional or possible cranial shaping, seven individuals also bore at least one dental filing or inlay, a modification that has been argued to signify special status within commoner and noble communities (Geller 2006b). Five individuals, however, had no modified teeth, and dental modification could not be determined in the case of four individuals. Hence, I propose that the shaping of infant crania did not necessarily dictate the modification of their permanent dentition later in life.

In other cases, bioarchaeologists have documented a link between cranial modification and ethnicity. Researchers working in the Andes, for example, have identified typological differences as evidence for the maintenance of ethnic boundaries among the Chiribaya (Lozada this volume; Lozada 1998; Lozada and Buikstra 2005) at San Pedro de Atacama, Chile (Gerszten 1993; Torres-Rouff 2002, 2009) and at Tiwanaku, Bolivia (Blom et al. 1998). Because researchers are still fleshing out the degree of ethnic differentiation among the Classic Maya, connecting ethnic identity to cranial modification is tenuous. As Sharer and Traxler (2006: 93–94) note, "Maya civilization comprises a multitude of ethnic and linguistic groups. Yet despite similar conditions in the Andes, the Inka were able to conquer and control a vast empire in a diverse environmental and cultural setting. [They] were motivated by an ideology that promoted their destiny to rule over their empires. Maya states were not organized to incorporate conquered territory and populations." This different political organization may have made such boundary maintenance unnecessary in the larger Maya world. While Tiesler Blos (1998) does not explicitly argue that shaped crania marked ethnic identity, she does make the case for boundary maintenance between discrete communities and has suggested that cranial styles from forty-one Maya sites in Mexico were shared among members of distinct residential groups, a contention that she supports with data from 403 crania (see Bonogofsky this volume for intrasite variation in the Levant). In comparison, the sample from northwestern Belize, which contains data from fourteen sites, only includes crania shaped in the tabular variety. Contrary to the argument Tiesler Blos (1998) makes, then, there is no evidence in this sample that different Maya communities favored specific styles. Rather, cranial modification indicates the materialization of shared cultural traditions and aesthetic ideals for Maya peoples from separate communities. Clearly, the bigger picture of ethnicity is very complicated, and pooling together distant regions may shed further light on the issue. But perhaps a more salient question pertains to the symbolic significance of the head: why modify crania?

A Matter of Scale: Individuals in Communities

Contingent on one's research questions, a population-based perspective is quite useful, as bioarchaeological studies of health, paleodemography, and paleopathology have underscored (e.g., Márquez Morfín and Storey 2005; Márquez Morfín et al. 2002; Storey et al. 2002; Wright and Chew 1998). We also know that mourners throughout the Maya world intentionally buried select decedents beneath structures that the living continued to use (e.g., Geller 2004, 2006b; Gillespie 2001, 2002; McAnany 1995; Webster 1997). Maya commoners during the Classic period, for instance, often buried deceased kin beneath their houses. These practices and spatial arrangements granted social viability to the biological dead and ensured an ongoing dialogue between the living and their powerful ancestors. But many burial samples also contain important and at times subtle information for which macro-scale analyses of observable patterns cannot always account. In the case of cranial modification, there is much about shared cultural practices and beliefs that we can learn from scaling down to the level of the community, family, and individual. A reduction in scale is especially constructive for thinking about commoner burials recovered from the minor center Dos Barbaras.

Located just west of the region's namesake, the Río Bravo, Dos Barbaras comprised at least five courtyards, Groups A through E (figure 10.2). This minor center resides on the periphery of two major centers: Dos Hombres and La Milpa (see figure 10.1). According to the site excavator, Brandon Lewis (personal communication, 2002), occupation extended from the Late Preclassic to the Late/Terminal Classic periods (ca. 400 BC–AD 900). As of 2001, seventeen individuals have been recovered from the site. Excavators unearthed the majority of these interments (n=14) in association with the residential structures arranged around Group B's courtyard. This location—atop a small ridge, in the center of the site, and associated with a stela—indicates importance within the community. Structures 11 and 6, in particular, contained multiple interments of decedents who are presumed to have had consanguineal and/or affinal ties (figure 10.3).

Structure 11 was an architecturally complex building. Numerous renovations and multiple interments qualify the building as the community residential and ritual center. Ten individuals in total were buried beneath this structure (Geller 2005). For several of these decedents, grave type, associated

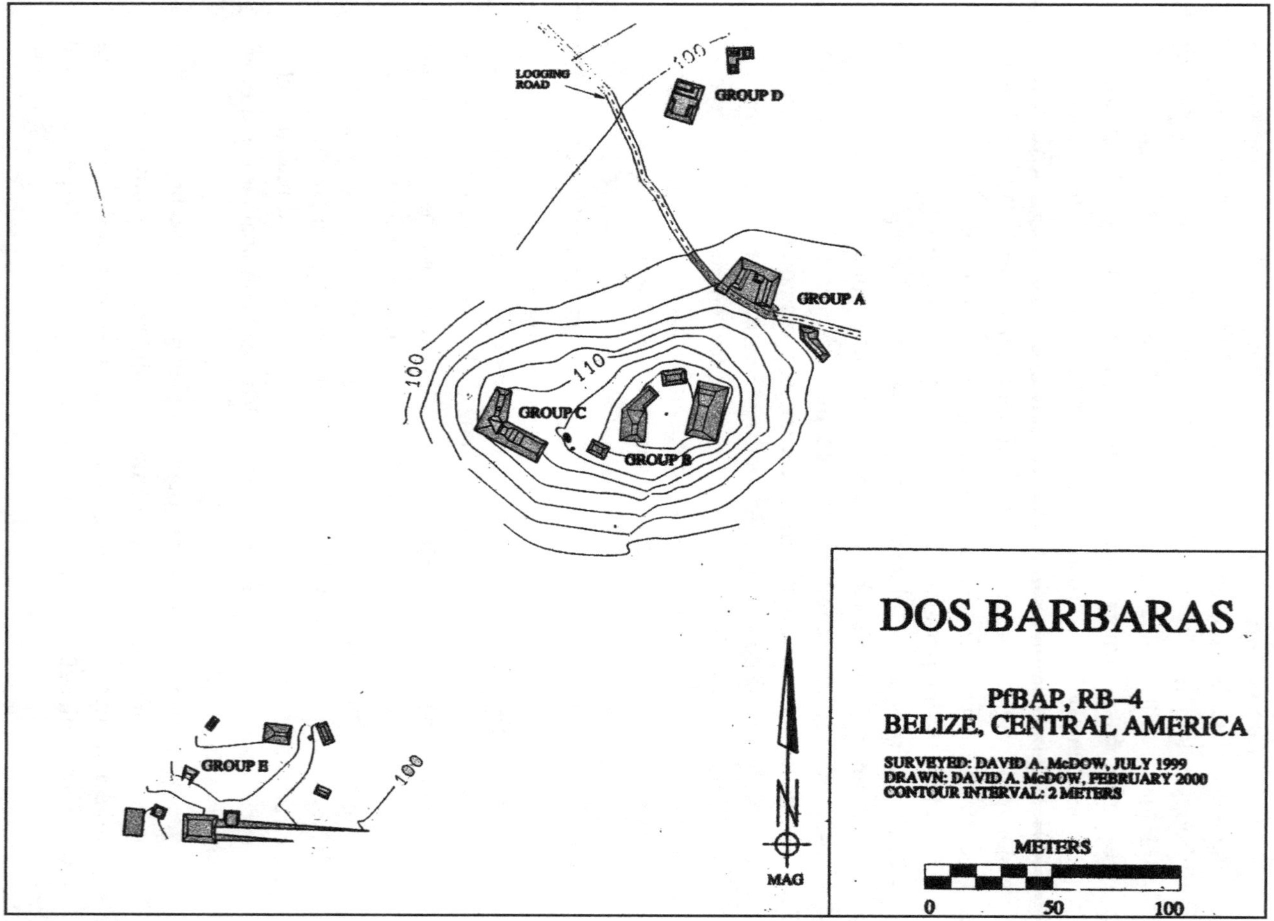

DOS BARBARAS

PfBAP, RB–4
BELIZE, CENTRAL AMERICA

SURVEYED: DAVID A. McDOW, JULY 1999
DRAWN: DAVID A. McDOW, FEBRUARY 2000
CONTOUR INTERVAL: 2 METERS

METERS

0   50   100

GROUP A

GROUP D

GROUP B

GROUP C

LOGGING
ROAD

100

110

100

100

GROUP E

MAG
N

Figure 10.2. Map of Dos Barbaras. Courtesy of Brandon Lewis.

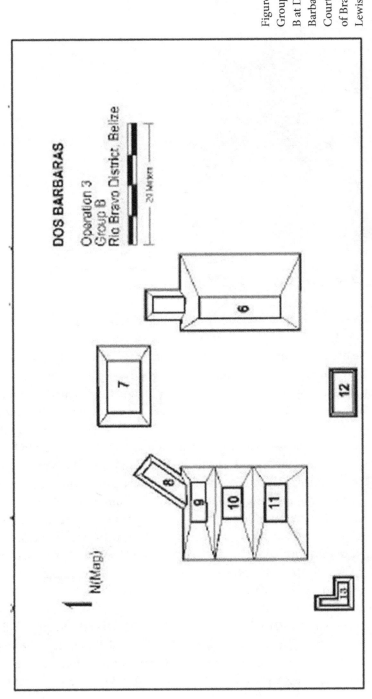

Figure 10.3. Group B at Dos Barbaras. Courtesy of Brandon Lewis.

Figure 10.4. Individual 35 interred beneath the floor of Room 2, Structure 6, Group B, Dos Barbaras.

architecture, and grave goods evoke ancestor veneration. Individual 22, a female 25–44 years of age, especially typified this ancestral status. Her Late/Terminal Classic capped cist, which kin had situated directly underneath a bench (or family altar), and unique grave goods—a polychrome plate fragment, stingray spine, and triangular jade pendant—signaled prominence acquired in life and after death. Despite these markers of ancestorhood, she exhibited no signs of cranial modification. Indeed, as Duncan has discussed (2009), the presence of an unshaped head by no means implied that Individual 22 was any less a fully embodied and important member of the community.

Yet contextualized analysis of those with cranial modification reveals similarly intriguing information about the formation and reformulation of social identity at Dos Barbaras. Just across the courtyard from Structure 11, to the east in Structure 6, the remains of two individuals with tabular cranial modification were recovered. Individual 35, mentioned earlier, was a male 20–30 years of age (figure 10.4). Individual 34 was an adult of unknown sex whose postcranial remains extended into the trench sidewall, thus remaining mostly unexcavated and unanalyzed.

Mourners had interred Individuals 34 and 35 beneath the plaster floors of separate though adjoining rooms (Room 3 and Room 2, respectively). Which individual was interred first is unclear, but both burials date to the Late/Terminal Classic period (ca. AD 700–900). No grave goods were found in association with either decedent. Their grave types were neither grand nor labor intensive. Mourners appear to have placed Individual 34 into the floor construction fill. For Individual 35, the parameters of an intentional pit grave were discernible. The fill directly associated with his remains was distinct from construction fill outside of the grave space. Grave builders appear to have excavated a pit into the floor and then sealed over the intrusion during a replastering episode. In the case of both decedents, the configuration of bodies positioned beneath residence living floors is suggestive of interaction between socially viable ancestors and their kin.

Altering Bodies to Embody Ideals

To initiate a discussion of cranial modifications in Individuals 34 and 35, a life-course approach is useful. Such an approach, according to Gowland (2006: 145), conceptualizes individual identities as complex, culturally contingent, and dynamic from conception to death. Data collected from the burials of Individuals 34 and 35 certainly facilitates consideration of identities as they shift from infancy to adulthood to ancestorhood. Intentional and unintentional changes to crania were the product of social practices that continued throughout the course of an individual's life. These practices, whether related to special events like birth or quotidian activities, set in motion a *process of becoming.*

This notion of becoming draws on Foucault's vision of docile bodies (Foucault 1977)—individual bodies that are subjugated, controlled, disciplined, and transformed through normalizing systems of power (e.g., military, schools, religious institutions). Yet as Meskell (1998: 141) stresses, a body is not only "a forum for display" of social norms and power relations. Processes of becoming that involve inscriptive practices also communicate information about an individual's experience of the world. These experiences may indicate internalization of or resistance to ideals and ideology. Ideas about bodily norms, transformations, and experiences then assist us in thinking about why members of the Dos Barbaras community decided to mold the crania of Individuals 34 and 35.

Physically and permanently molding infant crania facilitated culturally shaping, or socializing, individuals into viable and visually pleasing community members. These practices instigated a process of becoming, one which was intimately connected to life-cycle rituals associated with birth and cultural norms concerned with aesthetics. To highlight the importance of the head in this process of becoming, we can reflect on the multiple though related meanings of *baah* (Houston and Stuart 1998; Houston et al. 2006). According to Houston and his colleagues, the concept implies "body," though epigraphic and linguistic analyses also link it to "head" and "face." They (2006: 61) write, "The entries from Tzotzil and Yukatek Mayan define *baah* and its various forms as aspects of appearance, a recognizable 'visage' or overall mien, if always in a corporal, embodied sense. . . . The surface, the 'face,' does not so much mimic aspects of identity as realize them."

Although these authors are concerned with iconographic and glyphic images of bodies, the connection they identify between personal identity and the body may help us understand the motivations that undergirded cranial shaping. Modification of one's head would certainly work to shape or materialize personal identity. Self-expression on the part of the modifiee was of little importance, as he or she was too young to condemn or support these acts of alteration.

Houston and coauthors (2006: 62) continue to expand on *baah*: "Mayan script and language also make metaphoric use of 'head' as a means of exaltation, of designating someone as the principal member of a particular category of person." For example, the term *ba-al*, which they translate as "a woman's firstborn child," is salient for thinking about the bridge between infants, rituals related to birth, and shaped heads. Because all members of a community did not have shaped crania, it may be that mothers only molded the heads of their firstborn children. And for these individuals, their status would have been forever visible to the larger community.

One's position as firstborn may have also gone hand in glove with future expectations. I informally call this "getting a head start in life." As mentioned earlier, ethnohistory makes reference to the functional aspects of cranial shaping: that is, modifications facilitated the carrying of loads. Shaping of skulls soon after birth perhaps set the role of transporter or trader in motion by parents. This ascription of role may have signaled individual familial obligations or "occupational" identity in adulthood. Romano Pacheco (1987: 29) has proffered a similar notion, suggesting that stylistic differences marked distinct social statuses during the Classic period:

> En el caso de la deformación cefálica intencional encontramos que efectivamente existe cierta diferenciación por *status* social ya que el pueblo en general sólo podía imprimir a las cabezas de sus hijos la forma tabular erecta. En cambio, gobernantes, jerarcas, sacerdotes, guerreros y otros personajes de alto rango social, predestinados desde niños a ocupar las categorías de más alto renombre en la sociedad, se les conformaba la cabeza en el artificial modo tabular oblicuo. (emphasis in original)
> [In the case of intentional cephalic deformation we find that there effectively exists a certain difference by social *status* since common people

in general could only imprint the heads of their children in the tabular erect form. Instead, governors, leaders, priests, warriors and other persons of high social rank, predestined from birth to occupy the most renowned categories in society, had their heads shaped in the artificial style tabular oblique.]

Romano Pacheco (1987) based his statements on his iconographic analysis of Classic sculptures and painted images recovered from various Maya centers. A bioarchaeological analysis then extends his contribution by providing empirical evidence from contextualized human remains. I put forward an explanation for Individual 35's intentional *and* unintentional cranial modification below.

Individual 35 displayed an extreme type of tabular erect cranial modification. He had strong frontal flattening, as well as lateral bulging. Intriguingly, this individual also possessed a postcoronal depression. To reiterate, repeated use of a tumpline to transport heavy burdens could produce a transverse groove behind the coronal suture (Saul and Saul 1991: 154). We also see this postcoronal grooving in the historic-era skulls of Kwakuitl from British Columbia (Cybulski 1977), a group that modified infant crania and utilized tumplines to transport burdens (Curtis 1915: 4, 17; Jenness 1977 [1932]: 101, 150). Such an inadvertent mark speaks to the idea of practice making person, or bodily *hexis*, in the words of Bourdieu (1990: 69–70). That is, identities are materialized via repeated, culturally determined practices that are consciously and subtly reflected on the body. Likewise, Individual 34, whose parietal fragments exhibited lateral bulging, may have (re)produced this social identity through daily practices. Poor preservation, however, inhibited the identification of a groove on the cranial fragments of this decedent. The formation of individual identities thus may have commenced in infancy during ritual moments, as evidenced by the shaped crania of these two individuals. As the years went on, Individual 35's repetition of salient practices, marked by his postcoronal depression, perhaps served to maintain a social identity that had been preordained early in life.

Returning to the words of Romano Pacheco (1987), we may reflect further on the connection between stylistic types and identities shaped by political, economic, and social distinctions. As Romano Pacheco notes, tabular erect cranial modification reiterated (or possibly realized) the social positions of "el pueblo." Therefore, the fact that the crania of Individual 35, the resident of a minor center, was tabular erect in style may be more than coincidence. In comparison, the tabular oblique style occurs infrequently in the sample from the Río Bravo region. Indeed, the only two individuals with this style of modification were recovered in association with the region's major center, La Milpa.

Individual 114, a 20- to 30-year-old male, displayed a moderate degree of tabular oblique cranial modification. Excavators recovered his remains from beneath a bench in an elite residential group, an architectural feature that likely marked his ancestral identity. His burial, which was located just south of La Milpa's central Plaza A, dated to the Terminal Classic period (ca. AD 800–900). The second individual, Individual 94, a 20- to 30-year-old of indeterminate sex, exhibited an extreme degree of tabular oblique modification. This individual resided at La Caldera, a minor center located just three kilometers from La Milpa (Kunen 2001, 2004). Mourners had placed this decedent into a labor-intensive tomb, a grave type that occurs infrequently in the Río Bravo region ($n=12$; 9 percent of the total sample) and is generally found in association with monumental architecture. The tomb of Individual 94 was located beneath a structure adjacent to the center's main temple. Hence, architectural and spatial contexts indicate that Individuals 94 and 114 may have been of elite and quite possibly noble status. Perhaps the oblique style allowed nobles to embody the divine and replicate the aesthetically ideal. This idea builds on the suggestion made by Houston and colleagues (2006: 45) that modified crania symbolized ears of corn, a corpo-realization of the Maize God's conical head. Tabular oblique styles may have "imprinted" them as such early in life and represented a pointed contrast to the tabular erect modification of Individual 35.

Discussion of Semantic Sensibilities

Western scholars' fascination with the skull's malleability is longstanding, and the reasons for modification of newborns' crania have eluded researchers investigating the Maya for just as extended a time (Buikstra 1997: 227). The problem may stem in part from European stigmatization of native peoples' modifications in the wake of conquest and during colonialism. Derogatory characterization was one way by which conquistadores, chroniclers, and colonizers "othered" native peoples and, in so doing, justified their subjugation and exploitation (Geller 2004, 2006a). An especially dogmatic and influential seventeenth-century source for these disparaging attitudes was John Bulwer (1650), a British physician and natural philosopher whose central thesis in *Anthropometamorphosis* was that body modifications, regardless of type and degree, signified blasphemy, not beauty (Geller 2006a). Shaped crania appear to have produced a special revulsion in Bulwer. Indeed, the first edition's frontispiece depicted various thumbnail sketches of men's artificially "deformed" heads, about which he waxed caustically (figure 10.5).

Out of wise Nature's plastique hands thy *Head*
Came like a Ball of wax, oblongly spread:
Now'ts like, in its acuminated line,
A *sugar-loaf* or *Apple of the Pine*; *round*,
Nowt's *long*, now *short*, now *flat*, now *square*, now
Indented now like to a Foysting-hound;
Twas soft, now hard; it is a *Blockhead* made. (Bulwer 1650: A2)

Such poetry belies Bulwer's sentiments about the body's plasticity. Indeed, to manipulate and mold the head, he believed, ultimately produced a person of inferior intelligence, one without brains. Hence, the term *blockhead* does double duty, describing both morphology and behavior.

The presumption that (mis)shaped heads signal immorality and idiocy may linger, as evidenced by some contemporary scientists' use of the term *artificial cranial deformation* (e.g., Lekovic et al. 2007; Schijman 2005; Tubbs et al. 2006). Granted, the medical literature contains information about congenital anomalies that certainly qualify as cranial deformation (Krogman and İşcan 1986: 400). Craniostenosis, for instance, involves the premature closure

Figure 10.5. Frontispiece to John Bulwer's 1650 edition of *Anthropometamorphosis*.

of one or more cranial sutures, which produces a steeple-shaped, keel-shaped, or asymmetrical appearance (Maugans 2002; Moss 1958). One type of craniostenosis, known as positional plagiocephaly, is induced by unintentional external forces that flatten infant occiputs. Repeatedly placing infants on their backs, for instance, will produce these changes (Maugans 2002). In such cases, parents often seek medical assistance to rectify a "deformity" that they regard as pathological despite medical evidence to the contrary (Maugans 2002): helmets may even be used to remodel "abnormal" infant skulls. Cosmetic surgery presents an alternative corrective, though admittedly an extreme one that may endanger the individual's health to a greater degree than the perceived abnormality. The irony here is that heads are indeed (re)shaped to fit with our own aesthetic ideals. Hence, my semantic nitpicking is directed not at descriptions of congenital disorders as deformations but rather at scientists' identification of marks produced by cultural practices as "deformations" (e.g., Eppley 1996; Gerstzen and Gerstzen 1995). Additionally, medical researchers continue to explore the possibility that cranial "deformations" produced neurological impairments in children (e.g., Lekovic et al. 2007; Schijman 2005). The specter of Bulwer's blockhead thus continues to haunt even contemporary scientific studies.

Of course, anthropologists are not innocent of such semantic transgressions (although see Duncan 2009; Saul and Saul 1991; Saul and Saul 1997). The use of ethnocentric language in many research inquiries may unwittingly suggest that the intent of the modifier was to re-create the abnormal, grotesque, and defective. When significance is reduced to aesthetic, the complex ideological structures and social interactions that normalize and justify such transformations often go unexplored. To this end, my consideration of Maya cranial shaping has stressed the importance of contextualizing modifications in space and time, as well as regarding skeletal remains not as analytical endpoints but as dynamic entities whose morphology and meaning changed throughout an individual's life course.

Concluding Thoughts

Body modifications, whether intentional or the product of mundane and habitual action, are telling about social identity formation and maintenance of "insider" status. Contrary to historical accounts and modern scientific inquiries, I suggest that intentional cranial shaping was neither deforming nor pathological but a practice of considerable cultural significance. Cranial shaping for the pre-Columbian Maya, in particular, may have figured into the process of becoming a viable member within a community. Soon after birth, individuals would have been slotted into specific roles or prominent positions within their family. As the shaped crania of Individuals 34 and 35 illustrate, this status may have been shared by only a select few within the group. The repeated performance of certain practices later in life may have served to maintain related social identities during an individual's life, and prominence within the community would have in turn warranted assignment of an ancestral identity after biological death.

Stylistic differences within a larger region between tabular erect and oblique forms of cranial shaping perhaps signaled the complexities of social organization. The correlation of types with specific spatial location, architectural features, and material remains may offer evidence of sumptuary laws that regulated irreversible and indelible types of bodily alterations. Regardless of sociopolitical or economic differences, however, enactment of cranial shaping placed all who were modified on a path of identification that was preordained by modifiers. The permanence of in vivo cranial modification, then, provided a lasting reminder that far surpassed the moments of ritual or prosaic molding. For this reason, body modifications serve as important signs of identity formation, reiteration, and reformulation.

Of bodies born in postmodern moments, Bordo (1993) has argued that a paradigm of plasticity has come to replace understandings of the body's materiality as unalterable: that is, extreme bodily transformations—the body as "cultural plastic" (Bordo 1993: 266)—are specific to contemporary consumer capitalism and Western notions about individualism. Yet contrary to Bordo's premise, contemporary Western society is not unique in the links it forges between individual identities, material bodies, their plasticity, and cultural practices. The lesson learned from anthropological cases of bodily alterations, like that of pre-Columbian Maya cranial modification, is that societies through space and time—even societies without rampant consumer capitalism, philosophical individualism, advanced scientific technologies, and mass media imagery—have indelibly and extremely transformed bodies in the name of social norms, cultural values, religious or political ideologies, and aesthetic ideals.

Acknowledgments

The burials I discuss in this chapter were excavated from sites within and adjacent to the 250,000 acres owned by the Programme for Belize (PfB) in the Río Bravo Conservation and Management Area. I wish to extend my gratitude to the La Milpa Archaeological Project (LaMAP), Programme for Belize Archaeological Project (PfBAP), and Chan Chich Archaeological Project (CCAP) for sharing data. Frank Saul and Julie Mather Saul, under whose guidance I conducted doctoral research (Geller 2004), directed skeletal analyses for all three projects.

References Cited

Blackwood, Beatrice, and P. M. Danby. 1955. A Study of Artificial Cranial Deformation in New Britain. *Journal of the Royal Anthropological Institute of Great Britain and Ireland* 85 (1/2): 173–191.

Blom, Deborah E., Benedikt Hallgrímsson, Linda Keng, María Cecilia Lozada Cerna, and Jane E. Buikstra. 1998. Tiwanaku "Colonization": Bioarchaeological Implications for Migration in the Moquegua Valley, Peru. *World Archaeology* 30 (2): 238–261.

Bordo, Susan. 1993. "Material Girl": The Effacements of Postmodern Culture. In *The Madonna Connection: Representational Politics, Subcultural Identities, and Cultural Theory*, edited by C. Schwichtenberg, 265–290. Westview Press, Boulder, Colorado.

Bourdieu, Pierre. 1990. *The Logic of Practice*. Stanford University Press, Stanford.

Buikstra, Jane E. 1997. Studying Maya Bioarchaeology. In *Bones of the Maya: Studies of Ancient Skeletons*, edited by S. Whittington and D. Reed, 221–228. Smithsonian Institution Press, Washington, D.C.

Bulwer, John. 1650. *Anthropometamorphosis: Man Transform'd; or, the ARTIFICIAL Changeling. Historically Presented, in the mad and cruel Gallantry, Foolish Bravery, ridiculous Beauty, Filthy Finenesse, and loathsome Lovelinesse of most NATIONS, Fashioning & altering their Bodies from the Mould intended by NATURE, with a VINDICATION of the Regular Beauty and Honesty of NATURE, AND An APPENDIX of the Pedigree of the ENGLISH GALLANT*. J. Hardesty, London.

Curtis, Edward S. 1915. *The North American Indians*, vol. 10, *The Kwakiutl*. Classic Books, Murietta, California.

Cybulski, Jerome S. 1977. Cribra Orbitalia, a Possible Sign of Anemia in Early Historic Native Populations of the British Columbia Coast. *American Journal of Physical Anthropology* 47 (1): 31–39.

Dembo, Adolfo, and José Imbelloni. 1938. *Deformaciones intencionales del cuerpo humana de carácter étnico*. Biblioteca Humanior, Buenos Aires, Argentina.

Duncan, William N. 2009. Cranial Modification among the Maya: Absence of Evidence or Evidence of Absence? In *Bioarchaeology and Identity in the Americas*, edited by K. Knudson and C. Stojanowski, 177–193. University Press of Florida, Gainesville.

Eppley, Barry L. 1996. Literature Scans. *Journal of Craniofacial Surgery* 7 (4): 324.

Foucault, Michel. 1977. *Discipline and Punish: The Birth of the Prison*. Pantheon Books, New York.

Geller, Pamela L. 2004. Transforming Bodies, Transforming Identities: A Consideration of Pre-Columbian Maya Corporeal Beliefs and Practices. Unpublished Ph.D. dissertation, Department of Anthropology, University of Pennsylvania, Philadelphia.

———. 2005. Skeletal Analysis and Theoretical Complications. *World Archaeology* 37 (4): 597–609.

———. 2006a. Altering Identities: Body Modification and the Pre-Columbian Maya. In *The Social Archaeology of Funerary Remains*, edited by R. Gowland and C. Knüsel, 279–291. Oxbow Books, Oxford, U.K.

———. 2006b. Maya Mortuary Spaces as Cosmological Metaphors. In *Space and Spatial Analysis in Archaeology*, edited by E. Robertson, J. Seibert, D. Fernandez, and M. Zender, 37–48. University of Calgary Press, Calgary, British Columbia.

Gerszten, Peter C. 1993. An Investigation into the Practice of Cranial Deformation among the Pre-Columbian Peoples of Northern Chile. *International Journal of Osteoarchaeology* 3 (2): 87–98.

Gerszten, Peter C., and Enrique Gerszten. 1995. Intentional Cranial Deformation: A Disappearing Form of Self-mutilation. *Neurosurgery* 37 (3): 374–382.

Gillespie, Susan. 2001. Personhood, Agency, and Mortuary Ritual: A Case Study from the Ancient Maya. *Journal of Anthropological Archaeology* 20: 73–112.

———. 2002. Body and Soul among the Maya: Keeping the Spirits in Place. In *The Space and Place of Death*, edited by H. Silverman and D. Small, 67–78. American Anthropological Association, Arlington, Virginia.

Gowland, Rebecca. 2006. Ageing the Past: Examining Age Identity from Funerary Evidence. In *Social Archaeology of Funerary Remains*, edited by R. Gowland and C. Knüsel, 143–154. Oxbow Books, Oxford, U.K.

Houk, Brett. 1996. The Archaeology of Site Planning: An Example from the Maya Site of Dos Hombres, Belize. Ph.D. dissertation, Department of Anthropology, University of Texas at Austin.

Houston, Stephen, and David Stuart. 1998. The Ancient Maya Self: Personhood and Portraiture in the Classic Period. *Res* 33: 72–101.

Houston, Stephen, David Stuart, and Karl Taube. 2006. *The Memory of Bones: Body, Being, and Experience among the Classic Maya*. University of Texas Press, Austin.

Jenness, Diamond. 1977 [1932]. *The Indians of Canada*. 7th ed. University of Toronto Press, Toronto.

Krogman, Wilton M., and M. Y. İşcan. 1986. *The Human Skeleton in Forensic Medicine*. Charles C. Thomas, Springfield, Illinois.

Kunen, Julie L. 2001. Study of an Ancient Maya Bajo Landscape in Northwestern Belize. Unpublished Ph.D. dissertation, Department of Anthropology, University of Arizona, Tucson.

———. 2004. *Ancient Maya Life in the Far West Bajo: Social and Environmental Change in the Wetlands of Belize*. University of Arizona Press, Tucson.

Lekovic, G. P., B. Baker, J. M. Lekovic, and M. C. Preul. 2007. New World Cranial Deformation Practices: Historical Implications for Pathophysiology of Cognitive Impairment in Deformational Plagiocephaly. *Neurosurgery* 60 (6): 1137–1147.

Lozada Cerna, María C. 1998. The Señorío of Chiribaya: A Bio-archaeological Study in the Osmore Drainage of Southern Perú. Unpublished Ph.D. dissertation, Department of Anthropology, University of Chicago, Chicago.

Lozada Cerna, María C., and Jane E. Buikstra. 2005. Pescadores and Labradores among the Señorío of Chiribaya in Southern Peru. In *Us and Them: Archaeology and Ethnicity in the Andes*, edited by R. M. Reycraft, 206–225. Cotsen Institute of Archaeology, University of California, Los Angeles.

Márquez Morfín, Lourdes, Robert McCaa, Rebecca Storey, and Andres Del Angel. 2002. Health and Nutrition in Pre-Hispanic Mesoamerica. In *The Backbone of History: Health and Nutrition in the Western Hemisphere*, edited by R. Steckel and J. Rose, 307–338. Cambridge University Press, Cambridge.

Márquez Morfín, Lourdes, and Rebecca Storey. 2005. From Early Village to Regional Center in Mesoamerica: An Investigation of Lifestyles and Health. In *Ancient Health: Skeletal Indicators of Agricultural and Economic Intensification*, edited by M. N. Cohen and G. M. M. Crane-Kramer, 80–91. University Press of Florida, Gainesville.

Maugans, Todd. 2002. Commentary: The Misshapen Head. *Pediatrics* 110: 166–167.

McAnany, Patricia. 1995. *Living with the Ancestors: Kinship and Kingship in Ancient Maya Society*. University of Texas Press, Austin.

Meskell, Lynn. 1998. The Irresistible Body and the Seduction of Archaeology. In *Changing Bodies, Changing Meanings: Studies on the Human Body in Antiquity*, edited by D. Montserrat, 139–161. Routledge, London.

Moss, Melvin. 1958. Pathogenesis of Artificial Cranial Deformation. *American Journal of Physical Anthropology* 16: 269–286.

Romano Pacheco, Arturo. 1987. Iconografía Cefálica Maya. In *Memorias del Primer Coloquio Internacional de Mayistas, 5–10 de agosto de 1985*, 27–41. Instituto de Investigaciones Filologicas, Universidad Nacional Autónoma de México, Mexico City.

Saul, Frank P. 1972. *The Human Skeletal Remains of Altar de Sacrificios: An Osteobiographic Analysis*. Papers of the Peabody Museum of Archaeology and Ethnology, vol. 63, no. 2. Harvard University, Cambridge, Massachusetts.

Saul, Frank P., and Julie M. Saul. 1991. The Preclassic Population of Cuello. In *Cuello: An Early Maya Community in Belize*, edited by N. Hammond, 134–158. Cambridge University Press, Cambridge.

Saul, Julie M., and Frank P. Saul. 1997. The Preclassic Skeletons from Cuello. In *Bones of the Maya: Studies of Ancient Skeletons*, edited by S. Whittington and D. Reed, 181–195. Smithsonian Institution Press, Washington, D.C.

Schijman, Edgardo. 2005. Artificial Cranial Deformation in Newborns in the Pre-Columbian Andes. *Child's Nervous System* 21 (11): 945–950.

Sharer, Robert J., and Loa Traxler. 2006. *The Ancient Maya*. Stanford University Press, Stanford.

Storey, Rebecca, Lourdes Márquez Morfín, and Vernon Smith. 2002. Social Disruption and the Maya Civilization of Mesoamerica: A Study of Health and Economy of the Last Thousand Years. In *The Backbone of History: Health and Nutrition in the Western Hemisphere*, edited by R. Steckel and J. Rose, 283–306. Cambridge University Press, Cambridge.

Tiesler Blos, Vera. 1995. La deformacion cefalica entre los Mayas: Aspectos neurofisi-logicos. In *Memorias del Segundo Congreso Internacional de Mayistas*, 662–679. Centro Estudios Maya, Instituto de Investigaciones Filologicas, Universidad Nacional Autónoma de México, Mexico City.

———. 1998. *La costumbre de la deformación cefálica entre los antiguos mayas: Aspectos morfológicos y culturales*. Instituto Nacional de Antropología e Historia, Mexico City.

Tiesler Blos, Vera, and Arturo Romano Pacheco. 2008. El modelado del cráneo en Mesoamérica: Emblemática costumbre milenaria. *Arqueología Mexicana* 16 (94): 18–25.

Torres-Rouff, Christina. 2002. Cranial Vault Modification and Ethnicity in Middle Horizon San Pedro de Atacama, Chile. *Current Anthropology* 43: 163–171.

———. 2009. The Bodily Expression of Ethnic Identity: Head Shaping in the Chilean Atacama. In *Bioarchaeology and Identity in the Americas*, edited by K. Knudson and C. Stojanowski, 212–230. University Press of Florida, Gainesville.

Tozzer, Alfred M. 1941. *Landa's Relación de las cosas de Yucatán*. Papers of the Peabody Museum of American Archaeology and Ethnology, no. 18. Harvard University, Cambridge, Massachusetts.

Tubbs, R., E. G. Salter, and W. J. Oakes. 2006. Artificial Deformation of the Human Skull: A Review. *Clinical Anatomy* 19 (4): 372–377.

Webster, David. 1997. Studying Maya Burials. In *Bones of the Maya: Studies of Ancient Skeletons*, edited by S. Whittington and D. Reed, 3–14. Smithsonian Institution Press, Washington, D.C.

Wright, Lori E., and Francisco Chew. 1998. Porotic Hyperostosis and Paleoepidemiology: A Forensic Perspective on Anemia among the Ancient Maya. *American Anthropologist* 100 (4): 924–939.

11

How the Wari Fashioned Trophy Heads for Display

A Distinctive Modified Cranium from Cuzco, Peru, and Comparison to Trophies from the Capital Region

VALERIE A. ANDRUSHKO

The taking of human trophy skulls has a long and varied history in the pre-Columbian Andes, most notably among the Nasca of Peru's south-central coast (AD 1–750; see Forgey this volume). The later Wari Empire (AD 600–1000) of the central Peruvian highlands was also known to practice trophy-taking, as evidenced by a set of thirty-one trophy skulls from the heartland site of Conchopata. Now, the discovery of a distinctive modified cranium from Cuzco has expanded the known range of Wari trophy-taking and represents the first Wari trophy head discovered from the southern Peruvian highlands. The Cuzco modified cranium was found in 2006 at the site of Cotocotuyoc in the Huaro Valley, Peru. Through demographic analysis, the individual was determined to be an adult male. The modifications made to transform this individual into a trophy head were extensive—he was killed, scalped, and defleshed, and his nose and brain were removed. Following soft-tissue removal, multiple modifications were made to facilitate display: a large hole was punched in the back of the skull, tiny holes were drilled into the sides of the head with gold alloy tacks inserted (possibly to reaffix the scalp), and a bone insert and prosthetic teeth were fashioned to decorate the cranium.

In this chapter, I examine how trophy heads may be identified in the archaeological record and describe the site context in which a single Wari trophy cranium from Cuzco was found. I present the osteological analysis of the Cuzco cranium and detail its meticulous modifications, including evidence for scalping, defleshing, and brain removal. These results are synthesized and compared with Tung's (2007, 2008) analysis of thirty-one Conchopata trophy heads from the Wari heartland, revealing distinct differences between the Wari trophy head from the hinterland and those from the heartland. This comparison yields new information on the range and significance of trophy practices among the Wari and suggests additional avenues for research on Wari trophy skulls.

Introduction

Trophy-taking, the practice of removing the body parts of warfare victims for later display, has been documented in many prehistoric cultures worldwide (Chacon and Dye 2007a: 7; Keeley 1996; Walker 2000: 9). Once removed, the body parts were often modified with drill holes, polishing, pigments, incisions, and other alterations to facilitate display (Carneiro 1990: 204). In some cultures, trophies were thought to retain the spirit of the individual from which they were obtained, and their inclusion in rituals served to celebrate an avenged wrong or give thanks for supernatural assistance in victories (Chacon and Dye 2007b; Driver 1969; Seeman 2007: 171; Turney-High 1971: 197; see Bonogofsky and Graham this volume for examples from Melanesia). Trophies were also used as tangible proof of prowess in warfare, with individuals motivated to procure more trophies by the promise of increased social status, greater access to resources, and opportunities in marriage (Carneiro 1990; Mendoza 2007: 581; Mensforth 2007: 224; Smith 1993, 1997). For example, members of some Native American Northwest Coast groups who participated in trophy acquisition were known as "terrifying killers" (Ferguson 1984: 309), a standing that conferred compensation in ceremonial titles and prerogatives. These material gains represented a motivation for trophy-taking that complemented the religious aspects of the practice, implying both social and ideological significance for the taking of human body parts as trophies (Chacon and Dye 2007b: 630).

Among pre-Columbian groups in the Andes, the taking of human trophy skulls has a long and varied history (Benson and Cook 2001; Ogburn 2007; Rowe 1946: 279; Tung 2007; Verano 1995; Verano et al. 1999). The best-known example is the Nasca culture of the south-central coast of Peru (AD 1–750; Forgey this volume; Forgey 2006; Kellner 2002; Silverman 1993; Verano 2003; Williams et al. 2001). Some researchers have linked Nasca trophy heads to their warfare practices (Proulx 1989, 2001; Verano 1995), while others have posited a ritual explanation connected with ancestor veneration and fluctuating agricultural fertility (Carmichael 1994, 1995; Coelho 1972; Drusini and Baraybar 1989). While debate continues regarding the reasons for trophy-taking (Knudson et al. 2009: 4), the practice clearly played an important role in Nasca society. Over 150 trophy heads have been recovered (Tung 2007:

490), and depictions on Nasca ceramics suggest that successful headhunting was an important way to enhance power and status (Browne et al. 1993: 278; DeLeonardis 2000: 380).

Two recent discoveries shed light on trophy-taking in an Andean civilization that rose to prominence after the Nasca—the Wari Empire of the central Peruvian highlands (AD 600–1000). First, a group of thirty-one ritually buried trophy skulls was found at the Wari heartland site of Conchopata that showed a pattern of standardized modifications (Tung 2007, 2008; Tung et al. 2007). This extraordinary assemblage was the first trophy cache recovered from a Wari site (Tung 2008: 294), corroborating data from Wari iconography that attributed great social and ritual significance to trophy-taking (Cook 2001; Ochatoma and Cabrera 2002; Tung 2007: 496). The second discovery was a single distinctive modified cranium from the site of Cotocotuyoc in the Wari hinterland of Cuzco, Peru (Andrushko and Bellifemine 2006; Tesar and Rao 2007). This discovery, described in detail in the present chapter, represents the first Wari trophy head found in the Cuzco region. Moreover, it expands the range of known Wari trophy heads from their heartland into their southeastern hinterland, confirming that Wari trophy-taking was not merely a phenomenon of the empire's capital region. Together, these two discoveries provide a unique opportunity to examine how trophy heads were fashioned and displayed in Wari society.

Identifying Trophy-Taking in Archaeological Specimens

The practice of trophy-taking may be examined to provide a framework for identifying cases from the archaeological record. In this practice, body parts— often heads, limbs, or soft tissue such as scalps and ears—are removed at the time of death, instead of after the body has decomposed. Tool marks such as cut marks, chop marks, and scrape marks indicate that soft tissue was intentionally severed and removed perimortem (Allen et al. 1985; Milner et al. 1991; Owsley et al. 1977; White 1992). Trophy-taking may occur in contexts ranging from small raids and skirmishes to large-scale, organized battles, while victims may include those actively engaged in warfare as well as those swept up in the violence. After removal, the body part is modified in a way to facilitate public viewing, since trophy-taking requires an audience to maximize its symbolic power.

Ancestor veneration is frequently suggested as an alternative explanation for skull collecting and modification, whereby skeletal elements are removed from the burial context and retained as sacred keepsakes (Fenton 1991; Rakita et al. 2005). However, these cases often result in a different archaeological signature than trophy-taking, because venerated individuals are usually buried and later exhumed for removal of a part of the skeleton after decomposition of soft tissue. As such, no cut marks will appear on the bones when element removal occurs after the soft tissue has decayed. Demographic information may also help to distinguish cases of ancestor veneration from trophy-taking: trophy-taking may feature young- and middle-adult males, a demographic group associated with warfare, while venerated ancestors may feature older adults of both sexes (Finucane 2008: 75; Seeman 1988, 2007: 174; Verano 1995: 214; Walker 2001: 588). Finally, trophy-taking victims are expected to show significantly higher frequencies of both antemortem and perimortem trauma, reflecting their participation in violent conflict (Andrushko et al. 2005; Andrushko et al. 2010; Lambert 2002: 210; Tung 2008: 298; see Stojanowski and Duncan this volume).

Certainly, the archaeological signatures of these two practices may overlap, such that distinguishing trophy-taking from ancestor veneration may be difficult (Knudson et al. 2009: 4; see Valentin and Rolland this volume for examples from the Marquesas Islands). In some cases, in fact, they may be impossible to differentiate using osteological data alone (Forgey and Williams 2005: 274). Burial context may also fail to distinguish the two practices, because heads taken from both warfare victims and venerated ancestors may receive elaborate ceremonial treatment (Armit 2006: 3). In all cases, a comprehensive analysis is required that considers demographic information, trauma analysis, burial context, material culture, isotopic data (when available), ancient DNA, and intersite comparison (Finucane 2008; Tung and Knudson 2008; see Forgey this volume; Montgomery, Knüsel, and Tucker this volume).

Using this integrated perspective and the archaeological signature of trophy-taking victims described here—primarily adult males with indications of trauma, dismemberment, and postmortem modification—I turn now to a distinctive case of skull modification from the Cuzco region site of Cotocotuyoc, Peru.

Materials and Methods

Materials

The site of Cotocotuyoc, recently excavated by a team led by Mary Glowacki, is located forty-six kilometers southeast of Cuzco at an elevation of 3,200 meters above sea level (Glowacki 2002; Glowacki and Roman 2000; figure 11.1). Founded during the early part of the Wari occupation of Cuzco (ca. AD 600), the site occupation continued through the last phase of the Middle Horizon

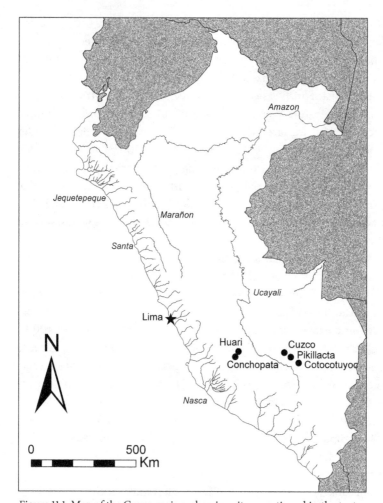

Figure 11.1. Map of the Cuzco region, showing sites mentioned in the text.

(ca. AD 1000), a time of violent conflict that required active defense of the Wari communities (Glowacki and McEwan 2001: 42). Several site character-istics indicate a settlement braced for intergroup conflict: a fortification wall, recovery of weaponry artifacts, and a location above the valley floor with stra-tegic views of the valley (Glowacki 2002: 272).

These archaeological data provide evidence for precipitating factors of Wari collapse in the Cuzco region. Glowacki's investigations into the terminal phase of Wari occupation at Cotocotuyoc indicate a population under duress, where political instability from environmental disruptions translated into substan-dard architecture and artifacts due to limited material resources (Glowacki

2005). Material evidence of violent conflict supports the notion that warfare and political instability contributed to the collapse of the Wari Empire in Cuzco (Glowacki 2002, 2005).

At the site of Cotocotuyoc, forty-five Wari burials were found during the 2005 and 2006 field seasons. Of the forty-five Wari burials, one isolated cranium (CC 48) was discovered with evidence of postmortem modification. The modified head was recovered in an elite section of the cemetery beneath carefully interred llama bones. In this section of the cemetery, high-quality ceramic artifacts and primary human interments were also found. Except for some postmortem damage to the right frontal, sphenoid, and parietal, the cranium was in excellent condition with no signs of weathering, cracking, bleaching, or flaking that might indicate exposure. Some root etching and adhering matrix were apparent on the cranial vault.

Methods of Analysis for the Modified Cranium

For CC 48, age was determined using the multiple criteria of dental development and eruption, dental wear, and cranial suture closure (Meindl and Lovejoy 1985; Smith 1984; Ubelaker 1999). Sex determination was also based on multiple criteria as outlined by Buikstra and Ubelaker (1994), using the sexually dimorphic characteristics of the nuchal crest, mastoid process, supraorbital ridge, and supraorbital margin. Data collection for bone modification was based on White's (1992) description of different types of tool marks such as cut marks and scrape marks.

Results

Sex, Age, and Trauma

CC 48 was determined to be a male based on his distinctive cranial characteristics: a pronounced nuchal crest, large mastoid processes, robust supraorbital ridges, and rounded supraorbital margins. Age was more difficult to determine, since none of the diagnostic postcranial elements (e.g., pubic symphysis or auricular surface) were available for analysis. Instead, age was determined primarily through cranial suture closure, a highly variable aging technique (Buikstra and Ubelaker 1994: 38). The cranial sutures of CC 48 were partially closed—none were completely open and none were completely obliterated. Based on this moderate degree of closure, CC 48 was estimated to be in the middle-adult age category (26–45 years). Arguing for the younger side of that age category, CC 48's dental wear was generally slight, suggesting that this individual had not consumed abrasive or fibrous foods for several decades.

Figure 11.2. Perimortem cut marks on posterior parietals with postmortem perforations at and above lambda.

(Individuals in this population over 40 years of age generally exhibited significant wear in their posterior dentition.)

This middle-adult male showed evidence for both healed and perimortem trauma. A healed, shallow depressed fracture to the right zygomatic, just lateral to the zygomaticofacial foramen, was small (4.7 millimeters in diameter) and round with no indications of fracture lines or subsequent infection. The two perimortem wounds—either of which may have been the mechanism of death—were found on the right and left posterior parietals (figure 11.2). The first perimortem cut was located on the right posterior parietal near the parietal eminence, with an ovoid shape of 20.0 millimeters (anterior–posterior [a–p]) × 4.31 millimeters (medial–lateral [m–l] at the widest point). The depth of this cut was 1.34 millimeters, with a classic perimortem signature including homogenous color for the modified and unmodified surfaces, crushing of the upper layer of bone, and slight peeling on the right lateral edge. The second perimortem cut was located on the left posterior parietal along the sagittal suture and measured 27.69 millimeters (a–p) × 6.05 millimeters (m–l at the widest point). The cut was 1.23 millimeters deep and showed the same perimortem characteristics as the first cut.

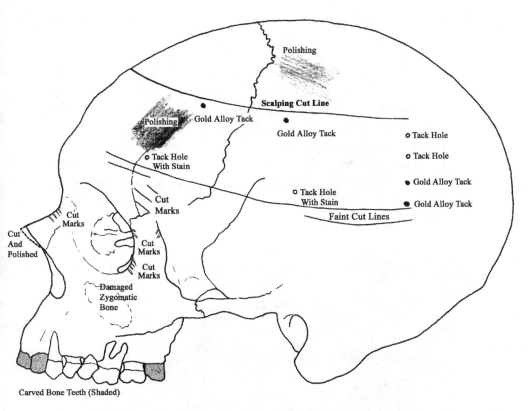

Figure 11.3. Sketch of the lateral view of CC 48, showing multiple modifications. Image courtesy of Louis Tesar and Viviana Bellifemine.

Bone Modification

The following eight types of modification were observed on CC 48 (figure 11.3): (1) removal of the entire basicranial region; (2) two perimortem circular perforations on the posterior cranium (one large, one small); (3) more than one hundred cut marks on the cranial vault and facial region; (4) scraping and polishing of the cranial vault; (5) modification to the nasal bones; (6) six small (≤1 millimeter) metal tacks inserted into the cranium, along with six additional small drill holes; (7) five prosthetic teeth inserted into open alveoli; and (8) one ovoid bone insert placed into the right posterior cranial vault.

(1) Cut basicranium: The occipital was cut in an arc that resulted in the removal of the entire inferior portion of the cranium (figure 11.4). The temporal bones were sliced through the external auditory meatus, as were

both sphenoids behind the lesser wings. The cut surface was very smooth, almost polished, and showed no flaking or chipping.

(2) Perforations: Two perimortem perforations, one large and one small, were located at the back of the cranium around the lambda region (see figure 11.2). At lambda, there was a large hole (24.8 millimeters in diameter) with irregular margins that showed no patina or smoothing. The hole was not drilled or cut but rather appeared punched out, due to the roughened margins. Superior to the larger hole, there was a much smaller perforation measuring 5.01 millimeters in diameter. This perforation had the same morphological characteristics of the larger hole and appeared to have occurred perimortem without any additional modifications such as smoothing.

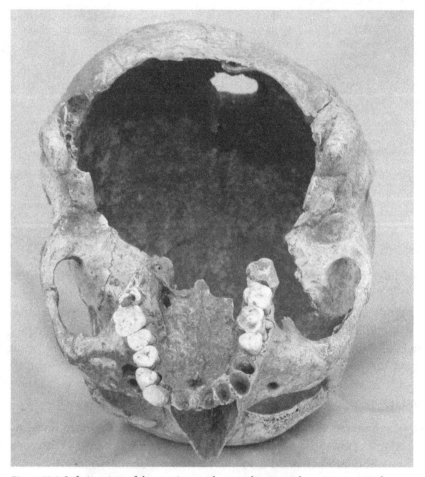

Figure 11.4. Inferior view of the cranium with entire basicranial portion removed.

(3) Cut marks: The two types of cut marks that were present included long, circumferential marks suggestive of scalping and short, clustered marks suggestive of defleshing (figures 11.5, 11.6).

The first scalping mark was a circumferential cut mark that swept from the left parietal to the midfrontal and onto the right parietal. A second set of circumferential cut marks crossed lower down on the forehead, also passing from the left parietal along the frontal and onto the right parietal.

The defleshing marks were concentrated on the facial bones but also extended to the cranial vault. A conservative estimate for the number of facial cut marks was forty-six: seven on the left zygomatic, fifteen on the right zygomatic, five on the left maxilla, four on the right maxilla, two on the left nasal, and thirteen on the right nasal. These cut marks ranged from 1.7 millimeters to 10.1 millimeters in length. Closely concentrated on most facial areas, these cut marks were oriented in all directions.

On the cranial vault, there was a cluster of cut marks on the left midparietal. The conservative count of cut marks within the cluster was twenty, with an average length of 30 millimeters. On the left frontal above the lateral orbit region, there was a cluster of very shallow cut marks, within an area measuring 27 millimeters (m–l) × 24 millimeters (a–p); approximately twenty-four cut marks were found in this area. On the right frontal,

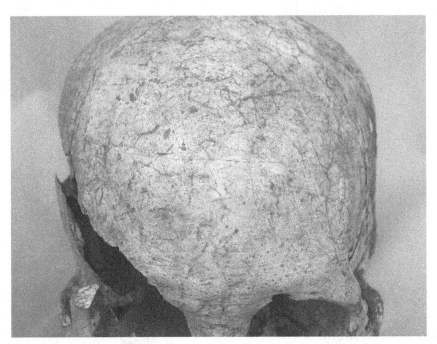

Figure 11.5. Anterior view of cranium with sweeping cut mark across the frontal.

a similar cluster of cut marks was located above the lateral orbit, within an area measuring 13 millimeters (m–l) × 28 millimeters (a–p). The conservative estimate for this cluster was fifteen cut marks, with some oriented vertically and others obliquely. There were also scattered cut marks around the cranial vault.

(4) Scraping and polishing: Small areas of the cranium were scraped on the ectocranial surface, which removed the first layer of compact bone and exposed the underlying trabeculae (figure 11.6). The scraped areas were polished and were most evident on the right and left temporal lines of the frontal.

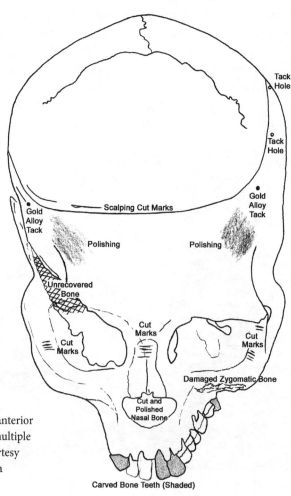

Figure 11.6. Sketch of the anterior view of CC 48, showing multiple modifications. Image courtesy of Louis Tesar and Viviana Bellifemine.

(5) Nasal bone modification: The projecting inferior edges of the right and left nasals were cut off and smoothed (figures 11.6, 11.7). The smoothed appearance extended to the top part of the right and left maxillary region of the nasal aperture but did not extend to the inferior portion of the maxilla around the nasal aperture.

(6) Metal tacks and associated drill holes: There were three sets of tiny drill holes, some filled with metal tacks (figures 11.3, 11.8). All of the holes appeared to be drilled rather than hammered, because there was no chipping

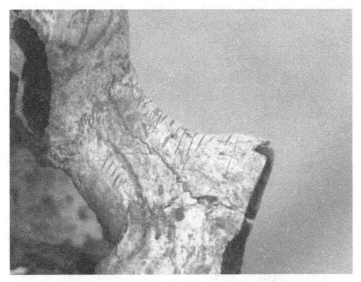

Figure 11.7. Cut nasals with multiple cut marks along nasal bridge.

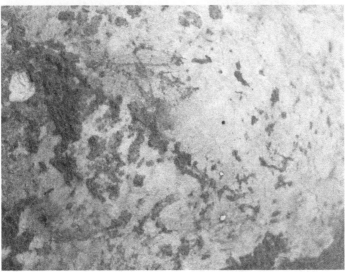

Figure 11.8. Tiny drill holes with two metal tacks on left parietal.

or impact scarring of the margins. When present, the metal tacks were uniform in size, approximately 1 millimeter in diameter, and made of gold alloy (Glowacki personal communication, 2007).

The first set of drill holes was found on the frontal, where two drill holes with metal tacks were present bilaterally along the right and left temporal lines. The height of the metal tacks on the frontal could not be measured because they barely extended past the ectocranial surface.

The second set of drill holes was found on the lateral surface of the anterior parietal. As with the drill holes on the frontal, these two drill holes were positioned symmetrically, one on each side of the cranium; each was filled with a metal tack. These metal tacks, like those on the frontal, barely extended past the ectocranial surface: on the right side, the metal tack extended 0.72 millimeters above the ectocranial surface, while on the left side the tack extended 0.32 millimeters above the ectocranial surface.

The third set of drill holes was located on the posterior parietals, where four holes were bilaterally symmetrical, positioned in a vertical line on both the right and left sides. On the right side, no metal tacks were inserted into the drill holes, while on the left side the bottom two holes had metal tacks and the top two did not. The holes were approximately 1 millimeter in diameter and were positioned equidistant from one another, approximately 10 millimeters apart.

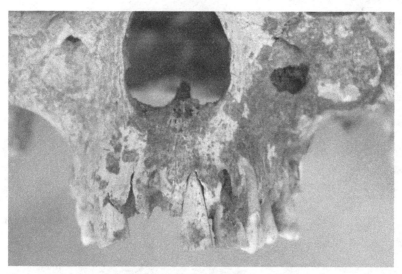

Figure 11.9. Anterior view of the maxilla showing prosthetic teeth in left central incisor, left lateral incisor, and right canine sockets.

None of the gold tacks were visible on the endocranial surface; therefore, given the thickness of the parietal vault, the tacks must have been less than 4.5 millimeters in length. All the drill holes were perfectly round with no damage at the margins of the holes, indicating that they had been drilled while the bone was still fresh.

(7) Artificial dental implants: There were five prosthetic teeth that appeared to be made of polished animal bone (figure 11.9). These implants were located in the sockets of the left first and second incisors, left third molar, right canine, and right third molar. The implants had been fashioned to mimic the morphology of the teeth they replaced with approximate sizes and cusp formation of permanent human dentition (figure 11.10). No wear was present on the occlusal surface of the teeth, confirming that they had been inserted after death.

(8) Ovoid bone insert: One bone insert was placed into the right posterior parietal, measuring 31.67 millimeters (a–p) × 4.9 millimeters (m–l), with an ovoid shape and sharply tapered ends (see figure 11.2). The parietal had been cut to perfectly accommodate the insert; this cut portion perforated the entire width of the cranium, with incised tool marks evident at the latero-inferior end of the insert. The bone insert appeared to be constructed from the same material as the prosthetic teeth.

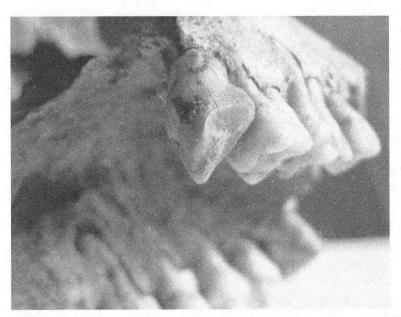

Figure 11.10. Lateral view of right maxilla showing cusp detail on prosthetic third molar.

Discussion

Was CC 48 a Trophy Head?

As discussed earlier in this chapter, identifying a trophy head from osteological data alone may be difficult. However, when all available lines of evidence are assessed for the Cotocotuyoc cranium, the data point to a trophy designation. First, the osteological evidence suggests that he was a warrior: his age and sex match the demographic group most likely to participate in warfare, while his traumatic injuries, both antemortem and perimortem, indicate that he engaged in and likely died from violent conflict. Moreover, his burial context matches that of Wari trophy heads found at other sites (Tung 2008). CC 48 was recovered in an elite section of the Cotocotuyoc cemetery, where several high-quality ceramic artifacts were found, and the decedent had lain beneath several carefully interred llama bones. This context of trophy heads, camelid bones, and high-quality ceramics has also been noted for the Wari capital region and appears to represent "part of an elaborate ritual complex within Wari society" (Tung 2008: 297). Material culture from the region also indicates the importance of Wari trophy-taking in Cuzco. A cache of warrior figurines was found at the nearby Wari site of Pikillacta in 2004, with one figurine depicting a fanged supernatural being holding a human trophy head (Arriola 2007).

Along with the age and sex data, evidence of trauma, burial context, and material culture, CC 48 also shows numerous modifications that suggest trophy-taking. The scalp and soft tissue of the face were removed, as evidenced by scalping and defleshing cut marks around the cranium. The entire inferior portion of the skull was cut away to remove the brain, a practice similar to that seen in other Andean trophy skulls (Browne et al. 1993: 285; Finucane 2008: 81; Verano 1995, 1997: 246; Williams et al. 2001). The individual's nose was also cut off, as is apparent in the cut to and polished appearance of the right and left nasal bones.

Once all the soft tissue had been removed, the cranium was modified for display. While the exact intentions of those who made these modifications cannot be determined, analogies from other Andean sites may shed light on these modifications.

The small metal inserts and associated drill holes were likely used to pin something on the surface of the skull, possibly part of the scalp and/or face that had been carefully removed. Similar cases in which the soft tissue and/or hair was reaffixed to the skull have been seen in trophy heads from the middle Majes Valley (Tung 2003: 262) and suggested for Nasca trophy heads as well (Browne et al. 1993: 286; Kellner 2006: 102).

Further modifications included a polished bone insert placed on the right side of the cranium and five prosthetic teeth inserted into open alveoli. His teeth were lost postmortem, so artificial teeth were likely constructed to make the head more complete and lifelike. The striking aspect of the teeth is how realistic they appear—the molar teeth have multiple rounded cusps, while the incisors have the more spatulate appearance of adult anterior dentition. There was no wear on the occlusal surfaces, indicating that these artificial teeth had been inserted after death. This appears to be the first archaeological example of multiple artificial teeth created for a trophy head in the Andes.

Finally, the two perforations at the back of the cranium may have been used to display the trophy head. At first glance, the positioning and size of these perforations are puzzling—one hole seems too large to pass a cord through, while the other seems too small. Moreover, the holes are not in the "normal" location for stringing up a trophy head, commonly located on the frontal bone of trophy heads from Nazca (Verano 1995; Williams et al. 2001). The holes in the back of the Cuzco cranium might have served to mount the head onto a wall, so that the face looked forward. This type of display—the tenoned head—is seen in sculptured heads on the upper walls of the temple at Chavin de Huántar (Burger 1992: 158). Indeed, the larger hole on the Cuzco trophy head appears to be in the ideal location for affixing it to a wall. However, because the Cuzco head was not discovered in such a state of display, this idea remains tentative until other Cuzco trophy heads are found.

Comparison to Wari Trophy Heads from the Capital Region

While there are no comparative specimens from the local region—CC 48 is unique among Wari sites in Cuzco—there is a set of trophy heads from Conchopata in the Wari capital region that provides an excellent comparative data set (Tung 2007, 2008; Tung et al. 2007). These trophy heads were recovered within one D-shaped and one circular ritual structure (Tung 2008: 297), both of which also held sacrificed camelids and ceramics with an elaborate iconography of warriors, weapons, and trophy heads (Ochatoma and Cabrera 2002).

Tung's extensive research on the thirty-one trophy heads from Conchopata revealed a standardized type of modification in the capital region (Tung 2008). Nearly 90 percent had a drilled hole on the superior cranium, with the majority positioned at or around bregma, and six occipital bones were also found with drill holes. The diameters of these drill holes were remarkably uniform, with very small standard deviations: 12 millimeters was the average for the superior holes (S.D.=2.84 mm), and 6.2 millimeters was the average for the occipital holes (S.D.=2.01 mm; Tung 2008: 299). Three mandibles also had drill holes. Cut marks were found on three zygomatic bones, one temporal at the mastoid process, and one occipital, indicating the removal of soft tissue. Eleven mandibles found in association with the modified crania also showed evidence of cut marks, and two showed evidence of chop marks. Adult males were overrepresented in the trophy head sample (88 percent of those sexed), and 42 percent of the adult trophy individuals showed evidence for trauma. Finally, twenty-eight of the thirty-one trophy heads had been completely burned.

When compared to the Conchopata trophy heads, the CC 48 Cuzco trophy head shows similarities, as well as distinctions. The similarities include the fact that CC 48 was an adult male with evidence of antemortem and perimortem trauma, resembling eight of the nineteen adult trophy heads from Conchopata (Tung 2008: 300). In addition, the osteological evidence is convincing for de-fleshing and dismemberment at both sites. And at both sites, the trophy heads were found in ritually significant spaces with camelid bones and ceramics, within regions where the material culture revealed iconographic evidence of trophy-taking. Yet the differences between the Conchopata and Cotocotuyoc heads are more striking. Most obvious is that CC 48 has two holes on the posterior portion of the cranium around lambda, whereas nearly 90 percent of the Conchopata heads show a drilled hole on the superior portion of the cranium. The metal tacks and tiny drill holes on CC 48 are absent from the Conchopata skulls, as are the ovoid bone insert and the prosthetic teeth. No mandible was recovered with CC 48, and no evidence of burning was found.

The differences between the Conchopata heads and CC 48 may relate to location. Conchopata, located near the Wari capital site, was an important ritual, domestic, and mortuary site in the heartland (Isbell and Cook 2002; Ochatoma and Cabrera 2002). In this context, we see a standardized approach to the manufacture of Wari trophy heads: deliberately positioned drill holes generally uniform in size and shape and a location ideal for suspending the head with the face forward. Tung (2007: 495, 2008: 303) interprets this standardization as a reflection of the authority of the Wari state in managing an important symbol of imperial power. In contrast, Cuzco was located at the southeastern-most border of the Wari Empire, roughly 250 kilometers from the Wari capital, long before Cuzco emerged as the capital of the Inca Empire. On the Wari border, away from imperial control of the capital, there would have been more leeway to construct and display material culture in a unique way—hence a trophy head much different from the standardized heads of the heartland. Cultural creativity in hinterlands has been documented in other Andean locales (Alconini 2004; Lau 2005; Van Gijseghem 2006) and possibly contributed to the distinctive Cuzco trophy head seen here.

Another explanation for the differences between the two sites is idiosyncratic variation. Because only one Wari trophy head has been recovered from Cuzco so far, there is no way to determine whether it is representative of a Cuzco style. Further discoveries of Wari trophy heads in Cuzco must be made to determine whether these modifications were standardized, like those of Conchopata, or highly variable. Clearly, we are just beginning to understand the range of ways in which Wari hinterland groups fashioned trophy heads for display.

Though much remains unknown about Wari trophy-taking practices, one thing is clear: the creators of Wari trophy heads spent considerable time and effort crafting these heads, transforming them from heads to ritual objects—a transformation that Tung (2007: 481) termed "from corporeality to sanctity." For the Conchopata trophies, this translated into a standardized modified skull with uniformly sized and positioned drill holes. For the Cuzco trophy head, this detail translated into a wealth of meticulous modifications, exemplified by the perfectly symmetrical, equidistant tiny holes filled with gold alloy tacks, as well as realistically shaped prosthetic teeth. The hours of concentrated effort required to fashion Wari trophy heads attest to their importance as objects of ritual significance and symbols of imperial authority (Tung 2007: 498).

Conclusions and Future Research

As determined in this study, the Cuzco trophy head was from an adult male with both healed and unhealed cranial injuries, suggesting that he engaged in and possibly died from trauma due to violent conflict. After death, his head was modified in a number of ways: his scalp was cut away and face defleshed, his nose was detached, and his brain was removed by cutting out the inferior section of his braincase. Then, tiny holes were drilled along the sides of his head, possibly to reaffix his face and/or hair, and larger holes were positioned in the back of his head, possibly to tenon the head to a wall for display. Finally, an ovoid bone insert was placed into the right side of his cranium and five prosthetic teeth were fashioned to replace ones lost after death.

Analysis on trophy heads from the Wari heartland has shown that these individuals are often identified as nonlocals based on strontium isotopic analysis of their teeth against known environmental ratios (Knudson and Tung 2007; Tung 2003; Tung and Knudson 2008). These data have been used to assert that at least some trophy heads represented individuals from outside the capital area who may have been perceived as enemies (Tung and Knudson 2008). The Cuzco trophy head similarly can be tested to detect his geographic origins. Strontium analysis has already been used to track prehistoric migrations in the Cuzco Valley region (Andrushko et al. 2009) and to examine a special group of child burials at the Cuzco site of Chokepukio (Andrushko et al. 2008). This type of research can now be extended to the Huaro Valley encompassing Cotocotuyoc to establish the local strontium signature and determine whether CC 48 deviates from this local signature. This would show whether the Cuzco trophy cranium came from the local Cuzco population or from an individual originating outside the Cuzco area, possibly from the Wari heartland or a different geographical region.

Though many questions remain regarding the identity and use of the Cotocotuyoc trophy head, great pains clearly were taken to meticulously transform him from a person into a sacred object. Also clear is that he was part of an extensive tradition of Wari trophy-taking that spanned the empire from heartland to hinterland. Wari iconography, such as the Pikillacta figurine of a supernatural being holding a human trophy head, further corroborates the importance of trophy-taking in Wari ideology. Additional findings of Wari trophy heads will help illuminate the full range of ways in which Wari trophy heads were fashioned for display throughout the empire.

Acknowledgments

I am indebted to Mary Glowacki, Nicolasa Arredondo, and Louis Tesar for including me in the Cotocotuyoc research project and for generously sharing their data. Their spirit of collaboration and commitment to scientific inquiry made this project an extraordinary experience. I gratefully acknowledge Tiffiny Tung for her exceptional work on the Conchopata trophy skulls that formed the comparative section of this study. Elva Torres, director of the Physical Anthropology Laboratory at the National Institute of Culture–Cuzco, deserves special thanks for her insight on ancient skeletal remains from Cuzco. Viviana Bellifemine provided essential help in cleaning and documenting the Cotocotuyoc trophy head with her meticulous drawings, and I am truly grateful for her assistance. I extend special thanks to Christopher Milan for drafting the map used in this chapter and to Deborah Andrushko for editorial assistance. I also thank Silvana Rosenfeld and Julie-Anne White for their company on the Cotocotuyoc project. Finally, I would like to express my appreciation to Michelle Bonogofsky for inviting me to contribute to this volume. This research could not have been completed without the generous support of the National Science Foundation, the Wenner-Gren Foundation, and the Connecticut State University–AAUP Research funds.

References Cited

Alconini, S. 2004. The Southeastern Inka Frontier against the Chiriguanos: Structure and Dynamics of the Inka Imperial Borderlands. *Latin American Antiquity* 15: 389–418.

Allen, W. H., C. F. Merbs, and W. H. Birkby. 1985. Evidence for Prehistoric Scalping at Nuvakwewtaqa (Chavez Pass) and Grasshopper Ruin, Arizona. In *Health and Disease in the Prehistoric Southwest*, edited by C. F. Merbs and R. J. Miller, 23–42. Anthropological Research Papers 34. Arizona State University, Tempe.

Andrushko, V. A., and V. Bellifemine. 2006. Descripción de restos oseos humanos de los contextos funerarios de Cotocotuyoc. Report submitted to the Instituto Nacional de Cultura–Cusco, Peru.

Andrushko, V. A., M. R. Buzon, A. Simonetti, and R. A. Creaser. 2008. Using Strontium Isotope Analysis to Investigate a Group of Child Sacrifices from the Inca Heartland. Paper presented at the 73rd Annual Meeting of the Society for American Archaeology, Vancouver.

———. 2009. Strontium Isotope Evidence for Prehistoric Migration at Chokepukio, Valley of Cuzco, Peru. *Latin American Antiquity* 20: 57–75.

Andrushko, V. A., K. A. Latham, D. L. Grady, A. G. Pastron, and P. L. Walker. 2005. Bioarchaeological Evidence for Trophy Taking in Prehistoric Central California. *American Journal of Physical Anthropology* 127: 375–384.

Andrushko, V. A., A. W. Schwitalla, and P. L. Walker. 2010. Trophy-Taking and Dismemberment as Warfare Strategies in Prehistoric California. *American Journal of Physical Anthropology* 141: 83–96.

Armit, I. 2006. Inside Kurtz's Compound: Headhunting and the Human Body in Prehistoric Europe. In *Skull Collection, Modification and Decoration*, edited by M. Bonogofsky, 1–14. BAR International Series 1539. Archaeopress, Oxford, U.K.

Arriola, C. 2007. Ofrenda guerra de Pikillacta. Paper presented at the 72nd Annual Meetings of the Society for American Archaeology, Austin.

Benson, E. P., and A. G. Cook, editors. 2001. *Ritual Sacrifice in Ancient Peru*. University of Texas Press, Austin.

Browne, D. M., H. Silverman, and R. Garcia. 1993. A Cache of 48 Nasca Trophy Heads from Cerro Carapo, Peru. *Latin American Antiquity* 4: 274–294.

Buikstra, J., and D. Ubelaker, editors. 1994. *Standards for Data Collection from Human Skeletal Remains*. Research Series 44. Arkansas Archaeological Survey, Fayetteville.

Burger, R. L. 1992. *Chavín and the Origins of Andean Civilization*. Thames and Hudson, London.

Carmichael, P. H. 1994. The Life from Death Continuum in Nasca Imagery. *Andean Past* 4: 81–90.

———. 1995. Nasca Burial Patterns: Social Structure and Mortuary Ideology. In *Tombs for the Living: Andean Mortuary Practices*, edited by T. D. Dillehay, 161–188. Dumbarton Oaks Research Library and Collection, Washington, D.C.

Carneiro, R. 1990. Chiefdom-Level Warfare as Exemplified in Fiji and the Cauca Valley. In *The Anthropology of War*, edited by J. D. Haas, 190–211. Cambridge University Press, New York.

Chacon, R., and D. H. Dye. 2007a. Introduction to Human Trophy Taking: An Ancient and Widespread Practice. In Chacon and Dye 2007c, 5–31.

———. 2007b. Conclusions. In Chacon and Dye 2007c, 630–653.

———, editors. 2007c. *The Taking and Displaying of Human Body Parts as Trophies by Amerindians*. Springer, New York.

Coelho, V. P. 1972. Enterramentos de cabecas de cultura Nasca. Unpublished Ph.D. dissertation, Department of Communication and Arts, University of São Paulo, Brazil.

Cook, A. 2001. Huari D-Shaped Structures, Sacrificial Offerings and Divine Rulership. In Benson and Cook 2001, 137–163.

DeLeonardis, L. 2000. The Body Context: Interpreting Early Nasca Decapitated Burials. *Latin American Antiquity* 11: 363–386.

Driver, H. E. 1969. *Indians of North America*. University of Chicago Press, Chicago.

Drusini, A. G., and J. P. Baraybar. 1989. Anthropological Study of Nasca Trophy Heads. *Homo* 41: 251–265.

Fenton, J. 1991. The Social Uses of Dead People: Problems and Solutions in the Analysis of Post Mortem Body Processing in the Archaeological Record. Unpublished Ph.D. dissertation, Department of Anthropology, Columbia University, New York.

Ferguson, R. B. 1984. A Reexamination of the Causes of Northwest Coast Warfare. In *War, Culture, and Environment*, edited by R. B. Ferguson, 267–328. Academic Press, Orlando, Florida.

Finucane, B. C. 2008. Trophy Heads from Nawinpukio, Peru: Physical and Chemical Analysis of Huarpa-Era Modified Human Remains. *American Journal of Physical Anthropology* 135: 75–84.

Forgey, K. 2006. Investigating the Origins and Function of Nasca Trophy Heads Using Osteological and Ancient DNA Analyses. Unpublished Ph.D. dissertation, Department of Anthropology, University of Illinois, Chicago.

Forgey, K., and S. R. Williams. 2005. Were Nasca Trophy Heads War Trophies or Revered Ancestors? Insights from the Kroeber Collection. In Rakita et al. 2005, 251–276.

Glowacki, M. 2002. The Huaro Archaeological Site Complex: Rethinking the Huari Occupation of Cuzco. In *Andean Archaeology*, vol. 1, *Variations in Sociopolitical Organization*, edited by W. H. Isbell and H. Silverman, 267–285. Kluwer Academic/Plenum Publishers, New York.

———. 2005. Excavations at Cotocotuyoc: New Data on the Wari and Lucre Occupations of the Huaro Valley, Cuzco, Peru. Paper presented at the 24th Northeast Conference on Andean Archaeology and Ethnohistory, Washington, D.C.

Glowacki, M., and G. F. McEwan. 2001. Pikillacta, Huaro, y La Gran region del Cuzco: Nuevas interpretaciones de la ocupacion Wari de la sierra sur. *Boletin de Arqueologica PUCP* 5: 31–49.

Glowacki, M., and N. Roman. 2000. *Valle de Huaro: Primera etapa: Reconocimiento sistematico de la superficie.* Informe preliminar. Instituto Nacional de Cultura–Cuzco, Peru.

Isbell, W. H., and A. Cook. 2002. A New Perspective on Conchopata and the Andean Middle Horizon. In *Andean Archaeology,* vol. 2, *Art, Landscape, and Society,* edited by H. Silverman and W. H. Isbell, 249–305. Kluwer Academic Press, New York.

Keeley, L. 1996. *War before Civilization.* Oxford University Press, Oxford.

Kellner, C. M. 2002. Coping with Environmental and Social Challenges in Prehistoric Peru: Bioarchaeological Analyses of Nasca Populations. Unpublished Ph.D. dissertation, Department of Anthropology, University of California, Santa Barbara.

———. 2006. "Trophy" Heads in Prehistoric Peru: Wari Imperial Influence in Nasca Head-Taking Practices. In *Skull Collection, Modification and Decoration,* edited by M. Bonogofsky, 101–111. BAR International Series 1539. Archaeopress, Oxford, U.K.

Knudson, K. J., and T. Tung. 2007. Using Archaeological Chemistry to Investigate the Geographic Origin of Trophy Heads in the Central Andes. In *Archaeological Chemistry: Analytical Techniques and Archaeological Interpretation,* edited by M. Glascock, R. J. Speakman, and R. Popelka-Filcoff, 99–113. American Chemical Society, Washington, D.C.

Knudson, K. J., S. R. Williams, R. Osborn, K. Forgey, and P. R. Williams. 2009. The Geographic Origins of Nasca Trophy Heads Using Strontium, Oxygen, and Carbon Isotope Data. *Journal of Anthropological Archaeology* 28: 244–257.

Lambert, P. M. 2002. The Archaeology of War: A North American Perspective. *Journal of Archaeological Research* 10: 207–241.

Lau, G. F. 2005. Core-Periphery Relations in the Recuay Hinterlands: Economic Interaction at Chinchawas, Peru. *Antiquity* 79: 78–99.

Meindl, R. S., and C. O. Lovejoy. 1985. Ectocranial Suture Closure: A Revised Method for the Determination of Skeletal Age at Death Based on the Lateral-Anterior Sutures. *American Journal of Physical Anthropology* 68: 57–66.

Mendoza, M. 2007. Human Trophy Taking in the South American Gran Chaco. In Chacon and Dye 2007c, 575–590.

Mensforth, R. P. 2007. Human Trophy-Taking in Eastern North America during the Archaic Period: The Relationship to Warfare and Social Complexity. In Chacon and Dye 2007c, 222–277.

Milner, G. R., E. Anderson, and V. G. Smith. 1991. Warfare in Late Prehistoric West-Central Illinois. *American Antiquity* 56: 581–603.

Ochatoma, J., and M. Cabrera. 2002. Religious Ideology and Military Organization in the Iconography of a D-Shaped Ceremonial Precinct at Conchopata. In *Andean Archaeology,* vol. 2, *Art, Landscape, and Society,* edited by H. Silverman and W. H. Isbell, 225–247. Kluwer Academic Press, New York.

Ogburn, D. 2007. Human Trophies in the Late Pre-Hispanic Andes: Striving for Status and Maintaining Power among the Incas and Other Societies. In Chacon and Dye 2007c, 505–522.

Owsley, D. W., H. E. Berryman, and W. M. Bass. 1977. Demographic and Osteological Evidence for Warfare at the Larson Site, South Dakota. *Plains Anthropological
Society Memoir* 13: 119–131.

Proulx, D. A. 1989. Nasca Trophy Heads: Victims of Warfare or Ritual Sacrifice? In
Cultures in Conflict: Current Archaeological Perspectives, edited by D. C. Tkaczuk
and B. C. Vivian, 73–85. University of Calgary Archaeological Association, Calgary, Alberta.

———. 2001. Ritual Uses of Trophy Heads in Ancient Nasca Society. In Benson and
Cook 2001, 119–136.

Rakita, G. F. M., J. E. Buikstra, L. A. Beck, and S. R. Williams, editors. 2005. *Interacting
with the Dead: Perspectives on Mortuary Archaeology for the New Millennium*. University Press of Florida, Gainesville.

Rowe, J. H. 1946. Inca Culture at the Time of the Spanish Conquest. In *Handbook of
South American Indians*, vol. 2, *The Andean Civilizations*, edited by J. H. Steward,
183–330. Bulletin of the Bureau of American Ethnology 143. Smithsonian Institution Press, Washington, D.C.

Seeman, M. 1988. Ohio Hopewell Trophy-Skull Artifacts as Evidence for Competition in Middle Woodland Societies Circa 50 b.c.–a.d. 350. *American Antiquity* 53:
565–577.

———. 2007. Predatory War and Hopewell Trophies. In Chacon and Dye 2007c, 167–
189.

Silverman, H. 1993. *Cahuachi in the Ancient Nasca World*. University of Iowa Press,
Iowa City.

Smith, B. H. 1984. Patterns of Molar Wear in Hunter-Gatherers and Agriculturalists.
American Journal of Physical Anthropology 63: 39–56.

Smith, M. O. 1993. A Probable Case of Decapitation at the Late Archaic Robinson Site
(40sm4), Smith County, Tennessee. *Tennessee Anthropologist* 18: 131–142.

———. 1997. Osteological Indications of Warfare in the Archaic Period of the Western
Tennessee Valley. In *Troubled Times: Violence and Warfare in the Past*, edited by D.
L. Martin and D. W. Frayer, 241–266. Gordon and Breach, Amsterdam.

Tesar, L., and Y. Rao. 2007. Wari Warfare and Trophy Taking: More Than Just a Skull.
Paper presented at the 72nd Annual Meeting of the Society for American Archaeology, Austin.

Tung, T. 2003. A Bioarchaeological Perspective on Wari Imperialism in the Andes of
Peru: A View from Heartland and Hinterland Skeletal Populations. Unpublished
Ph.D. dissertation, Department of Anthropology, University of North Carolina,
Chapel Hill.

———. 2007. From Corporeality to Sanctity: Transforming Bodies into Trophy Heads
in the Pre-Hispanic Andes. In Chacon and Dye 2007c, 481–504.

———. 2008. Dismembering Bodies for Display: A Bioarchaeological Study of Trophy Heads from the Wari Site of Conchopata, Peru. *American Journal of Physical
Anthropology* 136: 294–308.

Tung, T., M. Cabrera, and J. Ochatoma. 2007. Cabezas trofeo Wari: Rituales del cuerpo en el recinto ceremonial en "D" de Conchopata. *Revista de Investigacion, Universidad Nacional de San Cristobal de Huamanga, Peru* 15 (2): 216–227.

Tung, T., and K. J. Knudson. 2008. Social Identities and Geographical Origins of Wari Trophy Heads from Conchopata, Peru. *Current Anthropology* 49: 915–925.

Turney-High, H. H. 1971. *Primitive War: Its Practice and Concepts.* 2nd ed. University of South Carolina Press, Columbia.

Ubelaker, D. H. 1999. *Human Skeletal Remains: Excavation, Analysis, Interpretation.* 3rd ed. Taraxacum, Washington, D.C.

Van Gijseghem, H. 2006. A Frontier Perspective on Paracas Society and Nasca Ethnogenesis. *Latin American Antiquity* 17: 419–444.

Verano, J. W. 1995. Where Do They Rest? The Treatment of Human Offerings and Trophies in Ancient Peru. In *Tombs for the Living: Andean Mortuary Practices,* edited by T. D. Dillehay, 189–227. Dumbarton Oaks, Washington, D.C.

———. 1997. Advances in the Paleopathology of Andean South America. *Journal of World Prehistory* 11: 237–268.

———. 2003. Mummified Trophy Heads from Peru: Diagnostic Features and Medicolegal Significance. *Journal of Forensic Sciences* 48: 525–530.

Verano, J. W., S. Uceda, C. Chapdelaine, R. Tello, M. I. Paredes, and V. Pimentel. 1999. Modified Human Skulls from the Urban Sector of the Pyramids of Moche, Northern Peru. *Latin American Antiquity* 10: 59–70.

Walker, P. L. 2000. Bioarchaeological Ethics: A Historical Perspective on the Value of Human Remains. In *Biological Anthropology of the Human Skeleton,* edited by M. A. Katzenberg and S. R. Saunders, 3–39. Wiley-Liss, New York.

———. 2001. A Bioarchaeological Perspective on the History of Violence. *Annual Review of Anthropology* 30: 573–596.

White, T. D. 1992. *Prehistoric Cannibalism at Mancos 5MTUMR-2346.* Princeton University Press, Princeton.

Williams, S. R., K. Forgey, and E. Klarich. 2001. An Osteological Study of Nasca Trophy Heads Collected by A. L. Kroeber during the Marshall Field Expeditions to Peru. *Fieldiana: Anthropology,* n.s., 33. Field Museum of Natural History, Chicago.

12

Nasca Trophy Head Origins and Ancient DNA

KATHLEEN FORGEY

This chapter focuses on culturally modified human crania, or "trophy heads," from the Early Nasca phases (AD 1–450) of the Nasca culture (AD 1–750) of the South Coast of Peru, where they are ubiquitously represented and displayed, and their meaning is still debated. The two most prevalent explanations for trophy heads focus on ancestor worship (e.g., Carmichael 1988, 1995; Coelho 1972; Tello 1918) and warfare (e.g., Proulx 2001; Uhle 1914; Verano 1995, 2001); evidence of both can be found during the Early Nasca phases, a time of emerging social, political, and religious complexity. Each argument postulates different origins for the individuals whose heads were modified to become trophies—as Nasca or non-Nasca individuals, respectively. To date, explanations have been based on ethnography, ethnohistory, archaeological associations, osteology, and isotope signatures (as discussed later in this chapter). Trophy heads are recovered in a limited number of contexts at Nasca sites, primarily in caches of multiple heads—as many as forty-eight at one time (Browne et al. 1993; Proulx 2001)—or buried in jars.

Study of the context of Nasca trophy heads and the population affiliations of individuals represented by the heads has significant implications for work in other regions of the world (e.g., see Bonogofsky 2006). As demonstrated in the chapters of this book, the ritual treatment of heads and skulls occurs in various cultural and geographical contexts (e.g., Neolithic Near East, Iron Age Eurasia, and ethnographic Oceania). The same questions are emerging at all of these locations—who is represented by these heads? Are they ancestors of those who curated and interred them? Are they enemies from a separate ethnic group or population? This study demonstrates the utility of ancient DNA analysis in addressing these questions. Furthermore, as this example shows, unexpected results may force us to modify our reconstructions of ancient social structures.

This study is the first to incorporate ancient DNA analysis to explore Nasca trophy head origins. Seventy-three Early Nasca specimens, including nine trophy heads and the remains of sixty-four other individuals from the Nazca and neighboring Pisco and Acarí valleys were chosen for study. Mitochondrial DNA (mtDNA) variation was examined by restriction fragment length polymorphism (RFLP) analysis and by partial sequencing of an approximately 230–base pair (bp) fragment of the first hypervariable region (HVRI). Results indicate that the early Nasca people had a high degree of genetic diversity, which is in direct contrast to the limited variation observed in modern Andean populations. Additionally, spatial patterning of RFLP and HVRI sequence data was found among the three valley samples. Finally, limited data suggest that individuals whose heads were made into trophies were members of the Nazca Valley population. Throughout this study, the designation "Nasca" is used for the archaeological culture and "Nazca" for the geographic location and town, a distinction proposed by Silverman (1993).

Introduction

Bioarchaeological research uses biological methods to explore and better understand prehistoric human behavior (Buikstra 1977). One aspect of human behavior involved the taking and modification of human crania, or "trophy heads." Those associated with the Nasca culture from the South Coast of Peru retain the skull as well as the surrounding soft tissues. A perforation in the frontal bone was made to allow attachment of a suspensory cord, and a portion of the base of the skull was removed (figure 12.1). Additional modification was often made to soft-tissue structures, including inserting gauze into eye sockets and under cheeks and sealing the lips with acacia spines (Verano 1995).

Researchers have long debated the origin of and the role that trophy heads played in ancient societies. Iron Age Gaul (Armit 2006), ethnographic Melanesia (Bonogofsky and Graham this volume), and French Polynesia (Valentin and Rolland this volume) have received special attention. In the Americas, Nasca trophy heads have been the subject of great debate. Some researchers have argued that the heads belonged to deceased and revered ancestors; they have suggested that the heads may have been displayed in religious ceremonies (Carmichael 1994; Neira Avedaño and Coelho 1972; Tello 1918). Others have asserted that they represent trophies of war, taken from slain enemies (Proulx 1968; Uhle 1914; Verano 1995). Each argument postulates different origins for the individuals whose heads were modified to become these unique artifacts.

Recently the origin and application of Nasca trophy heads was systematically examined using osteological data taken from trophy heads from the

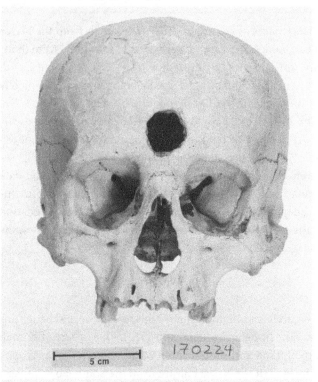

170224

5 cm

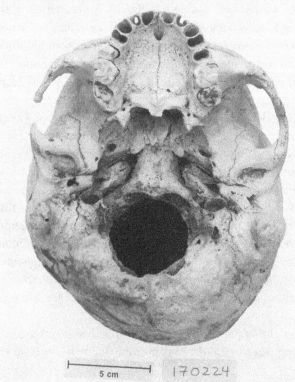

5 cm   170224

Figure 12.1. Nasca trophy head showing (*above*) frontal perforation and (*below*) posterior enlargement. FMNH 170224, A113587, A113590, reproduced with permission from the Field Museum of Natural History, Chicago. Photos by John Weinstein.

Kroeber collection (Kroeber 1937; Kroeber and Collier 1998, n.d.) at the Field Museum of Natural History in Chicago (Forgey 2006; Forgey and Williams 2005; Williams et al. 2001). The observed variation in age and sex distributions and in modification styles, over time and possibly space, suggests that trophy heads fulfilled multiple roles in Nasca society, despite the inability to identify the source population of the heads. Trophy heads have also been recovered from areas under later Wari imperial influence during the Middle Horizon period (AD 600–1000), with some significant differences in their method of preparation and geographic origin (Andrushko this volume; Kellner 2006; Tung 2008).

In this chapter, I use molecular techniques to investigate the genetic relationships between human trophy heads and other members of Nasca society. Data were obtained from trophy heads and comparative specimens from several Nazca Valley sites and from sites in two other valleys flanking the Nazca Valley to the north and south. Comparisons of these genetic data are then used to directly inform us of the origin of those individuals whose heads were made into trophies.

Background

The first evidence of the Nasca culture, which flourished during the Early Intermediate Period (AD 1–750), was discovered in 1901 by Max Uhle (1914). Based on ceramic stylistic similarities, he considered the Nasca culture to be a continuation of the earlier Paracas tradition, famous for its elaborate textiles and seated, flexed burials (Menzel et al. 1964) but sufficiently distinct to warrant its own classification. Its pottery was characterized by pre-fired slip painting depicting complex iconographic themes.

Now world famous for its fine polychrome pottery, textiles, and desert geoglyphs, Nasca material culture has a geographical distribution that spans a large portion of Peru's South Coast, including the area between the coast of the Pacific Ocean and the foothills of the Andes Mountains. It extends from the Chincha and Pisco valleys in the north to the Acarí Valley and beyond to the south (Silverman 1996, 2002; Silverman and Proulx 2002), a total area of some 10,750 square kilometers (ONERN 1971). The Nasca heartland encompasses the Río Grande de Nazca, its ten major tributaries, and the inland regions adjacent to them (figure 12.2).

The Nasca culture emerged during the Early Intermediate Period (table 12.1), which can be divided into eight chronological units, corresponding to the local Nasca ceramic styles (Dawson 1964; Rowe 1959; Schreiber 1998; Schreiber and Lancho Rojas 2003; Silverman and Proulx 2002). Nasca is generally

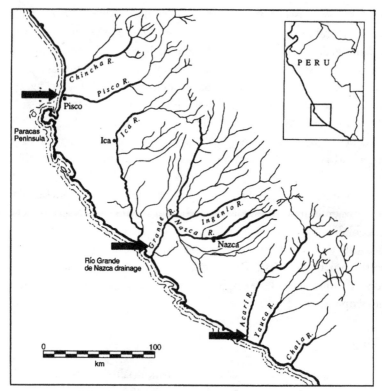

Figure 12.2. Peru's South Coast, with arrows showing valleys containing sites that yielded study specimens. After Williams et al. 2001: 3.

divided into three sociocultural phases designated as Early (AD 1–450), Middle (AD 450–550), and Late (AD 550–700) (Carmichael 1998; Schreiber 1998; Schreiber and Lancho Rojas 1995; Vaughn 2004; Vaughn and Neff 2004). Each phase is marked by changes in both material culture and settlement patterning.

The Early Intermediate Period was a time of dynamic change in the Nazca Valley; settlement patterns changed as people moved from many small scattered villages in the earlier phases to a small number of much larger towns in the later ones. Though Nasca society was certainly complex, recent analyses suggest that it most likely consisted of a network of small, loosely allied polities (Browne 1992; Silverman 1993) and had a level of social complexity characteristic of a chiefdom (Browne et al. 1993; Carmichael 1988, 1994).

The research discussed herein is derived primarily from materials dating to Early Nasca (phases 1–4), a time of emerging social, political, and religious complexity. During this time, Nasca trophy heads are depicted in contexts with various themes, including those surrounding birth, fertility, and death

Table 12.1. Chronology of the Nazca Valley

Estimated dates	Standard chronology	Phases	Culture names	Kroeber phases	Cultural events
AD 1476	Late Horizon				Inca conquest
	Late Intermediate Period	3–4		Late	Regional cultures reestablished
					Societal collapse
AD 750	Middle Horizon	2	Huaca del Loro	Nasca Y	Wari occupation
		(8) 1			
	Early	7	Late Nasca		Reorganization
		6		Nasca B	
	Intermediate	5	Middle Nasca		Transition
	Period	4		Nasca A2	
		3	Early Nasca	Nasca A1	Emergence of Nasca culture
		2		Nasca A0	
AD 1			Proto-Nasca/Montaña		
100 BC		1			
1000 BC	Early Horizon (phases 1–10)		Paracas		Initial permanent occupation
	Initial period				Unoccupied?
	Preceramic period				Temporary foraging occupations?

Sources: Adapted from Schreiber 1998; Schreiber and Lancho Rojas 2003; Silverman and Proulx 2002.

(Proulx 1968; Silverman and Proulx 2002), and are represented in the iconography of battles fought over agricultural land. Though Nasca iconography fulfilled a variety of functions, the general trend in trophy head imagery is change over time, with mythical and naturalistic themes dominating earlier periods and militaristic themes more often found in the later periods.

The Study

Ancient DNA (aDNA) studies (Kaestle and Horsburgh 2002; Stone 2000) have the potential to address ethnicity—whether or not a given individual was a member of a certain group or, alternatively, an outsider or enemy. Driving this study is the question of ancestor veneration or warfare-related activities. In genetic terms, the following can be assumed: (1) If the heads belonged to ancestors, they should be genetically similar to other skeletons buried at the same site, but (2) if the heads belonged to enemies or "outsiders," their genetic information would be genetically distinct and exhibit significant differences.

Genetic data from a subsample of trophy head individuals from the Kroeber collection (Kroeber 1937; Kroeber and Collier 1998, n.d.), which were previously examined using osteological techniques (Forgey 2006; Forgey and Williams 2005; Williams et al. 2001), were compared with data from three archaeological samples—in this case, from Early Nasca sites in the Nazca, Pisco, and Acarí valleys (figure 12.2). Sample selection was limited to those individuals from the Early Nasca phases because this is the time period during which, based on previous osteological analyses, there is the greatest likelihood that trophy heads would have belonged to ancestors. There is less evidence for ancestor-oriented ritual in the later periods.

Sampling

Sample selection and methods used were chosen to assess genetic variation of individuals living on Peru's South Coast during the Early Nasca phases. Cortical bone or tooth specimens were taken from a total of seventy-three individuals: nine trophy heads from the Nazca Valley and sixty-four comparative specimens from the Nazca, Pisco, and Acarí valleys. All nine trophy heads in this study were recovered from three Nazca Valley sites: five from Cahuachi, two from Cantayo, and two from Majoro Chico. The twenty-five Nazca Valley comparative specimens originated in these same sites.

The northern valley comparative sample of twenty-five specimens derives from the Chongos site in the Pisco Valley (Lanning 1960; Peters 1997; Silverman 1991; Wallace 1971, 1986). Chongos was first discovered in the 1950s by Dwight Wallace and yielded the well-preserved remains of more than seventy individuals. Chongos was occupied during the late Early Horizon into the Early Intermediate Period.

The southern valley comparative sample of fourteen specimens comes from the Tambo Viejo site in the Acarí Valley (Hrdlička 1914; Riddell 1985, 1986, 1989; Riddell and Valdez 1988; Rowe 1963; Valdez 1998). Remains from this site were first reported by Aleš Hrdlička in 1914 but were not identified as Nasca until decades later. Most of the Nasca material from Tambo Viejo dates to Early Intermediate phases 2 and 3, but some phase 4 materials have been found as well.

Methods

This ancient DNA study addressed genetic diversity on several levels. The primary goal was to answer the question of trophy head origins by genetically defining individuals whose heads were modified into trophies as either Nasca or non-Nasca individuals. However, to address this question, the amount of genetic diversity present among the groups who lived on Peru's South Coast during the Early Intermediate Period had to be determined first. This was accomplished by analyzing DNA data from comparative samples from three spatially distinct valleys: the Nazca, Pisco, and Acarí. Nasca trophy head genetic data were then compared to data from samples from these three valleys.

Having this South Coast data set extends our current knowledge about ancient New World genetic patterns from an area that is underrepresented in genetic studies of both living and ancient populations and contributes new information to our understanding of the population histories of ancient South Amerindians. As a technically demanding field, ancient DNA research is the subject of ongoing debate regarding methods and standardization of data. This study carefully considered extraction methods, critically evaluated the resulting data, and contributes to increased standardization in the field.

Ancient DNA analyses consist of a number of steps that I have outlined elsewhere (Forgey 2006). From bone preparation to extraction and analyses, extreme care was taken using molecular "clean room" protocols, which are rapidly becoming standardized in the field (Hofreiter et al. 2001; Kaestle and Horsburgh 2002; O'Rourke et al. 2000; Paabo et al. 2004). These consist of creating as sterile an environment as possible, including using a specially designed clean-room hood equipped with a high-efficiency particulate air filter with negative air circulation and ultraviolet lights. Work for this particular study was carried out in an ancient DNA lab at the University of Illinois at Chicago. Negative controls were used in all phases of extraction and initial amplification experiments.

Mitochondrial DNA has become the genome of choice for genetic anthropological studies on archaeological remains owing to several of its unique properties, which are also useful in studies using characteristically nonrobust ancient DNA (Avise et al. 1987; Brown and Pluceinnik 2001; Brown and Brown 1992, 1994; Hagelberg and Clegg 1991; Kaestle and Horsburgh 2002; O'Rourke et al. 2000; Sykes 1993; Wallace et al. 1999). In addition to the large number of mtDNAs per cell, the mitochondrial genome is relatively small, and its sequence is well known (Anderson et al. 1981; Andrews et al. 1999). Given that mtDNA is transmitted almost exclusively through the maternal line (Giles et al. 1980), no recombination occurs, and analysis is straightforward. Further, there are no known repair mechanisms for mutations that arise in mtDNA, so sequence changes evolve more rapidly than in nuclear DNA (Wilson 1985); this rapid rate of mutation has been useful in analyses of population structure (Stoneking et al. 1991). Finally, mtDNA mutations correlate with geographic regions of origin (Ballinger et al. 1992; Chen et al. 2000; Comas et al. 1996; Schurr 2002; Torroni et al. 1993, 1994, 1996, 1998), making mtDNA analysis ideal for studies focusing on individual identification, population history, and migration.

Mitochondrial DNA variation from all individuals, including those represented by trophy heads, was examined for this study by typing four restriction and one-length polymorphism used to define the four major founding Amerindian haplogroups: A, B, C, and D (Schurr et al. 1990; Torroni et al. 1992; Wallace et al. 1985), as well as the newly discovered Haplogroup X (Malhi and Smith 2002; Smith et al. 1999). After initial recognition sequences were obtained for regions that contain polymorphic sites defining Haplogroups A, C, D, and X, further restriction of the desired sequence fragments was performed. RFLP analysis was used to compare sample haplotype data with previously published RFLP data. Additionally, an approximately 230-bp fragment of the Hypervariable Region I (HVRI) of the mitochondrial D-loop was sequenced (Parr et al. 1996; Ribeiro–Dos Santos et al. 1996; Stone and Stoneking 1993, 1998). Unlike RFLP analysis, which examines regions of sequence changes, sequencing allows for the identification of individual "nucleotide-by-nucleotide" changes (Schurr 2002). In this study, sequencing was performed primarily to confirm restriction data. Sequencing experiments were carried out at the University of Illinois at Chicago; the final single-strand sequence electrophoresis runs were performed at the Field Museum of Natural History's Pritzker Laboratory.

Results

Ancient DNA is very hard to quantify, and yield must be experimentally determined. This was assessed by performing an initial postextraction polymerase chain reaction (PCR), with results demonstrating the presence or absence of ancient mtDNA in sufficient quantities to amplify by PCR. This was typically done using primers targeting the 9-bp deletion of the $COII$/tRNA^{Lys} intergenic region.

In this study, all seventy-three samples amplified for at least one of the mtDNA segments that can potentially identify New World founding haplotype restriction or length variants. But this figure is broadly inclusive and misleading and may not accurately reflect overall specimen extraction or DNA recovery success rate. Therefore, success rate was determined according to specific criteria based on the number of amplifications required to obtain an observable PCR product. The number of PCR reactions required to produce a positive result for each restriction marker was noted, and inclusion was based on those samples that amplified with three of the four primary Amerindian restriction markers by the second successful PCR attempt. Using this very conservative method, forty-eight of seventy-three samples yielded amplifiable DNA, for a success rate of 66 percent. This is comparable with other ancient DNA studies.

mtDNA RFLP Haplotype Results

Restriction analysis of the 48 samples resulted in assignment into one of the four major Amerindian haplogroups in 17 individuals, or 35.4 percent of the sample: 5 As, 6 Bs, 4 Cs, and 2 Ds (table 12.2). Some restriction markers for Haplogroup X were tested as well, but these were unsuccessful.

Definite haplotype assignment was given to those samples that always gave the same results. Possible haplotype assignment was given to those that contained at least one ambiguous result and required further analyses. The remaining thirty-one samples were grouped into an "undetermined" haplotype category either because they tested negative for all markers used to define the four primary Amerindian haplogroups or because data could not be obtained for one or more restriction primer sets after multiple PCR amplifications. These findings do not constitute evidence that these individuals were not Amerindian; rather, these results are likely related to the degraded quality of ancient DNA.

Table 12.2. Mitochondrial restriction haplotype data

Result	Haplotype					
	A	B	C	D	Undetermined	n
Definite	2	5	4	0	31	42
Possible	3	1	0	2	NA	6
Total	5	6	4	2	31	48

Partial Sequencing of HVRI of the mtDNA D-Loop Results

Sequencing experiments were performed to confirm restriction haplotype data and to gather more data to help characterize the undetermined group. Therefore, all study samples underwent sequencing experiments targeting a portion of the hypervariable region I of the mtDNA D-loop. Primers were used that amplify an approximately 230-nucleotide sequence fragment spanning the latter half of the HVRI, where the majority of nucleotide differences associated with the five Native Amerindian RFLP haplogroups are located.

Table 12.3 provides a summary of the HVRI-sequence haplotype results. Of the forty-eight samples containing sufficient DNA to be included in this study based on the RFLP exclusion protocol, forty-seven (98.0 percent) produced sequence data using the HVRI primers that amplify the larger 230-nucleotide sequence fragment. Only one specimen (FMNH 170221) failed to amplify this portion of the mtDNA sequence, although it did amplify using primers targeting smaller sequence fragments.

As shown in table 12.3, 10 specimens (20.8 percent) yielded sequence haplotype data: 7 As, 1 B, 1 C, and 1 X. The remaining 38 samples (79.2 percent) were assigned "undetermined" haplotype status, as sequence data failed to yield additional Amerindian haplotype data.

Table 12.3. Mitochondrial DNA sequence haplotype data

Result	Haplotype						
	A	B	C	D	X	Undetermined	n
Definite	4	0	1	0	0	38	43
Possible	3	1	0	0	1	NA	5
Total	7	1	1	0	1	38	48

Table 12.4. Combined RFLP and partial HVRI sequence data

	Total A–D, X	A	B	C	D	X	Undetermined
Total	22	9	6	4	2	1	26

Table 12.5. Combined RFLP and partial HVRI sequence data organized by valley

	Total A–D, X	A	B	C	D	X
Pisco	9	4	3	0	2	0
Nazca	5	1	1	2	0	1
Nazca trophy heads	3	1	0	2	0	0
Acarí	5	3	2	0	0	0
Totals	22	9	6	4	2	1

Summary of RFLP and Sequence Results

Tables 12.4 and 12.5 provide summaries of the RFLP and HVRI sequence results. Of the genetic material from the 48 individuals from the three-valley sample, RFLP and partial HVRI sequence data allowed for Native Amerindian haplotype determination for 22 individuals (45.8 percent): 9 As, 6 Bs, 4 Cs, and 2 Ds. An additional specimen exhibited the 16278 sequence variant that tentatively allows assignment into Haplogroup X. Haplotype designation could not be made for the remaining 26 individuals (54.2 percent of the total sample).

Discussion

As a result of this ancient DNA study, we can ask ourselves two questions: (1) What does this limited data set allow us to say? and (2) What are the possible explanations for the undetermined results?

The DNA data generated from these trophy heads and comparative specimens can provide important insights on prehistoric populations from Peru's South Coast. Mitochondrial DNA restriction and sequence data indicate that the Early Nasca people had a high degree of genetic diversity. In this study, evidence for all five of the known founding Amerindian haplogroup lineages, A–D and X (Brown et al. 1998; Malhi and Smith 2002; Shimada et al. 2004; Smith et al. 1999; Wallace et al. 1985), was present. This diversity has also been found among other pre-Hispanic coastal populations, including individuals of the Sican and Chirabaya Alta cultures (Williams et al. 2003; Shimada et al.

2003) and the individuals from Kilometer 4, a preceramic site (Cansino 2000). This diversity contrasts with studies of modern Andean populations, which exhibit significantly less variation (Bianchi et al. 1995; Lalueza Fox 1996; Merriwether et al. 1995, 1996; Rogan and Salvo 1990; Schurr et al. 1990; Torroni et al. 1992, 1993).

Intervalley variation during Nasca times, particularly in the later periods, holds great interest for archaeologists working on the South Coast. Data from this study, derived from Early Nasca phases, allow us to characterize the South Coast prior to these changes in material culture and settlement patterning, and establishes baseline information for comparison with later periods. The spatial patterning of RFLP and sequence data (table 12.5) shows that all three study valleys contained Haplogroup A and B individuals. Additionally, the Pisco Valley contained potential Haplogroup D individuals (to the exclusion of the other two valleys), and the Nazca Valley contained four Haplogroup C individuals and one potential Haplogroup X individual (to the exclusion of the other two valleys).

Comparison of trophy head samples with the comparative groups from the Nazca, Pisco, and Acarí valleys shows that Haplogroup C individuals ($n=4$) in this study were found only in the Nazca Valley, at the site of Cahuachi (table 12.5). Of the four Haplogroup C individuals, two are from trophy head individuals, one of whom was an adult female. These data suggest that Nazca Valley individuals may have been genetically distinct from those buried in the valleys to the north and south of them and that the trophy heads belonged to members of the Nazca Valley population. This could mean that peoples within the Nazca Valley were antagonistically taking heads from rival groups living in the same valley; however, it does not allow us to exclude closely related individuals as the source of the heads (i.e., Nazca Valley groups took heads from their own group members). These data lend support for claims that during earlier Nasca times, trophy heads may have come from members of Nasca society, possibly from ancestors or as a result of warfare between members of a single ethnic group. Data do not support the idea that trophy heads belonged to a non-Nasca group. These findings lend support to assertions by Brown (1995) that the early practice of ancestor veneration was replaced by the taking of enemy heads in later Nasca times. It also is consistent with what seems to be depicted iconographically at that time. Most recently, collaborative isotope studies by Knudson and colleagues (2009) lend further corroboration to these results.

Given the statistically small sample and the fact that the majority of individuals tested did not produce haplotype data, these results should be considered highly suggestive but not conclusive. Additional studies of ancient DNA on Nasca materials will help to clarify the degree of genetic diversity in the population and allow us to determine how representative these samples are of the Nasca as a whole.

The success rate of obtaining haplotype data in this study is comparable with other ancient DNA studies on samples from Peru. However, problems that plague aDNA studies in general (related to insufficient DNA yield) were also encountered. The nature of the ancient DNA evidence makes degradation, in particular, a constant challenge. A far less likely explanation for individuals in the undetermined haplotype category is that they represent additional founding haplogroups; this explanation cannot be completely ruled out (see Forgey 2006 for a detailed discussion of testing for these factors).

Conclusions

This is the first ancient DNA study to explore the genetic relationships among individuals and groups from the Nazca and surrounding Pisco and Acarí valleys. Within this sample, evidence for all five known founding Amerindian haplogroups was found. Further, genetic differences between valleys were found.

Results indicate that Early Nasca period trophy heads derive from the Nazca Valley population, in other words, from "insiders." These new genetic data provide a wealth of expectations for future studies to test in Nasca and ancient DNA research, as well as to address the universal question of who is represented by heads that have been deformed, disembodied, decorated, or otherwise modified from diverse regions of the world. Additional research on trophy heads should include increasing the existing data set with new sequence data generated from an expanded sample of trophy heads and comparative remains from later time periods. Future studies should also incorporate analyses of nuclear short tandem repeats (STRs), which will provide a more thorough picture of the genetic relationships among Nasca individuals. On a broader level, these data can be incorporated into existing New World ancient DNA findings to explore prehistoric migration patterns.

Various technical and analytical problems are inherent in ancient DNA research; detailed protocols will allow us to standardize ancient DNA research methods (see Forgey 2006 for an extensive discussion of standardization). Future studies will almost certainly improve DNA yields from ancient samples, and confirmatory protocols (and reporting) will strengthen existing data sets. In other words, our work has just begun.

Acknowledgments

This research was made possible by the generous support of the Wenner-Gren Foundation for Anthropological Research (Dissertation Fieldwork Grant #6795); Sigma Xi Grants-in-Aid-of-Research Program; the University of Illinois at Chicago; and the Field Museum of Natural History for numerous collaborative research grants. Thank you to Jonathan Haas, Gary Feinman, and Stephen Nash from the Department of Anthropology at the Field Museum of Natural History; to Susana Arce Torres, director of the Museo Regional de Ica; and to the late Francis Riddell from the California Institute for Peruvian Studies, for allowing me to examine and sample several individuals from the Nasca, Pisco, and Acarí valley collections, respectively. I would also like to thank Sloan Williams and the Department of Anthropology at the University of Illinois at Chicago for lending their support and laboratory facilities for this research and Kevin Feldheim from the Field Museum of Natural History's Pritzker Laboratory for his help during the sequencing portions of the ancient DNA research. Finally, my sincerest thanks go to Michelle Bonogofsky for inviting me to contribute to this important volume.

References Cited

Anderson, S., A. T. Bankier, E. G. Barrell, M. H. L. de Bruijn, A. R. Coulson, J. Drouin, I. C. Eperon, et al. 1981. Sequence and Organization of the Human Mitochondrial Genome. *Nature* 290: 457–465.

Andrews, K. G., I. Kubacka, P. F. Chinnery, R. N. Lightowlers, D. M. Turnbull, and N. Howell. 1999. Reanalysis and Revision of the Cambridge Reference Sequence for Human Mitochondrial DNA. *Nature Genetics* 23 (2): 147.

Armit, I. 2006. Headhunting and the Human Body in Prehistoric Europe. In Bonogofsky 2006, 1–14.

Avise, J. C., J. Arnold, R. M. Ball, E. Bermingham, T. Lamb, J. E. Neigel, C. A. Reeb, and N. C. Saunders. 1987. Intraspecific Phylogeography: The Mitochondrial DNA Bridge between Population Genetics and Systematics. *Annual Review of Ecology and Systematics* 18: 489–522.

Ballinger, S. W., T. G. Schurr, A. Torroni, Y. Y. Gan, J. A. Hodge, K. Hasson, K.-H. Chen, and D. C. Wallace. 1992. Southeast Asian Mitochondrial DNA Analysis Reveals Genetic Continuity of Ancient Mongoloid Migrations. *Genetics* 130: 139–152.

Bianchi, N. O., G. Baillet, and C. M. Bravi. 1995. Peopling of the Americas as Inferred through the Analysis of mtDNA. *Brazilian Journal of Genetics* 18: 661–668.

Bonogofsky, M., editor. 2006. *Skull Collection, Modification and Decoration*. BAR International Series 1539. Archaeopress, Oxford, U.K.

Brown, J. A. 1995. Andean Mortuary Practices in Perspective. In Dillehay 1995, 391–405.

Brown, K. A., and M. Pluceinnik. 2001. Archaeology and Human Genetics: Lessons for Both. *Antiquity* 75 (287): 101–106.

Brown, M. D., S. H. Hosseini, A. Torroni, and H.-J. Bandelt. 1998. mtDNA Haplogroup X: An Ancient Link between Europe/Western Asia and North America? *American Journal of Human Genetics* 63: 1852–1861.

Brown, T. A., and K. A. Brown. 1992. Ancient DNA and the Archaeologist. *Antiquity* 66: 10–23.

———. 1994. Ancient DNA: Using Molecular Biology to Explore the Past. *BioEssays* 16 (10): 719–726.

Browne, D. M. 1992. Further Archaeological Reconnaissance in the Province of Palpa, Department of Ica, Peru. In *Ancient America: Contributions to New World Archaeology*, edited by N. J. Saunders, 77–116. Oxbow Monograph no. 24. Oxbow Books, Oxford, U.K.

Browne, D. M., H. Silverman, and R. Garcia. 1993. A Cache of 48 Nasca Trophy Heads from Cerro Carapo, Peru. *Latin American Antiquity* 4 (3): 274–294.

Buikstra, J. E. 1977. Biocultural Dimensions of Archeological Study: A Regional Perspective. In *Biocultural Adaptation in Prehistoric America*, edited by R. L. Blakely, 67–84. University of Georgia Press, Athens.

Cansino, V. 2000. Kinship Determination of Individuals Buried at Kilometer 4, a Preceramic Archaeological Site on the Coast of Southern Peru. M.A. thesis, Forensic Science, College of Pharmacy, University of Illinois at Chicago.

Carmichael, P. H. 1988. Nasca Mortuary Customs: Death and Ancient Society on the South Coast of Peru. Ph.D. dissertation, Department of Archaeology, University of Calgary, Calgary, Alberta.

———. 1994. The Life from Death Continuum in Nasca Imagery. *Andean Past* 4: 81–90.

———. 1995. Nasca Burial Patterns: Social Structure and Mortuary Ideology. In Dillehay 1995, 161–187.

———. 1998. Nasca Ceramics: Production and Social Context. *In Andean Ceramics: Technology, Organization, and Approaches*, edited by I. Shimada, 213–231. University of Pennsylvania Museum of Archaeology and Anthropology, Philadelphia.

Chen, Y.-S., A. Olkers, and T. G. Schurr. 2000. Mitochondrial DNA Variation in the Southern African Kung and Khwe and Their Genetic Relationships to Other African Populations. *American Journal of Human Genetics* 66: 1362–1383.

Coelho, V. 1972. *Enterramentos de cabeças da cultura Nasca*, Universidad de Sao Paulo, São Paulo, Brazil.

Comas, D., F. Calafell, E. Mateu, A. Perez-Lezaun, and J. Bertranpetit. 1996. Geographic Variation in Human Mitochondrial DNA Control Region Sequence: The Population History of Turkey and Its Relationship to the European Populations. *Molecular Biology and Evolution* 13 (8): 1067–1077.

Dawson, L. E. 1964. Slip Casting: A Ceramic Technique Invented in Ancient Peru. *Ñawpa Pacha* 2: 107–112.

Dillehay, T. D., editor. *Tombs for the Living: Andean Mortuary Practices.* Dumbarton Oaks, Washington, D.C.

Forgey, K. 2006. Investigating the Origins and Function of Nasca Trophy Heads Using Osteological and Ancient DNA Analyses. Ph.D. dissertation, Department of Anthropology, University of Illinois at Chicago.

Forgey, K., and S. R. Williams. 2005. Were Nasca Trophy Heads War Trophies or Revered Ancestors? Insights from the Kroeber Collection. In *Interacting with the Dead: Perspectives on Mortuary Archaeology for the New Millennium*, edited by G. F. M. Rakita, J. E. Buikstra, L. A. Beck, and S. R. Williams, 251–276. University Press of Florida, Gainesville.

Giles, R. E., H. Blanc, H. M. Cann, and D. C. Wallace. 1980. Maternal Inheritance of Human Mitochondrial DNA. *Proceedings of the National Academy of Sciences* 77: 6715–6719.

Hagelberg, E., and J. B. Clegg. 1991. Isolation and Characterization of DNA from Archaeological Bone. *Proceedings of the Royal Society of London B: Biological Sciences* 244 (1309): 45–50.

Hofreiter, M., D. Serre, H. N. Poinar, M. Kuch, and S. Pääbo. 2001. Ancient DNA. *Nature Reviews Genetics* 2 (5): 353–359.

Hrdlička, A. 1914. Anthropological Work in Peru in 1913, with Notes on the Pathology of the Ancient Peruvians. *Smithsonian Miscellaneous Collections* 61 (18): 1–69.

Kaestle, F. A., and K. A. Horsburgh. 2002. Ancient DNA in Anthropology: Methods, Applications and Ethics. *Yearbook of Physical Anthropology* 45: 92–130.

Kellner, C. M. 2006. "Trophy" Heads in Prehistoric Peru: Wari Imperial Influence on Nasca Head-Taking Practices. In Bonogofsky 2006, 101–111.

Knudson, K. J., S. R. Williams, R. Osborn, K. Forgey, and P. R. Williams. 2009. The Geographic Origins of Nasca Trophy Heads Using Strontium, Oxygen, and Carbon Isotope Data. *Journal of Anthropological Archaeology* 28 (2): 244–257.

Kroeber, A. L. 1937. *Archaeological Explorations in Peru, part IV, Cañete Valley.* Anthropology Memoirs 2. Field Museum of Natural History, Chicago.

Kroeber, A. L., and D. Collier. 1998. *The Archaeology and Pottery of Nazca, Peru: Alfred L. Kroeber's 1926 Expedition.* Altamira Press, Walnut Creek, California.

———. n.d. Unpublished manuscript and field notes, Department of Anthropology, Field Museum of Natural History, Chicago.

Lalueza Fox, C. 1996. Mitochondrial DNA Haplogroups in Four Tribes from Tierra del Fuego–Patagonia: Inferences about the Peopling of the Americas. *Human Biology* 68 (6): 855–871.

Lanning, E. P. 1960. Chronological and Cultural Relationships of Early Pottery Styles in Ancient Peru. Ph.D. dissertation, Department of Anthropology, University of California, Berkeley.

Malhi, R. S., and D. G. Smith. 2002. Haplogroup X Confirmed in prehistoric North America. *American Journal of Physical Anthropology* 119 (1): 84–86.

Menzel, D., J. H. Rowe, and L. Dawson. 1964. *The Paracas Pottery of Ica: A Study in Style and Time*. University of California Publications in American Archaeology and Ethnology 50. University of California Press, Berkeley.

Merriwether, D. A., R. E. Ferrell, and F. Rothammer. 1995. mtDNA D-Loop 6-bp Deletion Found in the Chilean Aymara: Not a Unique Marker for Chibcha-Speaking Amerindians. *American Journal of Human Genetics* 56: 812–813.

Merriwether, D. A., W. W. Hall, and A. Vahlne. 1996. mtDNA Variation Indicates Mongolia May Have Been the Source for the Founding Population for the New World. *American Journal of Human Genetics* 59: 204–212.

Neira Avedaño, M., and V. P. Coelho. 1972. Enterramientos de cabezas de la cultura Nasca. *Revista do Museu Paulista*, n.s., 20: 109–142.

ONERN. 1971. *Inventario, evaluacion y uso racional de los recursos naturales de la costa: Cuenca del Rio Grande (Nazca)*. Oficina Nacional de Evaluación de Recursos Naturales, Lima, Peru.

O'Rourke, D. H., G. M. Hayes, and S. W. Carlyle. 2000. Ancient DNA Studies in Physical Anthropology. *Annual Review of Anthropology* 29: 217–242.

Pääbo, S., H. Poinar, D. Serre, V. Jaenicke-Sespres, J. Hebler, N. Rohland, M. Kuch, J. Krause, L. Vigilant, and M. Hofreiter. 2004. Genetic Analyses from Ancient DNA. *Annual Review of Genetics* 38: 645–679.

Parr, R. L., S. W. Carlyle, and D. H. O'Rourke. 1996. Ancient DNA Analysis of Fremont Amerindians of the Great Salt Lake Wetlands. *American Journal of Physical Anthropology* 99: 507–518.

Peters, A. H. 1997. Paracas, Topara and Early Nasca: Ethnicity and Society on the South Central Andean Coast. Ph.D. dissertation, Department of Anthropology, Cornell University, Ithaca, New York.

Proulx, D. A. 1968. *Local Differences and Time Differences in Nasca Pottery*. University of California Publications in Anthropology no. 5. University of California, Berkeley.

———. 2001. Ritual Uses of Trophy Heads in Ancient Nasca Society. In *Ritual Sacrifice in Ancient Peru*, edited by E. P. Benson and A. G. Cook, 119–136. University of Texas Press, Austin.

Ribeiro–Dos Santos, A. K., S. E. Santos, A. L. Machado, V. Guapindaia, and M. A. Zago. 1996. Heterogeneity of Mitochondrial DNA Haplotypes in Pre-Columbian Natives of the Amazon Region. *American Journal of Physical Anthropology* 101: 29–37.

Riddell, F. A. 1985. *Report of Archaeological Fieldwork: Tambo Viejo, Acari Valley, Peru, 1984*. Report no. 2. California Institute for Peruvian Studies, Sacramento.

———. 1986. *Report of Archaeological Fieldwork: Acari and Yauca Valleys, Arequipa, Peru, 1985*. Report no. 3. California Institute for Peruvian Studies, Sacramento.

———. 1989. *Archaeological Investigations in the Acari Valley, Peru: A Field Report*. Report no. 11. California Institute for Peruvian Studies, Sacramento.

Riddell, F. A., and L. Valdez. 1988. *Prospecciones arqueologicas en el Valle de Acari, costa sur del Peru.* Report no. 10. California Institute for Peruvian Studies, Sacramento.

Rogan, P., and J. J. Salvo. 1990. Molecular Genetics of Pre-Columbian South American Mummies. *UCLA Symposia in Molecular and Cellular Biology* 122: 223–234.

Rowe, J. H. 1959. Archaeological Dating and Cultural Process. *Southwestern Journal of Anthropology* 15 (4): 317–324.

———. 1963. Urban Settlements in Ancient Peru. *Ñawpa Pacha* 1: 1–27.

Schreiber, K. J. 1998. Afterword: Nasca Research since 1926. In *The Archaeology and Pottery of Nazca, Peru: Alfred L. Kroeber's 1926 Expedition,* by A. L. Kroeber and D. Collier, edited by P. R. Carmichael, 261–270. Altamira Press, Walnut Creek, California.

Schreiber, K. J., and J. Lancho Rojas. 1995. The Puquios of Nasca. *Latin American Antiquity* 6 (3): 229–254.

———. 2003. *Irrigation and Society in the Peruvian Desert: The Puquios of Nasca.* Lexington Books, Lanham, Maryland.

Schurr, T. G. 2002. A Molecular Anthropological Perspective on the Peopling of the Americas. *Athena Review* 3 (2): 62–107.

Schurr, T. G., S. W. Ballinger, Y. Y. Gan, J. A. Hodge, D. A. Merriwether, D. N. Lawrence, W. C. Knowler, K. M. Weiss, and D. C. Wallace. 1990. Amerindian Mitochondrial DNAs Have Rare Asian Mutations at High Frequencies, Suggesting They Derived from Four Primary Maternal Lineages. *American Journal of Human Genetics* 46: 613–623.

Shimada, I., K. Shinoda, S. Bourget, W. Alva, and S. Uceda. 2003. mtDNA Analysis of Mochica Populations: Results and Implications. Paper presented at the Midwest Conference on Andean and Amazonian Archaeology and Ethnohistory, Chicago.

Shimada, I., K. Shinoda, J. Farnum, R. Corruccini, and H. Watanabe. 2004. An Integrated Analysis of Prehispanic Mortuary Practices: A Middle Sican Case Study. *Current Anthropology* 45 (3): 369–402.

Silverman, H. 1991. The Paracas Problem: Archaeological Perspectives. In *Paracas Art and Architecture: Object and Context in South Coastal Peru,* edited by A. Paul, 349–415. University of Iowa Press, Iowa City.

———. 1993. *Cahuachi in the Ancient Nasca World.* University of Iowa Press, Iowa City.

———. 1996. The Formative Period on the South Coast of Peru: A Critical Perspective. *Journal of World Prehistory* 10 (2): 95–147.

———. 2002. *Ancient Nasca Settlement and Society.* University of Iowa Press, Iowa City.

Silverman, H., and D. A. Proulx. 2002. *The Nasca.* Blackwell Publishers, Malden, Massachusetts.

Smith, D. G., R. S. Malhi, J. Eshleman, J. G. Lorenz, and F. A. Kaestle. 1999. Distribution of mtDNA Haplogroup X among Native North Americans. *American Journal of Physical Anthropology* 110: 271–284.

Stone, A. C. 2000. Ancient DNA from Skeletal Remains. In *Biological Anthropology of the Human Skeleton*, edited by M. A. Katzenberg and S. R. Saunders, 351–371. Wiley-Liss, New York.

Stone, A. C., and M. Stoneking. 1993. Ancient DNA from a Pre-Columbian Amerindian Population. *American Journal of Physical Anthropology* 92: 463–471.

———. 1998. mtDNA Analysis of a Prehistoric Oneota Population: Implications for the Peopling of the New World. *American Journal of Human Genetics* 62: 1153–1170.

Stoneking, M., D. Hedgecock, R. O. Higuchi, L. Vigilant, and H. A. Erlich. 1991. Population Variation of Human mtDNA Control Region Sequences Detected by Enzymatic Amplification and Sequence-Specific Oligonucleotide Probes. *American Journal of Human Genetics* 48: 370–382.

Sykes, B. 1993. Less Cause for Grave Concern. *Nature* 366: 513.

Tello, J. C. 1918. *El usa de las cabezas humanas artificialmente momificadas y su representacion en el antiguo arte peruano*. Casa Editora de Ernesto R. Villanin, Lima.

Torroni, A., R. J. Bandelt, and L. D. Urbano. 1998. mtDNA Analysis Reveals a Major Late Paleolithic Population Expansion from Southwestern to Northwestern Europe. *American Journal of Human Genetics* 62: 1137–1152.

Torroni, A., K. Huoponen, and P. Francalacci. 1996. Classification of European mtDNAs from an Analysis of Three European Populations. *Genetics* 144: 1835–1850.

Torroni, A., M. T. Lott, M. F. Cabell, Y.-S. Chen, L. Lavergne, and D. C. Wallace. 1994. mtDNA and the Origin of Caucasians: Identification of Ancient Caucasian-Specific Haplogroups, One of Which Is Prone to a Recurrent Somatic Duplication in the D-Loop Region. *American Journal of Human Genetics* 55: 760–776.

Torroni, A., T. G. Schurr, M. F. Cabell, M. D. Brown, J. V. Neel, M. Larsen, D. G. Smith, C. M. Vullo, and D. C. Wallace. 1993. Asian Affinities and Continental Radiation of the Four Founding Native American mtDNAs. *American Journal of Human Genetics* 53: 563–590.

Torroni, A., T. G. Schurr, and C. C. Yang. 1992. Native American Mitochondrial DNA Analysis Indicates that the Amerind and the Nadene Populations Were Founded by Two Independent Migrations. *Genetics* 130: 153–162.

Tung, T. 2008. Dismembering Bodies for Display: A Bioarchaeological Study of Trophy Heads from the Wari Site of Conchopata, Peru. *American Journal of Physical Anthropology* 136: 294–308.

Uhle, M. 1914. *The Nazca Pottery of Ancient Peru*. Davenport Academy of Sciences, Davenport, Iowa.

Valdez, L. 1998. The Nasca and the Valley of Acari: Cultural Interaction of the Peruvian South Coast during the First Four Centuries AD. Ph.D. dissertation, Department of Archaeology, University of Calgary, Calgary, Alberta.

Vaughn, K. J. 2004. Households, Crafts, and Feasting in the Ancient Andes: The Village Context of Early Nasca Craft Consumption. *Latin America Antiquity* 15 (1): 61–88.

Vaughn, K. J., and H. Neff. 2004. Tracing the Clay Source of Nasca Polychrome Pottery: Results from a Preliminary Raw Material Survey. *Journal of Archaeological Science* 31 (11): 1577–1586.

Verano, J. W. 1995. Where Do They Rest? The Treatment of Human Offerings and Trophies in Ancient Peru. In Dillehay 1995, 189–227.

———. 2001. The Physical Evidence of Human Sacrifice in Ancient Peru. In *Ritual Sacrifice in Ancient Peru*, edited by E. P. Benson and A. G. Cook, 165–184. University of Texas Press, Austin.

Wallace, D. 1971. *Sitios arqueológicos del Peru (segunda entrega): Valles de Chincha y de Pisco*. Arqueológicas 13. Museo Nacional de Antropología y Arqueología, Lima.

———. 1986. The Topara Tradition: An Overview. In *Perspectives on Andean Prehistory and Protohistory: Papers from the Third Annual Northeast Conference on Andean Archaeology and Ethnohistory*, edited by D. H. Sandweiss and D. P. Kvietok, 35–47. Latin American Studies Program, Cornell University, Ithaca, New York.

Wallace, D. C., M. D. Brown, and M. T. Lott. 1999. Mitochondrial DNA Variation in Human Evolution and Disease. *Gene* 238: 211–230.

Wallace, D. C., K. Garrison, and W. C. Knowler. 1985. Dramatic Founder Effects in Amerindian Mitochondrial DNAs. *American Journal of Physical Anthropology* 68: 149–155.

Williams, S. R., K. Babrowski, V. Cansino, and K. Forgey. 2003. Ancient DNA Studies of Prehistoric Osmore Coastal Valley Residents. Paper presented at the 68th Annual Meeting of the Society for American Archaeology, Milwaukee, Wisconsin.

Williams, S. R., K. Forgey, and E. Klarich. 2001. An Osteological Analysis of Nasca Trophy Heads Collected by A. L. Kroeber during the Marshall Field Expeditions to Peru. *Fieldiana: Anthropology*, n.s., 33. Field Museum of Natural History, Chicago.

Wilson, A. C. 1985. The Molecular Basis of Evolution. *Scientific American* 253 (4): 164–173.

Contributors

Valerie A. Andrushko
Department of Anthropology, Southern Connecticut State University, New Haven

Heather Bonney
Human Remains Unit, Department of Palaeontology, Natural History Museum, London

Michelle Bonogofsky
Archaeological Research Facility, University of California, Berkeley

Margaret Clegg
Department of Genetics Evolution and Environment, University College London

William N. Duncan
Department of Sociology and Anthropology, East Tennessee State University, Johnson City

Kathleen Forgey
Department of Sociology and Anthropology, Indiana University Northwest, Gary
Department of Anthropology, Field Museum of Natural History, Chicago

Pamela L. Geller
Department of Anthropology, University of Miami, Coral Gables, Florida

Jeremy Graham
Victorian Institute of Forensic Medicine, Melbourne, Australia
School of Dentistry and Oral Health, La Trobe University, Bendigo, Victoria, Australia

Christopher J. Knüsel
UMR 5199, De Ja Préhistoire à l'Actuel: Culture, Environnement et Anthropologie (PACEA), Université de Bordeaux, Pessac, France

María Cecilia Lozada
Department of Anthropology, University of Chicago, Chicago

Janet Montgomery
Department of Archaeology, University of Durham, Durham, U.K.

Barra O'Donnabhain
Department of Archaeology, University College Cork, Cork, Ireland

Dmitry Razhev
Institute of Northern Development, Siberian Branch of Russian Academy of Sciences, Tumen

Noémie Rolland
INRAP (National Institute for Preventive Archaeological Research) 2, Paris, France

Svetlana Sharapova
Institute of History and Archaeology, Urals Branch of Russian Academy of Sciences, Ekaterinburg

Christopher M. Stojanowski
School of Human Evolution and Social Change, Center for Bioarchaeological Research, Arizona State University, Tempe

Katie Tucker
Department of Archaeology, University of Winchester, Winchester, U.K.

Frédérique Valentin
Archéologie et Ethnologie, CNRS (Centre National de la Recherche Scientifique), Nanterre, France

Index

Page numbers with *f* refer to illustrations.
Page numbers with *t* refer to tables.

Acari (site), 297*t*, 298

Acheulean age, 4

Achuar culture, 19, 113

Affinal ties, 82

Aging and the elderly, 18, 24–25, 89. *See also* Demographics

Aging methods: auricular surface, 205, 267; changes to pubis, 205; cranial suture closure, 267; dentition, 73–74, 76, 76*t*, 91, 155, 205, 267; epiphyseal fusion, 76; long bone diaphysis length, 76; nondestructive, 29–30, 70; pelvic fusion, 76; radiocarbon analysis, 220–21; radiography, 74

Agriculture, 22, 24, 162, 263

'Ain Ghazal (site), 4, 26, 27

Aitape, 70*f*

Alaska, 13, 18, 27

Aleut culture, 27

Algarrobal culture, 234

Amerindian haplogroups, 294, 295–97, 296*t*, 297*t*, 298

Ananyino (culture group), 204*f*

Anasazi culture, 2, 23

Ancestors: archaeology of, 34; context of skulls, 19–20; figurines, 87–88; head as seat of ancestorhood, 3, 34; *mbwan*, 83; misinterpretation of specimens, 68–70, 77, 91–92; relationship with enemies, 19, 82–83, 113; use of term, 34; worship (*see* Ancestor veneration)

Ancestor veneration: context, 20; figurines incorporating skulls, 87–88; *tiki* statues, 105; and trophy heads, 113, 263, 264–65, 292, 298

Anemia, 22, 23

Animals and animal remains: bones or spines as grave goods, 207, 208–9*t*, 234, 250, 276, 277, 278; collagen, 4; horses (*see* Horses and horseback riding); pigs (*see* Teeth, pig canines on trophy skulls)

Antemortem: tooth loss, 27; trauma, 265, 266, 278

Anthropology: forensics for population affinity assessment, 180–96; historical background, 13, 15–16, 20–21; interpretation based on "modern anthropological parallels," 68–69; limited access to archaeological specimens, 69, 205; limited access to data, 194; role of closure after defacement, 179, 194–95

Apotropaic devices, 17, 19, 20

Araha culture, 85

Arawe culture, 241

Archaeological research, 69–70, 205

Archaic period, 183

Architecture. *See* Building construction

Arikara culture, 187

Arm bones, 81

Arthritis, 27

...a: central, 202, 204, 220, 221; southern, 26, 220; western, 9
Asmat culture, 82
Aswad, 4–5
Australia. *See* Torres Strait Islands
Austria, 10
Avar culture, 10

Bamboo: burial effigy decoration, 80*f*; knives, 56, 58*f*, 59, 62; noseplug, 69*f*
Bark cloth. *See* Tapa cloth
Basket making, 27
Basque culture, 31, 188, 190*t*, 193
Beauty and youth: skull decoration and treatment reflecting, 29, 77–79, 86, 90; skulls of elderly not removed, 89. *See also* Fertility
Beeswax, 53, 54*f*, 56, 59
Belize, 241, 244*f*, 248*f*, 254. *See also* Maya culture
Biauricular breadth, 189
Bilobated form, 6
Bioarchaeology: as an integrative discipline, 1–2, 20, 21–22, 28, 34; definition, 1; emergence as a discipline, 21; history, 13, 20–21; language barrier, 65; limitations of data collection, 10, 193, 195; open source publishing for data exchange, 194; of the skull, overview, 20–22; thorough data collection to unravel context, 20, 67–68, 91–92. *See also* Biostressors; Challenges in bioarchaeology; Cultural considerations; Osteoarchaeologist; Political considerations; Religious or spiritual considerations; Societal considerations
Biocultural Adaptation in Prehistoric America (Blakely), 21
Biocultural factors, 24
Biological association. *See* DNA analysis; Morphometric analyses
Biostressors: anemia, 22, 23; arthritis, 27; brachycrania, 25; congenital defects, 25; cranial vault thickening with disease, 22; craniostenosis, 25, 256; craniosynostosis, 24; cribra orbitalia, 22; dental pathologies, 22, 23, 25–27; dolichocrania, 25; hydrocephaly, 12, 25; infection, 7, 22, 24, 35,

154; parasites, 22, 23; plagiocephaly, 15, 256; porotic hyperostosis, 22–23; scurvy, 22, 23–24; thalassemia, 22; tuberculosis, 22, 27; ulcers, occipital, 24
Bodo (site), 4
Body: as "a forum for display" of social norms, 251; context of long-term incarceration vs. execution, 135–36; as "cultural plastic," 257; head in the role of, 2, 15, 35, 179, 222, 252; interpretive potential through study of the skeleton, 28; public dissection, 130–32, 131*f*, 136
Body parts: execution by being drawn and quartered, 128–29, 128*f*, 130, 132, 134–35; genitalia attached to skull, 89; kept and lent by family members, 86; nose cut off, 276; worn by widow or warrior, 56, 84–85, 114
Bolivia. *See* Tiwanaku culture
Bone: arrowheads from, 208*t*, 211*f*; body adornment, 105, 114; grave goods, 208–9*t*, 210*f*, 211*f*; plates from, 205, 209*t*; utensils from, 6, 17, 205, 209*t*
Boundary or liminal locations, 132, 133–34, 134*f*, 236
Bowls, skulls as, 6
Brachycrania, 25
Brazil. *See* Kayabi culture
Britain: Bedfordshire, 9, 151; climate changes, 163–64; colonization by, 122, 187; Gloucestershire, 151; lifespan during Roman period, 152–53; London, 152–53, 153*f*; map, 124*f*; Outer Hebrides, 162, 166; Oxfordshire, 151; during reign of Septimius Severus, 145, 169–70; Roman period cemeteries, 151, 152–53, 153*f*, 164–66 (*see also* York); Winchester, 164–66, 165*f*, 168
Bronze, 208*t*, 209*t*, 210*f*, 214*f*
Bronze Age, 220
Building construction, 18, 133, 134*f*, 188
Burial/deposition: archaeological context, 17, 67–68; body placed on platform, 53, 56, 79, 99, 115; in a cave, 86, 115; effects on skulls over time, 267; with "extra" skulls, 3, 13–14, 81; flexed body, 289; in a foundation, 18; grave location and status, 31; with head missing, 3, 11–14,

179; under the house, 18, 86, 91, 247, 251; under important architecture, 247, 249*f*, 250, 254; intercutting of graves, 145, 147*f*; items buried with body (*see* Grave goods); kurgans, 31, 203, 204, 223; multiple burials in single grave, 145, 148*f*; under or in a tree, 85, 88, 115; rituals (*see* Mortuary practices); in rock crevice with bones rolled in a mat, 53, 85; at sea, 85; secondary, 85, 86; skull removed from internment after decomposition, 3, 14, 54, 85, 115; under standing stones, 83

Burial effigy (*rambaramp*), 79, 80*f*

Burned skulls, 278

Cabanas culture, 237

Caches, 12–16, 20, 26, 264, 276, 286

Calculus, dental, 27

Caldwell, Joseph, 187

Caldwell, Sheila, 183, 187

California, 22, 24, 25, 187

Calvaria, 31, 180, 181, 181*f*, 185–99, 186*f*, 192

Cambridge Anthropological Expedition, 51, 59, 65

Cannibalism, 2, 56, 59, 61

Carbon analyses, 55, 166, 220–21

Caries, dental, 22, 25–26

Cariogenic activity, 26

Çatal Höyük (site), 13, 14

Catholic Church, 180, 237, 242

Celt culture, 9, 35

Ceramics: Chiribaya, 234; Nasca, 264, 289; Sargat, 205, 208–9*t*, 211*f*, 213, 216*f*; Wari, 276

Ceremonies. *See* Rituals

CFIRMS. *See* Mass spectrometry, continuous-flow isotope ratio

Challenges in bioarchaeology: degradation of aDNA, 299; incomplete specimens, 188–89; labeling protocols in collections, 68–69, 77, 91, 113, 205; limited access to specimens, 69, 205

Charles Eaton shipwreck, 61

Children: exclusion from mummification, 18; firstborn, 87, 88, 252; high mortality

rates, 27; initiation rituals for males, 19, 82; parietal disk used as a rattle, 6; radiography and aging of modeled skull, 71–77, 75*f*, 91; skull decoration in Melanesia, 79, 81. *See also* Deformation of skulls

Chile, 5, 27, 235, 236, 237, 246

China, 11

Chiribaya culture: geography, 230, 230*f*, 231*f*, 236; high genetic diversity, 297; skull deformation (*see* Chiribaya skull deformation); social organization, 229–30

Chiribaya skull deformation: overview, 6, 32, 203, 236; skeletal evidence, 231, 232*f*, 233, 233*f*, 234*f*; societal context, 228–29, 233–35, 236–37; specimens, 230–31, 231*f*, 232*f*

Chi-square analysis, 233

Chumash culture, 187

Clay, 4, 6, 53, 54*f*, 74–79, 78*f*, 80*f*

Cleaning of skull. *See* Defleshing

"Clean room" protocols, 293

Climate change, 163–64

Coconut, 56, 79, 80*f*, 99

Colha (site), 12, 13

Collagen, 4, 151

Collaguas culture, 237

Collections, archaeological: data loss due to labeling protocol, 68–69, 77, 91, 113, 205; importance of objective data collection, 67–68; interpretation based on "modern anthropological parallels," 68–69

Color, symbolism, 103*f*, 113, 117, 237

Congenital defects, 15, 22, 25, 55, 255, 256

Contact, European, 115, 116. *See also* Britain, colonization by; Spain, colonization by

Container for skull or head: basket, 53, 83, 86, 89, 90; bowl, 85, 90; cane loop, 59; chest, 81, 90; jar, 286

Contextualization of the head: defacement, 179, 194–95; importance of objective data collection, 67–68; overview, 1–2

Copper, 17

Cord or rope for suspension of skull, 12, 69*f*, 102*f*, 104, 110*t*, 111*t*, 287

Cosmological events, 2, 9, 77

Cradleboards, 24, 243

Craniostenosis, 25, 255–56

Craniosynostosis, 24

Cranium: biostressors, 15, 22, 24, 25, 256; collections focused on, 15; cranial sutures, 25, 256, 267; cranial vault thickening, 22; modification (*see* Deformation of skulls; Perforations in skulls); morphology (*see* Morphology, craniofacial; Morphometric analyses, craniofacial); shape and masticatory function, 24, 25

Cremation, 85

Cribra orbitalia, 22, 23

CT scan, 16, 34

Cultural considerations: body as "a forum for display" of social norms, 251; body as "cultural plastic," 257; cultural bias of ethnographers, 67–68, 77, 254–56; language barrier, 65; material record contains "memory" of culture, 221

Curation, 15, 20, 34, 90

Currency, 59–60, 81

Cut marks: from bamboo knife, 62; on cranial vault, 106, 109*t*; with decapitation, 10, 12, 61–62, 148; Ireland skulls, 123, 129; on mandibles, 62, 62*f*, 63, 63*f*, 64*f*; from stone tools, 4; three-dimensional reconstruction, 64*f*; Wari skulls, 264, 267, 268, 269, 271–72, 273*f*, 277–78

Death. *See* Mortuary practices; Spirit of the dead

Decapitation: deposition and context of head after, 11–14, 179; execution cemeteries, 10; with human sacrifice, 10–11; in Irish literature, 126–27; osteological evidence, 61–63, 115, 123–24, 129; and public display (*see* Display of skull or head, to punish or dishonor); to punish the individual, 9, 10, 31, 127–29, 130*f*; to punish the soul, 30, 133, 135; to release the soul, 17; in representation of cosmic heroes, 9–10; of Roman monarchy, 170; Roman period York, 30–31, 148–52, 149*f*, 150*f*, 169–70; severed head talking or singing, 127, 133, 134; tools, 58*f*, 59; during war, 8, 9, 10, 11, 18, 19, 126

Decoration of skulls: of ancestor figure, 87–88; based on perception of beauty,

youth, and fertility, 70, 77–81, 83, 86, 90; of decapitated head for burial, 12; of decapitated head for skull-giving ceremony, 53–54, 54*f*; ear, 105; fabric, European, 101–2, 103*f*, 104*f*, 108*t*, 110*t*, 111*t*, 112–13, 117; of mummy, 56, 57*f*; noseplug, 69*f*, 99, 108*t*, 109*t*, 110*t*, 111*t*; representation of tattoos, 101, 102, 104, 104*f*, 108*t*, 111*t*; Sepik River Valley, 83; Solomon Islands, 84*f*; Torres Strait Islands, 28–29, 51, 56; trophy head, 59, 82; war canoe with trophy skulls, 114. *See also* Plastering and modeling of skulls

de Corpa, Pedro, 180, 183–85

Defleshing: in earth oven, 53, 59; of face to help fade memory of the newly dead, 19; manual (*see* Defleshing prior to decomposition); passive or "natural," 19, 112; submersion in creek, 53; in termite mound, 29, 53, 59, 60*f*

Defleshing prior to decomposition: overview, 3–4; Torres Strait Islands osteological evidence, 61–65, 62*f*, 63*f*, 64*f*; Wari osteological evidence, 271, 271*f*, 272*f*

Deformation of skulls: ban by the Catholic Church, 237, 242; to better carry loads, 243, 252, 253; by the Chiribaya (*see* Chiribaya culture); context of visual symbolism, 221–23, 251–52; geographic distribution, 202; Hippocrates on, 220; Iron Age, 220–21 (*see also* Sargat culture); at Jericho site, 7, 15–16, 23; by the Kwakuitl, 17, 253; as marker of group or status, 32, 202, 213, 222–23, 228–29, 233–37, 246, 252–53; by the Maya (*see* Maya culture); by the Nasca, 6; porotic hyperostosis and cribra orbitalia from, 23; process and techniques, 6, 24, 216–17, 228, 241, 242–43; as "process of becoming," 32, 242, 251–52, 253, 256–57; by the Sargat (*see* Sargat culture); semantic sensibilities, 255–56; shape as symbol of corn, 254; shape as symbol of landscape, 237, 238; shapes, 6–7, 221, 231, 232*f*, 237, 243; by the Tiwanaku, 234–35,

236, 238, 246; use of cradleboard, 24, 243; vs. craniostenosis, 25, 255–56

Deformed skulls, due to congenital defects, 15, 22, 25, 256

Demineralization, 25

Demographics: paleodemography, 76, 247; Roman period York cemetery, 151, 152–53, 153f; urban vs. rural populations, 143

Dentition: aging methods, 73–74, 76, 76t, 91, 155, 205, 267; CT scan analysis to determine presence or absence, 16; oblique radiograph through modeling material, 75f; pathologies, 22, 23, 25–27. See also Teeth

de Veráscola, Francisco, 184–85

Diaphysis length, 76

Diet and nutrition: biostressors from nutritional deficiency, 22–24; C4 plants and carbon isotope analysis of teeth, 166; coarse (see Teeth, attrition); and dental health, 26–27; health status as proxy for resource access, 22; iron, 22, 23; isotope analysis to identify locals vs. nonlocals, 30–31, 141–42, 166–70, 166t, 279–80, 298; pre-Inca Chiribaya, 229; seasonal starvation, 27; shift from gathering to agriculture, 22, 24; vitamin C (see Biostressors, scurvy)

Dismemberment. See Body parts; Execution, drawn and quartered

Display of body, 85, 123, 127–29, 128f

Display of skull or head: to bestow honor, 18, 126–27, 134; in boundary locations, 132, 133–34, 134f; as curio in 18th-century England, 30, 97, 117, 118; holes created in skull for, 6, 32, 269–70, 269f, 270f, 272f, 273–77; hung from neck of horse, 18; hung in tapa cloth, 99; Ireland, 30, 126–36; to prevent spirit's return, 82, 89; to punish or dishonor, 8–9, 30, 126, 130f, 133, 134, 185; suspensory cord or rope, 12, 69f, 102f, 104, 110t, 111t, 287; tenoned head on wall, 277; tied in groups, 82; on war canoe, 114; as a warning, 114, 134

Divination, 11, 29, 54–55, 56, 88. See also Magic and sorcery

DNA: degradation of aDNA, 299; rate of mutation of mDNA, 294

DNA analysis: methods, 287, 293–94; Nasca trophy head origins, 32–33, 292–99, 296t, 297t; overview, 15, 21

Dolichocrania, 25, 220

Dolls. See Figurines and dolls

D'Oyly, Capt., 61

Dreams, 54

Dura, 7

Dzhety-Asar (culture group), 204f

Economic considerations, 203, 218, 233, 234, 236, 238, 253

Ectocrania, 23, 272, 274

Ecuador. See Jivaro Achuar culture

Embalming, 85. See also Mummification

Emic explanation, 16

Enemies: archaeology of, 34; crania used in initiation ceremonies, 19; decapitation, 8, 9, 10, 11, 18, 19, 126; relationship with ancestors, 19, 29, 82–83, 113; trophies of war (see Scalping; Trophy heads and trophy skulls); and women, 58, 82

Enlightenment period, 136

Epicondyle, 27

Epiphyseal function, 76, 205

Eskimo culture, 27

Ethiopia, 4

Ethnographic studies: cultural bias, 67–68, 77, 254–56; gender bias, 86–87; limited access to specimens for anthropological study, 70; specimen labeling protocol and loss of data, 68

Ethnohistoric reports, 12, 32, 98, 114, 115, 229, 242–43

Ethnohistory, 234, 241, 252

Etic, 16

Eurasia: culture-group distributions, 204f; map, 203f; nomadism, 204, 218, 221, 223; scalping, 8; skull deformation, 220–21 (see also Sargat culture); Trans-Urals and western Siberia, 203

Europe: burial ritual of decapitated heads, 12; climate change, 164; colonization by, 115, 116 (see also Britain, colonization by; Spain, colonization by); decapitation, 8–9, 10, 17, 30–31; geology, 166, 167;

Europe—*continued*
  isotope analysis of teeth and origin of in-
    dividual, 166–67, 166*t*; medical treatment
    through trephination, 8; during the Ro-
    man Empire, 164, 170; scurvy, 23; trophy
    skull curio market of the 18th century, 30,
    97, 117, 118; use of fabric from, 101–2, 103*f*,
    104*f*, 108*t*, 110*t*, 111*t*, 112–13, 117. *See also*
    Roman period; *specific countries*
Evolution: abstract thinking, 222; craniofa-
    cial morphology, 24, 180, 183, 193
Execution: cemeteries, 10; decapitation in
    Roman period York, 151, 152, 169; drawn
    and quartered, 128–29, 128*f*, 130, 134–35;
    hanging, 130, 134
Extramasticatory function, 27
Eyes: cannibalism of the, 59, 61; gauze in
    eye sockets, 287; as seat of knowledge,
    105; skull decorations representing eyes,
    5*f*, 56, 72*f*, 74, 79, 99, 100, 108–11*t*, 112

Fabric: bark (*see* Tapa cloth); European,
    101–2, 103*f*, 104*f*, 108*t*, 110*t*, 111*t*, 112–13,
    117; pandanus fibers, 80*f*
FDB. *See* Forensic Data Bank
Feet, 56, 84–85, 202
Femur, 152
Fertility: granted by spirit of the dead, 90;
    rituals, 19, 79, 82; and treatment of skull,
    70, 77–81, 80*f*, 83, 86, 90
Fibula, 154
Figurines and dolls, 79, 87–88, 89, 276, 280
First hypervariable region (HVRI), 287,
    294, 296–97, 297*t*
Food: abrasive or fibrous (*see* Teeth, attri-
    tion); access to resources, 22, 23, 217;
    bone marrow, 2; C4 plants, 166; decom-
    position fluids as, 56; offerings as grave
    goods, 207*f*, 208–9*t*, 213. *See also* Diet
    and nutrition
Foramen magnum, 6, 56, 59, 109*t*
Fordisc software, 180, 182, 186, 187
Forensic Data Bank (FDB), 183, 186
Forensics. *See* Anthropology, forensics for
    population affinity assessment; Odontol-
    ogy, forensic
Fort King George (site): calvaria FKG-121,
    181*f*, 185–86, 186*f*, 188–89, 192–93, 192*f*;

constructing a comparative database,
    188–89, 190–91*t*, 195–96; historical and
    archaeological context, 31, 183–85; hu-
    man occupation, 187–88, 195–96; map,
    184*f*; methodological context, 181–83;
    population affinity assessment, 180–81,
    186–87, 193–95; principal components
    analysis, 189, 192–93, 192*f*
France, 8
French Polynesia. *See* Marquesas Islands
Funerary practices. *See* Mortuary practices

Genetic defects, 15, 22, 25, 55, 255, 256
Genetic studies. *See* DNA analysis
Genitalia, 89
Georgia, 187–88. *See also* Fort King George
Germany, 12–13, 111*t*, 167
Geronimo, 179
Glabella, 74, 189
Gold: beads, 212*t*; earrings, 212*t*, 214*f*;
    plaques, 213; tacks in trophy heads, 262,
    269, 269*f*, 272*f*, 279
Gorodetskaya (cultural group), 204*f*
Gran Chacoan culture, 6
Grave goods: Chiribaya, 234; in decapita-
    tion grave, 10, 14; Maya, 246, 250; place-
    ment within grave, 207*f*, 215*f*; Roman
    period York graves, 145–46; Sargat, 205,
    207–16; Wari, 276, 278
Grave robbers, 204, 205
Great Britain. *See* Britain
Greece, Ancient, 8
Greenland, 162
Guale culture, 183–84, 187, 192*f*

Haddon, Alfred, 51, 59, 65
Hair: beard or depiction of beard, 84*f*, 99,
    101; on burial effigy, 80*f*; and personhood,
    15; removal prior to mummification, 55;
    styled as in life, 75, 99–100, 101, 108*t*, 110*t*
Handedness, left- or right-, 24
Hands, 3, 56, 84, 114, 151, 152
Haplogroups, 294, 295–97, 296*t*, 297*t*, 298
Hat, representing head shape, 237
Hayonim (site), 16
Head. *See* Ancestors, head as seat of ances-
    torhood; Contextualization of the head;
    Personhood, head as the seat of; Soul,

head as the seat of the; Trophy heads and trophy skulls

Headhunting: disappearance after conversion to Christianity, 29, 51; enemies symbolically transformed into relatives, 19, 29; geographical distribution, 114; Melanesia, 81–83; Peru, 264 (*see also* Nasca trophy heads); raids, 14, 55, 58, 88; symbolic capital and power, 35, 81–82; taking name of the one slain, 82; Torres Strait Islands, 58–65. *See also* Trophy heads

Headless burial, 3, 11–14, 179

Headrest or pillow, skull as, 82, 83, 89

Health status, as proxy for resource access, 22

Health treatments, 8, 17

Holes in the skull. *See* Perforations in skulls

Hopewell culture, 14

Horse-harness, 208*t*, 213, 214*f*

Horses and horseback riding, 18, 32, 203, 208*t*, 212*t*, 218

Howells data set, 182, 183, 186

Huaca del Loro culture, 291*t*

Human sacrifice, 10–11, 13, 114

Hun culture, 202, 220, 221

Hunting, 55

Huon Gulf, 70*f*

HVRI. *See* First hypervariable region

Hydrocephaly, 12, 25

Hypoplasia, enamel, 27, 217

Iatmül culture, 70, 77–78, 78*f*, 81, 85, 90. *See also* Sepik River Valley

Iconography: decapitation and display of skulls in Ireland, 130*f*; execution in Ireland, 128*f*, 131*f*; Marquesas warrior with trophy skull, 97, 102*f*; Maya skull deformation, 243; Nasca, 292, 298; Wari warrior with trophy head, 277, 280

Identity. *See* Personhood, head as the seat of

Illinois, 8

Inca culture, 246, 278, 291*t*

Incision: cranial vault, 6, 275; for decapitation, 151; teeth, 7

Indonesia, 70*f*, 82, 87

Infection, 7, 22, 24, 35, 154

Inhumation, 13, 115, 145, 151, 152, 169. *See also* Burial/deposition

Initiation or rite of passage, 19, 82

Insiders: formation and maintenance of status as, 258; perceived as threat to political or social power, 122, 238; social differentiation among (*see* Social status); transformation of an outsider to, 29; transformation to an outsider, 30, 135

Insiders vs. outsiders: use of DNA analysis, 33, 292, 298; use of isotope analysis, 30–31, 141–42, 166–70, 166*t*, 279–80

Interobserver error, 193

Interpopulation, 182

Inuit culture, 162

Iraq, 17, 202

Ireland: conceptualization of the body and soul, 135–36; display of skull and body, 30, 122–35; Early Medieval period, 122–27; Early Modern period, 130–32; Late Medieval period, 127–30; map, 124*f*; Medieval Dublin, 124*f*; during Roman Warm Period, 164

Iron: collars or rings for prisoners, 123, 150, 150*f*, 154; grave goods, 205, 208–9*t*, 211*f*, 214*f*; knives, 59, 207*f*, 208*t*, 209*t*, 212*t*, 213; luxury goods, 214*f*; and nutrition, 22, 23; weapons, 205, 208–9*t*, 211*f*

Iron Age, 220. *See also* Sargat culture

Isotope analysis of teeth: and dental caries, 25; Greenland, 162; to identify locals vs. nonlocals, 30–31, 141–42, 166–70, 166*t*, 279–80, 298; methods, 142, 154–55, 157; Outer Hebrides, 162; overview, 21, 141–43, 162–63; Peru, 279–80; Roman period York, 30–31, 142, 156*t*, 157–67, 158*f*, 159*f*, 160*t*, 161*t*, 163*f*, 165*f*, 166*t*; seasonal data, 164

Itkul (culture group), 204*f*

Ivory, 105

Jericho (site): brachycrania and dolichocrania, 25; dental health, 26–27; magic and the use of skulls, 8; plastered and modeled skulls, 4–5, 5*f*, 16, 68; skull deformation, 7, 15–16, 23

Jewelry: disk of bone as an amulet, 8; earrings, 208*t*, 214*f*; enemy bone as a pendant, 114; kept with memento skull, 53; lower jaw and first cervical vertebrae as, 82, 86; necklace from teeth, 6, 19
Jewish culture, 17, 140*t*
Jivaro Achuar culture, 19, 113
Jordan, 4, 26. *See also* 'Ain Ghazal; Jericho

Kankanamun culture, 78, 79
Katakombnaya culture, 220
Kaulong culture, 17
Kayabi culture, 19
Kenyon, Kathleen, 68, 69–70, 91
Kiriwana culture, 86
Kiwai Papuan culture, 88
Knives: bamboo, 56, 58*f*, 59, 62; iron, 59, 207*f*, 208*t*, 209*t*, 212*t*, 213
Korwar, 87–88
Kurgans (burial mounds), 31, 203, 204, 223
Kwaio culture, 85
Kwakiutl culture, 17, 253

Labret ornamentation, 13, 27
Language considerations, 65, 105, 112, 252
Lapita culture, 3, 11, 13
Lead, 142, 157. *See also* Isotope analysis of teeth
Leg bone, 152, 154
Lifeway, 21, 32
Liminal locations. *See* Boundary or liminal locations
Lips: labret ornamentation, 13, 27; sealed with thorns, 12, 287; skull decoration representing, 101, 104*f*
Literature, descriptions found in: cultural bias toward Mayan skull deformation, 254–56, 255*f*; decapitation in Ireland, 126, 133
Literature, modern scientific: entrenchment of misinterpretations, 69–70; ethnocentric language, 255, 256

Mabuiag, Torres Strait Islands, 51, 52*f*, 53, 59, 60
Macfarlane, Rev. Samuel, 51
Macroscopic observation, 4, 8
Magic and sorcery: death charm, 89; decapitated head speaking or singing, 127, 133, 134; demons, 17; fertility (*see* Rituals, fertility); haunting by spirit of the dead, 60; insight into the future (*see* Divination); raising the dead, 17; use of head to identify person responsible for death, 54, 89; use of skull to ward off evil, 17–18, 19
Malekula, 70*f*, 79
Mandibles: degeneration, 27; osteological analysis, 112, 149*f*, 277–78; profile analysis, 64*f*; three-dimensional reconstruction, 64*f*; trophy, 59, 60, 62*f*, 63, 63*f*; vegetal link to skull, 54*f*, 100, 100*f*, 107*f*, 108–11*t*, 112, 116
Manus Island, 70*f*
Mari (spirit of the dead), 53, 54, 63
Mariana Islands, 26
Marquesas Islands: conversion to Christianity, 117, 118; effects of European contact, 115, 116, 117; geography, 98*f*; history, 97; trophy skulls (*see* Marquesas Islands trophy skulls)
Marquesas Islands trophy skulls: as ancestors or enemies, 113; description, 97–106, 100*f*, 103*f*, 104*f*, 107*f*; inventory in collections, 108–11*t*; as part of politico-religious system, 113–16; temporal variations of manufacture, 116
Marriage and matrimony, 15, 204, 223, 263
Masks, 4, 6, 55, 81, 83
Mass spectrometry, continuous-flow isotope ratio (CFIRMS), 155
Mastaba, 85
Masticatory function, 24–25
Maya culture: burial of decapitated heads, 12; geography, 244*f*; limitations of data, 10; skull deformation (*see* Maya culture skull deformation); social organization, 246, 247
Maya culture skull deformation: altering bodies to embody ideals, 251–54; bioarchaeological data, 243, 245–47, 245*t*; cultural bias of ethnographers, 254–56; ethnohistoric accounts, 242–43; individuals in communities, 247–51; overview, 25, 32, 203, 241–42
Mbwan, 83

Medical conditions. *See* Biostressors
Medical treatment, 8, 17
Melanesia: figurines incorporating skulls, 80*f*, 87–88; headhunting, 81–83; manipulation of body and spirit, 84–85; map, 70*f*; modeled and decorated skulls, 77–81, 89; mortuary practices, 3, 13, 18, 81, 85–87, 89–91; skull in trade and exchange, 16, 83; sorcery and divination, 29, 88–89. *See also* Indonesia; Kaulong culture; Lapita culture; Sepik River Valley; Solomon Islands; Torres Strait Islands
Melville, Herman, 99–100
Mementos or relics: body parts, 56, 84–85, 86; bones wrapped in tapa cloth after mummification, 115; given to widow, 53, 89; skull (*see* Mementos or relics, decapitated head or skull)
Mementos or relics, decapitated head or skull: decoration and skull-giving ritual, 53–54, 54*f*; modeling, 19, 53–54, 54*f*, 56, 89; overview, 3; re-use in ceremony or ritual, 54–55, 81, 83; use of tapa cloth (*see* Tapa cloth)
Mesolithic period, 7, 23, 24. *See also* Ofnet
Microevolution, 183, 193
Microstriation 2, 7
Middens, 17
Middle East. *See* Iraq; Jericho; Jordan; Syria
Missionaries. *See* Religious or spiritual considerations, conversion to Christianity
Mitochondrial DNA, 294. *See also* DNA analysis
Moche (cultural group), 10, 13
Modeling. *See* Plastering and modeling of skulls
Modern day: archaeological interpretation based on "modern anthropological parallels," 68–69; forensic odontology used with tsunami victims, 76; limitations of scientific literature, 69–70, 255, 256; skull trade, 179
Modification of skulls: postmortem (*see* Decoration of skulls; Defleshing; Incision; Overmodeling; Ovoid bone, prosthetic; Perforations in skulls; Plastering and modeling of skulls); premortem (*see* Deformation of skulls)

Mongolia, 202
Morphology, craniofacial: changes over time, 182–83, 193; congenital defects (*see* Deformed skulls); effects of age, 24–25; effects of masticatory function, 24; folk taxonomy of "social races," 180; forensic case from Spanish Colonial Georgia, 179–96; forensics used to return remains to appropriate community, 179–80, 194; historical studies, 20–21; modification (*see* Deformation of skulls)
Morphometric analyses, craniofacial: comparative craniometry methods, 15–16, 20–21, 181–83, 186, 189; Fordisc software, 182; Forensic Data Bank (FDB), 183, 186; interpopulation vs. intrapopulation variability, 182; methods, 181–83, 187; need for local population databases, 194; reification of racial types, 183, 187; W. W. Howells data set, 182, 183, 186
Mortuary practices: body placed on platform, 53, 56, 79, 99, 115; burial effigy, 79, 80*f*; extension of body, 11; to forget the newly dead, 19; furniture, 11, 14; grave goods (*see* Grave goods); hands positioned as though tied, 151; house burned down and new house built, 19; money in the hand, 81; orientation of the body, 12, 81; placement of grave goods, 207*f*, 215*f*; prone position, 10, 11, 18, 24, 89; sprawled or awkward position, 24, 151
Mouth, 55, 59, 71, 102, 104, 105
Muge (site), 7
Mummification: Marquesas Islands, 115; process methods, 55–56, 84–85; social context, 18, 115; Tlingit, 13; Torres Strait Islands, 55–56, 57*f*, 84
Musculation, 51
Mutations, genetic, 294
Mythology, 9–10. *See also* Power, head as the seat of

Nasal septa modifications, 67, 272*f*, 273, 273*f*, 276
Nasca (cultural group): ancestor veneration, 19, 292; burial with head missing, 3; carving the cranial vault, 6; geography, 287, 289, 290*f*; headhunting, 264 (*see also*

Nasca (cultural group)—*continued*
Nasca trophy heads); head to represent
entire person, 18; history, 290, 291*t*; skull
deformation, 6; social organization, 290;
timeframe, 262, 286, 289, 290
Nasca trophy heads: DNA analysis, 32–33,
292–99, 296*t*, 297*t*; osteological analysis,
288–89, 288*f*, 292; ritual burial, 12, 264;
specimens, 292–93
Native American Graves Protection and
Repatriation Act (NAGPRA), 194
Native Americans, 183, 194
Natufian period, 3, 14, 16
Natural Environment Research Council
(NERC), 155
Near East: Anatolia, 3, 13–14, 34; "ancestor
question," 19; Levant, 3, 14, 19, 23, 25, 34;
plastered and modeled skulls, 19, 21, 68,
77, 91; skull deformation, 7, 21, 23, 25. *See
also* 'Ain Ghazal; Çatal Höyük; Jericho;
Jordan
Neolithic period. *See* 'Ain Ghazal; Çatal
Höyük; Jericho
NERC. *See* Natural Environment Research
Council
NERC Isotope Geosciences Laboratory
(NIGL), 155
New Britain, 70*f*, 241
New Ireland, 70*f*, 81
Niches, 13, 85
NIGL. *See* NERC Isotope Geosciences
Laboratory
Nonresidents. *See* Outsiders
North America: African slaves in, 188;
Alaska, 13, 18, 27; British colonialism in
southeastern U.S., 187; burial with "extra"
skulls, 14; California, 22, 24, 25, 187;
carving the cranial vault, 6; craniometric
reification of Native Americans, 183;
decapitation, 13, 17; dental health, 26,
27; Georgia, 187–88 (*see also* Fort King
George); hydrocephaly, 25; Illinois, 8;
labret ornamentation, 13, 27; mummification, 13; North Dakota, 187; Northwest
Coast groups, 13, 17, 18, 253, 263; Ohio
River Valley, 14; plastering and modeling, 4–5; scalping, 8, 185; skull deformation, 17, 253; skull trauma patterns,

24; southwestern U.S., 2, 23; Spanish
colonialism in, 31, 188 (*see also* Fort King
George); trophy skulls, 18, 263
North Dakota, 187
Noseplug, 69*f*, 99, 108*t*, 109*t*, 110*t*, 111*t*
Nubian culture, 24
Nuku Hiva, Marquesas Islands, 98, 98*f*, 100*f*,
103*f*, 104*f*
Nut paste, 84*f*
Nutrition. *See* Diet and nutrition

Ob-Irtysh (culture group), 204*f*
Oblique, 76, 231
Oceania. *See* Melanesia; Polynesia; Torres
Strait Islands
Ochre, 4, 12, 13
Odontologist 7, 6
Odontology, forensic, 71–77, 75*f*
Offerings. *See* Grave goods; Rituals,
sacrificial
Ofnet (site), 12–13
Okunevskaya culture, 220
OPG. *See* Orthopantomograph
Orbitalia. *See* Cribra orbitalia
Orendorf, Ill. (site), 8
Origin stories, 2
Ornamentation. *See* Jewelry; Labret
ornamentation
Orthopantomograph (OPG), 74
Osteoarchaeologist, 10. *See also*
Bioarchaeology
Osteological analysis: abdominal stab-
bing, 152; decapitation (*see* Osteologi-
cal evidence for decapitation); of early
specimens, 15; polishing (smoothness) of
cut surface, 150–51, 272, 272*f*, 276; skull
deformation, 205, 216–19, 231–33, 245;
skull trauma by pointed object, 123, 125*f*;
through skull modeling material, 74;
trophy skulls, 106, 112–13, 262, 267–78,
288–89, 288*f*, 292
Osteological evidence for decapitation: Ireland, 123–24, 129; Marquesas Islands, 106;
Roman period York, 148–52, 149*f*, 150*f*;
Torres Strait Islands, 61–65, 62*f*, 63*f*, 64*f*
Osteology, 21, 22, 286. *See also*
Bioarchaeology
Osteometrics, 21, 74

Outsiders: cultural bias of ethnographers, 67–68, 77, 254–56; group identification by hat shape, 237–38; group identification by skull shape, 32, 202, 213, 222–23, 228–29, 233–37, 246; perceived as threat to political or social power, 122, 238; as spirit of the dead, 60–61; transformation of an insider to, 30, 135; transformation to an insider, 29

Outsiders vs. insiders: use of DNA analysis, 33, 292, 298; use of isotope analysis, 30–31, 141–42, 166–70, 166t, 279–80

Overmodeling, 29, 71, 74, 78f

Ovoid bone, prosthetic, 268f, 269, 275, 278, 279

Oxygen, 163, 164. See also Isotope analysis of teeth

Painting of skull: Marquesas Islands, 112–13; Melanesia, 79; overview, 4; Sepik River, 72f, 74, 77, 78f; Torres Strait Islands, 53

Paleoethnobotanist, 23

Paleopathology, 22, 25–27, 247

Palimbai, 81

Palm, 55, 56, 83

Papua New Guinea. See Kaulong culture; Sepik River Valley; Torres Strait Islands

Paracas culture, 289, 291t

Parasites, 22, 23

Parietal: cut marks, 154, 268, 268f, 271, 275; deformation, 6, 216, 221, 253; disk as rattle, 6; drill holes, 274; osteometrics, 189; overmodeled, 71; trephination, 7

Pathology, 22, 23, 25–27. See also Biostressors

Pazyryk (culture group), 204f

PCR. See Polymerase chain reaction

Perforations in skulls: for impalement, 123, 125f, 185, 186f; to insert tacks, 6, 32, 269, 269f, 272f, 273–75, 276; nasal septa modifications, 67, 272f, 273, 273f, 276; for suspension, 6, 270, 270f, 277, 288f; trephination, 6–8, 16, 22, 109t

Perimortem: cut marks, 125f, 168f; hanging body, 112; perforations, 269–70; soft tissue removed, 264

Personhood, head as the seat of, 3, 15, 16,

114. See also Trophy heads and trophy skulls

Peru: Cuzco, 265–66, 266f; decapitation with human sacrifice, 10; maps, 230f, 290f; Nazca Valley, 287, 290f, 291t, 299 (see also Nasca); skull deformation, 6, 234–35, 236, 237 (see also Chiribaya culture); Spanish colonialism in, 32, 237; trophy heads (see Nasca trophy heads; Wari culture)

Phenetic approach, 188, 193

Phytoliths, 27

Piercing as ornamentation, 13, 27, 202, 241

Pig tusk. See Teeth, pig canines on trophy skulls

Pisco Valley (site), 297t, 298

Plagiocephaly, 15, 256

Plaster, lime, 4, 14

Plastering and modeling of skulls: head as memento, 19, 53–54, 54f, 56, 89; interpretation, 5, 13–14; Jericho, 4–5, 5f, 16, 68; "masks" buried separately, 4; osteological analysis through, 74; overmodeling, 29, 71, 74, 78f; Sepik River Valley, 71–77, 72f

Polishing of cut surface, 150–51, 272, 272f, 276

Political considerations: Chiribaya, 231, 236–37; Franciscan friars in southeastern U.S., 184; Ireland, 133–34, 136; Marquesas Islands, 113–16; Solomon Islands, 114; Wari, 12, 32–33, 276–79

Pollen, 27

Polymerase chain reaction (PCR), 295

Polynesia, 16, 105, 113

Population-level considerations: general race vs. specific population, 193; interpopulation vs. intrapopulation morphometric variability, 182; population affinity assessment through forensics, 180–96; rate of mtDNA mutation, 294; urban vs. rural, 143

Porotic hyperostosis, 22–23

Portugal, 7

Postmortem modification. See Decoration of skulls; Defleshing; Incision; Overmodeling; Ovoid bone, prosthetic; Perforations in skulls; Plastering and modeling of skulls

Pottery. *See* Ceramics

Power: and eyes as expression of knowledge, 105; head as the seat of, 9, 35, 77–78, 81–82, 90, 127, 133; within the society (*see* Social status)

Prehistoric period: Britain, 19; diet and health, 25, 27; Eurasia, 6; migration, 279–80, 299; North America, 2, 23, 26; South America (*see* Nasca); South Asia, 26

Premortem modification. *See* Deformation of skulls

Principal components analysis, 189, 192–93, 192*f*

Profile analysis, 62, 64*f*

Protohistoric period, 13, 98, 114, 116

Provenience, 190*t*, 191*t*, 195

Punishment, 135–36. *See also* Execution

Race: craniometric reification of racial types, 183, 187, 193; folk taxonomy of "social races," 180; general race vs. specific population, 193, 195

Radiguet, Max, 99

Radiocarbon analysis, 55, 220–21

Radiographic aging methods, 34, 73–75, 75*f*, 91

Raids, headhunting, 14, 55, 58, 88

Rambaramp (burial effigy), 79, 80*f*

Reconstruction, three-dimensional, 62, 64*f*

Religious or spiritual considerations: Catholic Church ban of skull deformation, 237, 242; chief speaking on behalf of the gods, 115; conversion to Christianity, 29, 51, 65, 116, 118, 183–84, 241; defaced remains, 179–80, 195; Jewish Aramaic magic ritual, 17; Maize God of the Maya, 254; politico-religious system of Marquesas Islands, 113–16; purgatory and resurrection, 30, 133, 135; spirits (*see* Spirit of the dead); war between Christian Irish and pagan Viking groups, 127

Remembrance. *See* Mementos or relics

Restriction fragment length polymorphism (RFLP), 287, 294, 296–97, 297*t*, 298

RFLP. *See* Restriction fragment length polymorphism

Rite of passage, 19, 82

Rituals: agricultural, 263; burial (*see* Mortuary practices); "dead man's likeness" with mummy, 56; decapitation to portray mythic hero, 9–10; divination, 54–55, 88; fertility, 19, 79, 82; initiation or rite of passage, 19, 82; magic and sorcery, 17; manual defleshing prior to decomposition, 3–4; non-funerary, 13; prosperity, 79, 85; raising the dead, 17; rebirth, 85; sacrificial, 10–11, 13, 87, 88, 114, 234, 277; skull-giving, as memento for widow, 53–54; use of trophy heads, 19, 33, 82, 114, 263, 277; warrior, 114

Robusticity, 24, 289

Roman Empire, 158, 167–70

Roman period: historical context, 169–70; metal production and use of lead, 142; Romano-British cemeteries, 9, 151, 152–53, 153*f*, 164–66 (*see also* York)

Roman Warm Period, 164

Rope. *See* Cord or rope for suspension of skull

Russia, 116, 204–5

Sacrifice. *See* Rituals, sacrificial

Saka (culture group), 204, 210, 220, 221, 223

San Cristoval, 85

Sargat culture: archaeological evidence, 205–16; geography, 203, 203*f*; grave goods, 205, 207–16; skull deformation (*see* Sargat skull deformation); social organization, 203–4, 222–23

Sargat skull deformation: osteological analysis methods, 205; overview, 6–7, 31–32, 202; skeletal evidence, 216–19, 217*f*, 218*t*, 219*f*; specimens, 206*t*, 208–9*t*, 212*t*

Sarmatian culture, 204, 221

Sauromatian (culture group), 204*f*

Scalping: Ancient Greece, 8; Eurasia, 8; North America, 8, 185, 186; overview, 8, 82; South America, 8; by the Wari, 32, 262, 271, 271*f*, 276

Scandinavia, Vikings, 23, 127, 133–34

Sculptures. *See* Figurines and dolls

Scurvy, 22, 23–24

Scythian (culture group), 8, 9, 204*f*

Sedentism, 23, 31, 218, 220, 223

Sepik River Valley: forensic odontology of a child's skull, 71–77, 75*f*, 91; modeling the skull, 70, 71, 72, 74, 77; nondestructive aging methods, 29–30, 73–74; skull decoration, 70

Sex, biological: and decapitation, 10, 11; dental caries, 26; gender bias of ethnographers, 86–87; male overrepresentation in trophy heads, 278; sexing methods (see Sex determination); and skull deformation, 213, 229, 233, 236, 243, 245, 245t; skull trauma patterns, 24; trephination in women, 8

Sex determination, morphometric, 205, 267

Shang Dynasty, 11

Shell: with burial effigy, 80f; earrings, 105; grit used as tempering agent, 74; representing eyes, 5f, 56, 72f, 74, 79, 99, 100, 108–11t, 112; for sharpening bamboo knife, 59; skull decoration, 4, 78f, 84f

Shipwrecks, 60–61

Short tandem repeats (STR), 299

Shrines, 55, 90

Shrunken heads, 19

Siberia, 204–5, 220. See also Sargat culture

Sican culture, 297

Sickle-cell anemia, 22

Silicone cast, 62, 62f, 64f

Skull. See Burned skulls; Calvaria; Container for skull or head; Cranium; Display of skull or head; Mandibles; Mementos or relics, decapitated head or skull; Painting of skull; Perforations in skulls; Plastering and modeling of skulls; Trade and exchange of skulls

Skull fragments, 14, 30, 76, 82, 86, 91, 114

Skull pits, 11, 116

Smith, William Ramsay, 71

Social functions of the head, 16–20, 135–36. See also Power; Trade and exchange of skulls

Social permeability, 229

Social status: archaeology of elites, 34–35; burial position, 24; burial with inclusion of skulls, 3; chiefs, 79, 80f, 85–86, 114; color symbolism in decorations, 113; decapitation, 11, 126–27; grave furnishings, 11; labret ornamentation, 27; mana as sacred force, 105, 115; Roman Empire, 168–69; skull deformation as marker, 202,

213, 220, 222–23, 252–53; trophy head as status symbol, 29, 51, 58, 59–61, 83, 114, 263

Societal considerations: cohesion, 83, 86, 90; deformation of the skull as "process of becoming," 32, 238, 242, 251–52, 253, 256–57; group identification by hat shape, 237–38; group identification by skull shape, 32, 202, 213, 222–23, 228–29, 233–37, 246; maintenance of social stability, 115, 222; matrimonial diplomacy, 223; overview, 14–15, 16–20; social norms and appearance of the body, 251–52; status (see Social status)

Solomon Islands, 70f, 83, 84f, 85–86, 114. See also Kwaio culture

Sorcery. See Magic and sorcery

Soul, 135–36

Soul, head as the seat of the: decapitation to punish the soul, 30, 133, 135; decapitation to release the soul, 17; lack of belief, Torres Strait Islands, 65; mana as sacred force, 105, 115; Oceania, 65; overview, 3

South America: burial with head missing, 3; carving the cranial vault, 6; deformation of the cranium, 6, 7, 25, 229, 234–35, 236, 237 (see also Chiribaya culture); labret ornamentation, 27; mummification, 55; necklace from teeth, 6; plastering and modeling, 5; rituals to forget the newly dead, 19; scalping, 8; skull trauma patterns, 24; utensils from skull, 6. See also specific countries

Spain, colonization by, 31, 32, 188, 237, 241, 254. See also Fort King George

Spheno-occipital suture, 75

Spirit of the dead: fertility granted by, 90; haunting by, 60; mari, 53, 54, 63; mortuary rituals to prevent spirit's return, 18, 53, 84–85, 89; protection by, 9, 17, 85, 88, 90, 263; raising, 17; shipwreck victims as prior relatives, 60–61; trophy heads hung in groups to prevent spirit's return, 82; voyage to the land of the dead, 79

Splanchnocranium, 188

Statistical methods, 189, 192–93, 192f, 233

Statues, 105. See also Figurines and dolls

STR. See Short tandem repeats

Strangers. *See* Outsiders

Stressors. *See* Biostressors

Striations (decoration), 101, 104

Striations (physical), 2, 4, 7, 27

Strontium. *See* Isotope analysis of teeth

Subadult, 26, 51, 61, 71, 77, 153, 212*t*

Superstratum, 32

Supraorbital ridge, 24, 267

Syria, 5, 170

Tagar (culture group), 204*f*, 221

Tapa cloth: bones wrapped in, after mummification, 115; to distinguish ancestor from enemy skull, 113; entire skull wrapped in, 102, 104, 104*f*, 106, 108*t*, 111*t*, 113, 115; strip surrounding skull, 101, 103*f*, 108*t*, 110*t*; supporting hair locks, 101, 108*t*, 110*t*, 117

Taphonomy, 106, 221

Tasmola (culture group), 204*f*

Tattoos: as marker of social status, 202; Marquesas decoration on trophy skulls, 101, 102, 104, 104*f*, 108*t*, 111*t*; pre-Columbian Maya, 241

Teeth: attrition, 25, 27, 267; caries, 22, 25–26; dental calculus, 27; enamel hypoplasia, 27, 217; filing, 7, 241, 246; incision, 7; inlay, 7, 241, 246; isotope analysis (*see* Isotope analysis of teeth); landmarks of formation, 73; microstriation patterns, 27; necklaces from, 6, 19; as ornaments for decapitated head, 12; pig canines on trophy skulls, 97, 99, 100*f*, 105, 108*t*, 109*t*, 110*t*, 111*t*; premolar, 75*f*; prosthetic, 32, 88, 262, 269, 269*f*, 272*f*, 274*f*, 275, 275*f*, 277, 279; significance in Marquesas trophy skulls, 105; used as tools, 26, 27. *See also* Dentition

Thailand, 76

Thalassemia, 22

Tibia, 154

Tiwanaku culture, 234–35, 236, 238, 246

Tlingit culture, 13, 18

Torres Strait Islands: collection and preparation of relatives' heads, 53–56, 54*f*, 57*f*; conversion to Christianity, 29, 51, 65; decorated skulls, 28–29, 51, 53–54, 54*f*; defleshing of skull prior to decomposition, 3–4, 29, 59, 61–65; enemies symbolically transformed into relatives, 29; geography and map, 52–53, 52*f*; heads as memorials, 51–57, 83; location, 70*f*; mortuary practices, 85; mummification, 18, 55–56, 57*f*, 84; nonresidents spiritually transformed into relatives, 60–61; skull preparation in Western islands, 53–54, 54*f*; skull removed from internment after decomposition, 54, 85; sorcery, 54, 89; trophy heads as status symbols, 29, 51, 58–61, 83

Trade and exchange of skulls: European curio market of the 18th century, 30, 97, 117, 118; Melanesia, 16; modern, 179; Polynesia, 16; social cohesion through, 83; Torres Strait Islands, 29

Trans-Urals, 200, 203. *See also* Sargat culture

Trauma injuries: blunt force, 152, 153, 169; detachment of face from cranial vault, 185; impalement of skull, 123, 125*f*, 185, 186*f*; patterns, 24; perimortem, 12, 106, 107*f*, 152, 169, 265, 268; stabbing, 152, 170; in trophy-taking victims, 265, 268, 268*f*. *See also* Decapitation

Trephination, 6–8, 16, 22, 109*t*

Trilobed shape, 7

Trobriand Islands, 18, 70*f*, 86, 89

Trophy heads and trophy skulls: ancestor veneration and, 113, 263, 264–65; display to prevent spirits' return, 82, 89; European curio market of the 18th century, 30, 97, 117, 118; Marquesas Islands, 97–118, 100*f*, 103*f*, 104*f*, 107*f*; Melanesia, 82; osteological analysis, 106, 112–13, 262, 267–75; overview, 3, 18, 263–64, 287; as part of politico-religious system, 113–16; Peru (*see* Nasca trophy heads; Wari culture); processing methods, 59, 262, 274, 279, 287; ritually buried, 12, 263, 264, 278; ritual use of, 19, 33, 82, 114, 279; from shipwreck victims, 60–61; shrunken heads, 19; as status symbol, 29, 51, 58, 59–61, 83, 114, 263; Torres Strait Islands, 29, 51, 59–61, 83

Trophy mandible, 59, 60, 62*f*, 63, 63*f*

Tsantsa (shrunken head), 19

Tshuosh culture, 81
Tuberculosis, 22, 27
Tumpline to transport load by the head, 243, 253
Turkey. *See* Çatal Höyük
Turtle shell, 83, 101, 110*t*, 111*t*
Tzotzil Maya culture, 252

Ulcers, occipital, 24
Ural Mountains, 200. *See also* Sargat culture
Utensils from skeleton parts, 6, 17, 205, 209*t*
Uyuk (culture group), 204*f*

Vanikolo Island, 85
Vanuatu, 3, 69*f*, 70*f*, 79, 80*f*, 85
Viking culture, 23, 127, 133–34
Vitamin C. *See* Biostressors, scurvy

Warfare. *See* Enemies
Wari culture: cannibalism, 2; geography of Cuzco region, 265–66, 266*f*; history, 265–67, 278, 291*t*; skull trauma patterns, 24; suggestions for future research, 279–80; timeframe, 262; trophy heads (*see* Wari trophy heads)
Wari trophy heads: archaeological evidence, 264–65; osteological analysis, 6, 32, 262, 267–75, 277–78; sociopolitical context, 12, 32–33, 276–79

Warriors: body parts worn by, 114; iconography, 97, 102*f*, 277, 280; ornaments, 105, 114; rituals, 114. *See also* Scalping; Trophy heads and trophy skulls
Westo culture, 187
"White man," 60
Witchcraft. *See* Magic and sorcery
Women: low status, 24; matrimonial diplomacy, 223; mother controls decision to modify infant's skull, 242, 252; not taken prisoner or violated, 58; trephination in, 8

X-ray analysis. *See* Radiographic aging methods

York, Roman period (site): demographics of cemetery population, 151, 152–53, 153*f*; description, 31, 145–46, 146*f*, 147*f*, 168; geological setting, 143–44, 143*f*, 161–62; historical context, 169–70; isotope analysis, 30–31, 154–66; local vs. nonlocal indications, 166–70, 166*t*; map, 144*f*; osteological analysis, 148–52, 149*f*, 150*f*
York Archaeological Trust, 141
Yukatek Maya culture, 252

Zooarchaeologist, 23

About the Editor

Michelle Bonogofsky is the editor of *Skull Collection, Modification and Decoration* (2006) and the author of articles published in *Bulletin of the American Schools of Oriental Research, International Journal of Osteoarchaeology, Journal of Archaeological Science,* and *Paléorient.*

BIOARCHAEOLOGICAL INTERPRETATIONS OF THE HUMAN PAST:
LOCAL, REGIONAL, AND GLOBAL PERSPECTIVES

Edited by Clark Spencer Larsen

This series examines the field of bioarchaeology, the study of human biological remains from archaeological settings. Focusing on the intersection between biology and behavior in the past, each volume will highlight important issues, such as biocultural perspectives on health, lifestyle and behavioral adaptation, biomechanical responses to key adaptive shifts in human history, dietary reconstruction and foodways, biodistance and population history, warfare and conflict, demography, social inequality, and environmental impacts on population.

Ancient Health: Skeletal Indicators of Agricultural and Economic Intensification, edited by Mark Nathan Cohen and Gillian M. M. Crane-Kramer (2007; first paperback edition, 2012)

Bioarchaeology and Identity in the Americas, edited by Kelly J. Knudson and Christopher M. Stojanowski (2009; first paperback edition, 2010)

Island Shores, Distant Pasts: Archaeological and Biological Approaches to the Pre-Columbian Settlement of the Caribbean, edited by Scott M. Fitzpatrick and Ann H. Ross (2010)

The Bioarchaeology of the Human Head: Decapitation, Decoration, and Deformation, edited by Michelle Bonogofsky (2011; first paperback edition, 2015)

Bioarchaeology and Climate Change: A View from South Asian Prehistory, by Gwen Robbins Schug (2011)

Violence, Ritual, and the Wari Empire: A Social Bioarchaeology of Imperialism in the Ancient Andes, by Tiffiny A. Tung (2012; first paperback edition, 2013)

The Bioarchaeology of Individuals, edited by Ann L. W. Stodder and Ann M. Palkovich (2012; first paperback edition 2014)

The Bioarchaeology of Violence, edited by Debra L. Martin, Ryan P. Harrod, and Ventura R. Pérez (2012; first paperback edition 2013)

Bioarchaeology and Behavior: The People of the Ancient Near East, edited by Megan A. Perry (2012)

Paleopathology at the Origins of Agriculture, edited by Mark Nathan Cohen and George J. Armelagos (2013)

Bioarchaeology of East Asia: Movement, Contact, Health, edited by Kate Pechenkina and Marc Oxenham (2013)

Mission Cemeteries, Mission Peoples: Historical and Evolutionary Dimensions of Intracemetery Bioarchaeology in Spanish Florida, by Christopher M. Stojanowski (2013)

Tracing Childhood: Bioarchaeological Investigations Of Early Lives In Antiquity, edited by Jennifer L. Thompson, Marta P. Alfonso-Durruty, and John J. Crandall (2014)

The Bioarchaeology of Classical Kamarina: Life and Death in Greek Sicily, by Carrie L. Sulosky Weaver (2015)

Victims of Ireland's Great Famine: The Bioarchaeology of Mass Burials at Kilkenny Union Workhouse, by Jonny Geber (2016)

9 780813 061771